Monastic Culture
The Long Thirteenth Century

Monastic Culture

The Long Thirteenth Century
Essays in Honour of Brian Patrick McGuire

Editors:
Lars Bisgaard, Sigga Engsbro,
Kurt Villads Jensen and Tore Nyberg

University Press of Southern Denmark 2014

© The authors and University Press of Southern Denmark 2014
University of Southern Denmark Studies in History and Social Sciences vol. 480
Proceedings of the 33rd symposium organized by Centre for Medieval Studies,
University of Southern Denmark.
Printed by Specialtrykkeriet Viborg
Drawing of maps: Johnny G.G. Jakobsen
Cover: St Mary and child. Pilgrims' badge from Aachen found at the Swedish Cistercian monastery Alvastra (Photo Gabriel Hildebrandt 2011, Copyright SHMM).
Back: Part of the ruins of Alvastra (Photo Lars Bisgaard).

ISBN 978 87 7674 774 9

Printed with support from:
Carlsbergfondet
The Faculty of Humanities, University of Southern Denmark

University Press of Southern Denmark
Campusvej 55
DK-5230 Odense M
www.universitypress.dk

Distribution in the United States and Canada:
International Specialized Book Services
5804 NE Hassalo Street
Portland, OR 97213-3644 USA
www.isbs.com

Distribution in the United Kingdom:
Gazelle
White Cross Mills
Hightown
Lancaster
LA1 4 XS
U.K.
www.gazellebookservices.co.uk

Table of Contents

Introduction   7
Kurt Villads Jensen

The Innovational Power of Monastic Life in the Middle Ages   13
Gert Melville

An Intricate Web of Friends:
Unravelling the Networks and Personal Connections
of the two Lawrences of Durham   33
Mia Münster-Swendsen

An Ideal Clerical Administrator?
Reflections on the Thirteenth-Century Biography of Bishop Gunner   57
Sigga Engsbro

A Cistercian Sermon Collection from Løgum   81
Kurt Villads Jensen

Monasteries as Cultural Centres:
The Case of Schleswig-Holstein with Lübeck and Hamburg   103
Thomas Riis

Lordship over Monasteries in Twelfth and Thirteenth Century
Sweden and Denmark   119
Christian Lovén

Male Monastic Recruitment among the Cistercians
in Medieval Sweden, c. 1143-1450   149
Catharina Andersson

Networks, Contacts, and Change in Alvastra Abbey, c. 1185-1350   177
Elisabet Regner

Augustinian Canons and Benedictine Monks
in the Medieval Stavanger Diocese   197
Eldbjørg Haug

Dominican Experts in Medieval Scandinavia:
The Order of Preachers and the Dissemination of Knowledge
in Northern Societies   219
Johannes Schütz

Who ordered the Dominicans?
Initiators behind Dominican Convent Foundations
in Northern Europe, c. 1216-1350   241
Johnny Grandjean Gøgsig Jakobsen

The Cistercian Network: the Flemish Abbey
of Ter Doest and Scandinavia   269
Eric Delaissé

"Ex magno devotionis fervore…"
Danish Cistercians and the Apostolic Penitentiary
in the Later Middle Ages   285
Kirsi Salonen

Concluding Remarks: Monastic Culture in Northern Europe
in the long thirteenth Century, c. 1150-1350   297
Brian Patrick McGuire

Bibliography of Brian Patrick McGuire's published Works   309

Index   319

Introduction

Kurt Villads Jensen

The Medieval Centre at the University of Southern Denmark is the oldest medieval centre in Scandinavia and began shortly after the foundation of the university in 1966, as a loosely organised group of scholars from different institutes but with a common interest in the Middle Ages. Since 1976, the centre has organized an international congress each year in November, and the proceedings of almost all of these congresses have been published.

The articles in this collection were first presented and discussed at the centre's thirty-fifth congress in November 2011, the topic of which was *Monastic Culture in North Western Europe in the Long Thirteenth Century, c. 1150 – 1350*. The congress was held to honour Professor Brian P. McGuire who would retire from his chair at Roskilde University in the beginning of 2012. The topic chosen for the conference illustrates the research interests of Professor McGuire, but is also a contribution to an on-going research internationally and in Scandinavia.

In 2002, the Centre for Medieval Studies held its twenty-sixth Congress on early Scandinavian monasticism, which was an attempt to work backwards from what is known from the Scandinavian early Middle Ages into the nebulous preliminary stages of Christianity in Northern Europe.[1] It was a topic that had been the subject of a round table session at the International Congress of Historical Sciences in Oslo in 2000, which was among the incentives for deciding that the conference in Odense should be about monasticism.[2] The proceedings were published in 2006 and accompanied by several publications devoted to particular monasteries. 2003 saw the publication of an anthology on the Cistercian monastery of Øm in Jutland,[3] which had been inspired in its choice of topics and research questions by a similar investigation from 1997 of the Cistercian mother monastery in Denmark, Esrum,[4] to which Brian P. McGuire

---

1 Published in Bisgaard and Nyberg (2006).
2 Another important incentive was the publication of Tore Nyberg's book on monasticism; Nyberg (2000).
3 Gregersen and Jensen (2003).
4 Frandsen, Jørgensen, and Thortzen (1997).

contributed with an article on the background and the foundation of Esrum. In 2010 came a magisterial work on the history and architecture of Løgum monastery, which Brian P. McGuire has visited regularly for many years and to which he has introduced numerous students.[5] Similar books on Swedish monasteries have been published after conferences and studies, e.g. on Varnhem and on the two nunneries of Gudhem and Vreta.[6] An impressive and weighty publication of a conference on the Augustinian canonry of Dalby in Scania in 2010 appeared in 2012.[7] In Norway, medieval monasteries were fewer, and recent research has with few exceptions concentrated more on single aspects of monastic history than on broader, general aspects.[8] In Finland the situation has been similar, where much research has centred upon the Birgittine Order.[9]

Common for all these publications are not only a fresh view of the sources and new readings of old texts, but also an interdisciplinary approach and cooperation between historians, theologians, archaeologists, and scholars from other disciplines. The excavations of monasteries and the architectural studies of remaining buildings have been pursued without interruption since the late nineteenth century in Scandinavia and Northern Europe, and new studies add continuously to our knowledge. While this introduction is being written, there are for example promising excavations being conducted in pursuit of the least known and once most remote Danish Cistercian abbey of the Middle Ages, Ås monastery in northern Halland, near the very corner of the early three Scandinavian kingdoms. Nearby their sovereigns met at Kungälv (the *King's River*) in a collegiate Scandinavian spirit, one of the remarkable occasions of the early Middle Ages.[10]

The subject for this collection is not monastic history in general as part of the history of the surrounding societies. After each monastery had been founded, for whatever religious, political or economic reason, and after the foundation history had been recorded and put on parchment, there began the daily monastic work of all members of the community, expressed in the words *Ora et labora* – pray and work. The prayers of the monks have not been much studied in a Scandinavian and northern European context, and the work of the monks has

---

5   Sterum (2010).
6   Harrison et al. (2011); Hagberg (2009); Tagesson (2010). On Alvastra, see Regner (2005).
7   Borgehammar and Wienberg (2012). On Norwegian Monasteries, see Haugh (2008).
8   Exceptions are Haug (2005); Haug (2008).
9   E.g. Uotila (2011).
10 The meeting at Kungälv in 1101 between the kings of Denmark, Norway, and Sweden.

often been understood as manual work on their lands or fields, rather than the spiritual work on the field of the Lord. This approach has been in sharp contrast with what medieval monks themselves considered as their main task. Therefore, monastic culture is the focus of this publication, as it was of the symposium from which the contributions stem.

Monastic culture and way of thinking made its imprint on the sources so familiar to historians: the normative rules and statutes of the monasteries, written or material evidence of the monks' cultivation of the land and their craftsmanship, or their copying of books and illuminating of manuscripts, bearing witness to their artistic ambitions. And not least to consider is monastic ways of organization. All these sources manifest the abilities of monks and monasteries in creating social networks, and in their own understanding they aimed for networks for themselves and other friends of God. Their desire was to link men and angels together before God's face and to fight the devil and the powers of darkness.

Medieval monastic world was a multifaceted landscape, physically as well as spiritually. No monograph or collection of works can do justice to all aspects of it or comprise its entirety. The aim of the present collection is rather to present and discuss a number of the fundamental themes to understand better how the monastic world acted and thought, both internally and in relation to the surrounding society.

One such theme is the manifold *networks* that connected different monasteries with each other or with other elements of society. Learned networks were established among individuals who became friends and maintained and nurtured the links for years, also if they were separated by geographical distance, or they were created by for example the new mendicant orders that systematically disseminated knowledge. Aristocratic networks operated on a more local scale and established links to monastic institutions by donating children and economic support to them. Economic networks also functioned as means of communication that bound monastic centres together across regional boundaries. Ecclesiastical administrative networks became common European ones and connected even the most northern regions with the papal centres in Rome or Avignon.

Another central theme in this collection is the concept itself of *monastic culture*. We have considered what might be included within monastic life from our modern perspective, but also and especially from medieval ones. Were monastic institutions preservers of ancient knowledge which was slowly accumulated and added to, or were they innovative in combining selfreflection with active participation in worldly affairs? How was monastic life described in monastic texts, and were sermons different when directed to a monastic audience from those directed to lay persons?

The chronological frame for this collection is the long thirteenth century, ranging from around 1150 to about 1350. It was a particularly innovative and expansive period in the history of Europe with economic and intellectual growth, which saw the foundation of a number of institutions that are still of fundamental importance to modern societies. These include universities, parliaments, guilds and confraternities, international regulations of trade and warfare, but also a new and distinct monastic way of life, adopted by the old orders and promoted in the monasteries founded by the new orders, many of which are treated in this volume. It was also the period of the consolidation and unification of a common ecclesiastical legal system that for the rest of the Middle Ages covered all areas of Western Christendom, as the last contribution to this volume demonstrates.

Professor Brian Patrick McGuire's retirement from his professorship of medieval history was the incitement for the organizers to devote the 2011 symposium in Odense to him in recognition of what he has been and has done for medieval studies in Denmark and internationally, both for professional scholars and for the general public with an interest in the medieval universe.

Professor McGuire came to Denmark in 1971, with a newly awarded D.Phil. from the University of Oxford and a perspective from a historiographical tradition very different from the German-inspired approach among Danish historians. His influence upon Danish historical research cannot be overestimated. Professor McGuire has been instrumental not only in making Danish history research more international, but also in introducing to Denmark and Scandinavia history of mentalities, history of medieval spirituality. In short, he has been instrumental in teaching historians to take medieval man seriously. Monasteries and their monks and nuns, the spiritual literature and its authors, the search for God and truth in the middle of tedious intrigues, poverty and discontentment, the great men and women of a flourishing medieval culture, have been close to the heart of Professor McGuire.

Cistercians have played a prominent role in his research. One of his first comprehensive studies was his book on the Cistercians in Denmark, which came out in 1982 after the publication of more articles on aspects of the same topic. McGuire was not impressed by the spiritual grandeur of some of the monks in Esrum and Sorø – maybe he was disappointed by seeing them involved in petty quarrels about farms or the yield of farmlands. His work expanded rapidly in the following years and includes not only several biographies of Saint Bernard and a brilliant analysis of the fifteenth century Jean Gerson, but also studies devoted to earlier epochs of the Middle Ages. Among Professor McGuire's many impressing works stands his grand oeuvre on monastic friendship with its revolutionary insights into the sources of what kept monks together. The force of this indefinable metaphysic quality called friendship, the divine energy which Saint Bernard spread. In this book, and in his many other publications, Professor McGuire has delved into medieval monastic culture to an extent which few other modern scholars have achieved.

Literature

Bisgaard, Lars, and Tore Nyberg (ed.), *Tidlige klostre i Norden før 1200* (Odense, 2006).

Borgehammar, Stephan, and Jes Wienberg (ed.), *Locus Celebris. Dalby Kyrka, Kloster och Gård* (København, 2012).

Frandsen, S., J.A. Jørgensen, and Chr. G. Tortzen (ed.), *Bogen om Esrum Kloster* (Holstebro, 1997).

Gregersen, Bo, and Carsten Selch Jensen (ed.), *Øm Kloster - Kapitler af et middelalderligt cistercienser-abbedis historie* (Odense, 2003).

Hagberg, Markus, *Gudhems kloster* (Skara, 2009).

Harrison, Dick, et al. (ed.), *Varnhems kloster före Birger Jarl. Om klostrets rottrådar i tiden* (Skara, 2011).

Haug, Eldbjørg (ed.), *Utstein kloster og Klosterøys historie* (Rennesøy, 2005).

Haug, Eldbjørg, 'Challenges in the Research of Norwegian Monastic History' *American Benedictine Review* 59, no. 1 (2008), 64-96

Nyberg, Tore, *Monasticism in North-Western Europe, 800-1200* (Aldershot, 2000).

Regner, Elisabet, *Den reformerade världen. Alvastra kloster från medeltid til modern tid* (Stockholm, 2005).

Sterum, Niels T., *Løgum kloster, slot og by: "Pionerer i ødemarken"* 1-2 (Haderslev, 2010).

Tagesson, Göran, *Fokus Vreta kloster* (Stockholm, 2010).

Uotila, Kari (ed.), *Naantalin luostarin rannassa - arkipäivä Naantalin luostarissa ja sen liepeillä / Stranden vid Nådendals kloster - vardagen i klostret och dess omgivning* (Kåkenhus, 2011).

The Innovational Power of Monastic Life in the Middle Ages

Gert Melville

When thinking about monastic life in the Middle Ages, most people no longer automatically think of the strange aspect of the Dark Ages anymore, but rather remember that some of the most prominent personalities of European cultural history were formed by, and then in turn shaped, this way of life – people such as Benedict of Nursia, Bernard of Clairvaux, Thomas Aquinas, Savonarola, and even a certain Martin Luther. Monastic life also conjures up images of architectural marvels, such as the monastery of Mont-Saint-Michel on the Atlantic coast, the Charterhouse of Pavia, or the abbey of Cluny. These are only some of the highlights among thousands of Christian monasteries with tens of thousands of monks and nuns from Scandinavia and Scotland to Sicily, from Portugal to Poland and even Palestine, the Caucasus and China. It also brings to mind the fact that medieval monasteries were instrumental in, and at the forefront of, progress and innovations in medicine, territorial development and colonisation, architecture, science and technology.[1]

Nevertheless – all of these findings are no more meaningful than all those glossy coffee-table books about the medieval monastic world which only show a superficial interest in one of the marvels of our culture. In order to appreciate the actual cultural achievement of the medieval monasteries, the basis of monastic life needs to be explored more thoroughly. For this, the focus will have to be on the period of the eleventh to thirteenth centuries – an era which produced

---

[1] The following reflections are based on an article published in German as 'Im Spannungsfeld von religiösen Eifer und methodischem Betrieb. Zur Innovationskraft der mittelalterlichen Klöster', *Denkströme. Journal der Sächsischen Akademie der Wissenschaften zu Leipzig* 7 (2011), pp. 72-92. It presents the basic thesis of a long-term research project entitled 'Monasteries in the High Middle Ages: Laboratories of Innovation for European Life-Styles and Models of Order' ('Klöster im Hochmittelalter: Innovationslabore europäischer Lebensentwürfe und Ordnungsmodelle'), sponsored by the Saxonian Academy of Sciences and Humanities in Leipzig and the Heidelberg Academy of Sciences and Humanities, led by Gert Melville (Technische Universität Dresden), Bernd Schneidmüller and Stefan Weinfurter (both Universität Heidelberg).

a religious re-orientation of medieval society in so many different ways. Against the background of medieval ideas about God and man, individuality and community, faith and reason, we can find in the monasteries a world where order was rigorously sought and bold new life-styles developed. We can also find a world where people wrestled for truth and for an understanding of the earthly and the divine – or more simply, where they searched for a way to manage this life for the sake of the afterlife. Additionally, we will have to try and understand the motives, obsessions and desires of the people acting inside these monasteries, in order to acknowledge their specific contribution to European culture.[2]

I would like to suggest as a working hypothesis that if we did explore the basis of monastic life, we would find the following phenomenon: that medieval monasteries were veritable laboratories of innovation for European life-styles and organisational models; that they developed innovative achievements which could then be transferred to the secular world, or in other words to a world not under a monastic rule. I will explore this point of view for the remainder of my contribution. I will use both an approach that derives its essence from the field of cultural history as well as the methods of comparative monastic history[3] which focus primarily on an analysis of the variable basic structures of the *vita religiosa*.

A general characteristic of the Middle Ages would seem to have been the tendency to determine the immanence of secular existence strictly from a comprehension of divine transcendence – of a God who disposed of the world as a ruler, but who was not at the disposal of anyone. Christian faith was the basis of culture; it was present in all areas of life as a benchmark and final justification – in daily life, politics, law, economy, science and art.[4] Even though the *occulta cordis* – the secrets of the heart – could not be seen, it would have hardly been possible for anyone in the Middle Ages to withdraw from at least an outward acceptance of divine rule over the world.[5]

Monks and nuns were expected to do more than just follow God's commandments. In their desire for the sanctification of their souls, they had taken leave of the outside world, and they had subjected themselves obediently to the rigid rules of communal life in the monastery by renouncing their own will. This only made sense because in these monasteries – far away from impermanence and secured within the harmony of a strictly structured organisation – the most significant factor seemed embedded more fully there than anywhere else: not just to understand God's transcendence, but to make this transcendence immanent

---

2 A general survey can be found in Melville (2012).
3 Felten (2007).
4 Cf. the survey in Angenendt (2009).
5 Cf. Moos (2006); Melville (2011a).

in their souls by giving God a home in their souls in reciprocal love.[6] One had to strive for this union of the soul with God with religious fervour[7] – in its final rigour even with an ecstatic passion, and it was this union that was at the heart of monastic religiosity. Everything else can be explained through this.

Such a union could only be possible in the cloistered space of a monastic world which set itself apart from the secular world through a clear separation of interior and exterior.[8] In this context the important issue was not just the architectural and material construction of a separating wall; even more decisive was the inner disposition which produced a form of life which allowed the exclusion of the secular world.[9] 'Entering a monastery, he exchanges skin for skin and everything he has to his soul, while he removes the old and accepts the new man – entering into a new form of life.' The twelfth-century Abbot Peter of Moûtier-la-Celle used these words[10] to draw a clear spiritual boundary between the world and the monastery. To cross this boundary as an individual demanded an irreversible and 'total conversion of the heart to God (*conversio totalis ad Deum cordis*)'.[11] Whenever monks were called on to be willing and prepared to practise tolerance, silence, fasting and the renunciation of meat, manual labour, contemplation and vigils, and whenever pride and vainglory (*superbia*) were characterised as the worst vices while humility (*humilitas*) was seen to be the attitude that would lead to perfect virtue, the basic demands of this new domain of life and its behaviour patterns were outlined. And this new form of life could only be reached through just such a conversion.

Religious communities claimed to guarantee detachment from temporal mutability, by giving a symbolic expression to this detachment as well:[12] When men and women subjected themselves in the monastery to a daily routine of

---

6 On the (implicit) notion that man would become increasingly similar to God, as developed particularly by Bernard of Clairvaux, see Diers (1991), pp. 45-47. In analysing this notion, it has to be taken into account, however, that these ideals had to be fought for by individuals in each particular case, and that they were achieved in very different ways during the long history of monasticism.
7 This is clearly highlighted by Leclercq (1983), particularly pp. 109-116.
8 Cf. Melville (2005a); Melville / Müller (2010), pp. 107-118; Melville (2011b).
9 This can be seen particularly in Bohl (2000) who has shown that an interior/exterior dichotomy existed in the case of the mendicants just as much as it did for traditional monastic orders.
10 "De disciplina claustrali", Martel (1977), pp. 192, 194, with reference to Job 2, 4. To complete this internal step, the vow and its consecration were necessary institutional enactments of the sacral; cf. Breitenstein (2008).
11 "Epistola cujusdam de doctrina vitae agendae (12th century)", in Patrologia Latina 184, col. 1187.
12 On the following, see the in-depth discussion in Sonntag (2008).

recurring rhythms, and where they practiced in permanent repetition the daily sequences of services and prayers, sleeping and waking, work and food, they had a communal experience of cyclical time. This cyclical time broke into and negated the secular sequence of time, creating a symbolic prefiguration of timeless eternity. When what was seen as the eternal truth of divine revelation became permanently tangible to the senses in the liturgy, divine office, the singing of psalms, the Benedictine ritual of washing the feet of the poor, and also in the ordinary, daily work of listening to and reciting religious texts; or when the regularly occurring chapter of faults, where externally visible lapses were confessed in front of the community, was understood as a reflection of the Last Judgement, then this intended detachment of monastic life became the representation of the intention to achieve harmony between earthly existence and heavenly order, through actually lived and therefore institutionally strengthened practices.[13]

There were, however, two areas of particular tension in the attempt to live this religiosity: there was, on the one hand, the tension of the competition between the demands of the monastic community and the needs of the individuals inside the monastery who had to subject themselves strictly to the rules of the community despite (or even because of) the concern about their individual salvation; on the other hand, there was the basic tension between the transcendence of divine perfection and the status of both individuals and community who were still bound to an earthly, bodily materiality and were therefore understood to be deficient – a status which still needed to be perfected. These two areas of tension marked the normative corner-stones of religious life in the monastery – individual and community, this world and the next – and because these tensions could not ultimately be resolved, they needed to be kept in an even balance. Monastic life in its most perfect form could only work if these tensions were pragmatically managed. Because keeping this balance meant, in the first instance, the management of contingent disturbances,[14] the monks were adept at forming flexible and innovative solutions in order to attain their goals; solutions which were innovative in more ways than just their flexibility. I will try to clarify this.

Monastic life meant a life in transition which anchored a monastic community as a temporary point for the transition of the individual from earth to heaven. In accordance with this, the Rule of St Benedict already spoke of a 'school of

---

13 On monastic daily life, see also Moulin (1990).
14 Not least because members of a monastic community were not perfect and could therefore have a propensity to deviance. Cf. on this point Cygler (1992); Melville (1996); Füser (2000); Patzold (2000).

the Lord', or a 'workshop', in which the imperfect were being perfected.[15] The value of a monastic community therefore did not lie in itself, but in the fact that it supplied these 'tools',[16] with which individuals could lift themselves above earthly concerns and orient their entire life towards the perfect union of their souls with God. These tools encompassed both individual and social virtues, and they could be obtained in the care of the community. In order to use the tools, it was therefore necessary to subject oneself to the community for the sake of the perfection of one's spiritual welfare and salvation.

It is clearly discernible here how the poles of these two areas of tension are interlinked. In order to explore their inherent tension, however, it is now necessary to attempt a separate examination of these two poles.

To start with the community: Monastic rules shaped communities of mind and purpose which demanded of their members 'to be of one heart and soul' in accordance with the biblical text.[17] Justice was seen here as a significant social virtue which allocated 'to each his own', and which took into account the weaknesses of the individual as well as his or her strengths.[18] *Discretio* – the faculty of differentiation – was a key term in this context. In practice, this meant that there was a strict allocation of tasks according to the individuals' respective abilities. Additionally, medieval monasteries were able to conceive of communities which were highly efficient because they could demand strict obedience[19] on the one hand, and were therefore able to form a common, ordered 'battle line' against evil (an 'acies' as the Cistercian Bernard of Clairvaux had emphasised),[20] while on the other hand, despite all the demands on the individual, they validated individuals in a way that would best realise their strengths.

This is where we touch the other pole – the individual: monasteries also enabled a form of community which allowed for the responsibility of the individual and permitted him or her to pursue the perfection of his or her soul. The most significant example of this was the monastic practice of an individual examination of conscience. This *conscientia* was understood as *cordis scientia*, as the knowledge of the heart.[21] Particularly during the move towards spiritu-

---

15 "Constituenda est ergo nobis dominici scola servitii [...]"; Benedicti Regula (1977), prologue, line 45; "Officina vero, ubi haec omnia diligenter operemur, claustra sunt monasterii et stabilitas in congregatione": ibid., c. 4, line 78.
16 Cf. the passage "Quae sunt instrumenta bonorum operum": ibid., c. 4.
17 Cf. Schreiner (2002).
18 Breitenstein / Melville (2010); Breitenstein (2010).
19 Cf. Andenna / Barret / Melville (ed.) (2005).
20 Cf. for instance Bernard of Clairvaux, "Parabolae 3", in Jean Leclercq and Henri Rochais (ed.), Sancti Bernardi Opera, vol. 6.2, Rom 1970, pp. 261-303, here pp. 274-276.
21 In addition to Bertola (1970), see also Chenu (1969); for an overview, see Reiner

alisation in the eleventh and twelfth centuries,[22] the members of the monastic community learned to accept their conscience as an inescapable companion, to meet themselves in their conscience as individuals against the background of the precepts of their religious life, and to have only God as a partner who would look into their hearts. With key phrases such as 'Dare to recognise yourself' or 'If you follow your conscience, your own law will bind you',[23] monks and nuns practiced a form of behaviour that relied on its own judgement and not on that of others, for an examination of your own conscience would lead you to understand yourself better than anyone else. Only if you possessed a soul purified by the examination of your conscience would it be possible to furnish it as a home for the Lord. It was demanded of the members of the monastery as their highest ascetic goal and perfection to turn their senses away completely from the impressions of the outer world and to direct them only towards the soul as their inner cloister. The individual monk or nun should – literally – 'look' and 'listen' into their soul because only there, it was said, would they find and recognise God in reality.[24] This referred to the individual's personal path to God, and it also marked an individual territory which remained untouched by the norms of the community. The individual needed the community 'only' as a protective and reinforcing shell, but even then, it was the community which could help him or her to a charismatic dignity as a self-responsible individual before God.

There was therefore an offer of two routes for monastic life against the background of the dichotomy between imperfection and perfection: the path of organised community and the path of the individuality of the soul. Although they seem to contradict each other at first sight, neither of the paths could work without the other so that – as has already been sketched briefly – a permanent balance between the two had to be maintained.

We now need to explore the instruments that created and maintained this balance, and for that we need to come back to the thesis mentioned earlier, that it is exactly here that the innovative cradle of cultural achievements can be found.

Max Weber pointed out the paradox of the 'charismatic anti-rational and specifically anti-economic' habitus of the monastic ascetic who was looking for salvation on the one hand, and the 'rational achievements of monasticism' on the other. His explanation was, 'Asceticism becomes the object of methodical prac-

---

(1974), cols. 581-583; Krüger (1984).
22 The seminal work on this period of reform is Constable (1996).
23 "Meditationes piissimae", in Patrologia Latina 184, col. 494; "De interiori domo seu De conscientia aedificanda", in ibidem, col. 534.
24 Cf. Spijker (2004); and most recently Melville / Müller (2010), p. 111-114.

tices as soon as the ecstatic or contemplative union with God is transformed, from a state that only some individuals can achieve through their charismatic endowments, into a goal that many can reach through identifiable ascetic means.'[25] 'Rational achievements and practices' have now been introduced as the key terms.[26] In practice, we can speak of methodical rationality if a reflective and objectifying treatment of one's own actions or the actions of others is present, and if social action happens according to systematic design which also manages to grasp the conditions, modes and aims of action in a differentiated way. Medieval monasteries developed such a methodically implemented rationality in a pragmatic way, in order to maintain the spirit of their extra-temporal lifestyle in a form that was necessarily institutional.

The monasteries benefited in this context from their ability to use the necessary tools from the very beginning in an exceptional way: writing and literacy. To a large extent, writing as a basis of higher culture[27] had to be re-learned after the collapse of the ancient world, and it was only in the twelfth century that a revolution in writing began which spanned all aspects of civilization.[28] Monasteries, however, had been shaped by literacy in a fundamental way since Antiquity, in so far as their specific fundamental norms had been set down in writing – in the texts of their rules.[29] Better than any other institution, including ecclesiastical ones, monasteries managed over the centuries – including the crucial twelfth century – to use writing systematically as a repository for storage. This tool was the practical prerequisite for the rational fashioning of the life of the community, both as a whole and in its individual members,[30] and in addition to a vast literary production,[31] monasteries used it particularly in the

---

25 Weber (1980), p. 696.
26 On the corresponding conceptualisation of a key phase of the Middle Ages, see Wieland (1996), pp. 61-79. See also Moos (2001), pp. 303-310. On exemplary processes in the Middle Ages, see Melville (2005b).
27 Cf. Goody (1986).
28 Stock (1983); Keller (1990); Keller (1992). On a temporary flourishing of literacy even in the Carolingian era, see McKitterick (1995).
29 Among the oldest rules is that of Pachomius (ca. 292-348): see Rousseau (1999). At the same time there naturally remained a significant oral communication structure, as has recently and compellingly been shown for the High Middle Ages by Vanderputten (ed.) (2011).
30 A discussion of a broad range of such uses of writing in medieval culture from a comparative perspective can be found in Keller / Grubmüller / Staubach (ed.) (1992); Keller / Christel Meier / Scharff (ed.) (1999).
31 No topic was barred from literary production in medieval monasteries, because, together with the cathedral schools, these monasteries had practically a monopoly on learning well into the High Middles Ages. Even apart from this, however, it is particularly impor-

following fields of innovation: in paraenesis, that is, ethical instruction, and in law and administration.

Paraenetical texts had been produced more or less continuously since Late Antiquity, and in ever-increasing numbers since the eleventh century, in order to instruct monks and nuns in the basics of spiritual and moral progress.[32] The texts thereby gained a complementary function to the legal and administrative documents which focused on the affairs of the community. The texts' claim to validity rested on the fact that the types of behaviour they urged were seen as imperative and necessary to salvation; their validity was located solely in the conscience of each person and was therefore completely individual. In addition to the creation of a personal and inner acceptance of the monastic communal organisation, these texts also concerned the maxim of a spiritual formation of the individual and the demands, specifically on the soul, of a way of life which was individual and at the same time directed completely towards God. In this way, monasteries developed a mode of dealing with the Self for the first time in the Middle Ages.[33] They intended to describe the behaviours of the individual against the backdrop of this experienced and also preconceived world, and to analyse their definitive interior and exterior conditions and causes. They also intended to objectivise the normative structures derived from them, to understand the corresponding ideal values in abstract terms such as *caritas*, *pax* or *iustitia*, and thereby to establish them as guidance for their own behaviour.[34] In other words: individual action and aspiration, which were (as has already been mentioned) emphatically passionate, reappeared in a transpersonal conceptual framework which needed an act of rationally guided textualisation in order to become reproducible by and for the community.

In order to stabilise the community, its internal procedures were organised in the course of monastic history again and again through legal texts, such as rules

---

tant to emphasise that monasteries produced and transmitted texts in a highly rational fashion, in order to counteract the human tendency to forget, and in order to save for the future knowledge which was relevant to themselves as well as to the whole world. See the fundamental work of Leclercq (2008); cf. also the short survey in Milis (2002), pp. 85-107.

32 See Bynum (1979). Paraenetical texts could refer to the noviciate, but had a much larger scope and encompassed fundamentally all members of the order: see Breitenstein (2008), passim; and more recently on a significant form of transmission Breitenstein (2009).

33 See the collection of essays in Melville / Schürer (ed.) (2002).

34 See the survey of Leclercq (1963) and more recently, the case-study of Breitenstein / Melville (2010); Melville (ed.) (2011).

and written *consuetudines*, statutes, decisions of general chapters etc.,[35] which regulated the admission of members, the investiture of offices, and their relationship with the surrounding society, and which provided material resources and monitored their use. Monastic rules and the norms which derived from them in the form of written customs, statutes etc. assigned roles and competencies; they attempted to prevent deviance and imposed sanctions if this failed. Thereby, a field of behavioural structures, which were all related to this organisation, was established in a highly rationalised way, regulating spiritual, material and economic matters and day-to-day life, as well as the use of space and the rituals enacted there, food and clothing etc. In addition, they provided regulations for the relationship with the monastery's surroundings in an accurate, detailed and indispensable manner.

It was only through the medium of such legal and administrative texts (including in the area of the economy) that the modes of action which they demanded could then be practiced and acted upon by all those concerned in as similar a way as possible, independent of location or situation.[36] Additionally, the corporate leadership of monastic associations or orders inevitably needed a system of norms that rested on a general consensus, which showed itself independent with regard to the individual, and was binding for everyone in the same way – including those who were its guardians.[37] This independent validity, however, presupposed writing as an objective carrier of knowledge, which made any arbitrary interpretation or change impossible, or at least exposed such arbitrariness, and which made changes or annulments possible only if these were agreed on by the community.[38] This rational codification of objective law made the legislative and judicative practice in monastic communities adaptable in the face of the contingent disturbances mentioned earlier, and they were therefore

---

35 On this, see Andenna / Melville (2005).
36 Cf. Melville (1991); Schreiner (1992a).
37 It was part of the Benedictine tradition that the abbot could not order anything against the norms of the rule: "Extra Deum nihil agas, extra Benedictum nihil praecipias", as it was phrased by the above-mentioned Abbot Peter of Moûtier-la-Celle, "Epistolae I, 31", in Patrologia Latina 202, cols. 439-441. An analogous attitude can be seen in the more recent statutory laws from the twelfth century onward. The abbot of Cluny, as head of an order emerging from an association, stated succinctly in his promulgation of the Cluniac statutes of 1200: "[...] etiam nos ipsos legi subjicimus [...].": Charvin (1965), p. 41.
38 This concern for textual integrity is clearly articulated in the prologues of the Premonstratensian statutes which state that nobody was allowed to change, add or subtract anything according to his own will ("si mutare vel addere vel minuere nulli quitquam propria voluntate liceat"); Lefèvre / Grauwen (ed.) (1978), p. 1.

able to initiate reforms in order to maintain those things through change which seemed worth preserving.[39]

Against the background of this struggle for perfection both tools – the texts of legal organisation and the paraenetical texts – symbolised the claims to validity of the whole community, as well as of the individual. But what made these texts special was that while their contents juxtaposed the internalised passion of the individual ascetic and the 'methodical practices' of an institutional community, these contents were shaped as transpersonal patterns of organisation in a similarly rational structure. For both types of text had an identical aim: because of their equally normative character, the opportunity presented itself, in a way that was actually enforceable, to see the religious fervour of each individual as being consistent with the demands of communal organisation and vice versa.[40]

This specifically monastic set of tools constituted the basis for concrete institutional forms which can quite clearly be characterised by the Weberian term of 'methodical practices'. – For the remainder of my lecture, I would like to present a few examples of how innovative achievements could firmly arise from this.

Monasteries were the first communities in the Middle Ages which prospectively created organisational forms which could claim to enable and determine both goal-oriented and uniform actions in any future decision-making. In an introductory passage to the Cistercian *Carta caritatis prior* from the early twelfth century – probably the first medieval text that deserves to be called a 'constitution' – this principle was formulated in the form of a programme (and then put into practice): 'In this decree the above-mentioned brothers decided, and determined for their successors, through which contract, in which manner, or rather, with what love their monks should remain united and inseparable in spirit, although scattered among abbeys in many parts of the world in body.'[41] The Cistercians became an exemplar for other monastic associations; their model – the order as the new form of organisation for regular life – gained general acceptance. They created the general chapter both as a symbolic institution which represented the entirety of the order and as an organ of legislation and ultimate control. With the general chapter they also reached the perfection of any prospective creation: an authority of perpetual correction, which was necessary

---

39 Important aspects of this are discussed in Klaus Schreiner (1992b), pp. 311-333.
40 On this, see Melville (1996), pp. 167-171.
41 "Hoc etiam decretum cartam caritatis uocari censebant, quia eius statutum, omnis exactionis grauamen propulsana, solam caritatem et animarum utilitatem in diuinis et humanis exequitur." (*Carta Caritatis Prior*, prologue 4); Waddell (1999), p. 274.

to maintain the original impetus; other orders, particularly the Dominicans in the early thirteenth century,[42] developed these structures further. For instance, they introduced for the first time a system of democratically elected delegates to legislative assemblies, or the obligation to pass new legislation three times; for practical reasons they were also the first to create statutes the violation of which meant a breach of the law, but not a sin (which would have imperilled the soul), and thereby they separated morality and positive law.[43]

Additionally, monasteries were the first to draw up plans for architectural spaces which corresponded to the differentiated multipolarity of communal life in a functional way – as can be seen in the early medieval apparent 'utopia' of the St. Gallen Abbey Plan.[44] They were the first ones who, in order to realise the rational thought of self-sufficiency, built up economic empires with overwhelming success,[45] but they were also the first ones to make work acceptable as a methodical concept in the context of the guiding principles of their spirituality.[46] All monastic associations and orders were able to create efficient communication networks spanning all of Europe, which enabled them to exchange political analyses, as well as information about economic performance, disciplinary matters, methods of building construction and similar topics, all of which could be disseminated quickly by their distribution centres.[47] It was the Franciscans who, together with the Dominicans, dared to go on missions even into Muslim territories, having meticulously planned their expeditions, and who crossed the borders of the known world and forced a re-writing of geography. Examples such as these could easily be multiplied.

The rationality of an organisation to be perfected also guaranteed the best possible development of practices of communal or individual piety in the framework of the liturgy, divine office or individual contemplation. William of Saint-Thierry for instance characterised the cell prepared for eremitical life within the monastery as an enclosed space which, for those full of piety, was not a prison but a home of peace (a *domicilium pacis*). The door to this cell did not hide anything, but made withdrawal from other parts of the mon-

---

42 See in detail Galbraith (1925); on their place in contemporary structures, see Schmidt (1999).
43 This was the case in the particular legislation of the Dominicans and was then adopted by other orders. See Cygler (2001).
44 Hecht (1983); Zettler (2005). On its further development, see for instance Untermann (2010).
45 For a significant example, see most recently Rösener (2009).
46 Cf. Schreiner (2006), pp. 133-170.
47 Cf. Andenna / Herbers / Melville (ed.) (2012).

astery possible.[48] In this space the monk would be 'utterly locked out from the world' and at the same time 'locked in with God', according to William's emphasis.

Members of a monastic community tested the borders of rational understanding by using the method of so-called symbolism[49] and later scholastic dialectics[50] while simultaneously and radically forcing these borders open through individual mystical experiences.[51] For monastic organisation allowed in principle a deeply internalised, and often ecstatically lived spirituality, although this was occasionally realised in a radical and even revolutionary way. These cases showed, however, how monastic life was located liminally between orthodoxy and heresy[52] and what forces of retardant discipline were necessary to maintain the balance of zealous passion and the 'methodical practices' of the community. But even so, the guidelines of the law and the call of conscience would not have had an effect if there had not been a 'total conversion of the heart to God' which had already rigorously grasped the individual's entire self. Monasteries were therefore the first forms of community in the Middle Ages which showed consistently in their daily life that the pragmatics of life could not be led without a transcendent reference to sense-giving values and norms to which the individual felt committed in his heart. And they showed that the pragmatics of life could in the final analysis only succeed if one identified oneself deep in one's heart emotionally, even passionately with its rules.

From this collaboration of an internalised faith with the pragmatic organisation of life, members of monastic communities drew the innovative strength to fashion their own, still temporal world in a way that would leave hope for entry into heaven. This meant entering far into new territory which established a new organisation and which was methodically directed by the principles of the rational, and from an analytical point of view, this provides the justification for speaking of medieval monasteries as 'laboratories of innovation'.

But even if the innovative efforts of the monasteries primarily happened for the sake of their own stability, and even if they were geared strictly towards the demands of a world set apart, as has been sketched here, a world which had created for itself a separate interior and fenced itself off from all the exterior, it

---

48 Déchanet (ed.) (1975), p. 168. On the development of the medieval monastic cell, see Lentes (1998), pp. 125-164.
49 Cf. Dempf (1954), pp. 229-284.
50 Cf. Chenu (1969).
51 From the rich literature on mysticism, see particularly McGinn (1992-2005); Ruh (1990-1999); Langer (2004); Weiß (2006).
52 On this, see the seminal work by Grundmann (1935; 1977).

is still necessary to ask to what extent these innovative achievements had a significant effect on the secular world outside the monasteries.

But in order to do so, the actual relationship between the monastery and its environment has to be examined briefly. Only thus can we clarify the extent to which the secular world of the Middle Ages was prepared to accept innovations from an apparently very strictly secluded monastic world.

'Le monastre est en meme temps la cellule d'une cité terrestre', is how Marie-Dominique Chenu quite rightly emphasised[53] this in continuation of an Augustinian dichotomy. Indeed, history shows that the monasteries were able to give significant impulses to their surrounding environment even beyond the boundaries of their separated existence, and that they were also able to connect with that environment both politically and economically.

Thus, the monastery could provide a crucible for the fundamental but diverging needs of medieval society. Monks and nuns did not just provide an example, through their lives, of how to realise the ethical principles of the Christian faith, they also promised the extra-monastic world a secure repository for investments both in piety and in the secular business of economy and politics. From the very beginning of the Middle Ages some monasteries had accumulated enormous estates through donations and property transfers, and these estates could include not just lordship over people, but also tithes, as well as parochial, customs, mining and market rights. The new reform movements of the eleventh and twelfth centuries, however, and particularly the Cistercians, focused their criticism of Benedictine monasticism on just this point: they accused the traditional abbeys of feeding on the blood of the people by collecting tithes.[54] Poverty movements arising out of contemporary eremitical circles, and sustained later by the mendicant orders of the thirteenth century, therefore refused any common property and presented to the world a model of voluntary poverty as a spiritual way to salvation.[55]

The extent to which all these monastic forms were accepted by the secular world is astounding, albeit in different ways and at different times, as is the extent to which the monastery as an institution appeared throughout the Middle Ages as an integral part of separate noble, urban and universal-ecclesiastical spheres.[56] In the face of this acceptance (which was never self-evident, and often

---

53 Chenu (1966) p. 230.
54 Cf. Melville (2009), p. 29.
55 Cf. Little (1983); Kehnel / Melville (ed.) (2001).
56 From a broad range of scholarship, see Schreiner (1989); Milis (1999); Kleinjung (2008).

had to be gained and re-gained),[57] members of monastic communities were fundamentally able to teach men in the secular world how to live lives pleasing to God, to show them through their example ways into the interior of their souls, and to interpret for them in a programmatic way nature, life and the afterlife in sermons, for which they had created specialised orders.

From this point of view, there were no obstacles in principle to the transfer of innovation, and monastic achievements were therefore available to the secular world, wherever and whenever they were transferable in actuality and despite their connection to the specificity of the monastery. – There were two possibilities here. One constituted an immediate influence on contemporary affairs during the Middle Ages; this refers really just to a transfer from the monastic to the secular world which did not alter the substance of monastic values. The other one needed a much longer time to take effect; it involved a secularisation of monastic values which in the final instance made their monastic origin irrelevant.

On the first possibility: because the pragmatics of a methodically implemented rationality was functionally open, and could therefore be used both in religious and secular forms of life, everything derived from these innovations was at least potentially transferable to the extra-monastic world. Examples are the parliamentary organisation introduced by the orders in order to supervise the executive, or the elaboration of statute legislation which could resist arbitrary attacks and which at the same time was adaptable to new situations through the systematic introduction of legal amendments, or the creation of a body of law the sanctions of which were not linked to salvation, or a division of labour that was determined exclusively by ability. These all represented innovative institutions which could profitably be transferred to the secular world, and which filled, among other things, the needs of the developing urban communities of the twelfth and thirteenth centuries.[58] In more general terms, monastic structures could therefore offer their secular environment nothing less than models for the rationality of planning, the creation of norms, the division of labour, the allocation of resources, economic operating efficiency and a responsible handling of both property and a lack of possessions. Through the rational shaping of social systems that had been tested out in the monasteries they could also prepare the way to state formation which began its development in this period.

On the second possibility: It has been shown that one of the particular innovative achievements of the monasteries had been their very specific handling of absolute values. This had been deeply internalised in their souls and was determined by total devotion to religious fervour; it was therefore in its

---

57 See the striking observations of Schmidt (2009).
58 See for instance Busch (1991).

essence individual and unreservedly emotional – and therefore necessarily radical and anti-institutional. At the same time, it was institutionally bound, subject to discipline and humility, framed by a community of peace, and held by rules and rituals which were based on differentiation or *discretio*. Through this seeming paradox, European culture acquired a model which allowed it to see a link between individually experienced religiosity and the regularity of practical rationality in such a way that the two levels did not neutralise but sublimate each other. This opened up a new type of ethics which was fundamentally human and humane, and which accorded humanity the dignity of the right measure even when faced with the precept to follow absolute demands.[59] In order to transfer this humanity to the secular world, however, it was necessary to renounce monastic religiosity as its transcendent foundational element.

Literature

Sources

Benedicti Regula, ed. Rudolphus Hanslik, (Wien, 1977).

Charvin, Gaston, *Statuts, chapitres généreaux et visites de l'ordre de Cluny* vol. I (Paris, 1965).

Déchanet, Jean (ed.), *Wilhelm von Saint-Thierry, Lettre aux frères du Mont-Dieu* (Paris, 1975).

Lefèvre, Placide Fernand, and Wilfried Marcel Grauwen (ed.), *Les statuts de Prémontré au milieu du XIIe siècle* (Averbode, 1978).

Martel, Gérard de (ed.), *Pierre de Celle, L'école du cloître* (Paris, 1977).

Waddell, Chrysogonus, *Narrative and Legislative Texts from Early Cîteaux. Latin Text in Dual Edition with English Translation and Notes* (Cîteaux, 1999).

Studies

Andenna, Cristina, Klaus Herbers and Gert Melville (ed.), *Die Ordnung der Kommunikation und die Kommunikation der Ordnungen im mittelalterlichen Europa*, Bd. 1: *Netzwerke: Klöster und Orden im 12. und 13. Jahrhundert* (Stuttgart, 2012).

Andenna, Cristina, and Gert Melville (ed.), *Regulae - Consuetudines - Statuta. Studi sulle fonti normative degli ordini religiosi nei secoli centrali del Medioevo* (Münster, 2005).

Andenna, Giancarlo, Sébastien Barret and Melville, Gert (ed.), *Oboedientia. Zu Formen und Grenzen von Macht und Unterordnung im mittelalterlichen Religiosentum* (Münster, 2005).

Angenendt, Arnold, *Geschichte der Religiosität im Mittelalter* (3rd ed. Darmstadt, 2009).

Aulinger, Gislar, *Das Humanum in der Regel Benedikts von Nursia. Eine moralgeschichtliche Studie* (St. Ottilien, 1950).

Bauer, Gerhard, *Claustrum animae. Untersuchungen zur Geschichte der Metapher vom Herzen als Kloster* (München, 1973).

Bertola, Ermenegildo, *Il problema della coscienza nella teologia monastica del 12 secolo* (Padova, 1970).

---

59 Cf. Aulinger (1950).

Bohl, Cornelius, *Geistlicher Raum. Räumliche Sprachbilder als Träger spiritueller Erfahrung, dargestellt am Werk "De compositione" des David von Augsburg* (Werl, 2000).

Breitenstein, Mirko, and Gert Melville, ´Gerechtigkeit als fundierendes Element des mittelalterlichen Mönchtums´, in *Bilder – Sachen – Mentalitäten. Arbeitsfelder historischer Kulturwissenschaften, Wolfgang Brückner zum 80. Geburtstag*, ed. Heidrun Alzheimer et al. (Regensburg, 2010), pp. 33-42.

Breitenstein, Mirko, ´"Ins Gespräch gebracht": Der Dialog als Prinzip monastischer Unterweisung´, in *Understanding Monastic Practices of Oral Communication (Western Europe, Eleventh – Thirteenth Centuries)*, ed. Steven Vanderputten (Turnhout, 2009), pp. 205-229.

Breitenstein, Mirko, ´Gerechtigkeit als Leitidee und Ordnungsprinzip im frühen Cisterzienserorden´, *Analecta Cisterciensia* 60 (2010), p. 225 - 262.

Breitenstein, Mirko, *Das Noviziat im hohen Mittelalter. Zur Organisation des Eintrittes bei den Cluniazensern, Cisterziensern und Franziskanern* (Berlin, 2008).

Busch, Jörg W., ´Zum Prozeß der Verschriftlichung des Rechtes in lombardischen Kommunen des 13. Jahrhunderts´, *Frühmittelalterliche Studien* 25 (1991), pp. 373-390.

Bynum, Caroline, '*Docere verbo et exemplo*'. *An Aspect of Twelfth-Century Spirituality* (Missoula, 1979).

Chenu, Marie-Dominique, *La théologie au XIIe siècle* (2nd ed. Paris, 1966).

Chenu, Marie-Dominique, *La théologie comme science au 13e siècle* (3rd ed. Paris, 1969).

Chenu, Marie-Dominique, *L'éveil de la conscience dans la civilisation médiévale* (Montréal/Paris, 1969).

Constable, Giles, *The Reformation of the Twelfth Century* (Cambridge, 1996).

Cygler, Florent, ´L'ordre de Cluny et les "rebelliones" au XIIIe siècle´, *Francia* 19 (1992), pp. 61-94.

Cygler, Florent, ´Une nouvelle conception de la culpabilité chez les réguliers. Humbert de Romans, les Dominicaines et "principe de la loi purement pénale" au XIIIe siècle´, in *La culpabilité*, ed. Jacqueline Hoareau-Dodinau and Pascal Texier (Limoges, 2001), pp. 387-401.

Dempf, Alois, *Sacrum Imperium. Geschichts- und Staatsphilosophie des Mittelalters und der politischen Renaissance* (Darmstadt, 1954).

Diers, Michaela, *Bernhard von Clairvaux. Elitäre Frömmigkeit und begnadetes Wirken* (Münster, 1991).

Felten, Franz Joseph, `Arbeit, Armut und Askese und die Folgen bei den frühen Zisterziensern´, *Cistercienser Chronik* 108 (2001), pp. 59-87.

Felten, Franz Joseph, ´Wozu treiben wir vergleichende Ordensgeschichte?´, in *Mittelalterliche Orden und Klöster im Vergleich. Methodische Ansätze und Perspektiven*, ed. Gert Melville, Gert / Anne Müller (Berlin, 2007), pp. 1-51.

Füser, Thomas, *Mönche im Konflikt. Zum Spannungsfeld von Norm, Devianz und Sanktion bei den Cisterziensern und Cluniazensern (12. bis frühes 14. Jahrhundert)* (Münster, 2000).

Galbraith, Georgina Rosalie, *The Constitution of the Dominican Order: 1216 to 1360* (Manchester, 1925).

Goody, Jack, *The Logic of Writing and the Organization of Society* (Cambridge, 1986).

Grundmann, Herbert, *Religiöse Bewegungen im Mittelalter. Untersuchungen über die geschichtlichen Zusammenhänge zwischen der Ketzerei, den Bettelorden und der religiösen Frauenbewegung im 12. und 13. Jahrhundert und über die geschichtlichen Grundlagen der deutschen Mystik* (Berlin, 1935, reprint Darmstadt, 1977).

Hecht, Konrad, *Der St. Galler Klosterplan* (Sigmaringen, 1983).
Kehnel, Annette, and Gert Melville (ed.), *In proposito paupertatis. Studien zum Armutsverständnis bei den mittelalterlichen Bettelorden* (Münster, 2001).
Keller, Hagen, Klaus Grubmüller, and Nikolaus Staubach (ed.), *Pragmatische Schriftlichkeit im Mittelalter. Erscheinungsformen und Entwicklungsstufen* (München, 1992).
Keller, Hagen, Christel Meier, and Thomas Scharff (ed.), *Schriftlichkeit und Lebenspraxis im Mittelalter. Erfassen, Bewahren, Verändern* (München, 1999).
Keller, Hagen, 'Die Entwicklung der europäischen Schriftkultur im Spiegel mittelalterlicher Überlieferung. Beobachtungen und Überlegungen', in *Geschichte und Geschichtsbewußtsein. Festschrift Karl-Ernst Jeismann*, ed. Paul Leidinger and Dieter Metzler (Münster, 1990) pp. 171-204.
Keller, Hagen, 'Vom "heiligen Buch" zur "Buchführung". Lebensfunktionen der Schrift im Mittelalter', *Frühmittelalterliche Studien* 26 (1992), pp. 1-31.
Kleinjung, Christine, *Frauenklöster als Kommunikationszentren und soziale Räume. Das Beispiel Worms vom 13. bis zum Beginn des 15. Jahrhunderts* (Korb am Neckar, 2008).
Krüger, Friedhelm, 'Gewissen, III. Mittelalter und Reformationszeit, 1. Mittelalter', in *Theologische Realenzyklopädie* 13 (1984), pp. 219-221.
Langer, Otto, *Christliche Mystik im Mittelalter. Mystik und Rationalisierung - Stationen eines Konflikts* (Darmstadt, 2004).
Leclercq, Jean, *L'amour vu par les moines au XIIe siècle* (Paris, 1983).
Leclercq, Jean, *L'amour des lettres et le désir de Dieu. Initiation aux auteurs monastiques du Moyen Âge*, (4th ed. Paris, 2008).
Leclercq, Jean, *Otia monastica. Etudes sur le vocabulaire de la contemplation au moyen âge* (Roma 1963).
Lentes, Thomas, 'Vita perfecta zwischen Vita communis und Vita privata. Eine Skizze zur klösterlichen Einzelzelle', in *Das Öffentliche und das Private in der Vormoderne*, ed. Gert Melville and Peter von Moos (Köln/Weimar/Wien, 1998), pp. 125-164.
Little, Lester Knox, *Religious Poverty and the Profit Economy in Medieval Europe* (Ithaca, NY, 1983).
McGinn, Bernard, *The Presence of God, A History of Western Christian Mysticism*, 4 vols., (London/New York, 1992-2005).
McKitterick, Rosamond, *The Carolingians and the Written Word* (3rd ed. Cambridge 1995).
Melville, Gert, and Markus Schürer (ed.), *Das Eigene und das Ganze. Zum Individuellen im mittelalterlichen Religiosentum* (Münster, 2002).
Melville, Gert (ed.), *Aspects of Charity. Concern for One's Neighbour in the Medieval vita religiosa* (Berlin, 2011).
Melville, Gert, and Anne Müller, 'Franziskanische Raumkonzepte. Zur symbolischen Bedeutung des inneren und äußeren Hauses', *Revue Mabillon* 21 (2010), pp. 105-138.
Melville, Gert, 'Der Mönch als Rebell gegen gesatzte Ordnung und religiöse Tugend. Beobachtungen zu Quellen des 12. und 13. Jahrhunderts', in *De ordine vitae. Zu Normvorstellungen, Organisationsformen und Schriftlichkeit im mittelalterlichen Ordenswesen*, ed. Gert Melville (Münster, 1996), pp. 153-186.
Melville, Gert, 'Die Zisterzienser und der Umbruch des Mönchtums im 11. und 12. Jahrhundert', in *Norm und Realität. Kontinuität und Wandel der Zisterzienser im Mittelalter*, ed. Franz Josef Felten and Werner Rösener (Berlin, 2009), pp. 23-43.

Melville, Gert, 'Im Zeichen der Allmacht. Zur Präsenz Gottes im klösterlichen Leben des hohen Mittelalters', in *Das Sichtbare und das Unsichtbare der Macht. Institutionelle Prozesse in Antike, Mittelalter und Neuzeit*, ed. Gert Melville (Köln/Weimar/Wien, 2005a), pp. 19-44.

Melville, Gert, 'Inside and Outside. Some Considerations about Cloistral Boundaries in the Central Middle Ages', in *Ecclesia in medio nationis. Reflections on the Study of Monasticism in the Central Middle Ages*, ed. B. Meijns and S. Vanderputten (Leuven, 2011b), pp. 167-182.

Melville, Gert, 'Stephan von Obazine. Begründung und Überwindung charismatischer Führung', in *Charisma und religiöse Gemeinschaften im Mittelalter*, ed. Giancarlo Andenna, Mirko Breitenstein and Gert Melville (Münster, 2005b), pp. 85-102.

Melville, Gert, 'Tegumenta virtutis und occulta cordis. Zur Wahrnehmung religiöser Identität im Mittelalter', in *Religiöse Erfahrung und wissenschaftliche Theologie. Festschrift für Ulrich Köpf zum 70. Geburtstag*, ed. Albrecht Beutel and Reinhold Rieger (Tübingen, 2011 a), pp. 277-290.

Melville, Gert, 'Zur Funktion der Schriftlichkeit im institutionellen Gefüge mittelalterlicher Orden', *Frühmittelalterliche Studien* 25 (1991), pp. 391-417.

Melville, Gert, *Die Welt der mittelalterlichen Klöster. Geschichte und Lebensformen* (München, 2012).

Milis, Ludo, *Angelic Monks and Earthly Men. Monasticism and its Meaning to Medieval Society* (2nd ed. Woodbridge/Rochester, 1999).

Milis, Ludo, *Les moines et le peuple dans l'Europe du Moyen Âge* (Paris, 2002).

Moos, Peter von, 'Herzensgeheimnisse (occulta cordis). Selbstverwahrung und Selbstentblößung im Mittelalter', in *Peter von Moos, Gesammelte Schriften zum Mittelalter, Bd. 2: Rhetorik, Kommunikation und Medialität*, ed. Gert Melville (Münster/Berlin, 2006), pp. 5-28.

Moos, Peter von, 'Krise und Kritik der Institutionalität. Die mittelalterliche Kirche als „Anstalt" und „Himmelreich auf Erden"', in *Institutionalität und Symbolisierung. Verstetigung kultureller Ordnungsmuster in Vergangenheit und Gegenwart*, ed. Gert Melville (Köln/Weimar/Wien, 2001), pp. 293-340.

Moulin, Léo, *La vie quotidienne des religieux au Moyen Âge. X^e - XVe siècle* (Paris, 1990).

Patzold, Steffen, *Konflikte im Kloster. Studien zu Auseinandersetzungen in monastischen Gemeinschaften des ottonisch-salischen Reichs* (Husum, 2000).

Reiner, Hans, 'Gewissen', in *Historisches Wörterbuch der Philosophie* 3 (1974), cols. 574-592.

Rösener, Werner, 'Die Agrarwirtschaft der Zisterzienser: Innovation und Anpassung', in *Norm und Realität. Kontinuität und Wandel der Zisterzienser im Mittelalter*, ed. Franz-Josef Felten and Werner Rösener (Berlin, 2009), pp. 67-95.

Rousseau, Philip, *Pachomius. The Making of a Community in Fourth-Century Egypt* (Berkeley, 1999).

Ruh, Kurt, *Geschichte der abendländischen Mystik*, 4 vols. (München, 1990-1999).

Schmidt, Hans-Joachim, 'Klosterleben ohne Legitimität. Kritik und Verurteilung im Mittelalter', in *Institution und Charisma. Festschrift für Gert Melville zum 65. Geburtstag*, ed. Franz Josef Felten, Annette Kehnel and Stefan Weinfurter (Köln/Weimar/Wien, 2009), pp. 377-400.

Schmidt, Hans-Joachim, 'Legitimität von Innovation. Geschichte, Kirche und neue Orden im 13. Jahrhundert', in *Vita religosa. Festschrift für Kaspar Elm zum 70. Geburtstag*, ed. Franz J. Felten and Nikolaus Jaspert (Berlin, 1999), pp. 371-391.

Schreiner, Klaus, '"Brot der Mühsal". Körperliche Arbeit im Mönchtum des hohen und späten Mittelalters. Theologisch motivierte Einstellungen, regelgebundene Normen, geschichtliche Praxis´, in *Arbeit im Mittelalter. Vorstellungen und Wirklichkeiten,* ed. Verena Postel (Berlin, 2006), pp. 133-170.

Schreiner, Klaus, ´Dauer, Niedergang und Erneuerung klösterlicher Observanz im hoch- und spätmittelalterlichen Mönchtum. Krisen, Reform- und Institutionalisierungsprobleme in der Sicht und Deutung betroffener Zeitgenossen´, in *Institutionen und Geschichte. Theoretische Aspekte und mittelalterliche Befunde,* ed. Gert Melville (Köln/Weimar/Wien, 1992b), pp. 295-341.

Schreiner, Klaus, ´Ein Herz und eine Seele. Eine urchristliche Lebensform und ihrer Institutionalisierung im augustinisch geprägten Mönchtum des hohen und späten Mittelalters´, in *Regula Sancti Augustini. Normative Grundlage differenter Verbände im Mittelalter,* Gert Melville and Anne Müller (Paring, 2002), pp. 1-48.

Schreiner, Klaus, ´Mönchsein in der Adelsgesellschaft des hohen und späten Mittelalters. Klösterliche Gemeinschaftsbildung zwischen spiritueller Selbstbehauptung und sozialer Anpassung´, *Historische Zeitschrift* 248 (1989), pp. 557-620.

Schreiner, Klaus, ´Verschriftlichung als Faktor monastischer Reform. Funktionen von Schriftlichkeit im Ordenswesen des hohen und späten Mittelalters´, in *Pragmatische Schriftlichkeit im Mittelalter. Erscheinungsformen und Entwicklungsstufen,* ed. Hagen Keller, Klaus Grubmüller and Nikolaus Staubach (München, 1992a), pp. 37-75.

Sonntag, Jörg, *Klosterleben im Spiegel des Zeichenhaften. Symbolisches Denken und Handeln hochmittelalterlicher Mönche zwischen Dauer und Wandel, Regel und Gewohnheit* (Berlin, 2008).

Spijker, Ineke van't, *Fictions of the Inner Life. Religious Literature and Formation of the Self in the Eleventh and Twelfth Centuries* (Turnhout, 2004).

Stock, Brian, *The Implications of Literacy. Written Language and Models of Interpretation in the 11th and 12th Centuries* (Princeton/New York, 1983).

Untermann, Matthias, ´Innovative Architektur. Das Beispiel der Zisterzienser´, in *Verwandlungen des Stauferreichs: drei Innovationsregionen im mittelalterlichen Europa,* ed. Bernd Schneidmüller, Stefan Weinfurter and Alfried Wieczorek (Darmstadt, 2010), pp. 230-245.

Vanderputten, Steven (ed.), *Understanding Monastic Practices of Oral Communication (Western Europe, Tenth-Thirteenth Centuries)* (Turnhout, 2011).

Weber, Max, *Wirtschaft und Gesellschaft* (5th ed. Tübingen, 1980).

Weiß, Bardo, *Ekstase und Liebe. Die Unio mystica bei den deutschen Mystikerinnen des 12. und 13. Jahrhunderts* (Paderborn 2006).

Wieland, Georg, ´Rationalisierung und Verinnerlichung. Aspekte der geistigen Physiognomie des 12. Jahrhundert´, in *Philosophie im Mittelalter. Entwicklungslinien und Paradigmen,* ed. Jan P. Beckmann, Ludger Honnefelder and Gangolf Schrimpf (2nd ed. Hamburg, 1996), pp. 61-79.

Zettler, Alfons, `Der Himmel auf Erden... Raumkonzepte des St. Galler Klosterplans´, in *Virtuelle Räume, Raumwahrnehmung und Raumvorstellung im Mittelalter,* ed. Elisabeth Vavra (Berlin, 2005), pp. 35-46.

An Intricate Web of Friends:

Unravelling the Networks and Personal Connections of the two Lawrences of Durham

Mia Münster-Swendsen

Once a marginal subject, friendship and the relationships between individuals and communities are now at the forefront in the social and cultural history of the Middle Ages. This is not least due to Brian Patrick McGuire's seminal study on monastic friendship from 1988, which became the starting point of a large and still expanding body of scholarship on medieval friendship and network formation.[1] Friendships and personal connections are now seen as the main structures governing medieval "face-to-face society", thus transcending the individual, personal and "psychological" level. This essay represents an attempt to trace such connections in more minute detail – a type of prosopographic work that is both time-consuming and often tedious - but which may serve to show the remarkable density and interconnectedness of overlapping personal and communal networks and hopefully, in conjunction with similar studies, provide further insights into how friendship functions and what it means in a specific historical or social context.

Writing this essay has given me an opportunity to revisit one of my former research topics, namely the intellectual milieu of the monastic cathedral chapter of Durham, including one of the most intriguing, prolific, yet least studied monastic authors of twelfth-century England, Lawrence of Durham (c. 1100x1110-1154).[2] Moreover, it provided a chance to engage with an old problem that had

---

1   It is striking today to read its opening line: "Friendship is hardly a subject which seems conducive to academic treatment...", McGuire (1988), Preface, p. vii. An earlier version of the paper that became this essay was presented at the seminar workshop 'Social Networks and Institutional Friendships" of members of the *British Academy Network on Medieval Friendship Networks* (which ran from 2004-10) in March 2009.
2   For a general introduction to Lawrence of Durham and his works, see Rigg (1992), pp. 54-61 and Münster-Swendsen (2005), pp. 151-168. Lawrence's major work, the Biblical epos *Hypognosticon* is the only one of Lawrence's works that has received a thorough study, see Daub (2005).

nagged me for some time, but which I had not managed to write up on. Some readers will remember Sir Richard Southern's struggles to distinguish between two Peters of Blois. In a similar manner, scholars working on Lawrence of Durham will soon discover that here is a similar case of mistaken or conflated identities. There appear to be *two* Lawrences of Durham: exact contemporaries, both of them writers and intellectuals, and both moving in the same circles. In the case of these two Lawrences, it is my contention that unravelling their personal networks is the only way that may enable us finally to disentangle the two. Moreover, this nitty-gritty prosopographical detective work also reveals a fascinating web of connections comprising several of the most important monastic learned communities in England and converging in the extremely influential Abbey of St Victor in Paris.

Since the historical background might be unfamiliar to some readers, let me briefly recount the main events: The monastic chapter of Durham[3] had seen its share of upheavals during the troubles of King Stephen's reign in the 1130s, culminating in the usurpation of the episcopal see by the allegedly brutal oppressor William Cumin, who was finally ousted in 1144 after years of bitter and often violent conflict.[4] For a few years the Durham chapter was at peace under Bishop William of St Barbara, electing Lawrence as prior in 1149[5] (he was apparently

---

3   The cathedral chapter of secular canons had been replaced by Benedictine monks in the early 1080s, during the episcopacy of William of St Calais/Carileph (1081-96). The prior of the Durham Chapter, second only to the bishop, held abbatial status. On the prior's liberties, see the charters of Archbishop Thomas of York and William the Conqueror, printed as appendix 5-8 in Raine, *Historiae Dunelmensis Scriptores Tres* (1839), pp. 11-18. The role of the Durham Archdeacon seems to have been a recurrent source of conflict.

4   On the so-called "Cumin-affair", see Young (1979) and Young (1994), pp. 353-68. A brief summary of these particular events and Lawrence's involvement in them can be found in Münster-Swendsen (2012), pp. 159-62. The main contemporary sources to the affair are John of Hexham's *Historia* and the anonymous continuator to Symeon of Durham's *Libellus de exordio*. William Cumin belonged to a powerful clerical family and was the chancellor of King David of Scotland, former member of the English royal chancery (as member of the *familia* of chancellor Geoffrey Rufus later bishop of Durham (1133-41), as well as archdeacon of Worcester. Supported by King Henry II and Archbishop Theobald of Canterbury, William Cumin quickly regained his positions and prestige after the debacle at Durham. The reports of his ruthlessness by Lawrence of Durham in his *Dialogi* and the anonymous continuator of Symeon of Durham's *Libellus* may have been strongly exaggerated.

5   These dates can be established from the charter material and its witness lists. In 1147, a Lawrence, presumably the later prior, appears as subprior (no. 36, p. 142). Four other genuine Durham charters from the period 1149-52 mention a Prior Lawrence (nos. 32

sub-prior from 1147). However, after the death of Bishop William in November 1152, Durham again found itself in turmoil over an episcopal election. After some deliberation and the gentle prodding of the ecclesiastical power-broker par excellence of these years, Bishop Henry of Winchester (a.k.a. Henry of Blois), the chapter finally voted unanimously for the young treasurer and archdeacon of York, Hugh of Puiset, a candidate below canonical age. The election immediately met with strong opposition from a formidable Cistercian duo comprising the Archbishop of York, Henry Murdac, Hugh's (and the Durham chapter's) archenemy,[6] and none other than Bernard of Clairvaux. The main electors, including prior Lawrence, were promptly excommunicated by the Archbishop who, despite pleas and acts of penance, refused to lift the sentence.[7] The only option left was to appeal directly to Rome, though with Bernard's and Henry's close friend Eugenius III on the papal throne, the prospects for winning a case against this powerful Cistercian party were not good. The Durham election dispute bears a strong resemblance to the earlier one at York. The opposition was the same Cistercian trio, which had succeeded in removing the royal candidate from the archiepiscopal see creating a remarkable and, for the Durham electors, dangerous precedent. Nevertheless, in late summer 1153 a delegation consisting of Hugh of Puiset (the bishop-elect), Prior Lawrence, Archdeacon Wazo, and an uncertain number of Durham notables left for Rome. In his *Little Book on the Life and Miracles of Godric of Finchale*, one of the few sources for these events, Reginald of Durham recounts that on the eve of departure, a *Magister* Law-

---

D, p. 130; 39, p. 158; 41, p. 164) see *Durham Episcopal Charters 1071-1152*, ed. Offler (1968). A note in the *Feodarum prioratus Dunelmensis*, ed. Greenwell (1872), p. 129 mentions a grant by Prior Lawrence.

6   Henry Murdac, originally a member of the York cathedral chapter and a master of theology, had been persuaded by his friend Bernard of Clairvaux to become a Cistercian monk at Clairvaux, where he met and befriended the future pope Eugenius III. In 1144 Henry was back in Yorkshire, becoming abbot of Fountains, and on 7 December 1147, after the deposition of Archbishop William fitzHerbert, a nephew of King Stephen, he was consecrated Archbishop of York. The consecration was met with fierce opposition from the York cathedral chapter, led by the treasurer, Hugh of Puiset, whom Henry promptly excommunicated and for most of his archiepiscopacy, Henry was absent from York. He died on 14 October 1153 and William fitzHerbert was reinstated but died the year after, in 1154, in suspicious circumstances. He was later canonised – twice – as a saint. On the York dispute, see Councils and Synods (1981), pp. 810-13; pp. 817-20 as well as the *Vita sancti Willelmi*, ed. Raine (1886), pp. 270- 78. Various scholars have presented their differing views of the episode, most recently Norton (2006). Two classic articles on the subject are Poole (1930) and Knowles (1936).

7   On the controversy surrounding Hugh's election, see Scammell (1956), pp. 13-21. As to how stubbornly Henry upheld the excommunication, reports vary.

rence visited the hermit to hear his advice. The holy man replied with a chilling prophecy: "He said to him, 'You two Lawrences are now preparing to journey to Rome, but from this day on neither of you two will ever return here, nor will you ever behold Durham again.'" ('Ad quem ille, "Vos," inquit, "duo Laurentii, nunc Romam disponitis proficisci, sed nunquam vos utrique amodo huc eritis ambo redituri, sed neque Dunelmum amplius aspecturi".')[8]

Reginald then writes that a trembling Master Lawrence abandoned the trip – as well as his secular habit – and became a monk at St Albans and, several years later, abbot of Westminster. Auspicious news of the pope's death[9] reached the travelling Durham delegation as they were about to cross the Alps,[10] and in Rome, Prior Lawrence succeeded in persuading the new pope, Anastasius IV, to consecrate Durham's chosen candidate.[11] Tragically, the Prior fell ill and died in an unnamed French village on the return trip. His remains were later transported back to Durham.

So here, as announced, we have two Lawrences, exact contemporaries, involved in the same affair, both writers and men-of-letters, both of Durham. Reginald was careful to distinguish between the two men by their titles. Yet this has not hindered a persisting confusion between the two, which may have originated as early as the late twelfth or thirteenth century. The earliest example I have so far been able to find is in the admittedly unreliable Peterborough Chronicle for the year 1163 recording the translation of Edward the Confessor as 'procurata per Laurentium, ex priore Dunelmensi, Westmonasterii abbatem…'[12]

Two Lawrences are not found in the York continuation of Hugh the Chanter's Lives,[13] nor in the anonymous Durham continuation of Simeon's *Libellus* that treats these events.[14] In these sources, there is only the prior, and he is men-

---

8 Reginald of Durham, *Libellus*, ed. Raine (1845), pp. 233.
9 Eugenius III died 8 July 1153, followed closely by Bernard of Clairvaux on 20 August and Henry Murdac on 14 October. No doubt, the sudden disappearance of the entire group of opponents was highly conducive to the Durham legation's success.
10 Geoffrey of Coldingham, *De statu ecclesiae*, ed. Raine (1839), p. 6.
11 The bull of pope Anastasius IV, which is probably spurious, credits Lawrence personally for securing papal support. Hugh was consecrated on 21 December 1153. The document is printed as appendix 28 in Raine, *Historiae Dunelmensis Scriptores Tres* (1839), p. 34.
12 *Chronicon Angliæ Petriburgense*, ed. Giles (1845), p. 98
13 The continuator mentions the three main electors: Lawrence the Prior, and the archdeacons Wazo and Ranulph. Continuator of Hugh the Chanter (of York), *Addition to the lives by Hugh the Chantor*, ed. Raine (1886), p. 226.
14 Continuator of Symeon of Durham, *Libellus de exordio*, ed. D. Rollason (2000), in the variant section, pp. 321-23.

tioned by his title, not his name. Equally, Geoffrey of Coldingham's much later, thirteenth century chronicle is very detailed when it comes to Prior Lawrence's involvement, but no second Lawrence is mentioned. Thus apart from Reginald, only one other main source for the events in 1153 and 54 mentions two Lawrences. Like the anonymous York continuator, John of Hexham names prior Lawrence together with the archdeacons Wazo and Ranulf as the main electors. But he notes that a *Magister* Lawrence was excommunicated together with these.[15] The members of the party that left for Rome are not named, but John notes that *Magister* Lawrence detached himself from them, became a monk at St Albans and shortly thereafter abbot of Westminster. John does not report the prior's death in France.

The conflation of the two Lawrences seems to have originated already in the thirteenth century and it would be perpetuated by the early-modern antiquarians, notably John Leland (1503-52).[16] In Browne Willis's *A History of the Mitred Parliamentary Abbies and Conventual Cathedral Chapters* (1718) the confusion is complete. The index nominorum distinguishes between two Lawrences, but appears to get them mixed up. The entry for "Laurence Abbat of Westminster" refers to page 202 in the text; however on that page (in the list of abbots in the section on Westminster), the reader encounters the following:

> 17. Laurence, Prior of Durham, who obtained from Pope Alexander the 3rd to himself, and his successors, the privilege of using the Mitre, Ring, and Gloves. He died April 11 an. 1167 and was buried by his successor under a marble stone with the effigies of an Abbat carved upon it, having his inscription fixed on or near his tomb, in memory of him".[17]

If we are looking for the entry on "Laurence Prior of Durham", the index gives the following note: "preferred to the Abbacy of Westminster" and refers the reader to page 259 (in the list of priors, Durham section), which yields the following description:

---

15 John of Hexham, *Historia* (continuation of Symeon of Durham, *Historia regum*), ed. Arnold (1885), p. 329.
16 Leland (1709), pp. 204-5. Since Leland's groundbreaking *Commentarii de scriptoribus Britannicis* (published in print edition by Anthony Hall in 1709) became the foundation for later antiquarians' lists, the confusing of the two Lawrences came to be repeated. I have retained the original spelling in the quotations from the early modern scholars.
17 Willis (1718), p. 202. To my knowledge Willis is the only source for these obituary verses, which he printed below the entry: 'Clauditur hoc tumulo vir quondam clarus in orbe,/ qui præclarus erat hic locus, est et erit./ Pro meritis vitæ dedit illi Laurea nomen,/ detur ei vitæ Laurea pro mentis.'

"5. Laurence. Elected the same year [1149], a man of singular Prudence and Learning, as the many Books he wrote manifest. Bale erroneously says, he was promoted to the Abbacy of Westminster. He died in France on his Return from Rome, at the latter end of the year 1153. However his bones were afterwards brought hither, and deposited in the Priory Cemetery."[18]

So Willis appears to be correcting a mistaken identification, attributed to John Bale, who based his catalogue on Leland's, but seems to have got the dating of the prior's death wrong. According to contemporary sources that mention the prior's demise, together with the commemorative material in Durham (registers of obits, the Durham *Liber vitae*) Lawrence died in spring 1154 and the commemoration date is set to 15 kalends of April (18 March).[19] That both Lawrences are commemorated in the sections for April in the Durham memorial sources may also have added to the confusion, although the Durham *martyrologium* is careful to make the distinction between the two.[20] In his updated catalogue (1748), based on Leland, Thomas Tanner reprinted Leland's entry on "Laurentius Dunolmensis", but inserted a footnote (c) concerning the year of the prior's (and author's) death: "Hic Lelandus aperte hallucinatus est; nam Laurentius archidiaconus Dunelm. postea monachus Albanensis, factus erat abbas Westmonast. multos annos post obitum Laurentii prioris."[21] That the other Lawrence was a former archdeacon of Durham cannot possibly be the case, no list of archdeacons mentioning a Lawrence, so in correcting one mistake Tanner merely made another. A certain degree of confusion and uncertainty still appears among the few modern scholars who occasionally mention either of these Lawrences.[22]

---

18 Willis (1718), p. 259.
19 A.G. Rigg's biography of prior Lawrence in the Oxford DNB gives the dates 16 or 18 March 1154. Rigg (2004).
20 *Excerpta ex obituario ecclesiae Dunelmensis* (1841), p.142. Lawrence of Westminster appears in a group that includes Aelred of Rievaulx.
21 Tanner (1748), p. 472.
22 A. Young contends that 'Henry Murdac may still have had Master Laurence in mind in 1153 when he objected to Durham's choice of Hugh of Puiset.' Young (1994), p. 363. This hypothesis seems doubtful. If the reports of Reginald of Durham and John of Hexham are correct, this *Master* Lawrence was one of the electors and excommunicated together with the others by the archbishop. A. Lawrence-Mathers states that *Prior* Lawrence had probably travelled in France earlier, that is, before the fateful trip of 1153, but she provides no reference to evidence. See Lawrence-Mathers (2003), p. 145. Presumably this assumption comes from the rather vague statements in Raine's introduction to his edition of Lawrence's *Dialogi*. Lawrence-Mathers also assumes that the Lawrence who grew up in Waltham, Essex, and later became prior of Durham is

Prior Lawrence's connections

It may seem paradoxical that the prior and illustrious author's connections are more difficult to trace than those of the other, to modern scholars lesser known, Lawrence. The former, that is, Lawrence the Prior, is strangely reluctant to mention contemporaries by name except for the Durham bishops, and most of his *dramatis personae* appear to be fictional characters. One of the few exceptions is a certain Gervase, to whom Lawrence's main work, the *Hypognosticon*, is dedicated. To my knowledge, no one has yet tried to identify this Gervase.

While there are several Gervases in the twelfth-century parts of the *Durham liber vitae*, the nearly 4000 hexameters that make up the *Hypognosticon* are – in my opinion – too grand a gesture to be dedicated to a simple fellow member of the community. Hence, this Gervase would be someone worthy of a work of this magnitude, someone who would appreciate such a work, an individual who was known to Lawrence personally, as the wording in the dedication suggests, but not necessarily intimately. He would be someone seen as 'inspiring poetical composition' but not a recipient who had directly requested a work from Lawrence, as the author states it was written on his own initiative (but with Gervase functioning as a kind of muse) in the spare time between administrative duties at the episcopal palace.[23] I think I have managed to boil it down to two possible candidates, both of whom would connect Lawrence, the monk-courtier and future prior, to wider circles outside Durham. However, given the lack of central pieces of information, these possible identifications must remain hypothetical.

In 1133, around the same time as the *Hypognosticon* is generally thought to have been composed, we find a Gervase as sub-prior of the Benedictine Abbey of St Mary, York, where he is involved in ongoing internal reform struggles that end with a number of monks, including this Gervase, leaving York and creating Fountains Abbey. In 1139 he became abbot of Louth Park, a daughter house of Fountains, from where he retired some ten years later, shortly before his death,[24] at a time when the monastic community had grown from the original twelve to a crowd of over a hundred monks.[25] Thus with Gervase of Louth Park we have

---

    identical to the Lawrence in the letter of Bernard of Clairvaux and William of Rievaulx of 1143 and hence that the later prior, not the *magister*, was the Cistercians' favourite episcopal candidate after William Cumin's reign. Lawrence-Mathers (2003), p. 145.

23 Lawrence of Durham, *Hypognosticon*, ed. Daub (2002), pp. 69-70.

24 On this Gervase, see Talbot (1951), pp. 32-45. After his retirement he slips out of sight. The much later *Chronicle of Louth Park* surprisingly has no mention of Gervase, the founding abbot. Information on his earlier career is dependent on sources from Fountains Abbey.

25 Talbot (1951), p. 36: 'This dedication, however, shows us that he not only kept in contact with literary men of his time, but also provided the necessary stimulus for the

an important, albeit now largely forgotten, figure among the Cistercians in the north. What makes him particularly likely as a candidate for being Lawrence's unidentified dedicatee is his reputation as an ardent book-lover and patron of writers. From Robert, the future prior of Bridlington (c. 1147-50), Gervase requested a gloss on the minor prophets[26] and hence a Biblical epos such as the *Hypognosticon*, focussing on the Old Testament, might have suited his theological interests and perhaps also, literary taste.

Another possible identification of Lawrence's friend/patron Gervase, though it may be a long shot, has larger political ramifications. He might be none other than the powerful and controversial Gervase of Blois, the son of King Stephen who became abbot of Westminster in 1137. As abbot this Gervase made himself very unpopular: Osbert of Clare, his prior, even managed to procure a papal letter of sanction against him,[27] and he was eventually deposed in c. 1157 by Henry II on a charge of gross financial mismanagement and replaced by none other than our Durham man, the *Magister* Lawrence. Yet Gervase of Blois' reputation within the church establishment might have been wholly different in the 1130s. Was our author attempting to flatter a member of the royal family? While both possibilities open up interesting perspectives, none of them can be proven with certainty and I therefore hesitate to enter into further speculation as to how such connections might have influenced Lawrence's career. It is enough to say that for some reason, in the 1130s, at a time where he was enjoying tremendous personal success in Durham, as he was careful to stress in several of his works, it seems as if Lawrence was also seeking patronage outside his own community.

The Letter to Aelred

Before moving on to the other Lawrence (of Westminster), I will briefly touch on the question of the future prior Lawrence's intimate connection to Aelred of Rievaulx. The sole piece of evidence for this friendship is the dedicatory letter attached to the new Latin Life of St Brigit of Kildare that Aelred's father, Eilaf, had requested from a Durham author named Lawrence.

The *Vita Brigidae* and thus, presumably, the letter to Aelred, can be dated relatively safely to around 1133, mainly because Lawrence addresses Aelred as

---

    production of their works.' There has been some speculation that Gervase was the one who asked Aelred of Rievaulx to compose the *Speculum caritatis*. See Talbot (1951), p. 36.

26 Lawrence-Mathers (2003), p. 182.

27 Gervase was apparently planning to sell the relics of Edward the Confessor. On his role in the canonisation, or rather lack thereof, see Scholz (1961), pp. 38-60.

member of the royal household (*dispensator domus regis*) of David I of Scotland – a title Aelred held at the end of his court-career, before becoming a monk in 1134. Thus Eilaf was still alive - he died in 1138 after having taken the Benedictine habit at Durham. But why, then, was the *Vita* dedicated to Aelred and not to the man who originally requested it?[28] Lawrence mentions Eilaf as the commissioner, and as one of his personal friends, but gives no hint as to why he thought the son should be the dedicatee instead – and neither why Eilaf wanted a *vita* of this particular Irish saint in the first place. A few hypotheses must suffice for now. Firstly, Lawrence (whichever it was) may have thought that Aelred was in a better position to appreciate its Latinity: A large part of the dedicatory letter concerns matters of rhetorical composition and Lawrence praises Aelred's learned diligence, even while the latter is caught up in the cares of the court. Secondly, he may have hoped by this gift to revive an old relationship. Finally, Lawrence may well have had a political agenda, after all, Aelred could serve as an important link to the Scottish royal court. So both men were involved in the highest political circles of the North at the time when the letter must have been composed. The situation was therefore that of a courtier-scholar writing to a fellow courtier-scholar. The annoyances of court life were a theme that Prior Lawrence would later revisit in the *Hypognosticon* and the *Dialogi*, but being a commonplace among writers who were also courtiers, this cannot be used as evidence for attributing the *Vita* and the letter to Aelred to the future prior. The modern scholars who have used the letter, and who have done so mainly to shed light on an otherwise elusive period in Aelred's life, generally contend that Lawrence was (or had been) a sort of mentor, perhaps even teacher, of the young Aelred, when the latter was at school in Durham.[29] This interpretation is based on Lawrence's amiable yet magisterial, 'lecturing', tone in the letter.

---

28 In his biography of Aelred, McGuire wondered about this too, suggesting Lawrence's change of the dedicatee "indicate that even before he arrived at Rievaulx, Aelred had a reputation as a writer". McGuire (1994), p. 43.

29 As the letter's editor contends 'We may take it for granted that Laurence was a former master and guide for the boy Aelred...' Hoste (1960), p. 261. The monastic historian Chrysogonus Waddell has no doubts that Lawrence was Aelred's "former teacher from Durham, now become a monk in that community". Waddell (2006), p. 58. This statement seems to suggest that Lawrence taught in Durham, before joining the Benedictine chapter, but according to the autobiographical snippets that Lawrence occasionally gives in his writings, Lawrence moved straight from Waltham Abbey, where he was schooled among the secular canons, to become a Benedictine monk at Durham. Though his self-description as episcopal courtier and causidicus in the prologue to the *Hypognosticon*, Lawrence's self-description in the *Dialogi* expressly problematises his double role of monk and courtier. Where Waddell got his information from is not clear.

He addresses Aelred fondly as his 'dearest friend' and commends the fact that Aelred, even when engulfed in the cares of the king's court, maintained his love of learning (*litterae*) and studious pursuits. There is little doubt who was (or at least who thought himself to be) the intellectually superior.

The *Vita* (and hence the letter) has generally been accepted as the future Prior Lawrence's work, but I should like to question the certainty of that attribution. The only firm evidence that suggests that the author *was* the future prior of Durham, and not the other Lawrence, is the direct reference to a copy of Cicero's *De amicitia* in the letter to Aelred - the book that would inspire Aelred's own later work on friendship. From the Durham library list of the late twelfth century, we know that Prior Lawrence owned a copy which he donated to the chapter library,[30] yet Cicero's work was not a rarity in the northern monastic milieus, nor in Durham it seems, where several copies could be found. What puzzles me among other things is that the *Vita Brigidae* is not included in the main Durham codex of Lawrence's collected *oeuvre*.[31] It was also omitted from John Leland's otherwise fully comprehensive list of Lawrence's works which includes several minor works now considered lost, hence Leland was not just copying the contents list of the aforementioned Durham manuscript.[32] Moreover, it is intriguing to note that one of the three extant manuscripts of the *Vita Brigidae*, which is found in a twelfth-century compilation from Hexham now at the Bodleian Library (Cod Laud misc. 668), also contains several works by Aelred, but that none of them contains any of the other known works by "Laurentius Dunelmensis." Why, if the author was indeed the later *Prior* Lawrence was the *vita* kept separate from the other works? In fact it even looks as if there is safer evidence for a close connection between the *other* Lawrence, the later abbot of Westminster, and Aelred, namely in Aelred's preface to the *vita* of Edward the

---

30 *Catalogi veteres librorum* (1838), p. 8. The list of Prior Lawrence's books include a glossed psalter by Magister Anselm and another by Magister Ivo. Commentaries on the Letters of St Paul, on Isaias, two books of sermons by Bernard of Clairvaux, a *versarius* (perhaps a collection of Lawrences own poetical works?) and "Tullius de Amicitia". The main invemtory of the library also lists Cicero's *De amicitia* (in two copies). *Catalogi veteres*, p. 4.

31 Durham University Library, MS Cosin V. iii. 1 (mid-12th century), which contains the *Consolatio de morte amici*, the *Hypognosticon* with its two prologues, the five forensic *Orationes*, the *Rhitmus* (Easter play) and the *Prosa de resurrectione* connected to the latter. Apart from the *Vita Brigidae*, Lawrence's *Dialogi* is the only other of Lawrence's known, extant works not included in the splendid codex. This omission of this particular work may have been due to its politically controversial nature. See Münster-Swendsen (2012), pp.169-70.

32 The Durham manuscript was well known to the early-modern antiquarians.

Confessor, a work commissioned by Abbot Lawrence, which implies some kind of family connection. It is obviously also quite possible that *both* Lawrences were friends of Aelred. No doubt, being Durham men, they would all have known each other personally.

Magister Lawrence's network and itinerary

As soon as we leave Durham, we lose sight of *Prior* Lawrence so this is the time to properly introduce the other Lawrence, the *Magister* of Reginald's tale, and his much larger circle of friends. Most of the extant evidence concerns his abbacy of Westminster, spanning from 1158 until his death in 1173x75, and consists of charter-material[33] but luckily we do have a few letters that provide much safer ground on which to establish his personal network.

I have so far only found two pieces of evidence regarding Master Lawrence's whereabouts before the events of 1153, and neither is entirely solid.[34] First, from c. 1143, we have a short letter from Bernard of Clairvaux and William of Rievaulx (abbot 1132-45) to Prior Roger of Durham that was inserted in a Durham manuscript (MS B. IV.24, fol 96). The letter was printed by Thomas Rud in his catalogue of the Durham library[35] and is not to be found in the modern editions of Bernard's letters. The context appears to be an episcopal election dispute and the letter commends its bearer, a certain Magister Lawrence, to the prior of Durham (Lawrence's predecessor).[36] Most scholars have followed Rud in reading it to suggest that this Lawrence was the Cistercian party's candidate (there is some disagreement as to which Lawrence it refers to), but I cannot see anything in it that directly supports such a reading. The letter merely introduces Lawrence, not as a contender for a bishopric, but rather as a mediator. So at this point this Lawrence – whichever one it was - was not only still on friendly terms with Bernard and his circle, he even worked on their behalf, as the letter states.

---

33 Apart from the later charter material from his abbacy of Westminster, a confirmation of a gift to Fountains Abbey of the Archbishop Henry Murdac of York is attested by a Magister Lawrence (no. 113 in *English Episcopal Acta:York 1070-1154*, p. 86. He also appears in the witness list of a spurious Durham charter confirming the privileges of the church of Durham and its prior in regard to the archbishopric of York.

34 There is also an act of Archbishop Henry Murdac attested by a Magister Lawrence, but I am not sure what to make of that, see no. 113 in *English Episcopal Acta: York 1070-1154*, ed. Burton.

35 Rud (1825), pp. 208-9.

36 After some general comments on election procedure the letter concludes: 'Sit vobis commendatus Magister iste Laurentius, tum propter nos amicus vestros, tum quia fideliter et efficaciter pro vobis laboravit in hoc negotio.'

Second, and even more intriguing, is a letter from a Lawrence to his friend Maurice, contained in several Continental and English manuscripts, and possibly written at about the same time.[37] The purportedly 'private' letter forms the introduction to a rendition of Hugh of St Victor's work on the sacraments (in one of its many versions known as the *Sententiae de diuinitate*), hence its wide distribution.[38] This Maurice is in all probability the same as the one who was educated at Durham and left for Rievaulx in the late 1130s where he succeeded William as abbot in 1145. Maurice did not himself study at St Victor, but he had advised Lawrence to do so, as the letter-writer acknowledges. Lawrence tells us that the work, of which he names himself as *artifex* rather than *auctor*, is a collection of lecture notes which he on behalf of his fellow students took down while at school. Thus the text is an early example of the scholastic *reportatio* genre. The letter offers direct evidence that Lawrence was a student of Hugh of St Victor in Paris, i.e. that he must have studied there some time before 1141/42. But how can we be absolutely certain which Lawrence – not least since the works usually ascribed to the prior show vestiges of Victorine thought? The *Hypognosticon*, for example, shares the same plan of the ages of the world as the one stipulated in Hugh's *De sacramentis*. The *reportatio* is likewise structured according to this plan. Yet if the later Prior Lawrence had indeed spent years studying at St Victor, there is nothing in the frequent autobiographical remarks in his works that suggests this, the only place of study that Lawrence mentions being his birthplace, Waltham.[39] Is it likely that a man with such a prominent educational background as St Victor would have provided would fail to mention it? Hardly.

It should be noted that Hugh of St Victor's own preface to his work on the sacraments contains a warning to readers to discard (or at least correct) certain unauthorised copies of his work in circulation. This might well refer to the *reportatio* or to a similar type of text, which, contrary to Hugh's wishes, contin-

---

37 The most recent, though incomplete, edition is in Berndt (2005), p. 165. A complete transcript is provided by Bischoff (1935), p. 250. Bischof only lists two manuscripts containing the letter, the one in the Bodleian Library and the other found in Breslau (provenience unrecorded). Rodney Thomson mentions two others, one from Durham and one with a Cistercian provenance. See Thomson (1982), p. 46.
38 The identification of this Lawrence with Lawrence, later abbot of Westminster was made by Croydon (1950), 160-71. This brief study is still the starting point for scholars working on Lawrence of Westminster. The twelfth-century Durham library catalogue contains a *Sententiae Magistri Hugonis*, but I am not aware if anybody has tried to identify this particular text among the extant manuscripts at Durham. *Catalogi veteres librorum ecclesiæ cathedralis Dunelmensis* (1838), p. 3.
39 Lawrence of Durham, *Dialogi*, ed. Raine, pp. 40-1.

ued to circulate. Constant Mews recently made me aware of two manuscripts containing a twelfth century French/Continental introduction to prominent authors of theology in which a Lawrence of Durham turns up side-by-side with Hugh of St Victor and Bernard of Clairvaux.[40] The introduction does not refer to any of the later Prior's works, and the context suggests it must refer to Magister Lawrence. So the works of both Lawrences were circulating on the Continent, in roughly the same learned milieus, and it is likely that even contemporary schoolmen would have thought them to be one and the same person.

No doubt the most interesting aspect from an intellectual history perspective is the Victorine link but before returning to it, let us follow Master Lawrence's footsteps after he abandoned the trip to Rome in 1153 and make a stop at St Albans. As Rodney Thomson has shown so vividly in his survey of the St Albans manuscripts, the abbey was a major centre of learning in the mid-1100s. Thus if a schoolman like Master Lawrence wanted to take the monastic habit, St Albans might be an obvious choice. Moreover, there were close institutional and personal links between the communities of Durham and St Albans. At St Albans, Lawrence seems to have been received with enthusiasm. According to the *Gesta abbatum* he was made prior of St Albans within a year or two after his arrival. Unfortunately the *Gesta* gets things slightly muddled up when Lawrence appears in the context of a dispute involving a certain Alchinus, sometimes spelled Alquinus or Alechinus.[41] Let us just call him Alcuin. In 1146 Abbot Geoffrey of St Albans died and dissension arose concerning the election of his successor. A party supporting prior Alcuin promptly elected him, but the election was quashed by royal intervention, and Stephen got a certain Radulf installed instead. As the head of the opposition Alcuin was persecuted by the new abbot and eventually forced to flee to Westminster where, according to the *Gesta*, he was warmly received by Abbot Lawrence, who made him prior -- this according to the St Albans historical tradition of Matthew Paris and Thomas Walsingham, which places these events in the later 1140s. Their judgment of Alcuin's character, as a well-meaning man unjustly persecuted, is contradicted by a contemporary anonymous letter of a St Albans man to a friend which deals at length with the affair from an eye-witness perspective.[42] This letter does not mention any Lawrence and here Alcuin is clearly a most unpleasant character. That it was Lawrence as abbot of Westminster who took Alcuin in can't possibly fit if Alcuin's persecutor was Abbot Radulf who died in 1151, years before Lawrence even considered changing Durham for St Albans. In that case,

---

40 Evreux MS 137 and Rouen MS 553.
41 *Gesta abbatum*, ed. Riley, pp. 109-110; 112.
42 Letter 10 of the *Epistolae ad Amicum*, ed. Colker (1975). pp. 108-12.

the Westminster abbot who received the prior on the run must have been the aforementioned Gervase of Blois (the possible dedicatee of Lawrence the prior's *Hypognosticon*). Yet why would the *Gesta abbatum* present Lawrence as Alcuin's generous saviour?

Ecclesiastical controversies – of which there were plenty in England in the 1140s and 1150s – generate excellent and informative sources. Indeed, many of the individuals of this period are only known to us because they were involved in scandal. Yet a toxic environment of rumour and political intrigue also erects a smoke-screen for the non-contemporary observer. Understandably, but annoyingly for us, the anonymous letter-writer of St Albans requested his recipient to keep his name and that of any others involved a secret. We may never know which part, if any, Lawrence played in the Alcuin-affair, yet some sort of link seems to have existed between the two and I think we might safely add Alcuin to Lawrence's growing list of friends. It is probably no coincidence that this Alcuin would later, like his abbot at Westminster, be solemnly commemorated in Durham. Here he occupies a prominent place in the Durham obituary side by side with none other than the celebrated hermit-saint Godric of Finchale.[43] After his abrupt move, Lawrence's relationship with the St Albans community became somewhat strained. The *Gesta abbatum* reports that the new abbot of Westminster responded with unseemly ingratitude to a gift from Abbot Robert (1151-68), an event probably connected to the series of bitter property disputes between the two abbeys, which may well have been initiated by Lawrence.[44] Judging from the sources concerning his abbacy, Lawrence was involved in prolonged series of lawsuits trying to regain what had been lost due to his predecessor's ineptitude.

Throughout the latter half of the twelfth century St Victor maintained a strong English and especially northern presence; equally there was lots of activity especially in the 1160s when the abbey exchanged scholars with both St Albans and Westminster. It is likely that Lawrence's stay in St Albans created, or at least strengthened, a direct link to St Victor that was maintained after his departure. A prior G of St Albans corresponded with Prior Richard of St Victor regarding the exchange of students and the prior and later abbot of St Albans, Simon (1167-83), also wrote to Richard of St Victor requesting copies of some

---

43 *Excerpta ex obituario ecclisiae Dunelmensis*, (1841), p 143: For XII Kalends of June (21 May): '..Godricus heremita de Finchalle, et Alequinus prior Westmonasterii, monachus ecclesiæ Sancti Albani. Pro his duobus fiat annuatim servitium plenary, sicut pro monachis nostris professis.'.
44 See *Gesta abbatum*, ed. Riley, pp. 133-34.

of Hugh's works and making arrangement to send a St Albans scholar there to make them. In fact most of Richard's extant correspondence consists of letters to or from St Albans.[45] At Westminster, Lawrence too kept up his Victorine connections. In one letter he addresses Abbot Ernis of St Victor as 'his most beloved kinsman' and commends a certain John, a kinsman of the prior of Westminster (Alcuin?) to be accepted as a student at the school.[46] Another letter of his commends another John, Lawrence's own nephew – adding to the influx of prospective English students at St Victor.[47]

It is no wonder that Durham, St Albans and Westminster had long-standing, formalised confraternity agreements with each other. Commemorative sources from Durham clearly show the connections to the two other communities – in the part of the obituary that records confraternities, Westminster and St Albans are even mentioned together in the same entry.[48] The connections to St Victor seem to have been less formal, relying upon individuals and their personal friendships. The Victorine obituary contains no Westminster people, but among Westminster's charters, a confraternity agreement with St Victor exists. It was drawn up between 1173 and 1175, shortly after Lawrence's death, in all probability as an attempt to formalise and solidify an already existing connection that the abbey of Westminster owed primarily to its deceased abbot and his excellent personal network.

Excursus: Lawrence of Durham on Friendship.

Most learned celebrations of the virtues of human friendship begin with the end, so to say, that is, they appear in the context of loss and from the experience of grief. Cicero's much imitated dialogue took its departure from a friendship lost. Equally, the perhaps most eloquent and sensitive investigator of human

---

45   Richard of St Victor, *Epistolae*, PL 196 col. 1225A-1230C: I. Abbot Ervisius and Richard to Robert of Hereford col. 1225A regarding studies at St Victor; VI. Prior G of St Albans to Richard (venerable lord and friend) col. 1227D Commending his nephew Matthew.; VII. Prior G of St Albans to Richard (venerable friend) col. 1228A; Regarding the same Matthew and his studies at St Victor.; VIII. Brother S of St Albans to Richard (venerable brother and friend) col. 1228C; IX. Brother M of St Albans to Richard col. 1229A; X. Brother M of St Albans to Richard col. 1229C. M refers to the prior of St Albans as his friend.; XI. Prior G of St Albans to Richard (venerable friend) col. 1230B commends a brother M. The letters together provide a glimpse of criss-crossing connections between individual members of the two communities.
46   In Ernis's letter collection, no. VII. PL 196, col. 1385C ff.
47   The letter is edited by Luchaire, (Paris,1889), p. 108. Cited by Croydon (1950), p. 170.
48   *Excerpta ex obituario ecclesiae Dunelmensis* (1841), p.135

friendship, Aelred of Rievaulx, was spurred on by the loss of his friend Simon, as he mentions in his *Speculum caritatis*, his major work on the theory of human and divine love. Discontinuity, it seems, is more often than not the context for writing on friendship. Lawrence of Durham's longest exposition on the theme also appears in a text mourning the loss of a close friend: the great prosimetrum *Consolatio de morte amici*.[49] Though Lawrence's *Consolatio* was clearly modelled upon Boethius' *De Consolatione Philosophiae*, a central text in the medieval scholarly curriculum, contrary to its model the consoler is a fellow human being: he is cast as one of Lawrence's close friends, yet he remains anonymous and unidentifiable.[50] The friend whose death he mourns is a certain Paganus, to whom Lawrence became strongly attached from his early years as a *novus miles* (Lawrence's term for a novice monk)[51] at Durham, and it was through Paganus that Lawrence met a great number of other important friends.[52] According to the internal evidence provided by the *Consolatio*, Paganus was a member of the Durham community (but not necessarily therefore a monk), but like so many of Lawrence's friends, he cannot be identified with any certainty. There are two men named Paganus, a knight (*miles*) and a fellow brother, in the excerpts of the Durham obituary printed by the Surtees Society.[53] More intriguingly, the witness list to a 1127 grant by Ranulf Flambard, then bishop of Durham, contains a Paganus, nephew of the powerful and controversial bishop.[54] Lawrence had only praise for the otherwise much-loathed Bishop Ranulf and it is quite likely that it was his connections to this influential family collective that paved the way for Lawrence's own rise to prominence. However, like other *dramatis personae* in Lawrence's works, the elusive Paganus might just be a pseudonym. The literary self-portrait that this author draws here is complex and contradictory. Just as would be the case in his later work, the *Dialogi*, in which the author expertly plays with the distinction between his literary persona and actual self, the "Lawrence" we meet in the *Consolatio* is not meant as a realistic depiction and does not necessarily reflect the opinions of the author. Lawrence presents himself and his own misfortune as an exemplum on the destructive powers of grief and loss of self-control, here expressed in the mourner's continual shedding of

---

49 The attribution to the later prior Lawrence seems certain – the work is the first in the "commemorative" codex mentioned earlier and internal evidence and autobiographical information link it to the other works that can safely be attributed to the prior.
50 Indeed, the dialogue seems rather to be an interior one, in which the Consolator reflects the author's conscience or, for want of a better term, "super ego".
51 Lawrence of Durham, *Consolatio*, 3.3, ed. Kindermann, p. 141.
52 Lawrence of Durham, *Consolatio*, 3.6, ed. Kindermann, p. 143.
53 *Excerpta ex obituario ecclesiae Dunelmensis* (1841), p. 141 ('Paganus miles') and p. 146.
54 Aird (1998), p. 203.

'unmanly' tears.[55] A long prosimetric dialogue ensues employing a remarkable array of different and often difficult verse forms, through which the general therapeutic programme is gradually unfolded, leading the protagonist towards enlightenment, which here means the acceptance of the inevitable transience of things. On the surface, this text (in contrast to most of Lawrence's other literary works) looks unremarkable. The ideal of perfect friendship found here closely follows the general twelfth-century ethical tenets. Yet when considered within the frames of the discourse on sublime friendship, Lawrence's preoccupation with his loss of a number of prize possessions gotten through the friend, such as power, status, honour, and riches (the more base utilitarian aspects of friendship), is striking. According to the ideal, selfish yearning after material gain and similar shallow motives should be banished from true friendship, in fact they are directly detrimental to the appropriation of *virtus*, the means and end of friendship. The Lawrence-figure in the *Consolatio* is wholly caught up in his own loss, and mourning the lost friend almost seems to be merely a pretext for indulging in his own emotions. Accordingly, the *Consolator* directly accuses Lawrence of weeping for pain that the loss has caused him, rather than for Paganus himself.[56] As the dialogue unfolds it reveals the extreme self-centeredness of the sufferer: grief, the inevitable result of forming close human relationships, is certainly not a virtue.

The paradoxes also thrive in Lawrence's treatments of the distinction between *amicitia* and *amor*[57] – a theme he returned to in the *Hypognosticon*. In book five the praise of friendship is set in the context of the Old Testament story of David and Jonathan.[58] Like Aelred, Lawrence extols the venerable pact - the *fedus venerabile*, between the two – even though their closeness spells grief when Jonathan dies.[59] The high flown lecture on the virtue of friendship is later followed by a prolonged discourse on love (*amor*) centering on the pain and confusion resulting from the 'noxious' arrows of 'the boy' (Amor) which leads straight to the excursus entitled 'Conflictus amoris et rationis'.[60] The latter is drenched in metaphors of warfare and carnage. No skill in medicine can remedy the wounds

---

55 Lawrence of Durham, *Consolatio*, 6.13-15, ed. Kindermann, pp. 159-60.
56 Lawrence of Durham, *Consolatio*, 4.9, ed. Kindermann, p. 146.
57 In a somewhat cryptic sentence that draws attention to the distinctions between friendship and love as well as public and private, the Consolator characterises Paganus as "your private friend, or, rather, public love."("Paganum, tuum privatum amicum, immo amorem publicum.."). Lawrence of Durham, *Consolatio*, 4.9, ed. Kindermann, p. 146.
58 Lawrence of Durham, *Hypognosticon*, ed. Daub, pp. 151-52.
59 Compare with McGuire's discussion of the David-Jonathan theme in McGuire (1988), introduction pp. xvii-xviii and Aelred's use of it pp. 321-22.
60 Lawrence of Durham, *Hypognosticon*, ed. Daub, pp. 169-75.

inflicted by passionate love – which is 'furor' – rage and madness. Contrary to such unreason, friendship is rational, though it still involves *amor*, but in a form kept strongly in check by the exercise of virtue and self-control. Hence, *amicitia* stands in direct opposition to passionate love, whether the latter expresses itself in the immature love among boys, or the love of women. This is why one cannot form real friendships with either; they are, as Lawrence also stresses in a poem, 'as fleeting as the breeze'.[61] Such inconstancy is irreconcilable with true friendship. Love obscures reason and inspires doubt, as Lawrence stresses in a stanza on the doubting Thomas in the Easter play.[62] Yet in other instances, Lawrence praises *amor* as a great spiritual teacher[63] just as he also applied the term to his relationship with Paganus in its positive aspect and to the emotional bond between David and Jonathan. Hence, since Lawrence often does not distinguish clearly between higher and lower forms of *amor*, his evaluation of the ethical value of passionate human love remains ambiguous, perhaps deliberately so.

The result of the therapy in Lawrence's *Consolatio* is that friendship is refashioned as transcending death, but also therefore as being somehow detached from and independent of the beloved object: the human friend. Because real love is immortal and ought to remain constant, it cannot be dependent upon the physical presence of another person – fleeting and inconstant as human life is. Indeed, the mourner is cured by the acknowledgement that everything flows, that nothing in this world is permanent, and that true happiness is found in detaching oneself from anything that, because of its passing nature, may cause grief. This is wholly consistent with Lawrence's profound Stoicism, but it also seems to be at odds with the notion that involving oneself in friendship with mortal beings may lead to the highest good.

Though they moved within similar milieus and intellectual frameworks, Lawrence's thoughts on love and friendship seem to differ from those of Aelred of Rievaulx. The same goes for the two writers' depiction of their monastic milieus: The warmth and humanity of Aelred's community of friends is absent in Lawrence's exposition which focuses on impermanence and loss. Moreover, though Lawrence too was a monk, the monastic context of spiritual friendship is also remarkably absent, and compared to Aelred's works, the whole setting seems

---

61 The poem *Aura puer mulier*, a reprimand to a fickle friend, has been attributed to Lawrence of Durham. For an edition, see Mozley (1942). The attribution seems sound, because there is an echo of the poem in Lawrence's *Consolatio de morte amici*, ed. Kindermann, p. 169 and Lawrence here claims the verses as being his ("Versus quidem meos recognosco...").

62 Lawrence of Durham, *Rhitmus*, v. 87, ed. Kindermann, p. 97.

63 Lawrence of Durham, *Hypognosticon*, ed. Daub, p. 225.

removed from the close-knit monastic community. Indeed, Lawrence frequently depicts himself as standing somehow outside the protective cloistered environment and the friends (fictional or real) that he converses with are also, it seems, outsiders. Lawrence's literary persona in both the *Consolatio* and in the *Dialogi* is from the outset that of a troubled man – the most prevalent emotion on display is despair.

Judging from the odd self-portrait he drew in his many writings, Lawrence did not find the tranquillity and personal fulfilment that Aelred would discover among his fellow Cistercians. Throughout Lawrence's adult life, Durham remained in almost perpetual conflict, and being more a courtier than a monk, he frequently found himself in the midst of it. Though seemingly an adept power-broker – a man who did not need the advice of others, as Geoffrey of Coldingham would later state it – Lawrence's position and personal security seem to have been precarious almost continuously since the death of his main patron, Bishop Geoffrey Rufus in 1141. It is entirely possible that the turmoil in Durham caused Lawrence to develop a more pessimistic and more cynical view of human friendship than Aelred, who had the luck of dying peacefully, surrounded by his friends, whereas Lawrence, left behind by the bishop whose see he has just secured, expired in an unknown French village in 1154.

Concluding remarks

Let us return to Reginald's story of Godric of Finchale's prophecy: "You two Lawrences are now preparing to journey to Rome, but from this day on, neither of you two will ever return here, nor will you ever behold Durham again." From here the two Lawrences part ways and the author continues: "And thus the dreadful forebodings of the man of God were fulfilled, and before one year had passed they were known and proved by many, as Master Lawrence was recounting all of this to several persons; having become abbot of Westminster, he went to Durham several years later and explained all of this to the brethren in chapter."[64]

Surely, this is not exactly the most convincing example of the hermit's prophetic powers: after all it tells us that *contrary* to the divinely inspired forebodings, one Lawrence *did* eventually return to Durham to tell his tale. His oral testimony was

---

64 'Sic itaque viri Dei dira præsagia completa sunt, et ante anni unius exitum magistro Laurentio hæc omnia pluribus referente, a multis cognita et experta sunt, qui Westmonasterii abbas effectus, post annos plures Dunelmum venit, et hæc omnia coram fratribus in capitulo enarravit.' Reginald of Durham, *Libellus*, ed. Raine, p. 233.

probably *the* source of the story for the two writers who recounted it in detail, Reginald of Durham and the chronicler John of Hexham. Had *they* not retold the story as involving *two* Lawrences, we may not have been made aware of the existence of another Lawrence, who would so easily be confused with the prior. To claim that the two were indeed one and the same person would require the prior to have succeeded in a remarkable vanishing stunt, i.e. being presumed dead and then turning up at St Albans as another person with the same name. Unlikely, but not impossible. Stranger things are known have happened. Thus, to truly discard this fanciful hypothesis one needs to find traces of the other Lawrence before the prior's death, and however scant, there are indicators of the existence of a Magister Lawrence in the Durham milieu. If the *Vita Brigidae* and the letter to Aelred (before 1133) can be safely attributed to him, which the Aelred-link might be seen to suggest, and not to the later prior, this would strengthen the argument further – and also explain why the *vita* was never copied together with the other works of Lawrence of Durham, which tend to appear together. Nevertheless, it is still an imperfect picture that emerges from this jigsaw puzzle. As medievalists we habitually, however grudgingly, have to make interpretations *e silentio* and rely upon mere conjecture. In the case of the two Lawrences, the silences may sometimes speak volumes when the sources do not. This is very much the case here, where my ability to distinguish between them to a large degree comes to depend upon Prior Lawrence's silences, most significantly his failure to mention any Victorine connections in his works. The prior was not loath to boast of his education and intellectual skills, so if he had received part of his education at St Victor, the most prominent school in Paris at the time – as one Lawrence certainly did – it is unlikely that he would not have mentioned it.

Prior Lawrence would repeatedly draw attention to the importance of friendship *per se* – and to the crucial role that his friends had played in the making of his personal career. The other Lawrence, while abbot of Westminster, made good use of his old contacts in England and abroad and his continuously expanding network to the benefit of both his community, his personal friends, himself and his kinsmen. On the more general level, the fierce political and ecclesiastical conflicts in the middle decades of the twelfth century, particularly those affecting Durham, St Albans, Westminster, and York, also reveal the functioning of monastic friendship-networks in creating, accelerating and solving disputes.

Literature

Manuscript sources
MS Durham University Library, Cosin V. iii. 1 (12th century).

Printed sources
Catalogi veteres librorum ecclesiæ cathedralis Dunelmensis, ed. Surtees Society (London, 1838).
Chronicon Angliæ Petriburgense, ed. J. A. Giles (London, 1845).
Continuator of Hugh the Chanter (of York), 'Addition to the lives by Hugh the Chantor', ed. J. Raine in *Historians of the Church of York,* Rerum Britannicarum Medii Ævi Scriptores vol. 2 (London, 1886), pp. 220-227.
Councils and Synods with Other Documents Relating to the English Church I. Part II (1066-1204), ed. D. Whitelock, M. Brett and C. N. L. Brooke (Oxford, 1981).
Durham Episcopal Charters 1071-1152, ed. H. S. Offler (Gateshead, 1968).
English Episcopal Acta: Durham 1153-1195, ed. M. G. Snape (Oxford, 2002).
English Episcopal Acta: York 1070-1154, ed. J. E. Burton (Oxford, 1988).
Epistolae ad Amicum, ed. M. Colker, *Analecta Dublinensia* (Cambridge (Mass.), 1975).
Ervisius/Ernisius of St Victor, 'Epistolae', ed. J. P. Migne, *Patrologia Latina* 196, col. 1385C.
Excerpta ex obituario ecclesiae Dunelmensis, ed. in *Liber vitæ ecclesiæ Dunelmensis*, Surtees Society (London, 1841), pp.135-52.
Geoffrey of Coldingham, 'De statu ecclesiae Dunelmensis', ed. J. Raine in *Historiae Dunelmensis Scriptores Tres,* (Edinburgh, 1839).
Gesta Abbatum monasterii Sancti Albani, vol. I, A.D. 793-1290, ed. H. T. Riley (London, 1867).
Hugh of St. Victor, 'De sacramentis legis naturalis et scriptae', ed. J.P. Migne, *Patrologia Latina* 176, cols. 0017-0042.
John of Hexham, 'Historia' (continuation of Symeon of Durham, *Historia regum*), ed. T. Arnold in *Symonis monachii opera omnia: Historia regum eadem historia ad quintum et vicesimum annum continuata, per Joannem Haugulstadensem. Accedunt varia* (London, 1885), pp. 284-332.
Lawrence of Durham, *Hypognosticon,* ed. S. Daub, *Gottes Heilsplan – verdichtet: das Hypognosticon des Laurentius Dunelmensis* (Erlangen, 2002).
Lawrence of Durham, *Dialogi,* ed. J. Raine, *Dialogi Laurentii Dunelmensis Monachi ac Prioris*, (Edinburgh, 1880).
Lawrence of Durham, 'Orationes', ed. U. Kindermann, 'Die fünf Reden des Laurentius von Durham', *Mittellateinisches Jahrbuch* 8 (1971), pp. 108-141.
Lawrence of Durham, *Consolatio de morte amici,* ed. U. Kindermann, *Laurentius von Durham Consolatio de morte amici* (Erlangen/Nürnberg, 1969).
Lawrence of Durham, 'Vita Brigidae', ed. Smedt and Backer in *Acta Sanctorum Hiberniae* (Edinburgh 1896), pp. 3-76.
Lawrence of Durham, 'Rithmus Laurentii de Christo et eius discipulis', ed. U. Kindermann, 'Das Emmausgedicht des Laurentius von Durham', *Mittellateinisches Jahrbuch* 5 (1968), pp. 79-100.
Lawrence of Durham, 'Aura puer mulier', ed. J. H. Mozley, 'The collection of medieval Latin verse in MS Cotton Titus D. xxiv', *Medium Ævum* 11 (1942), p. 44.

Lawrence of Durham, 'Epistola ad Ethelredum' (Letter to Aelred of Rievaulx), ed. A. Hoste, 'A Survey of the Unedited Work of Laurence of Durham', *Sacris Erudiri* 11 (1960), pp. 163-65.

Lawrence (of Westminster?), ‚Reportatio', transcript by B. Bischoff, 'Aus der Schule Hugos von Skt Viktor', Beiträge zur Geschichte der philosophie und theologie des Mittelalters, suppl. III. I. *Aus der Geisteswelt der Mittelalters* I (Münster, 1935), p. 250.

Liber vitae ecclesiae Dunelmensis (facsimile), ed. Surtees Society (London, 1923).

The Priory of Hexham, its Chroniclers, Endowments, and Annals, vol. I, ed. J. Raine (Edinburgh, 1864).

Reginald of Durham, *Libellus de vita et miraculis S Godrici Heremitæ de Finchale*, ed. J. Raine (London & Edinburgh 1845). (The tale of the two Lawrences is on pp. 232-233).

Reginald of Durham, *De admirandis beati Cuthberti virtutibus*, ed. J. Raine (London 1835).

Richard of Hexham, 'De gestis regis Stephani', ed. R. Howlett in *Chronicles of the Reigns of Stephen, Henry II and Richard I* (London, 1886), pp. 152-178.

Richard of St Victor, 'Epistolae', ed. J. P. Migne, *Patrologia Latina* 196 cols. 1225-1230.

Symeon of Durham (Continuator of), 'Libellus de exordio', ed. D. Rollason, *Symeon of Durham. Libellus de exordio atque procursu istius, hoc est Dunelmensis, ecclesie* (Oxford, 2000), pp. 266-323.

'Vita sancti Willelmi', ed. J. Raine, *The Historians of the Church of York and its Archbishops*, vol. 2 (London, 1886), pp. 270-91.

Studies

Aird, W. M., *St Cuthbert and the Normans: The Church of Durham 1071-1153* (Woodbridge, 1998).

Berndt, R. (ed.), *Schrift, Schreiber, Schenker: Studien zur Abtei Sankt Viktor in Paris und den Viktorinern* (Berlin, 2005).

Croydon, G. E., 'Abbot Laurence of Westminster and Hugh of St Victor', *Medieval and Renaissance Studies* 2 (1950), pp. 160-71.

Daub, S., *Von der Bibel zum Epos: Poetische Strategien des Laurentius am geistlichen Hof von Durham* (Cologne/Weimar/Vienna, 2005).

Knowles, D. 'The Case of Saint William of York', *Cambridge Historical Journal*, 5, 2 (1936), pp. 162-77 (appendix pp. 212-14).

Lawrence-Mathers, A., Manuscripts in Northumbria in the 11th and 12th Centuries (Woodbridge, 2003).

Leland, J., *Commentarii de Scriptoribus Britannicis (Ex Autographo Lelandino nunc primus edidit Antonius Hall, A. M. Coll. Reg. Oxon. Socius)* vol. 1 (Oxford, 1709).

Luchaire, A., Études sur quelques MSS de Rome et de Paris (Paris, 1889). (The edition of Lawrence of Westminster's letter is on p. 108).

McGuire, B. P., *Friendship and Community: The Monastic Experience 350-1250* (Kalamazoo, 1988).

McGuire, B. P., *Brother and Lover: Aelred of Rievaulx* (New York, 1994).

Münster-Swendsen, M., 'Setting Things Straight: Law, Justice and Ethics in the Orationes of Lawrence of Durham', in *Anglo-Norman Studies XXVII*, ed. J. Gillingham (Woodbridge, 2005), pp. 151-168.

Münster-Swendsen, M., 'Irony and the Author. The Case of the *Dialogues* of Lawrence of Durham', in *Modes of Authorship in the Middle Ages,* ed. Slavica Rankovic, Else Mundal, Aidan Conti, Ingvild Brügger Budal og Leidulf Melve (Toronto, 2012), pp. 159-62.

Norton, C., *St William of York* (Woodbridge, 2006).

Poole, R. L., 'The Appointment and Deprivation of St. William, Archbishop of York', *The English Historical Review* 45, 178 (1930), pp. 273-281.

Powicke, F. M., 'Maurice of Rievaulx', *The English Historical Review* 36, 141 (1921), pp. 17-29.

Rigg, A. G., *A History of Anglo-Latin Literature 1066-1422* (Cambridge, 1992).

Rigg, A. G., 'Durham, Lawrence of (c.1110–1154)', *Oxford Dictionary of National Biography*, (Oxford, 2004) [http://www.oxforddnb.com/view/article/16167, accessed 24 Aug 2012]

Ronquist, E. C., 'Friendship in Laurence of Durham', *Classica et Mediaevalia* 35 (1984), pp. 191-213.

Rud, T., *Codicum Manuscriptorum Ecclesiae Cathedralis Dunelmensis. Catalogus Classicus descriptus a Thoma Rud* (Durham/London, 1825).

Scammell, G. V., *Hugh du Puiset: A Biography of the Twelfth-Century Bishop of Durham* (Cambridge, 1956).

Sharpe, R., *A Handlist of the Latin Writers of Great Britain and Ireland before 1540, Additions and Corrections* (Turnhout, 1997-2001).

Scholz, B. W., 'The Canonization of Edward the Confessor', *Speculum* 36, 1 (1961), pp. 38-60.

Talbot, C. H., 'The Testament of Gervase of Louth Park', *Analecta Sacri Ordinis Cisterciencis* 7 (1951), pp. 32-45.

Tanner, T., *Bibliotheca Britannico-Hibernica sive de Scriptoribus qui in Anglia, Scotia, et Hibernia ad saeculi XVII initium floruerunt, literarum ordine juxta familiarum nomina dispositis commentarius* (London, 1748).

Thomson, R. M., *Manuscripts from St Albans Abbey 1066-1235* (Woodbridge, 1982).

Waddell, C. 'The Hidden Years of Ælred of Rievaulx: The Formation of a Spiritual Master', *Cistercian Studies Quarterly* 41. 1 (2006), pp. 51-63.

Willis, B., *A History of the Mitred Parliamentary Abbies and Conventual Cathedral Chapters* (London, 1718).

Young, A., 'The Bishopric of Durham in Stephen's Reign" in *Anglo-Norman Durham 1093-1193*, ed. D. Rollason, M. Harvey and M. Prestwich (Woodbridge, 1994), pp. 353-68.

Young, A., *William Cumin: Border Politics and the Bishopric of Durham 1141-1144* (York, 1979).

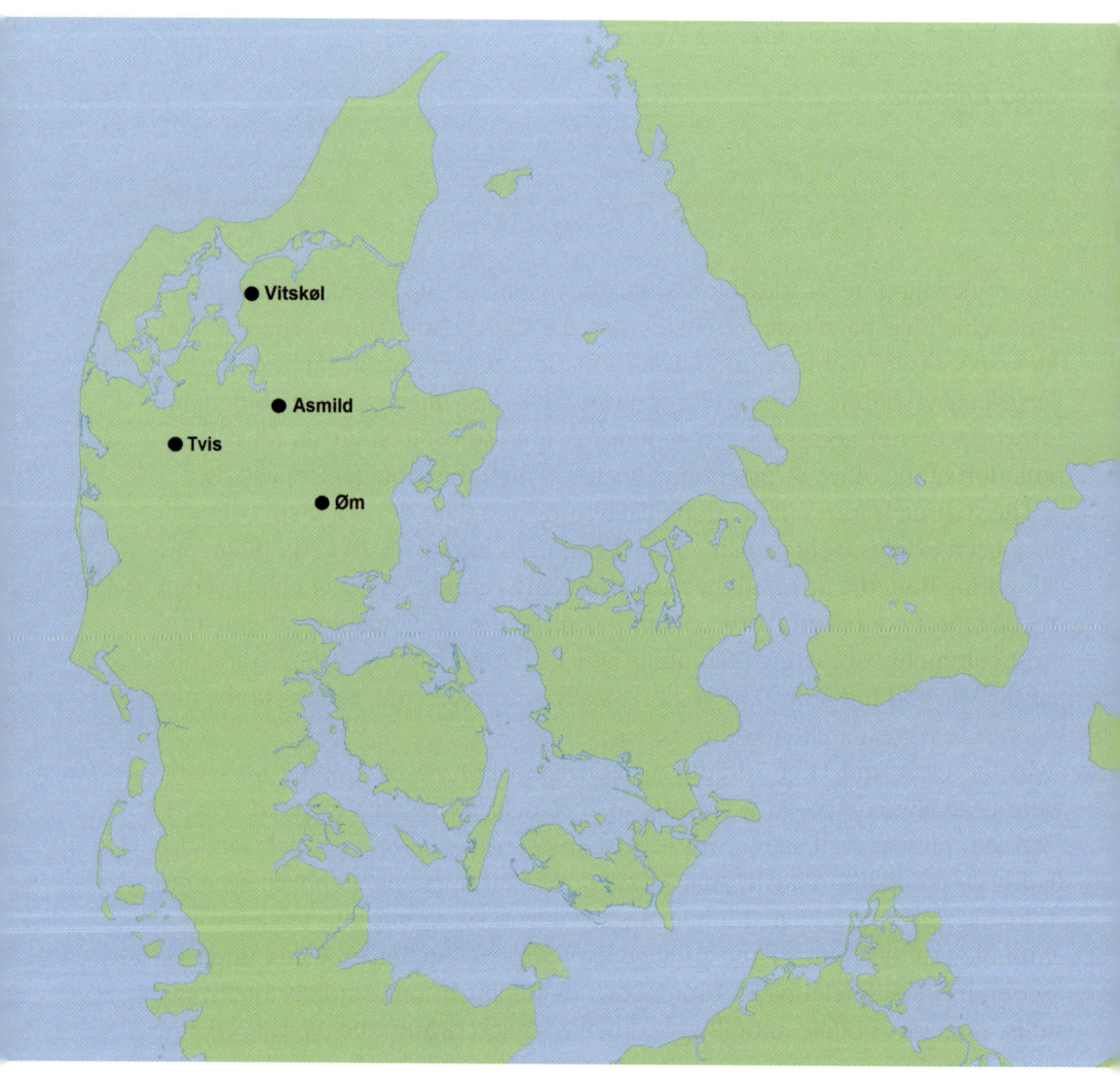

Monastic locations cited in the article.

An Ideal Clerical Administrator? Reflections on the Thirteenth-Century Biography of Bishop Gunner

Sigga Engsbro

The understanding of ideal and reality in medieval biographical works is an issue which has been extensively discussed within scholarship in the past decades, specifically within cultural history in the context of what can be defined as *Vorstellungsgeschichte*.[1] From the perspective of *Vorstellungsgeschichte* biographical works do not necessarily convey reality but rather illustrate an ideal representation of the office or position in society which the protagonist possessed.

The stylistic features of biographical writing and their development over time have been exhaustively explained by Berschin in his survey of Latin biographical writing from the third till the early thirteenth century. There is a wide variety of subgenres contained in the definition of medieval biography of which the most commonly occurring ones about official figures such as bishops or abbots are the *vita* and the *gesta*. The *gesta* typically emphasizes the actions of the protagonist to a greater extent than the *vita*.

In the Early and High Middle Ages in Latin Europe biographical accounts were generally composed according to typological schemata inspired by classical antiquity as well as by early Christian practices; select classical standards had been modified to a Christian context. For instance, biographical accounts from the Early and High Middle Ages only rarely supply the reader with a chronological account of the protagonist's actions but rather focus upon his accomplishments relating to topics such as his birth, outstanding intellectual skills, exercise of office, morally good behavior and death. The typical ordering of a biography according to topoi rather than a strict chronology within a moralizing frame draws upon Suetonius in the Latin tradition if not on the Greek tradition in the generation after Aristotle. To be noted in this respect is that the Christian tradition of biography in its multitude of genres had been fused with Christian concepts of duty and morality. Here the thought of imitation and

---

[1] See e.g. the description of the typical abbot in the context of "Vorstellungsgeschichte" by Goetz (2007), pp. 297.

exemplum constituted the most common strand within biographical writing in the Latin Middle Ages.[2]

Description of character was a central issue in classical biographical works of Greek as well as Latin origin and was undertaken by describing occurrences in private/official life; here episodic narratives serve as a didactic tool to delineate the moral characteristics of the protagonist.[3] Thus, I perceive biographical works written in the Early and High Middle Ages typically as didactic works which were primarily written for the purpose of improvement in life morally as well as practically. In these works the actions of the protagonists were described with a moralizing evaluating vocabulary; value judgments, thus conveying to the reader or hearer which actions should be emulated and which should be avoided.

Bishops' Biographies

In the Early and High Middle Ages men holding high offices either of a royal or clerical rank were the common subject for biographical accounts. Here the bishop is the most frequent subject of biographical accounts. The genre of bishops' biographies flourished particularly from the tenth to the early thirteenth century in Latin Europe. Bishops' biographies have been exhaustively researched within German historiography for the tenth through the twelfth centuries. In this respect in the past decades the concept of ideal representation has become a subject of greater interest, whereas in an earlier tradition the statements upon the bishop's conduct were often taken at face value.[4]

I suggest that bishops' biographies can be understood as manuals of how to attain a bishopric according to contemporary standards. In lengthier early and high medieval biographical accounts of bishops the protagonist is typically portrayed as near-perfect in all aspects of his life i.e. he fulfills the duties inherent in his office.

Thus, I believe that first and foremost the protagonist of a bishop's biography should serve as an example for the appropriate dual practical and moral behavior in the capacity of bishop as well as a role model for good behavior for all

---

2 Berschin (2004), pp. 69-71.
3 Averintsev (2002), pp. 21-26.
4 The importance of contemporary societal developments and/or political circumstances for changes in representation has been underlined by e.g. Jaeger and Haarländer; Jaeger (1985), pp. 25-30; Haarländer (2000), pp. 1-3, 16-28. The most relevant early work is Oskar Köhler's "Bild des Geistlichen Fürsten in den Viten des 10., 11. und 12. Jahrhunderts" from 1935.

Christians in general. Even though exemplum literature is a phrase frequently applied to biographical literature as such, the best-known and first actual bishop's biography occurring in a Danish context – the rather lengthy biography of Gunner, bishop of Viborg (c. 1152-1251) – has not yet been examined thoroughly from the perspective of continuity of genre and episcopal ideals. This biography has often been viewed by scholarship as a reliable source for the everyday life of a bishop due to its realistic depiction of a bishop's actions; e.g. the absence of miracles has been noted. Here scholars are typically not taking into account that Gunner's behavior is at all times praised and idealized.

Gunner's biography was most likely written at Vitskøl monastery by an anonymous Cistercian monk in the years 1264-67. Gunner was bishop of the diocese of Viborg from 1222-51 and had prior to that, in the years 1216-1222, occupied the office as abbot of Øm, a monastery of the Cistercian order. This biography has attracted much attention from Danish scholars. This is primarily due to the vivid depiction of Gunner's actions and behaviour in everyday life in a realistic, rather down-to-earth manner, uncommon for the few other biographical documents preserved from the period. Today Gunner is known for his abilities as a scholar of great eminence within the context of law as well as for his political acumen. Another reason for the interest in Gunner's biography is the probability of his participation in the composition of the law of Jutland completed in 1241.[5]

With my article I wish to underline that our comprehension of this particular biography of Gunner will benefit from being placed in a wider European context. Here one should look at the traditions of biographical writing in neighbouring Germany as many of the key elements which Jaeger explicates as typical for a bishop's biography c. 950-1220 in the German realms also apply to the biography of Gunner. I here wish to emphasize the didactic purpose of the biography in the context of tradition: Namely, to present the protagonist as an outstanding example so that his behavior can serve as guidance for others practically and morally, in the case of Gunner specifically meant for other members of the Cistercian order to emulate. Thus, the didactic rather than the commemorative aspect should be seen as the main purpose of writing.

The most recent and thorough discussion of the biography of Gunner can be found in the article by Brian Patrick McGuire, "Monastic and Episcopal Biography in the Thirteenth Century" from 1983. Here McGuire has made the first beginnings in integrating the understanding of exemplum literature into the analysis of Gunner's biography. The following part of my article should be viewed as a comment upon the many interesting issues that McGuire addresses

---

5   Jørgensen (1931), p.18, 24; Skyum-Nielsen (1966), p. 146-147; Christiansen (1981), pp. 168-169; Jansen (1991), pp. 120-123.

in his analysis of Gunner's biography. McGuire seeks to place the biography in a wider, primarily Cistercian, context and notes that this biography does not appear to be very similar to other episcopal biographies written by Cistercians in the twelfth-thirteenth centuries and sees the current conditions of the Cistercian order in Denmark as the reason for this deviation from common Cistercian practice.[6] Here McGuire emphasizes the divergences between the depiction of Gunner and other representations of bishops written by Cistercians in the twelfth-thirteenth centuries and interprets the biography of Gunner as an indicator for a unique understanding of the role of the bishop in a Danish Cistercian context. I do not question that the situation of the Cistercian order at the time of writing could have influenced the emphasis upon successful administration and material abundance in Gunner's biography. However, I wish to accentuate the probability that the traditional image of the bishop as a good administrator and educator was also seen as laudable in a wider Cistercian context consistent with the common practice within pre-existing traditions of writing bishops' biographies. Primarily, the focus upon Gunner's perfect exercise of administrative episcopal duties is very similar to descriptions of traditional practices of biographical writing in neighbouring Germany from the tenth to the early thirteenth century.[7]

Even though there were divergences between the depiction of bishops in biographies written by Cistercians in the twelfth-thirteenth centuries and Gunner's biography, it may be argued that the depiction of Gunner was actually in close agreement with the episcopal ideal displayed by the most prominent and authoritative Cistercian author Abbot Bernard of Clairvaux (c. 1090-1153) in works such as *De Moribus et Officio Episcoporum* and *De Consideratione*. In both these works the views presented conform to idealized representations of bishops in the tenth-thirteenth centuries in the German realms. Bernard of Clairvaux describes the appropriate behavior of a bishop and explicitly outlines the suitable virtues of a bishop as well as his correct social conduct. Particularly, the bishop should honor his office and thus take upon him the responsibility for both the spiritual and the material welfare of his subjects. Here it is stated that endeavors to increase the wealth and status of the bishopric should be pursued by the bishop.[8] Thus, it may be fruitful in regard to the Cistercian factor to com-

---

6   McGuire, (1983), pp. 209-211, 214.
7   See e.g. Jaeger (1985) or Stephanie Haarländer (2000).
8   Bernard of Clairvaux, *De Consideratione*, book 2, chapter 8-13; *De Moribus et Officio Episcoporum*, chapter 31- a further argument for the similarity between the views of Bernard of Clairvaux and the views of Gunner's biographer is the similar reference to Timothy (1,3,5) regarding the care for the household. See *De Consideratione*, book 4,

pare the description of virtuous behavior in Gunner's biography with the description of the necessary virtues in the episcopal office in the aforementioned works by Bernard of Clairvaux.

Hagiography?

The importance of Gunner's biography has been emphasized by Danish historians as a significant and singular occurrence in Danish medieval biographical literature within a secular context rather than a hagiographical one.[9] However, as McGuire has noted, it is unfortunate to interpret Gunner's biography without recourse to hagiographical traditions or rather, I would add, to Christian traditions of biography within the church. Bishops' biographies have typically been labelled as hagiography within an older tradition of scholarship but this definition is increasingly questioned on several accounts, specifically in regard to the near absence of miracles in the description of the bishop from the tenth century onwards. Miraculous events have typically been seen as a common denominator for hagiographical works which were written to underline the sanctity of the protagonist. Hagiography as such is a problematic definition for biographical works, specifically those describing bishops. Firstly this definition was not applied by the medieval scholars themselves, but rather was used when referring to the Hagiographa in the Old Testament. Secondly, from the tenth century onwards specifically within the context of episcopal biography in Latin Europe the depiction of bishops as mediators of miracles is quite rare.[10] Thus, the typical biographical accounts of bishops from the tenth century onwards rather emphasize their administrative competence, intellectual ability, progress in the *artes liberales*[11] and correct ethical behaviour in accordance with classical political ethical philosophy in the tradition of Plato, perhaps by way of mediators such as classical philosophers, primarily Cicero or Christian mediators such as Boethius or the church fathers Augustine and Gregory the Great.[12]

---

chapter 17; *Vita Gunneri*, chapter 6 (quotation in footnote 41). I will not go into a discussion of the appropriate virtues for a bishop displayed in these works by Bernard of Clairvaux, even though they may also be said to be exemplified in Gunner's biography.
9   See e.g. Jørgensen, (1931), p. 18.
10 See definition and function of hagiography by Schmale (1985), pp. 112-115, 160-162. For a discussion of hagiography see Berschin, (1986), p.17-18, 22; Berschin, (2004), p. 43.
11 The seven *artes liberales* comprise grammar, rhetoric, dialectic, arithmetic, geometry, astronomy and music.
12 Gregory the Great is also directly mentioned in a Cistercian context. See e.g. the description of Sven in a laudatory manner. Øm *Exordium*, chapter 31. It can also be ar-

Literary Role Models

McGuire discusses whether the author of the biography of Gunner could have used literary role models such as the fifth century *Vita Martini* by Sulpicius Severus, the eleventh-century Adam of Bremen's *Gesta Hammaburgensis* or the Chronicle of the Bishops of Ribe.[13] According to McGuire, these works were most likely available to the author of Gunner's biography. McGuire dismisses the possibility that Gunner's biography could be influenced by or imitate other literary products. However, he does mention that Bishop Sven of Aarhus may have constituted the only concrete model for the biography of Gunner in a practical sense.[14]

I quite agree that the depiction of Sven of Aarhus in the thirteenth century *Øm Exordium* (Exordium Monasterii Caræ Insulæ) may have constituted a probable role model for the writing of Gunner's biography but not merely due to a shared historical situation.[15] Contrary to McGuire, I believe that the similarities between these accounts may be explained on account of literary imitation as well as continuous traditional understanding of the ideal exercise of the bishop's office.[16]

In this respect I wish to emphasize that there is a high probability that Adam of Bremen's *Gesta Hammaburgensis* constituted a source of literary influence for the biography of Gunner, specifically with regard to structure and the illustration of daily life in the lengthy account of Archbishop Adalbert of Hamburg-Bremen as well as the general moralizing tenor of the gesta. Also, the use of anecdotes to display appropriate moral conduct may be discerned in the description of Adalbert and in this case also manners at table are of the essence – although negatively for Adalbert whereas this is positive in the biography of Gunner.[17]

In general the greatest divide between these two works is that the biographical account of Adalbert primarily serves as an explanation for the problems that the archbishopric of Hamburg-Bremen faced in the later eleventh century. This

---

gued of late Carolingian bishop's lives that this shift takes its beginnings in the later ninth century e.g. to be seen in the ninth century bishops' biographies of Ansgar and Rimbert of Hamburg-Bremen.

13 McGuire (1983), p. 209.
14 McGuire (1983), p. 214.
15 The Øm *Exordium* was written at the Cistercian monastery of Øm. The biographical account of Bishop Sven was written in the early thirteenth century while the Øm *Exordium* giving brief accounts of successive abbots and controversies as a continuous work was broken off around 1267.
16 McGuire (1983), p. 215.
17 Adam of Bremen, *Gesta Hammaburgensis*, book 3, chapter 39-40, Biography of Gunner, chapter 8, chapter 12.

appears in the eyes of the biographer to be due to Adalbert's moral shortcomings. In contrast the behaviour of Gunner is throughout displayed as laudable to imitate and the good reasons for conduct which could be reproached by contemporaries is here explained:

> In his guest quarters he (Gunner) used to drink from a particular small silver vessel observing (his drinking) with attentive care so that he did not drink more on one day than another, keeping the same measure; For he made a very small ball of bread for each emptied vessel and placed it secretively under the small napkin in front of him. Once, when it (this practice) was evident to master Abbot Sven, who had been his chaplain earlier and therefore was knowledgeable of him, then he was delicately surveying it and secretly removed some of the small balls, so that he made him drink more than he was used to so that he yielded to cheerfulness in his household. Shortly after when the bishop discovered it, he immediately ceased to drink and then he said in agreeable and elegant words: "I have become a fool (in glorying); you have compelled me."[18]

In this respect the behaviour of Gunner at table is displayed in a more humorous tone showing his good intentions, even though he was exceeding the golden mean in his drinking. And it is emphasized that the reasons for his excessive drinking is to be found in the fault of the abbot.

To a minor extent the *Vita Martini* by Sulpicius Severus may have been consulted by the author of Gunner's biography as one of the essential role models for biographical writing in the Early and High Middle Ages within a clerical context. In the *Vita Martini* it is outlined how one may attain salvation without achieving martyrdom, primarily through virtuous deeds. The purpose of the work is stated as serving as an exemplum for others, which was more often than not stated in the prologue of biographies.[19] The depiction of virtuous behaviour by way of exemplary episodes as such is also a common trait in Gunner's biog-

---

18 Biography of Gunner, chapter 12: "Solebat bibere de quodam vasculo argenteo, (in infirmitorio suo) diligentem curam habens, mensuram eandem seruando; vt uno die plus quam alio non biberet, mensuram eandem seruando; nam ad quodlibet vasculum exhaustum minimam pilulam de pane fecit et secrete sub mappula ante se posuit. Quod quidam dompnus abbas, videlicet Sueno, qui capellanus suus prius fuerat, conscius sibi subtiliter perpendens, quasdam pilulas secrete subtraxit, vt eum plus bibendo, quam solitus esset, letiorem redderet in domo sua. Quod episcopus Paulo post recognoscens bibere statim desijt, blandis verbis et graciosis dicendo : "Factis sum insipiens, vos me coegistis. " Here the citation of Gunner's words is directly borrowed from II Cor 12,11.
19 Severus Sulpicius, *Vita Sancti Martini*, chapter 1, 7, chapter 2,2, chapter 13, 9, chapter 25, 5-8, chapter 27.

raphy, admittedly in a worldlier manner than is the case in *Vita Martini*. Furthermore in the *Vita Martini* there is specifically a depiction of conduct at table also referring to the bishop's humble conduct and honour owed to clerical office.[20] However, the depiction of the bishop's virtuous conduct by way of example is a common trait in most Latin Christian biographies, at least until the early thirteenth century. Due to generic difference however, as well as the setting in a different age when Christianity had not yet been institutionalized, the *Vita Martini* displays a quite different understanding of the proper conduct of episcopal office than is seen in the biography of Gunner. In the *Vita Martini* the strength of Christian beliefs and the struggle and success of Martin in displaying the power of faith are at the center. In the biography of Gunner the demands of a successful administration of a well-established institution in a Christian society are emphasized. Thus, the influence from the depiction in the *Vita Martini* can mainly be seen in the depiction of virtuous conduct, i.e. the virtues considered exemplary in a bishop.

More similarities may however be found between the description of Bishop Gunner, Bishop Sven and Bishop Adalbert, due to the more institutional focus. Thus, inspiration for the author was probably primarily found in the biography of Sven from the *Exordium of Øm* as well as the eleventh century work by Adam of Bremen the *Gesta Hammaburgensis*, these being the most immediate role models.

Furthermore in a wider Latin European perspective relating to currents within contemporary learned culture McGuire also notes the possibility that influences from Aristotle's *Ethics*[21] may be seen in Gunner's biography, specifically in regard to the display of generosity and liberality with money. Here McGuire primarily underlines that the study of Aristotle's *Ethics* was revitalized in the later thirteenth century. He refers to the Christianization of the concepts of *magnamitas* and *honor* by Thomas of Aquinas and notes that similar concepts are applied in Gunner's biography. In this respect McGuire sees Gunner's biography as a product displaying a changing view of ethics and human behaviour; here material surplus and rank are combined as commendable in a virtuous man.[22] However, more recent research has shown that the concepts of *magnamitas* and *honour* were quite central issues within the bishops' biographies already in the tenth century and these concepts may just as well have been based upon Ciceronian notions. The material display of high office was quite unproblematic

---

20 Severus Sulpicius, *Vita Sancti Martini*, chapter 20; Vita Gunneri, chapter 8.
21 Probably hereby the work *Nicomachean Ethics* by Aristotle is understood.
22 McGuire (1983), pp. 228-230.

in the tenth-twelfth centuries.[23] For bishops the amassing and display of material wealth to the benefit of the bishopric was actually considered a proof of the bishop's good conduct of office. Here the conduct of office in an honourable manner included the dual material and spiritual care for the subjects' well-being, ultimately leading them towards salvation. Also, I would suggest that the deployment of the concept of honour had not changed significantly from the tenth century to the thirteenth century in the episcopal biography. The concept of honour does not refer only to the attainment of high office in the world and the visualization of material goods suitable for persons of high rank, but also to the display of honourable conduct in the world.

Here I would suggest that the honour owed to the episcopal office is primarily depicted in the bishop's responsible conduct fulfilling his dual obligation as a public figure providing the community with spiritual and material care. This may be defined as a traditional trait of episcopal biography particularly from the tenth to the early thirteenth century. In respect to the concept of honour as responsible conduct towards the community in his care, Gunner's biography is clearly influenced by classical concepts of ideal behaviour for those in position of authority, specifically in the tradition of Plato, also encompassing the moral philosophical works by Aristotle, Cicero as well as the Greek and Latin Church fathers.

It may remain an open question which of the above-mentioned philosophers/church fathers the biographer more closely relies upon as there is no reference in the biography to any of them. It may be a matter of an Aristotelian concept, but also the much nurtured Ciceronian views, or maybe rather traditions building upon the church fathers such as Augustine and Gregory the Great? Common to all the above-mentioned authors is the perception that the exercise of high office implies responsibility towards the subjects governed in terms of both moral and material welfare.

Vita or Gesta?

The biography of Gunner was probably part of a larger work, now lost, and it is highly speculative to expound upon the specific genre of the work into which the biography was incorporated. There is no doubt however, that the biography of Gunner represents a diversion from the structure of this work, as there are

---

23 See Jaeger (1994) for a thorough discussion of the Ciceronian elements honor and magnamitas in an episcopal context in the tenth-twelfth centuries. McGuire concretely notes in his article (1983), p. 205: "..for our author *honor* means high office in the church, whether secular or monastic".

some explanatory phrases in the prologue on the reasons for its incorporation as well as a reference to two abbots, presumably of Vitskøl, to be described at a later point in the same work.

The Latin title commonly used to designate the biography of Gunner is "Vita Gunneri Episcopi Vibergensis". This title is the invention of the editor Geertz as the original manuscript itself was without title. McGuire suggests that Gunner's biography was originally part of a lost *Vitae Abbatum* of the monastery of Vitskøl.[24] I believe that it is quite credible that this work depicted the lives of the abbots at Vitskøl, but I would argue that the structure of the biography of Gunner more likely may point to the genre of "gesta" rather than the genre of "vita abbatum".

The *vita* usually begins with a description of the protagonist's descent and development in childhood and youth ultimately leading to the assumption of office, while this description is typically lacking in the *gesta* or is not very extensive; here the exercise of office constitutes the main focus and is frequently evaluated in a moral tenor.

This may be underlined by the probability that the most immediate literary role model for Gunner's biography was the *Gesta Hammaburgensis* written by the cleric Adam of Bremen in the 1070s. In this *gesta* there is e.g. no description of Bishop Adalberts' progress in life before the accession to episcopal office. Bishop Adalbert is the most explicitly described bishop in this work. Gunner's biography, similar to the depiction of Adalbert, also begins with the description of the circumstances for the assumption of office and makes no reference to either his descent or his progress in childhood and youth. Thus, I would assume that the biographical genre of the Latin *gesta* most likely is what we encounter in Gunner's biography.[25]

No matter whether the biography of Gunner's structural composition is that of a *vita* or a *gesta* the adherence to exemplum literature must be emphasized; this biography is moralistic in a panegyrical manner and the description of correct actions and behaviour as bishop dominates.

Gunner, a nearly Perfect Cistercian Administrator?

In lengthier biographical accounts of bishops in either *vita* or *gesta* from the tenth-twelfth centuries the perfect fulfilment of the requirements of the office is generally mirrored in terms of the duality of office encompassing both the

---

24 McGuire, (1983), pp. 202-203. For the sake of transparency i.e. to facilitate finding the source I have chosen to specify the biography of Gunner as *Vita Gunneri* in the footnote apparatus.
25 Berschin, (2004), vol. 5, p. 27-28.

outer, worldly and inner, spiritual obligations towards his subordinates, often underlining his abilities in administrative affairs, intellectual skills and virtuous behavior. In Gunner's biography the *vita activa* as active involvement in the matters of the world is also clearly on display. This is the ideal behaviour for a bishop rather than the *vita contemplativa*; the typical life style relating to withdrawal from the world which was viewed as appropriate for the ordinary monk. It is the notion of the *vita activa* as appropriate for a bishop that we also encounter in Gunner's biography, even though it is at times described how Gunner sought to follow the monastic practices of withdrawal and prayer. Here we encounter a typical topos present in bishops' biographies, namely the tension between *vita contemplativa* and *vita activa*: the wish of the bishop to withdraw from the world to the benefit of his own salvation succumbs to the understanding of the bishop's duty as caring for his subjects in the world. Thus, Gunner follows the golden mean rather than monastic ascetic practices because of the duties inherent in episcopal office. Emphasis on the adherence to monastic ideals specifically in the sense of asceticism or contemplation is not uncommon within bishop's biographies in general. However, neither monastic asceticism nor contemplation seems to be of particular consequence in the depiction of Gunner, who is rather described as adhering to Cistercian monastic practices due to reverence for the order.

Explicit monastic elements as such are hard to come by in this biography, excepting the emphasis on adherence to Cistercian liturgical practice which, however, is not described in detail. Therefore it is hard to infer something substantial with regard to the Cistercians except that the author describes Gunner's devotion to the Cistercian order in a laudatory manner – a dominant theme throughout the biography.

The many references to the Cistercian order and the bishop's reverence for the order do not blur the fact that the biography of Gunner conveys a typical representation of the ideal exercise of a bishop's duties. The qualities of Gunner enumerated and described in detail in the biography are in agreement with the traditional view of the courtly administrator bishop much loved by king and venerable members of society typical for the tenth-twelfth centuries. Here the emphasis on honourable manners, profound knowledge of the liberal arts, just and able administration of property is remarkably similar. Nonetheless, the economic abilities admittedly appear very conspicuous and are more explicitly described in the biography of Gunner than is usually the case.

Gunner is depicted as an authoritative father figure who takes care of both the temporal and spiritual needs of his flock with just administration and government. Here the emphasis upon Gunner's magnificence and successful material and spiritual care for the household and subjects in the diocese provides the guideline in the narrative. The bishop displays spiritual care for the subjects mainly through means of correction and admonition as a superior authority. In terms of material care he applies just arbitration and prudent foresight to meet the material needs of the household and subjects. The dispensation of justice is frequently described in a material sense; the penitence of the perpetrator is specified in kind or money. Gunner is also described as receiving money in exchange for his exercise of justice.

Here the practical approach of the bishop to issues such as the correct legal procedures is at all times indicated, e.g. his leniency towards women who in their sleep had accidentally killed their babies. This incident also serves to illustrate his charity/love towards his neighbour, also a significant element within Cistercian ideology. Thus the bishop's rational and practical approach is underlined as the incidents at hand are described within a realistic frame. Here Gunner's sharp mind is praised and depicted as the determining factor for his actions and success in his results.

The ideal of the administrator bishop expressed in Gunner's biography may also be compared to another and earlier thirteenth century Danish Cistercian biography, the account of Bishop Sven of Aarhus in the *Øm Exordium*. Both of these biographical accounts deal with the bishop's exercise of office and are of a panegyrical character. The main focus in both biographical accounts is how these bishops benefited the order and, in the case of Gunner how members of the order would continue to benefit by his example. In this respect it is particularly interesting that there is a shared emphasis upon material assets rather than spiritual contemplation.

However, administrative qualities were not only valued in bishops. The biographical account of Gunner as an abbot as well as the biographies in the *Øm Exordium* are also revealing with respect to the ideal requirements for abbots. However, the worldly administrative qualities of abbots are accounted for rather briefly in comparison with the biographical account of Sven.

In the *Øm Exordium* rather than merely focusing on spiritual qualities, the abbot's ability to maneuver in the world is commemorated in a positive manner. It even appears as unbecoming in an abbot when he does not accord enough attention to the temporal aspects of office.

In the *Øm Exordium* Gunner's conduct of office while he was abbot is compared with that of his successor; it is apparent that Gunner was perceived as an extraordinarily able abbot. The value accorded to the worldly aspect of the work of an abbot is here quite evident. In order to be a good abbot successful dealings with secular matters appear to be a necessity and often serve as the justification for promotion to higher ranks, as is explicitly explained in the case of Abbot Nicholas in the outline of his exercise of abilities in inner and outer affairs:

> The ninth was Master Nicholas the second, and he was brought up from boyhood in the discipline of the monastic order, a man who was fortunate in all his dealings and who also for some time was prior in the house, in secular dealings he was very persistent and sufficiently instructed in the inner concerns. Finally, the rumour of his flexibility and honourable character travelled to many and he was transferred from us to the "mother house" [Vitskøl] where he was distinguished with the burden of greater honors.[26]

Abbot Nicholas is thus apparently promoted to higher honours because of his skillful conduct in secular dealings as well as his honourable character. Here higher honours are synonymous with greater burdens; that is greater responsibilities.

The responsibility of office is also explicitly stated in the biographical accounts of the bishops Sven and Gunner. Here the depiction of Sven differs in scope from the biography of Gunner as the establishment of claims upon property which he had bequeathed to the Cistercians take up most space as documentation for the Cistercians' legitimate possession. This concern should be seen in the context of the "exordium" genre, wherein the beginnings of the order/monastery are laid out, so that later claims in relation to privileges and territory may be justified. The mentioning of the testament in the biography of Gunner reflects the same tradition of administration and economic provision also to be seen in the account of Sven.

Exemplum

We will never know the specific purpose of the larger work from which the biography of Gunner is extracted, and its genre will remain unclear. However, in the biography of Gunner it is evident that the dual spiritual and material benefit to the Cistercian order is the central theme as it also was in the biography of Sven in the Øm Exordium. In the biography of Gunner members of the Cistercian order are encouraged to follow his example, whereupon salvation, success in life and honourable office will follow:

> As there already has been mention of Master Gunner, who at that time was abbot of Øm, and as he was a renowned member of our order, I cannot pass him by in si-

---

26 Øm Exordium, chapter 36, p. 194 "Nonus fuit dominus Nicolaus secundus, et ipse in monastici ordinis disciplina a puero enutritus, uir in cunctis prospere agens, qui et ipse aliquando priorabatur in domo, in agendis secularibus multum strenuus et in interioribus satis edoctus. Fama tandem agilitatis et honestatis ad plurimos peruolante, ad matrem domum ea nobis aufertur, onere maioris honoris insignitus."

lence; rather I shall briefly say something about him for those who wish to hear. For if someone from our order perhaps should wish to follow the example of his life and appearance, this (endeavour) will make it possible for them to obtain salvation of the soul and advancement and honours in life.[27]

Thus, to follow the example of Gunner will result in dual benefits, spiritual as well as material. Here reaping worldly benefits such as promotion to higher rank and obtaining honours are mentioned in the same breath as salvation of the soul.

Sven's status as an example to be followed is also expressed directly in the text as was the case in Gunner's biography. But Sven is present mainly as an example for visitors to the Cistercian order; Sven can be imitated by them in the manner in which he shows reverence for the customs of the Cistercian monks as he leaves his horse at the gate of the monastery.[28]

The main difference between these two accounts lies in the fact that the exhortation to imitation of his life and character for members of the Cistercian order is explicitly present in the biography of Gunner while it is rather implicit in the biography of Sven, as his function as an exemplum is only presented in respect to his reverence for the order.[29] In the biography of Gunner it is explicitly stated that the intention behind describing the life of Gunner is in terms of his example, which can inspire members of the Cistercian order to imitate him.

The positive evaluation of attainment of high office and rank in society abounds in the biography of Gunner. The examples of his fortunate exertion of influence on his surroundings are numerous. Here the benefit of being educated by Gunner is described as resulting in promotion to high office:

> However none of the clerics, rough in their ways, who came to him and stayed for some years and followed him, failed to make progress in what is required of a clergyman as well as in honourable manners in a marvellous way.[30]

---

27 *Vita Gunneri*, chapter 1 "Cum autem de dompno Gunnero, tunc abbate in Cara Insula, mencio iam habetur, et ipse nobile membrum fuit nostri ordinis, non possum pertransire cum silencio, quin aliqua de eo breuiter dicam audire volentibus; quia, si aliqui de ordine nostro exemplum vite sue et formam fortasse sequi voluerint, illis potest fieri ad salutem anime et ad vite profectum et honorem."

28 Øm *Exordium*, chapter 31, p.188. It is rather vague who Sven's imitators are but probably non-Cistercian visitors to the monastery.

29 The depiction of Sven is also highly laudatory due to his position as one of the monastery's founders, although his initial resistance towards the order is mentioned this soon gives way to panegyrics. Øm *Exordium*, prologue, chapter 1, 22-24, 31, 35.

30 *Vita Gunneri*, chapter 5. "Nullus autem clericus ita rudis ad eum venit et in obsequio

Here the duality of practical skill in terms of knowledge and of spiritual accomplishment in the instilment of honourable morals appears to be central.

In the ordering of the examples of persons who, due to the influence of Gunner, achieved promotions to higher office, monks are mentioned first, whereas the secular clergy comes second. This is just another indication of the significance given to monks of the Cistercian order. Specifically, in this first clarification of Gunner's beneficial influence it is pointed out that three monks attached to him as chaplains later received the office of abbot in the Cistercian monasteries, respectively of Tvis and most likely Vitskøl. The two abbots of Vitskøl are described as presiding over the monastery in a useful way but it remains rather vague whether it is their practical wordly or inner spiritual qualities which are seen as useful in their leadership. Or maybe both qualities?[31]

Members of the secular clergy are described as receiving office as bishops, provosts or masters. The Bishop John of Børglum in this respect constitutes the most outstanding example in this enumeration of men who attained higher rank due to their education by Gunner and receives much more attention and space than any of the others.[32] Thus it is only holders of high ranking office who receive mention by name in Gunner's biography.

The magnificence of Gunner as bishop is expressed in terms of his relations with others, be it matters of education, rank or the dispensing of justice. Rank and the duties that come with it appear to be of importance in both biographical accounts of Sven and Gunner, but this is especially the case in Gunner's biography, which repeatedly mentions his keeping company with members of the nobility and emphasizes the king's appreciation of him. In this respect it is notable that persons who outrank the bishop, such as king and archbishop, are also described as showing their reverence and love for him as if he were their father. This emphasis can serve to underline his importance as an authoritative figure deserving respect due to his ability, merit and rank.

Also, in the case of Gunner the presence of nobility during the writing of the testament may also have served to underline its trustworthiness and validity on the basis of the high rank of his witnesses:

> He suffered from this illness through all the summer and in the autumn, having made clear his last will to all the nobles of his diocese and having regulated all his

---

suo iugiter per aliquot annos permansit, quod non tam in clericatura quam in morum honestate proficeret miro modo."
31 *Vita Gunneri*, chapter 5.
32 Ibid.

affairs from his sick bed, he ended his days at Asmiald, in the year of the lord 1251, on the day of the Martyr St. Genesius, a Friday and in the sixth hour.[33]

With a phrase coined by Jaeger in connection with the conduct of bishops in the German realms, it may be described as a display of aristocratic deference when Gunner shows reverence to abbots who are beneath him in rank. The Ciceronian phrase from *De Officiis* may convey this sentiment: "The higher we are placed, the more humble we should behave."[34] This statement is actually also present in the work *De Moribus et Officio Episcoporum* by Bernhard of Clairvaux.[35] Here the display of humility is repeated as a main guideline for virtuous behaviour; where respect for rank is also emphasized as a central obligation in the office of bishop.

In Gunner's biography his humility is emphasized on various occasions, specifically in regard to his behavior towards the Cistercian abbots as well as towards other bishops. He shows great reverence for Cistercian abbots and does not allow them to be inconvenienced and forced to submit or yield to him because of the bishop's higher rank. The use of signs of office in everyday life such as a silver cup at meals is explained through respect for the office of bishop, but the tone appears defensive:

> However, he always had his silver cups carried by his cupbearer not because of pride or empty glory but because of the honour he was obliged to show according to his official position. For at this time this was an appropriate custom with all lords and honourable men of the land. [36]

Thus a pre-existing code of behaviour appropriate for men of high rank such as bishops and abbots is as depicted here not far from the courtly behaviour on display in Adam's depiction of table manners in his account of Bishop Adalbert of Bremen in the eleventh century.

---

33 *Vita Gunneri*, chapter 13. "Quam infirmitatem per totam estatem sufferens et in autompno in bono testamento coram omnibus nobilioribus sue dyocesis (sua ordinans, in infirmitorio suo) finiuit dies suos Asmiald, Anno domini M.CC.L.I., die sancti Genesij martyris, feria sexta et hora sexta."
34 Cicero, *De Officiis*, book 1, section 90.
35 Bernard of Clairvaux, *De Moribus et Officio Episcoporum*, chapter 31.
36 *Vita Gunneri*, chapter 8. "Portari autem secum semper fecit per pincernam suum suos ciphos argenteos, non propter superbiam vel inanem gloriam, sed propter ministerij sui debitam honorificentiam, quia illis temporibus hec consuetudo apud omnes dompnos et precipuos terre celebris et condecens habebatur."

Secular Sanctity and the Responsibility Derived from Rank?

The phrase secular sanctity coined by Thomas Noble may help to clarify both the importance of high rank in society as well as the emphasis on the bishop's closeness to members of the aristocracy and king which is similarly to be seen in the biography of Gunner and Sven. In Noble's terminology secular sanctity denotes a common noble ethos among the Carolingian nobility which was promoted from the time of Charlemagne in the aristocratic elite, both lay and ecclesiastical. Within this frame it was required of the nobility to assume a common responsibility for the Christian people and lead an active public life serving as examples for the public. [37] Thus, by secular sanctity is meant an elitist understanding of the responsibility to serve God by serving Christian society (*Civitas Dei*) through one's actions as an exemplary figure and thereby achieving saintly status. Leadership in this form is perceived as divinely ordained and fundamentally good. The understanding of the reciprocal connection of high office in society with the duties towards subordinates may be discerned in a multitude of bishop's biographies from the tenth through the twelfth centuries. However, if we apply the definition by Noble to the biographical accounts of Sven and Gunner it should be adapted in the sense that rank and outstanding abilities, rather than adherence to the nobility, determine responsibility, and the duties merely pertain to the good of the household and/or monastic community rather than all of Christendom.

The preoccupation with rank and leadership as well as the worldly duties deriving from it in the service to God are explicitly present in the description of Sven. Sven was not allowed by the abbot to become a mere monk as he would be of higher utility to God in his office as bishop and thus earn the honour of eternal salvation. If he protected the servants of the lord, they could live in peace and pray much more than Sven himself would be able to do if he was living a life of contemplation in the monastery:

> This would have been fulfilled in deed if the lord abbot had not been opposed to it asserting to him that it is of greater benefit for attaining the honour of eternal bliss if he placed himself as a wall for the house of the lord against the attacks of evil men and protected the servants of God under the wings of his defense and kept them warm, so that because of this many could be alive and in the tranquility of peace serve God and also pray in great abundance for him, than if he himself alone resided in the quiet monastery grounds and relinquished the lord's boat with the rope cut off in the waves to be shaken severely by the many temptations and disturbances of this world.[38]

---

37 Noble (2007), p. 8.
38 Øm *Exordium*, chapter 22."Quod profecto opera adimplesset, si domnus abbas non

Thus, Sven is obliged to relinquish his wish for the contemplative life due to the obligations of his office as well as his outstanding abilities.

The sanctity of Gunner must also clearly be seen in his perfect exercise of the public office as bishop, as the typical signs of sanctity such as miracle-working, prophesies, inner spirituality and ascetic behaviour are lacking:

> Even though from ancient times it has been said that achievement of honourable office often changes the character, this man was previously holy and perfect which at that time was heard from all. However, when he was elected and made bishop he began to be holier and even more perfect towards God as well as towards his neighbour and the people of the temporal world due to a change [effectuated] by the hand of the elevated one [God].[39]

The portrayal of Gunner's holiness is seen not only towards God but towards his nearest and those in the temporal world. The distinction between his nearest and those belonging to the temporal world may point towards the significance given to the household in the biography. This distinction is to my knowledge not a typical feature of earlier biographical accounts of bishops in the German realms.

In the biography of Gunner the bishop's public life in and for the community is at the center, rather than his personal life. Here social interaction with the members of the household is of the highest importance. It is thus not a saint in the traditional mould performing miracles whom we encounter in the biography of Gunner but rather a public figure who through his perfect exercise of office, in acknowledgment of the duties derived from his high rank and ability, will attain salvation.

Government and Material Provision

Successful endeavours to provide for the material well-being of those in his charge and to increase the status and wealth of the bishopric are frequently underlined in a laudatory manner in the biographical accounts of Gunner and

---

obstitisset, affirmans maioris esse meriti ad promerendam eterne felicitates gloriam, si se opponeret murum pro domo domini contra malignantium incursiones et seruos dei sub alis sue defensionis protegeret atque foueret, ut ex hoc multi possent in pacis tranquilitate uiuntes deo serurire et pro eo copiosius orare, quam si ipse solus in terra claustralis quietis residens dominicam nauiculam abscisco fune inter fluctus huius seculi conquassandam reliqueret ad multorum scandalum et perturbationem."

39 *Vita Gunneri*, chapter 2. "Igitur cum dictum sit ab antiquis, quod honores sepe solent mores mutare, hic prius sanctus et perfectus dum ab omnibus audiebatur, electus et episcopus factus sanctior et perfectior mutacione dextere excelsi cepit existere, siue ad deum siue ad proximum et seculum."

Sven, and this concern is quite in accordance with the admonition to bishops in the writings of Bernard of Clairvaux. Preoccupation with the adequate provision for the material needs of the household however is also present in bishops' lives from the tenth through twelfth centuries.[40]

In Gunner's biography many elements can foremost be understood in terms of the display of dutiful fatherly care towards the people under his direct jurisdiction, the household. This may be inferred from the allusion to the words of Paul in the first letter to Timothy (1,3,5): "As he said in the words of Saint Paul: The man who does not know how to govern his own household, in what way could he have care for God's church?"[41] In order to underline Gunner's abilities in the supervision of his household the bishop's behaviour in daily life and the fulfilment of his duties within the diocese are described in detail. Regarding the household it is the care for the material necessities in life which receives most attention. Its members receive fair, just and adequate treatment in matters of food, clothing, education and economy. Here social behaviour is of central concern, but in relation to the care for the physical well-being of the household rather than the poor.

The material aspect is also what springs to mind in the description of Sven, specifically in the abundance of testamentary gifts of property explicitly reported in the Øm Exordium. In this respect it is noteworthy that there is also a record of the testament in the biography of Gunner, but this is done in passing rather than explicitly outlining details, as is the case in the Øm Exordium.

The economic aspect receives much attention and is shown in diverse fields such as Gunner's procedure in regard to equipping knights for the king's expeditions; he skillfully foresees the expenses of each and makes a full report on them. Interestingly, in the description of the education available at Gunner's court the economic element is introduced. Better and cheaper than study in Paris is education at the court of Gunner. This question may have been a subject of discussion when the biography was written; it appears superfluous to support study at the schools in Paris when a better education might be achieved at Gunner's court.[42] However, this comment is ambiguous in character, as Gunner himself is noted as receiving his education in Paris in the company of Cardinal Gregory, who later helps arrange Gunner's election to the office of bishop. However, it is quite probable that the author is negatively disposed towards new

---

40 A similar emphasis upon the bishop's material care for the household may e.g. be seen in the tenth century Vita Oudalrici, chapter 5.
41 Vita Gunneri, chapter 6. "Dicens illud sancti Pauli: Qui familiam suam regere nescit, ecclesie dei diligentiam quomodo habebit?"
42 McGuire (1983), pp. 226-228.

independent practices in Paris and rather welcomes the educational practices of the cathedral school as sufficient.

In the context of material provision poverty does not constitute a significant theme in either of these biographical accounts but rather, in Sven's case, the bishop's adequate means to serve the Cistercians' worldly needs, and in the case of Gunner, mainly care for the household, monastic clergy and men in power, such as the aristocracy and the nearby town. Here both accounts deviate from the ideal Cistercian practice of almsgiving, as well the commonplace topos of caring for the poor in German bishops' biographies. It does thus not seem of consequence in the exertion of episcopal office in a Danish Cistercian context to care for the poor – no almsgiving is mentioned. This is also the case in the description of Sven, except in designating the poor in Christ, that is the Cistercian monks, as worthy of alms. Here the hospitality of the bishops is described primarily as extended to abbots and monks of the order. It is even implied that to honour the office of bishop is synonymous with showing hospitality to monks.

Cathedral School?

The description of the manner in which Gunner educated his clerical subjects to their high standards of morality and knowledge is intriguing first and foremost because of the emphasis upon personal imitation. Here we meet what Jaeger has phrased as charismatic learning, a model of learning connected to the cathedral school, viewed as contrary to the text-oriented education received at the independent schools of Paris.[43]

Gunner's superior skills in the *artes liberales* compared to those of scholars studying in Paris are also displayed as the attainment of superior moral and intellectual skills at his court. Here the focus is primarily upon abilities in dialectical argument or logic as well as morality whereas Scripture as such does not receive similar attention. In the following example Gunner's superiority in dialectical argument is displayed in comparison to recently educated clerics arriving from Paris:

> His perspicacious intellect and his knowledge of the science of the liberal arts and of sacred Scripture was so great, that when highly intellectual and sharp minded clerics came back from studying in Paris, he often silenced them with a single question within a horned syllogism.[44]

---

43 Jaeger (1994), p. 325.
44 *Vita Gunneri*, chapter 4. "*In arcium liberalium et sacrarum sciencia scripturarum tam pers-*

The intellectual ability of Gunner is thus unquestionable and the author even notes that the education achieved at the court of Gunner is equal if not superior to that of the schools of Paris, and at a much lesser expense.[45]

Another central feature of education in a cathedral school context was the dual concept of education encompassing both training in the *artes liberales* as well as moral conduct.

The description of the moral education supplied by Gunner may be seen for example in the references to his employment of his sentences of the saints, verses of poets and other analogies.[46] Gunner is portrayed as a living exemplum in accordance with the concept of charismatic learning, for he impresses his image upon his students in the fields of moral and intellectual learning. Is it a continuation of the twelfth-century cathedral school which lives on at the court of Gunner?

Concluding Remarks

The figure of Gunner is intriguing from a national Danish perspective but from a wider Latin European perspective appears to primarily reflect the traditional episcopal ideal present in early and high medieval tradition as governor of his flock, skillfully administering material resources and admonishing his subjects to display virtuous behaviour. This view of the good conduct of a bishop was also in close agreement with the admonitory writings to bishops by the most influential twelfth-century Cistercian author, Bernard of Clairvaux.

However, it may be that views among Danish Cistercians of the good conduct in the office as abbot differ from the common understanding of the obligations of an abbot in thirteenth century Latin Europe. The differences in the duties inherent in the exercise of abbatial or episcopal office were rather emphasized in a wider Latin European context. Here the main deviance may be that Danish Cistercians acknowledged that the dutiful and good exercise of the office of abbot or bishop entailed a wide range of similar activities which were to the material and spiritual benefit of the community. Specifically, with Gunner's biography at hand the monastic reader was equipped for every aspect of behavior in public office. Thus, it does not appear to have been perceived as problematic in a Danish Cistercian context to follow the example of administrator bishops in the thirteenth century, as this practice was rather welcomed. An abbot who was

---

picaci calluit intellectu, vt, cum clerici satis subtiles et acuti de Parisiensi studio redissent, ad vnam sepius questionem eos cornuto concluderet sillogismo."
45 *Vita Gunneri*, chapter 5.
46 *Ibid.*

imitating Gunner's example would thus be an apt administrator with a firm grip on the economy, caring for his household, and maintaining close ties to king and nobility to ensure the safety of the bishopric. In respect to education he would excel in the liberal arts and moral conduct. Here his levels of knowledge, abilities of discernment and dialectical argument would be superior to those of his surroundings.

Literature
Sources
Adam of Bremen, 'Gesta Hammaburgensis ecclesiae Pontificum', in *Quellen des 9. und 11. Jahrhunderts zur Geschichte der Hamburgischen Kirche und des Reiches*, ed. and transl. Werner Trillmich (Darmstadt, 1968), pp. 160- 503.
Bernard of Clairvaux, 'De Consideratione ad Eugenium Papam', ed. Jean Leclercq and Henri Rochais in *Sancti Bernardi Opera* vol. 3 (Rome, 1957), pp. 379-494.
Bernard of Clairvaux, 'De Moribus et officio episcoporum', ed. Jean Leclercq and Henri Rochais in *Sancti Bernardi Opera* vol. 7 (Rome, 1974), pp. 100-131.
Cicero, 'De Officiis', ed. Page et al. in *Cicero. De Officiis*, (London and New York, 1921).
'Exordium Caræ Insulæ,' ed. M. Cl. Geertz in *Scriptores Minores Historiæ Danicæ* 2, reprint (København, 1970), pp. 158-264.
Gerhard, 'Vita Oudalrici', ed. Waitz, transl. Kallfelz in *Lebensbeschreibungen einiger Bischöfe des 10.-12. Jahrhunderts* (Darmstadt, 1973), pp. 46-167.
Rimbert, 'Vita Anskarii', ed. Waitz, transl. Trillmich in *Quellen des 9. und 11. Jahrhunderts zur Geschichte der Hamburgischen Kirche und des Reiches*, (Berlin, 1961), pp. 16-133.
'Vita Gunneri', ed. M. Cl. Gertz in *Scriptores Minores Historiæ Danicæ* 2, reprint (København, 1970), pp. 265-278.
'Vita Rimberti', ed. Waitz in *Vita Anskarii auctore Rimberti accedit Vita Rimberti*, reprint of the edition from 1884, (Hannover, 1977).

Studies
Averintsev, Sergei, 'From Biography to Hagiography', in *Mapping Lives. The Uses of Biography*, ed. Peter France and William St. Clair (Oxford/New York, 2002), pp. 19-36.
Berschin, Walter, *Biographie und Epochenstil im lateinischen Mittelalter. Von der Passio Perpetuae zu den Dialogi Gregors des Großen,* vol.1 (Stuttgart, 1986).
Berschin, Walter, *Biographie und Epochenstil im lateinischen Mittelalter. Kleine Topik und Hermeneutik der mittellateinischen Biographie,* vol. 5 (Stuttgart, 2004).
Christiansen, Tage E., 'To gejstlige typer fra Valdemarstiden', in *Middelalder, Metode og Medier*, ed. Karsten Fledelius, Niels Lund, and Herluf Nielsen (København, 1981), pp. 167-181.
Dierksmeier, Claus, and Anthony Celano, 'Thomas Aquinas on Business and the Fulfillment of Human Needs', in *Humanistic Ethics in the Age of Globality,* ed. Claus Dierksmeier et al. (New York, 2011), pp. 60-75.
Jaeger, Stephen, *The Origins of Courtliness. Civilizing Trends and the Formation of Courtly Ideals 939-1210* (Philadelphia, 1985).

Jaeger, Stephen, *The Envy of Angels. Cathedral School and Social Ideals in Medieval Europe 950-1200* (Philadelphia, 1994).
McGuire, Brian Patrick, *Conflict and Continuity at Øm Abbey* (København, 1976).
McGuire, Brian Patrick, 'Monastic and Episcopal Biography in the Thirteenth Century. The Danish Cistercian Account of Bishop Gunner of Viborg', *Analecta Cisterciensia* 39 (1983), pp. 195-230.
Jørgensen, Ellen, *Historieforskning og Historieskrivning i Danmark indtil Aar 1800* (København,1931).
Haarländer, Stephanie, *Vitae Episcoporum. Eine Quellengattung zwischen Hagiographie und Historiographie, untersucht an Lebenbeschreibungen von Bischöfen des Regnum Teutonicum im Zeitalter der Ottonen und Salier* (Stuttgart, 2000).
Jansen, Chr. R., 'Et menneske på Jyske Lovs tid: bisp Gunner', in *Jydske Lov 750 År*, ed. Ole Fenger and Chr. E. Jansen (Viborg, 1991), pp. 109-123.
Noble, Thomas, 'Secular Sanctity; Forging an Ethos for the Carolingian Nobility', in *Lay Intellectuals in the Carolingian world*, ed. Janet Nelson and Patrick Wormald (Cambridge/ New York, 2007), pp. 8-36.
Skyum-Nielsen, Niels, 'Kanslere og Skrivere i Danmark 1252-1288', in *Middelalderstudier tilegnede Aksel E. Christensen*, ed. Tage E. Christiansen, Svend Ellehøj, and Erling Ladewig Petersen (København, 1966), pp. 141-184.

Monastic location cited in the article.

A Cistercian Sermon Collection from Løgum

Kurt Villads Jensen

Cistercian studies in Denmark have become a lively and thriving research area since the 1970s, thanks to the enthusiasm and massive contribution of Professor Brian Patrick McGuire. Together with a few other Danish scholars he has also been extremely influential in discussing and introducing the history of mentalities, the history of spirituality, the history of friendship etc. In short, he has taught a whole new generation of Danish historians to take medieval people seriously.

Against this background, it is perhaps somewhat surprising that no one has really worked with the Cistercian sermon material preserved from Danish collections. Sermons were not mentioned in McGuire's comprehensive study of *The Cistercians in Denmark* from 1982, which may reflect the specific historiographical tradition in Denmark. At that time, only one lone scholar had worked thoroughly with medieval preaching,[1] and medieval sermon collections from Denmark have remained unedited.[2] Although internationally the topic was major and growing, and in spite of the thriving milieu in neighbouring Sweden, which had begun the systematic exploration of the huge collection from Vadstena Monastery preserved in the University Library of Uppsala,[3] it was virtually ignored in Denmark.

The aim of this article is to present a first and preliminary reading of one sermon collection which was copied and to some extent also composed in the Cistercian monastery of Løgum in Southern Denmark. It will be argued that this collection was for internal use among the monks in the monastery and not a guide for preaching to the world outside. This fact is indicated by the lack of themes that were common in other sermon manuals as for example the call for penitence, and likewise by a tendency towards spiritual or allegorical interpretations of certain passages from Scripture which in other contexts were used much more literally.

---

1   Riising (1969).
2   With one exception, Liber Petri Mathiae, which was published online by Anne Riising c. 2008.
3   Anderson & Borgehammar (1997); Anderson (2010); Anderson (2011).

This sermon collection is now preserved in the Universitäts- und Landesbibliothek in Halle in Germany, whose holdings include three manuscripts formerly belonging to the Cistercian monastery of Løgum in Southern Jutland. One of these, Y c 2 in quarto, is a miscellanea of theological and mystical texts.[4] The first 111 folios consist of a *nucleus theologie,* a basic and very variegated collection of essential knowledge for a theologian plus some texts to inspire reflecting upon God. They include several of the thirteenth century mendicant great theologians: the Franciscan Master General Bonaventura (obs. 1274) with his *Lignum vite;* the Dominicans Jacobus de Benevento (obs. after 1271) with *Expositio super credo;* Huge Ripelin de Argentina (obs. 1268) with his *Compendium theologie veritatis;* and Arnoldus Leodiensis (obs. 1310) with the *Alfabetum narrationum,* together with the Franciscan Conradus de Saxonia (obs. 1279) and his *Speculum Beate Marie Virginis.* These texts are simultaneously expositions of fundamental dogmas, exempla and miracles, and some very mystical texts with meditations upon the humanity and divinity of Christ.

As a part of this handbook in theology is also included a *Speculum dominicale,* a collection of model sermons for the liturgical year.[5] It is undated and with no indication of author, but it is a reasonable guess that it is relatively contemporary with the other texts surrounding it, i.e. from the last decades of the thirteenth century, although to judge from the authorities referred to it may actually be older. To judge from the content and especially from the constant references to Saint Bernard, it must have been written by Cistercians. It may or more probably may not originally have been written by a monk from Løgum, because at least one further copy and probably three more have survived in England.[6] In any case, the sermon manual and the theological texts were all copied in the late fourteenth century by a Peter the Dane in Løgum, so we are here getting as close as we can to what was actually preached and discussed among the Cistercians in one of the monasteries in medieval Denmark.

Peter the Dane opens the whole codex with a brief introduction explaining the purpose of the work, decorated with a finely coloured initial in blue and red, of which there are only a few examples in the manuscript. The most inferior of all brethren in Løgum, he has collected these works and excerpts from

---

4 Cf Schipke und Heydeck (2000), 112; Langkilde (2005), 13. Description of the content of the manuscript, see the bibliography at the end of this article.

5 Fol. 5va-33va.

6 Ms Oxford Merton College ms. 112 (s. XV) seems to contain the same text, cf. Schneyer (1965), 140, 192, 474. Riising (1969), 51 and note 18 refer to it as Merton ms 18, which must be a typing error. Lincoln Cathedral Library B. 6. 5. also includes part of this text, see Schneyer (1965), 140; as does British Museum Harleian 1744, see Schneyer (1965), 523.

different theologians, from various doctors of the church, to help the young in their studies, and because no one any longer has the gift of knowing everything or remembering everything, but the divine is everything, and therefore it is necessary to know it.[7]

Sermons can be studied from a number of perspectives – as sources for theology, social history, linguistics etc. Here, my aim is to use them to sift out what they reveal about the self-understanding of Cistercians, and about their attitude to the spiritual and material world surrounding them.

The present sermon collection is not a clear-cut case of sophisticated scholastic sermons, intended for promoting debate among learned colleagues, but on the other hand it is not uninfluenced by the scholastic obsession with well-ordered argumentation.

Each Sunday sermon opens with a short quotation from the Bible, and continues immediately: "This can be understood in three different ways" – or in two ways or in four, but most often in three different ways. To each of these aspects is devoted a paragraph, which contains some general observations and a number of quotations from Scripture or from authorities to substantiate them. All these references, however, are not presented in a well-ordered hierarchical structure, but loosely grouped together in an uneven fashion, almost as if the author is leaping from one association to the next. The collection belongs rather to the genre of monastic sermons whose main analytical tool was to *ruminare*, to chew upon the same texts again and again, until they reveal a higher or hidden meaning, and until seeming contradictions within the texts disappear.

An example of these expansions of the biblical quotation into different aspects or associations is the sermon for the First Sunday in Lent, based on Matt 4,1:[8]

'Jesus was led into the desert by a spirit to be tempted by the devil'.
In these words three things are to be noted.

---

7   *Omnibus hoc scriptum cernentibus uel legentibus frater minimus monachorum loci dei salutem in uero omnium saluatore. Quin labilis est hominum memoria. nec superest aliquis cui omnia scire datum est. memoriamque habere omnium. quia diuinitatis est totius.* Fol 1va.
8   *Ductus est Ihesus in desertum a spiritu ut temptaretur a dyabole. Jn uerbis istis tria possunt notari.*
    Ductus saluatoris, quia uoluntarius. ibi. ductus est. Qui enim duceri non uiolenter set sponte ducitur. ...
    Locus pene et horroris. quia solitarius. ibi. in desertem. Desertus postest dici mundus. ...
    Visus naturam temptatoris. quia temerarius. Que enim maior temeritas quam temptare dominum suum. ... Fol. 11vb.

> The way the Saviour was led, that it was voluntarily, when it is said 'he was led'. For He cannot be led by violence, but only freely. ...
> It was a place of torment and horrors, where it is said: 'in the desert'. The desert could be said to be this world. ...

It is further explained that Jesus was led *sponte,* by His own free will, because He did it for our sake, God was not forced to follow the devil and resist temptation. The desert, it is explained, is this life, filled with solitude and wild beasts.

The *temptator,* the devil, is everywhere, and we can never be secure from his temptations, we can never become so secluded from the desert of this world that the evil cannot reach us – if he could tempt even the Lord himself. This last statement is not elaborated further, but it must have held a special warning for Cistercians living in a monastic community: despite having left the outside world and having secluded themselves from the desert, the devil can still reach out for and get to them.

The impossibility of leaving the world totally offers a clue as to the intended audience. This collection of sermons is for internal use, and intended to provide inspiration for preaching within the walls of the monastery. This is not stated directly anywhere in the text, but it can be inferred from the main content or the main message of the sermons. In the following, the aim is firstly to give an impression of this central message, and secondly to present some specific topics in the text – plus some that are not included or touched upon in the sermons, although one might have expected they would be.

Central message

The author of these sermons reveals attitudes that are complex or at least divided in their nature. On the one hand, he is firmly convinced about the love of God; on the other hand he is not a happy man, but finds that life is bad.

The love of God, the *dilectio, caritas,* or *amor,* is probably the most common theme in the collection. It appears again and again, associated with scriptural verses where one would have expected it but also with verses where this theme might not have been anticipated. God's love is the reason for belief, for faith, for salvation, and for other manifestations of love, as the love towards God and towards your neighbour, the love of justice etc.[9]

Love is bisected – *bifurcata* – and consists of love of neighbour and love

---

9   *Quia ipse spiritus sanctus amor est siue caritas qua diligimus dominum et proximum. que caritas est in nobis. ita ud nos afficiat diligere dominum et proximum.* Fol. 19ra.

for the Lord, as is explained in one sermon.¹⁰ It is also bisected from another perspective in consisting both of man's love towards God, and of God's love towards man, although this concept of double love is expressed much less directly in the collection. It is, however, fundamental for the whole theological understanding, and the objective and subjective love of God are interdependent. Our love towards God is necessary, because He loved us first.¹¹ And conversely, if we want to be loved, we must love – *si vis amari ama*.¹²

The Incarnation is the most magnificent expression of God's love. Because of His love for the poor, which in this context means all humankind, God humiliated Himself and descended from His throne to stay with us in poor huts,¹³ in the *tugurium,* a word which would have reminded the Cistercian about the shed in the cucumber field, the daughter of Sion in Isaiah 1,8, the sinful people from the sole of the foot even unto the head with no soundness, but wounds and bruises and putrefying sores. Christ died for our sins for many reasons, but first among them was to prove his love for us.¹⁴

Love of God is also the ultimate cause behind *amicitia,* friendship, which is mentioned only in passing and without being much elaborated upon. *Amicitia* is basically the love of one's neighbour; it is synonymous with *caritas,* and is the prerequisite for being encompassed by love. 'We should increase in *amicitia*. Because if we want to be loved (*amari*) by the angels, it is necessary for us to love (*amare*) others, and the more we are connected to each other, the stronger is the love (*caritas*).'¹⁵ Amicitia is, what brings people together.¹⁶

Amor is an ambiguous word in Latin, and so in these sermons. It can be elevated and divine, but it can also designate very plain and mundane lust and carnal desire. Who was wiser than Salomon, the preacher asks, and nevertheless he was besotted by love for women, *amore mulierum*.¹⁷ That kind of love is a dangerous enterprise and will lead to perdition and hell. There is light in hell, it is explained, not to make it a nice and comforting place (*nec ad solacium*) but as a torture, so that the condemned souls can see the torments of those with whom they have sinned in love, *amore*.¹⁸ This use of the word *amor* is, how-

---

10 Fol. 12va.
11 Fol. 19ra.
12 Fol. 8rb.
13 Fol. 28va.
14 Fol. 25 ra.
15 Fol. 8rb.
16 *ad quod congregat homines amicitia est*. Fol. 9rb.
17 Fol. 10va.
18 *lucebit ignis ille ad aliquid. scilicet ad torquendum. ut reprobi uideant eos in pena quorum amore peccauerunt in seculo*. Fol 31vb.

ever, rare. In most contexts in this text, it refers to the love of God towards his creatures.

The love of God is not treated exhaustively in one single sermon, but is a theme scattered around in the whole collection. It functions as the background or the basis for all other theological reasoning in the text, which of course is not surprising.

The second topic is addressed much more directly. Expressed in concentrated form, it says that life is dust and ashes and nothing at all. This is stated on one of the first pages of the codex, in one of the small marginal verses that are lavishly distributed throughout the work:

> *Quid nisi terra sumus. sed terra quid est nisi fumus*
> *Sed numquid est fumus. nos nichil ergo sumus*
> We are nothing but earth, but earth is nothing but smoke,
> but smoke is nothing, and therefore so are we.

This attitude to life is fundamental for many of the sermons and for the whole work. One example is the sermon for the Third Sunday of Advent on John 1,22: *Quid dico de te ipso.*[19]

The Pharisees ask John the Baptist: 'What do you say about yourself?' The answer is not, as in the gospel, that 'I am a voice of one crying in the Wilderness, "Make straight the way of the Lord",' but 'I am dust and ash, sick and fragile, a distorted image of God, a useless minister of His.'[20]

We are made of dust and return to ashes, but from ashes we shall again be resurrected or reinstated. And then the Cistercian preacher, obviously interested in hard science, immediately explains that when dust combines with humidity, it becomes mud – *lutum*. Humidity is this present life, which then, consequently, when combined with the human who is dust, becomes a muddy matter. A minor digression follows, on steam or mist and vapour, which can be either

---

19 *Ego dico me esse puluerem et cinerem. infirmum et fragilem. deformatam ymaginem. ministrum inutilem. ...*
   Puluerem et cinerem. puluerem quia de puluere factum, cinerem quia in cinerem restituendum. puluis adueniente humore fit lutum. Humor adueniens est uita presens. Philosophus in 1º[,18] metheorologica. vapor est duplex. uapor et humidus et siccus. et in uapore humido est uapor siccus. et in uapore sicco est humidus. ...
   Job. 30[,19]. Comparatus sum luto. quo ad primum. et assimulatus sum fauille et cineri quo ad secundum et ceteri. ... Fol. 7ra.
20 Thomson (1989), 265, refers to the same reading in a manuscript in Lincoln Cathedral Chapter Library, which I have not yet had the opportunity to consult.

humid or dry, according to Aristotle. And this explains, via a reference to Peter the Lombard, why Job can lament both that he is comparable to mud, and that he is similar to ember and ashes. This neatly illustrates the non-linear, associative argumentation of the author.

Other sermons continue the same theme over several folios: 'The whole world is in evil, that is, placed in evil. And the longer the world lasts, the more evil it will accumulate.'[21] The first half of the sentence is a quotation from 1 John 5,19, but the pessimistic realisation that it becomes worse and worse is added by the Cistercian preacher. Similarly in another formulation: 'All wisdom is from God the Lord. But the wisdom of the world is not from God. Therefore, there is no wisdom in the world.'[22] Again, while the first part is a quotation (from Sirah 1,1), the second term of the syllogism is the author's own, as well as the conclusion which from a formal philosophical point of view is neither necessary nor apparent. Such sweeping generalisations are not uncommon in these sermons. Without peace, it is impossible for man to be happy or content – *iocundus*. But it is obvious that there are wars in the world, and in the present state, there is no real peace, and therefore man can never be fully content.[23]

This fundamental attitude to the world is expressed in concentrated but comprehensive form with reference to Saint Paul, that all temporal things are but dung, compared to knowing Christ. The Cistercian preacher continues that this world is full of dung, and he asks, 'What is this world then, except a sewer, for dung' – a *cloacha stercorum*. To stress the point, he ends the sermon by stating that those who love the world, are like the world – dung.[24]

There is not much joy in the world, except the joy of being loved by God and of loving your neighbour. The negative impression of the material world stems from the conviction that it easily leads into temptation, but perhaps also from an implicit wish to identify with Christ? In the few instances where He is mentioned as something more than just divine and love, Christ is connected to humility and humiliation. The whole sermon collection ends with the passion of Christ and the flagellation and crucifixion 'between two rob-

---

21 *Totus mundus in maligno. id est in malo positus est. et quanto diutius durat. tanto magis maliciam suam cumularet.* Fol. 7vb.
22 *Omnis sapientia a domino deo est. et cetera. Sed sapientia mundi non est a deo. ergo non in mundo sapientia.* Fol. 7vb.
23 Fol. 15rb.
24 *Si enim temporalia sunt stercora. ut dicit apos Phil. 3[,8]. Omnia detrimentum feci et arbitror ut stercora. Sed mundus iste plenus est stercoribus. Quid igitur est mundus nisi cloacha stercorum. … Qualis ergo mundus tales sunt eius amatores.* Fol 7vb.

bers', and the last words are 'Behold and see if there is any pain comparable to my pain.'[25]

Other examples from this collection could be produced and analysed, but the aforementioned must suffice to illustrate what is the second most important theme in this collection of Cistercian sermons. This attitude to the world has been neatly and precisely summarized elsewhere in a short verse: 'Life is a piece of shit, when you look at it,' from the very last scene of the Monty Python movie *Life of Brian* from 1979.

Major authorities

Authorities are referred to extensively throughout the sermons and to a degree that reflects both an author with a well-educated background and a library giving access to all standard reference works.

First among the authorities are evidently the Scriptures, mainly the Old Testament, with the Psalms and Isaiah as the most commonly quoted. Many of the quotations from the Bible are not exact, but differ a little in word order or in phrasing. This could indicate that the author is quoting from memory, from different versions of the Text, or from the liturgy.

Among older authorities outside Scripture, Aristotle and Augustine are the most prominent, and the philosopher is referred to much more often than the church father. The *poeta*, Ovid, is also quoted on several occasions. There are, in addition, surprisingly many references to John Chrysostomos, and a few to Origen. Among modern authorities, Anselm is mentioned in some places, and more space is devoted to Peter Comestor's *Historia ecclesiastica* and to the *magister*, Peter the Lombard, which should not surprise anyone. The *Glossa ordinaria* is also used frequently to provide interpretations of sentences or of singular words. The overwhelming authority is, however, Bernard of Clairvaux. He is not referred to in all sermons, but in most of them. Many references are precisely specified, so the original text can easily be located and consulted.

The quotations should probably not be understood as definite and exhaustive, but as starting points. When the preacher went to consult these authorities and had a closer look at the specific quotations, he would often find himself in the middle of a longer discussion, which can have inspired him to further elaborate on the theme of the sermon. This suggestion is built on

---

25 *Attendite et uidete si est dolor sicut dolor meus,* fol. 33va. And pain is a good thing for the Christian doing penance: *penitens semper debet dolere et de dolore gaudere. sed quia hoc non est ex se. set ex dono dei. ideo si doleat consolatur eum deus.* Fol. 30va.

an initial impression of the text and should be investigated more thoroughly before drawing any definite conclusions, but at least it seems to indicate that this sermon manual was intended as part of a continuous meditation or a continuous dialogue which took place within the monastery – not as definitive statements about the Christian faith that should be communicated to the laity.

Missing messages

These sermons were not intended to be delivered in ordinary parish churches or to a lay audience. This is evident not only from their composition, but also from their content and especially from what they do not contain, themes that are not included.

The call for penitence was one of the main purposes of most sermons to the laity throughout the Middle Ages. It is mentioned in this collection only in three instances, in which the main aim is not directly to induce the listener to seek penitence. In one, it is explained that the moral understanding of the conversion of water into wine during the wedding in Cana is that man can be transformed from a state of sin to a state of glory by means of penitence. Wine is stimulating, refreshing, and warming, in the same way as the thought of the coming glory.[26] It is also explained in another sermon that the effect of grace is fulfilled in heaven, in two ways. Those who have never sinned can enjoy the eternal punishment of the sinners, and those who have sinned but escaped eternal punishment because of penitence can enjoy the same sight while praising God.[27] In another instance, it is stated that contrition of the heart prepares the way for penitence, but it is not specified what this penitence may consist in.[28] Such is the case also in another sermon where penitence is mentioned. It is said directly in simple words that the penitent should feel pain – *debet dolere* – but not how.[29] A natural explanation for this lack of detail with regard to penitence is that the life in a monastery was an exercise of penance in itself and did not need to be further elaborated upon.

Similarly, there is almost no mentioning of the redemption of mankind be-

---

26 Fol. 8vb.
27 ... *ergo in celis erit plena promissio ibi erit et plena gratiarum actio. et hoc duplici de causa. primo ex parte eorum qui non peccauerunt et penam peccatorum videbunt. Ps. [58,11] Letabitur iustus cum viderit vindictam. 2o ex parte eorum qui peccauerunt. et per penitenciam de periculo euaserunt. illi dicent. benedictus dominus qui non dedit nos in captionem dentibus eorum* [Ps 124,6]. Fol 10ra.
28 Fol. 11vb.
29 Fol. 30va.

cause of the Incarnation. This is somewhat peculiar because one would have expected the redemption to be a recurrent theme in all kinds of preaching. It may simply have been subsumed under the meditations about the love of God towards his creature.

Hell is not totally absent, but the author neglects most of the excellent opportunities for providing elaborate details on the horror of hell to cause fright and exhort believers to refrain from sin. The longest description comes towards the end of the collection. It rightly stresses that hell is an extremely horrible place with a vehement fire, but then immediately slips into considerations of the physical nature of this eternal fire, which is not fuelled by anything – *nullam substantiam consumit*. Therefore it cannot create light, but is an obscure fire with shadowy flames. This view is stated with reference to Chrysostomos, but an alternative interpretation is offered by Gregory, who has claimed that the fire in hell gives enough light for the sinners to see the torments of the others.

After this digression into the nature of hellfire, which is interesting but not of much use in calling repentant sinners to penance, comes a short mnemonic verse listing the infernal punishments: 'As shadows, worms and mourning, as cold and thirst, so is this fire, as hunger, stench, derision, and demon's horror.' But worse than all these horrors is the *privatio Christi*, the circumstance that the damned shall not see Christ: for if they could see the face of God, they would feel no punishment, no pain, no sorrow.[30]

The internal or monastic purpose of these sermons may also be seen from the very few references to daily life and the social context. In one place, a parallel is made to an earthly king who returned from afar, but was not received with proper respect. He therefore punished those who had shown contempt towards him. Similarly, the king of heaven came to his own, and his own did not receive

---

30 *Conuersacio reproborum est formidolosa et non mirum. quia cum locus ille sit tenebrosus. constat quod ualde horribilis. sed cum ibi sit ignis uehemens. ardet quidem. non tamen lucet ad solacium nec tamen nullam substantiam consumit. Sap. 17. Nulla uis poterit lumen eis prebere. etc. Crisostomus. Nec aeris quid ipsius erit ullum solacium in inferno aut lucis. circumdabunt enim loca penarum tenebre exteriores. et ille ignis sicut non materiam habet consumendi ita nec illuminandi. set est ignis obscurus et flamma tenebrosa. Gregorius. tamen dicit. quod lucebit ignis ille ad aliquid. scilicet ad torquendum. ut reprobi uideant eos in pena quorum amore peccauerunt in seculo. Versus de penis inferni. Sicut tenebre vermes. luctus. frigus. sitis. ignis. Esuries. fetor. irrisio. demonis horror. Set superat cunctas xristi priuatio penas. Ysidorus l' sol' Quod si faciem dei omnes in carcere inferni inclusi viderent. nullam penam. nullum dolorem. nullamque tristiciam sentirent.* Fol. 31vb.

Him, so they sinned even more.[31] Kings are also mentioned as those who can make laws, just as the King of heaven can.[32]

Merchants are mentioned only twice: first the evil ones who gold-plate plain metal and sell it as gold,[33] second as the provident merchant who is very economical and does not spend the commodity of which he has little, and therefore we should not spend this short life on futile exercises but beware of the hour,[34] in the same way as the labourers in wintertime who eagerly rush to their work because the days are short.[35]

The only other civil occupation outside the monastery mentioned is that of the falconer. It is used as a fine and clear illustration of the point to be stressed, but the author mixes two incompatible applications of the metaphor, and so he does not emerge as the most systematic thinker. First he relates that the Lord is calling us back, just as the good falconer calls back the falcon, also when it does not want to return to his hand. Then he quotes Bernard to the effect that Christ has ascended to the heights so that He can be seen by everybody. The result is thus that Christ is simultaneously both the falconer and the falcon, which makes the parallel less effective.[36]

Elsewhere in the codex the point is made that the preacher should consider which audience he is addressing. Two examples are given, namely how one should open a sermon to monks, and how one should open one to a lay audience. The former case should go something like: "Most reverend fathers and most beloved brethren. Your minds, your consciences, your understandings far supersede those of secular persons because of the laudable way you have chosen to arrange the present life, and because of the fine aspirations you have for the life to come."[37]

The approach to a lay audience was to be very different. As they do not understand sacred matters, there is no reason to preach to them in Latin, and it

---

31 *Si rex terrenis ueniret a remotis in terram propriam. et nemo ipsum reciperet. constat quod contemptores grauiter puniret. ... Sed rex celestis in propria uenit et sui eum non receperunt. Joh. i°. Jdeo. magis peccauerunt.* Fol 6vb.
32 Fol. 22va.
33 Fol. 7va.
34 Fol. 11va.
35 Fol. 11va.
36 *... sed dominus nos misericorditer reuocauit more boni falconarii qui falconem redire nolentem reclamat. sicut dicit Bernardus. Xritus in altum ascendit. ut ab omnibus uideretur. clamauit ualide ut ab omnibus audiretur. lacrimas adiecit ut eum compateratur.* Fol. 12rb.
37 *Prologus ad clericos. Domini reuerentissimi et patres dilectissimi. Mentibus vestris melioribus. et conscientiis magis intelligibilioribus longe ab aliis secularibus propter laudabilem vie presentis conuersationem et amabilem uite sequentis aspiracionem ...* Fol 44va

would in any case be boring for them and detract from their devotion. Therefore one should preach to them briefly in their own language and use examples from what was generally talked about or from practical matters. The preacher should express this directly to them in his opening address: "As you do not understand Holy Scripture, listen carefully and remember what I tell you to do in your mother tongue, for if you don't do it, what will you tell the Judge at the Last Judgement, and you will have to pay back for your disobedience, and you will never see God."[38]

The remainder of this article will concern specific themes, which in other contexts could have been used to preach a message very different from the one here.

The first concerns the second Sunday after Epiphany with its text about the wedding in Cana, which is classic in all medieval sermons and was often used to teach the right relationship between man and woman, or to expound canonical teaching about marriage and the licit and illicit degrees of marriages. This is not the case here.

The sermon opens with the very short statement that the parable is a recommendation of the institution of marriage, because Jesus and the disciples attended it. If it had not been advisable, they would not have done so, and therefore marriage is a sacrament.

Immediately afterwards, the wedding is used in a spiritual exegesis and it is stressed rather that the sacrament of marriage is a symbol for the spiritual unity or union between Christ and the church. Marriage is good for three different reasons: for faith, for children, and for the sacrament. And it is then explained that the transformation of the elements from water to wine has a moral interpretation and parallels the transformation from sin to glory. Water is cold and unstable, just as the sinner who lacks the warmth of charity.[39] This sermon is not

---

38 *Jnfirmioribus et simplicioribus istorum sacrorum intellientibus non est necesse in lingua latina loqui cum inde tedium audientium generetur et deuocio tolletur. quampropter breuiter proponendi et faciliter animaduerti potest propter causas satis notabiles et rationabiles. ...*
[Prologus ad laicos.] Vobis sacram scripturam non intelligentibus attendite diligenter et memoriter tenete et opere perficite que lingua materna exprimo diuina gratia adiutus. quod nisi feceritis quod vobis dicuntur coram equissimo iudice deo pro inobdientia rationem pro eisdem estis reddituri et numquam deum visuri. Fol. 44va.

39 *Jn isto ewangelio tria tangimus que in nuptiis istis contigerunt. Primum est commendatio matrimonij ibi. ...*
Signum est spiritualis vnitatis christi et ecclesie. ...
Nupciale bonum tripertitum est. fides. proles et sacramentum. ...
Transmutatio elementi. scilicet aque in vinum. ...Moraliter aquam in vinum mutare est. sta-

much help for the priest explaining to his community who could legitimately be married to whom, or how a married couple should live together. It is much more suited for an audience for which the word 'marriage' would immediately be understood as referring to the spiritual union between man and God.

The second example concerns the commandment that *thou shall not kill*. The argument is that killing is against the will of God, against the law of nature, and against divine commandment. Then it is explained that that there are several ways of killing – *modos occidendi*: lack of love, which is to kill the heart; deducting from truth – small lies – which is to kill with the mouth; deducting from piety, that is deducting in alms to the needy, which is killing by deed.[40]

There is nothing whatsoever in this sermon about warfare which is unusual. There is nothing about physical killing, except that it is better to be killed by the sword than starving to death. Most others might have used the opportunity to relate to realities in society and explained when killing was actually permitted, as it would be in cases of just wars, or when a king or prince is exercising justice and uses capital punishments against robbers and homicides, or against heretics or in defence against attacks from infidels. It would have been appropriate to quote St. Augustine that it is not against the Gospel to use the sword, if a higher authority concedes it or commands it.[41] In this sermon, on the contrary, it is stated that if nobody dares to go against the command of an earthly king, how much more should they then obey when killing is prohibited by the celestial Lord.

---

tum culpe in statum glorie commutare. Aqua est frigida. insipida et instabilis. ita peccator frigidus est. quia non habet feruorem caritatis. Fol 7vb-8ra.

40 *De ewangelio Mt 5. Non occides etc. Non sit ocidendum patet plurimis rationibus. primo quia uoluntati dei est contrarium. eze. 19. Nolo mortem peccatoris. 2o nature legi oppositum. /22va/ Lex nature est. quod hoc quod oderis tibi fieri. videre ne alteri facias. Omne enim animal naturaliter fugit mortem. Vnde legitur de xristo. Mt. 14. quod appropinquante morte. cepit pauere et tedere. igitur nullus deberet uelle occidere. 3o in lege diuina prohibitum. Exo. 20. Sed si rex uel princeps aliquis terrenus aliquid prohiberet quis contrairet. quantomagis rex celestis prohibet.*
Sciendum est plures esse modos occidendi. videlicet:
Per defectionem caritatis. quod est homicidium cordis. ... Per subtractionem ueritatis. quod et homicitium oris. ... Per subtractionem pietatis. uel victum subtrahencio ab indigentibus uel fraudem faciendo operantibus. quod est homicidium operis. ... et certe crudelius occidit qui uictum subtrahit quam qui gladio occidit. Fol. 22r-22va.

41 Augustinus, *Contra Faustum Manichaeum*, lib. 22, cap. 70, in PL 42, 444. From here included in Corpus Iuris Canonici, Decretum C. 23, q. 4, c. 36, in CJC, ed. Friedberg, I, 916. Cf. in general F. H. Russell 1975.

A parallel approach is actually taken when the author discusses the word of Jesus in John 20,19, *pax vobis* – peace be to you.[42] Peace can be three things, one of which is the establishing of security – *stabilimentum securitatis* – but as there is war on earth, nobody will ever be totally secure, except in the next life. The whole discussion about peace is concerned with achieving peace in heaven and is in no way connected to peace on earth.

The third example concerns the time of salvation, the *ecce nunc tempus acceptabile*. This is of special interest, because it was used by St. Bernard as an important theme for his sermons at the time of the Second Crusade in 1147. He may have believed that the end of time was near, although that theme is ambiguous. In any case, he argued that it was the right time for missions and crusading, that it was the right time for creating martyrs and for gaining more indulgence than ever before. It was the right time for sinners to be accepted into heaven.[43] This aspect of Bernardine theology is conspicuously absent from the present sermon collection. Instead, the sermon immediately turns into an interesting linguistic and philosophical discussion about what the small adverb 'nunc' means.

Nunc designates the present, but the present is a dubious concept. Part of it has already passed, part of it is yet to come. Here it is fitting to quote the philosopher: "What is gone, is no longer the future". The present is of no permanence, *instabilem*. From here, the sermon continues, via Seneca, to the notion that we all die every day, because the remaining part of our life diminishes every day. Our time is short and we had better use it well, is the conclusion.[44]

The fourth example is from John 6, 9-11 about Jesus' miracle of feeding the multitude.[45] The text is 'There was a boy who had five loaves'. It would have

---

42 Fol. 15rb.
43 Kahl (1992); Fonnesberg-Schmidt (2007), 152-153.
44 Ecce nunc tempus acceptabile. *ecce nunc dies salutis. Hic tangimur tria. Vite breuitas.* <u>ecce nunc</u>. *temporis oportunitas. ibi* <u>tempus acceptabile</u>. *spiritualis sanitas. ibi* <u>dies salutis</u>. *Dico ergo sic.*
    Ecce nunc. instans modicus ad viuendum. quod patet in dubio aduerbio. ecce nunc. quorum utrumque presens tempus demonstratur. sed presens est cuius pars preterit et pars futura est. preteritum irremeabilem. Philosophus. Que preteriit non est amplius futurum. Presens est instabilem. Iob 17. Numquam in eodem statu permanet. idem 33. Nescio quam diu subsistam. Seneca. Cotidie morimur cotidie aliqua pars uite nostre diminuitur. et tunc cum crescimus uita decrescit. hunc ipsum diem quam agimus cum morte diuidimus futurum inopinale. Fol. 11va.
45 *Subjectione filialis. ibi. puer. fili enim flexibiliores sunt ad obediendum quam senes. ideo de facili iuuentus flectitur et trahitus ad arbitrium colentis.* ...

been obvious to discuss miracles, or to preach about the sustenance and abundance and bread as gifts from God.

Instead, the sermon first reflects upon the fact that it is a boy. This is because young people are more obedient towards older ones, and the older they get, the less flexible they are to change their minds. The relevance this has for the Gospel text is not clear. From this point, the author continues with the obedience a son should show towards his father, and from there the transition to talking about the Trinity is not difficult. The loaves provide spiritual sustenance – *refectio spiritualis*. The first loaf is the person of God the Father, who is one and yet divided in three.

The fifth example concerns women. Man is born of woman,[46] which in other sermons could be a point of departure for moving on to the fact that Jesus too is born of a woman. From here, it would be obvious to either reflect upon the double nature of Jesus, or to tell about the Virgin Mary. But she is surprisingly absent from these sermons and mentioned in only one place, which quotes Bernard to the effect that the breasts of Mary and the wounds of Jesus are the signs of charity.[47]

These sermons, however, do include a few remarks about the nature of women in general. They are more fragile, because they are colder than the male sex, and therefore mankind, born of women, is also fragile. This should actually mean that men are colder than men. The argument is totally illogical, but substantiated by reference to both Aristotle and Augustine.[48]

In a short discourse about the devil, it is stated that the woman was seduced in Paradise, not the man, but this is no wonder: women are weaker in the spirit, they are more prone to lying and being unchaste, and they are easier to deceive than men.

Vir non est seductus set mulier. quia stultior. De animalis lib. Mulieres sunt debiles spiritui et mendaces magis et inverecunde et de facili decipiuntur.[49]

 Refectio spiritualis. ibi. quinque panes. primus panis est patris persone. qui cum sit vnus tamen tria est diuisus. …Fol. 13ra.
46 Fol. 18vb.
47 *Bernardus. Mater ostendit filio pectus et ubera. filius ostendit patri latus et uulnera. non potest esse repulsa. ubi tot et tanta occurrunt caritatis insignia.* …, fol. 24va.
48 *Job homo natus est de muliere etc. et homo fragilis. Cum enim mater sit fragilis. constat quod proles. ut dicit philosophus de animalibus libro 15. Geniti assimilantur generatibus, non in naturali creatione tamen. sed et in rebus accidentibus, quia natura feminarum est debilis. scilicet minoris caloris maribus. Augustinus de uerbis domini. Quid fragilius uase* …. Fol. 18vb.
49 Fol. 8vb.

The sixth example is an interpretation of Matthew 7,15: Beware of false prophets. This would be a standard point of reference to warn against heretics or ill educated preachers or any kind of wrong teaching. Instead, it is explained that there are three kinds of false prophets, the flesh, the world, and Satan. The flesh promises sex, the world riches, and Satan promises things that cannot be delivered and which do not belong to God's justice.[50]

The seventh and last example treats a theological matter as complicated as predestination, beginning from Matthew 21: 'Many are called upon, but few are elected'.

All are called, because in this life both the good and the evil alike are invited to blessedness. How is this compatible with hell and eternal punishment? The solution is to discuss the two different meanings of the verb 'to be' – all are being called, but 'to be' can have two meanings, 'to be' and 'really to be'. The good ones predestined for salvation really are called, the evil ones are also summoned, but only provided and as far as they listen to the preaching.[51] Again, this is an interesting discussion from a theological and linguistic point of view, but hardly a matter that one would expect to find in a sermon to a broader public.

These sermons were most probably intended for use within Cistercian monasteries such as Løgum, but this purpose is not all that apparent. There is no direct mentioning of monastic life, and what one could call specific monastic ideals in these sermons are few.

One such may be the praise of stability. There is no sign of modern management language about flexibility and adaptability or readiness to change. On the contrary: only God is totally unchangeable, according to Boethius, but the more man loves mobility and change, the lower and more inferior he becomes, and the more he sins. 'For nobody can love change and himself remain unchanged.'[52]

On the other hand, the Cistercian author does not use the occasion to argue for the supremacy of the monastic life, not even when it would have been obvious given the context. The soul is the precious treasure that we carry through life,

---

50 Fol. 23va-23vb.
51 *Vocati sunt. Jn presenti vita omnes sunt uocati boni et mali. Mt 21. Quoscumque inueneritis ad nupcias. Cum igitur duplex sit esse. esse et uere esse. illud vere est quod bene est. et quod bene est et bonum est. mali igitur non sunt quia boni non sunt. Licet igitur uocati sunt uniuersi. tamen modi vocandi sunt diuersi. Boni enim uocantur per predestinationem. id est per eternam electionem. Ro. 6. Quos predestinauit hos et uocauit. etc. Mali uocantur per exhotacionem. quia deus neminem uult perire. set omnes ad agnitionem sui uenire. Prouerbi. 1. Vocaui et renuistis.* ...Fol. 30rb
52 ... *nemo namque potest mobilia diligere et ipse immobilis stare.* Fol. 24ra.

and we must guard it just as travellers with a fortune in money who are to travel through a forest with robbers. They wait until they can form a company large enough for travelling together, and they bring armed guards with them.[53] So likewise is the spiritual life where we journey with the soul. Here it would have been easy to continue and recommend the community of other monks in a monastery and explain that they would be the strongest company to travel together with on a spiritual journey with the soul. But this idea is not directly expressed.

Analyzing sermon collections

In 2005, the Swedish historian of monastic life and spirituality Alf Härdelin discussed the traditional division of sermons into scholastic and monastic sermons and claimed that it is a challenge to understand the monastic sermons and analyse and present them to others, because we normally tend to use scholastic language to describe the monastic sermon. We use a hierarchically ordered, linear chain of argumentation, and therefore we have difficulties in grasping the logic behind the circular, associative sermons.[54]

Instead, he suggested the use of the concept of clusters of words or clusters of pictures, real or imagined. It becomes then "rather a question of literary analysis and poetical listening than the usual writing of the history of dogmas of the systematic theology."[55]

These clusters cannot be precisely defined, and it is impossible to categorize any single theme, object, or word as included in or excluded from the cluster. It all depends upon the context they are used in and whether or not they have many and strong relations to other elements. Such relations could also be called simply associations. An example of a specific and strong form for relations would be medieval etymologies. They are strong because medieval authors would normally know the agreed etymologies of different words, and new etymologies could not be formed arbitrarily and by free association. In contrast to modern linguistics, however, medieval words could have several and different etymologies. Words were in themselves clusters *en miniature*.

Härdelin suggests that clusters in medieval monastic theology cannot be defined precisely, but at least often center around some basic themes of action.

The first is moving and connecting two worlds, either vertically up and down or horizontally between past and future: from heaven to earth with the incar-

---

53 Fol. 30 ra.
54 Härdelin (2005), pp. 319-320.
55 "Kanske måste det då mera bli fråga om littteraturanalys och poetiskt lyssnande än om den vanliga systematikens dogmehistorieskrivning." Härdelin (2005), p. 322.

nation, from earth to heaven with resurrection, the soul descending in sin and ascending in grace, miracles coming down from saints in heaven and martyrs ascending, etc.; horizontally it is from Creation to Last Judgment, from the birth to the death of Jesus, paralleling the sequence from birth to death of individuals, life as a pilgrimage towards the true fatherland, the heavenly Jerusalem, life as sailing on the sea with Peter to steer the boat towards the safe haven, etc.

A second theme is the desert with all its temptations and dangers, but also spiritual development through loneliness and meditation. A third theme is the divine marriage with all the language of love, from almost carnal to totally spiritual, the love that unites what is fundamentally different, the divine and the earthly, Christ and the church as the body of believers, etc. A fourth theme is the dwelling place, the house or temple or tent or holy mountain. A fifth is the feast with food and drink and guests invited to join the table of the host, at the Eucharist of the Lord.[56] More themes could perhaps be added, but Härdelin has pointed to the most important, and it also becomes clear that many biblical or theological elements can be used and reused in different clusters according to where the author puts the emphasis.

Does the idea of clusters work for this collection? Does it help to understand the text better? Yes and no. It is often difficult to follow the associations from one reference to the next. Perhaps the solution to this problem is to work the other way around. It may be that the author of this sermon collection has chosen his themes first, or has been inspired to concentrate upon one theme, and then has begun browsing around and found references that complemented or expanded the theme.

This way of working may also take the sting out of some of the criticism aired above, for example that Jesus could be at the same time a falconer and a falcon. In a hierarchical scholastic either-or theology, it would not have made much sense, but in a monastic both-and cluster theology, the two mental pictures equally well illustrate the movement from heaven to earth and from earth to heaven, and thereby how the sinner is lifted up and freed from sin because of Jesus. This method also helps understanding why some possible and common interpretations are totally absent from this sermon collection, for example a discussion about when it is actually possible and legal to kill others. From a scholastic point of view in which a concept should be defined precisely and exhaustively, one cannot discuss killing without mentioning legitimate killing. If the interpretative frame or the cluster is spiritual killing, it is not necessary at all.

---

56 Härdelin (2005), pp. 322-375.

Today we would Google a few key words; in the Middle Ages the Cistercians studied books; but fundamentally it is the same epistemological process. Maybe we are better able today, because of our Google-mentality, to begin to understand medieval monastic attitudes to texts. Härdelin's theory of clusters may be a help also to better understand this collection from Løgum, if we do not leap from one association to the next, but begin with a central theme and then expand by building reference upon reference, in an ever-expanding web.

Conclusion

This collection, which was used by the Cistercians in Løgum, must have been composed by a well-educated theologian who probably had access to a fine library. He chose not to work in a strictly scholastic way but rather to concentrate on certain themes and explain and illustrate them by associative elements and by a substantial amount of quotations from a wide range of authorities.

From the interpretations and themes chosen, it is very likely that the collection was intended for internal use in the monastery and not as a preparation for preaching to lay people outside the walls. This orientation, of course, does not mean that the monks in Løgum were not involved in the affairs of the outer world, but that this world was not considered of great importance or interest for the spiritual well-being of the brethren.

Medieval sermons constituted a flexible genre that could easily change and incorporate other interpretations, so we should be careful and not draw too far-reaching conclusions based on one single collection. Nevertheless, through these sermons today preserved in Halle, we can get very close to the lived life and mental world of the Cistercians in Løgum.

Literature

Manuscript sources
Ms Halle Y c 2 in quarto
Description from Schipke und Heydrek (2000), 112:
Nummer 155, sign. Y c 4° 2
Pergament. 184 Bl. 23,5 x 19,5 . Løgumkloster (Schleswig). 14 Jh., Ende.
1r Excerpta. 1va – 111 va Nucleus theologiae mit zahlreichen Überschriften, darin u.a. (35ra-42ra) Bonaventura: Lignum vitae, (51va-55vb) Jacobus de Benevento: expositio super credo (Auszüge), (56ra-78ra) Conradus de Saxonia: Speculum BMV, (80ra-111va) Hugo Ripelin de Argentina: Compendium theologicae veritatis (Auszüge), (112ra-183rb) Arnoldus Leodiensis: Alphabetum narrationum.
Schreiber: Petrus Dan.
Vorbesitzer: Zisterzienserklöster Løgum (Schleswig).

Printed sources

Augustinus, *Contra Faustum Mahichaeum*, ed. J. P. Migne, in *Patrologia Latina* 42, cols. 207-518.

CIC: *Corpus Iuris Canonici*, vol 1-2, ed. Aemilius Friedberg (Graz, 1959 [1. ed. 1879]).

Liber Petri Mathiae Curati Ecclesie Sancti Petri Ripis, ed. Anne Riising, on http://static.sdu.dk/mediafiles//Files/Om_SDU/Institutter/Ihks/Projekter/Middelalderstudier/Ny_Peder_Madsen.pdf (Odense, s.a.).

Studies

Anderson, Roger, 'Sermon Manuscripts of Different Kinds', *Medieval Sermon Studies* 55 (2011), pp. 31-44.

Anderson, Roger, 'Att predika och berätta historier', in *Den medeltida skriftkulturen i Sverige. Genrer och texter,* ed. Inger Larsson et al. (Stockholm, 2010), pp. 155-170.

Anderson, Roger, and Stephan Borgehammar, 'The Preaching of the Birgittine Friars at Vadstena Abbey (ca. 1380-1515)', *Revue Mabillon* 69 (1997), pp. 209-236.

Fonnesberg-Schmidt, Iben, *The Popes and the Baltic Crusades 1147-1254* (Leiden, 2007).

Härdelin, Alf, *Världen som yta och fönster* (Stockholm, 2005).

Kahl, H.-D., 'Crusade Eschatology as Seen by St Bernard in the Years 1146 to 1148', *The Second Crusade and the Cistercians,* ed. Michael Gervers (New York, 1992), pp. 35-47.

Langkilde, Birgitte, *Libri monasteriorum Danicorum mediae aetatis – index ad tempus compositus / Danske middelalderklostres bøger – en foreløbig registrant* (Århus, 2005).

McGuire, Brian P., *The Cistercians in Denmark* (København, 1982).

Riising, Anne, *Danmarks middelalderlige prædiken* (Odense, 1969).

Russell, F. H., *The Just War in the Middle Ages* (Cambridge, 1975).

Schipke, Renate, and Kurt Heydeck, *Handschriftencensus der kleineren Sammlungen in den östlichen Bundesländern Deutschlands: Bestandsaufnahme der ehemaligen Arbeitsstelle «Zentralinventar Mittelalterlicher Handschriften bis 1500 in den Sammlungen der DDR» (ZIH)* (Wiesbaden, 2000).

Schneyer, J., *Wegweiser zu lateinischen Predigtreihen des Mittelalters* (München 1965).

Thomson, Rodney M., *Catalogue of the manuscripts of Lincoln Cathedral Chapter Library* (Cambridge, 1989).

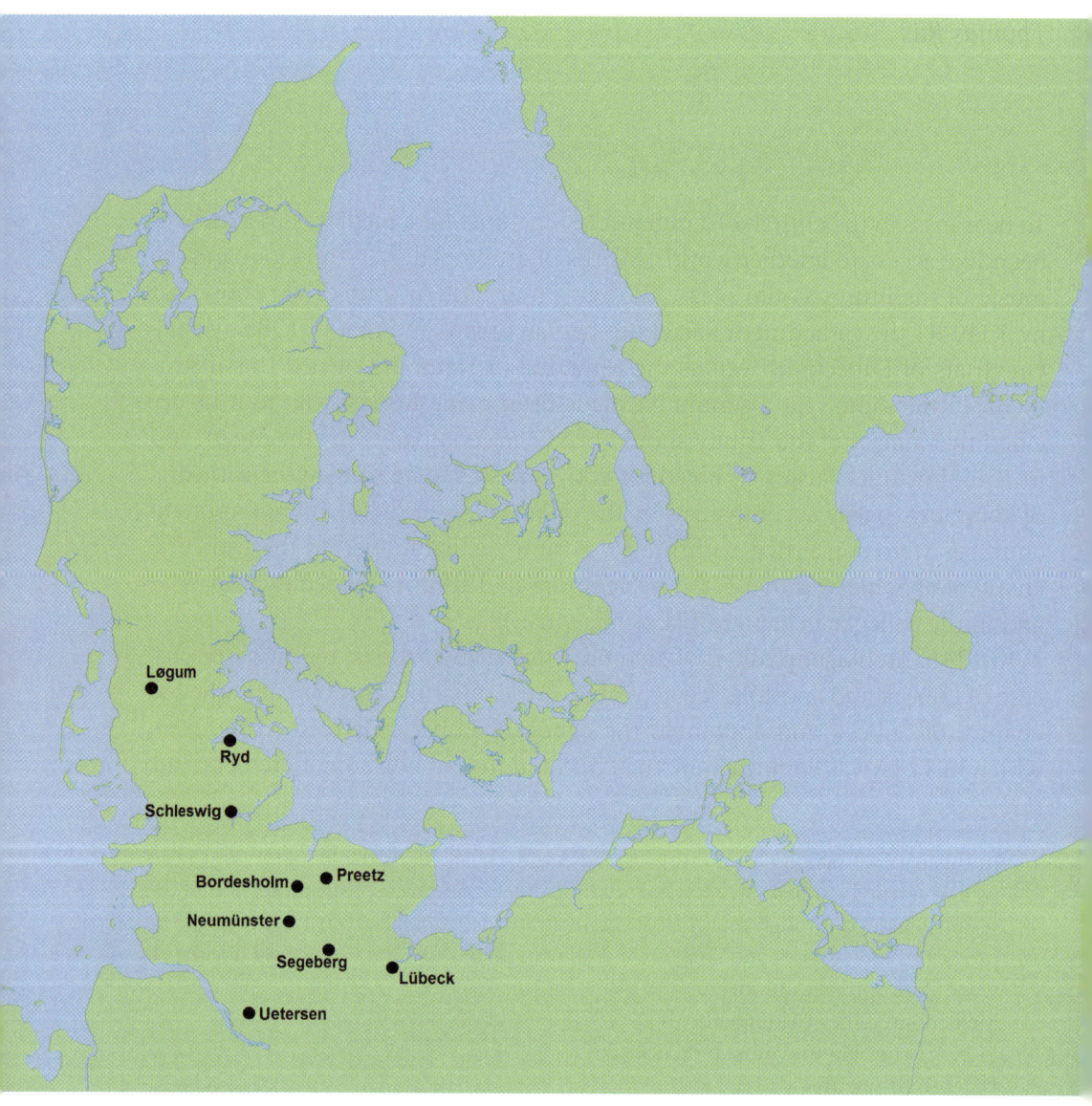

Monastic locations cited in the article.

Monasteries as Cultural Centres: The Case of Schleswig-Holstein with Lübeck and Hamburg

Thomas Riis

To hear mass in the church of a rich monastery must for a medieval layman have been like access to another world.[1] Works of art embellished the room and the music of the liturgy could please the ear. From written sources we know that by 1340-41 the cathedral of Ratzeburg had an organ[2] and that in 1386 also the Greyfriars of Lübeck[3] as well as the cathedral of Hamburg owned this instrument. In the same year a certain Nicolaus Brun made his last will; in it he decided that a mass of the Trinity should be sung accompanied by the organ[4] and in 1389 Johannes Puster arranged for votive masses to be sung in the cathedral of Hamburg, partly accompanied by the organ.[5] Especially the more important churches were concerned with music: a cantor is mentioned in the cathedral chapters of Schleswig in 1271,[6] of Hamburg in 1286,[7] of Ratzeburg in 1395,[8] and in the collegiate chapter of Haderslev in 1371.[9]

In 1248, Archbishop Albert of Livonia, Estonia and Prussia, regent of the diocese of Lübeck and apostolic legate, founded the office of cantor in the cathedral chapter of Lübeck and appointed the canon of Lübeck Gerhard to the post, which in 1249 was confirmed by the Pope and the Archbishop of Bremen – the

---

1   In this paper, I take „culture" in the broad sense, i.e. the fine arts, literature, music, as well as learned studies (divinity, history etc.). My paper gives a first impression of the results obtained through the work at the Institute of History, University of Kiel, on the project on monasteries and chapters in Schleswig-Holstein, Hamburg and Lübeck, cf. www.klosterprojekt.uni-kiel.de.
2   Meklenburgisches Urkundenbuch IX, 1870, nos. 6067 and 6145.
3   Lübeckisches Urkundenbuch IV, no. 474.
4   DD 4 R. III no. 58.
5   SHRU VI, no. 480.
6   DD 2. R. II no. 160.
7   SHRU II no. 688.
8   Meklenburgisches Urkundenbuch XXII no. 12809.
9   DD 3. R. IX no. 52.

latter obliged the cathedral of Lübeck to adopt the liturgy of Bremen.[10] Seven years later, in 1256, the bishop of Lübeck again founded the office of cantor, describing the revenue assigned to the office.[11]

Some years later, the tasks of the cantor were defined by the bishop and the cathedral chapter. Assisted by another canon, he should lead the singing in the choir at important feasts and take care of the organs and organize the divine services. From this description we may perhaps infer that already in 1259 the cathedral of Lübeck had an organ.[12] The last will of a later cantor tells us that school pupils did service in the choir both at night and in the daytime,[13] probably meaning their assistance in the canonical hours.

The performance of music can be proven only for the major churches: a good example is the *Marienklage* (Mary's lamentations) composed at Bordesholm about 1476, which requires five voices; it was performed as part of the services during Holy Week.[14] However, we may assume that also in the minor churches music must have played a role. Thus in his last will written in 1313 the cantor of Lübeck left three marks to the church of Malente (Eastern Holstein) "…ut Antiphonarium unum scribi faciant pro ecclesie necessitate." [15] We may thus safely assume that music was performed in most monasteries and not only to the minimal extent required by the divine offices.

Artistic activities

Obviously, one cannot exclude the presence of artists among the inhabitants of the monasteries in Schleswig-Holstein, but as a rule the sources do not allow us to identify them or their works.

Only from the Benedictine nunnery of Preetz by Kiel has a tapestry from the fourteenth century survived. It is an embroidery on linen made by the nun M. Schinkel; it shows the Annunciation of the Virgin.[16] Another embroidery on linen was also made at Preetz in the first half of the fourteenth century, but in this case we do not know the artist's name. Its motive was the Dormition of the Virgin.[17]

---

10 Urkundenbuch des Bistums Lübeck I, nos. 101 and 105-106.
11 Ibid., no. 125. The repetition of the foundation could have been necessary, because the initial founder was only the regent, not the bishop of the diocese.
12 Ibid., no. 139 (7.3.1259).
13 Ibid., no. 281 (1280s), probably their assistance in the canonical hours is meant.
14 Lorenzen-Schmidt & Pelc (2006), p. 75 (Dieter Lohmeier).
15 Urkundenbuch des Bistums Lübeck I no. 445 p. 540.
16 Kloster Preetz, Wandbehang.
17 Ibid., Hungertuch.

A related work of art has also survived from the convent of Uetersen by Hamburg (Cistercian nuns), but from the years around 1480. As at Preetz, it must have been made in the monastery itself, but the artist remains anonymous. Also here we find embroidery on linen, and the Crucifixion is the central theme. It must obviously have been intended for the altar of the convent's church.[18]

Book production

Each monastery had to have a minimum of books: a missal, a gradual, a breviary, a book of hours, possibly also a Bible or at least the New Testament. These books were indispensable for the mass or the hours. Life in this world necessitated legal knowledge, thus in the monastic libraries legal books are often mentioned: canon law, Roman law, and obviously the secular law of the region. Where the texts were copied remains mainly obscure, as the existence of scriptoria is seldom mentioned in the sources. It is however probable that in the fourteenth century illuminated manuscripts were produced at Segeberg.[19] Towards the end of the fifteenth century the scriptorium was still active, at any rate the accounts of the monastery from the 1480s inform us that medicine had been bought for the rubricator, i.e. the painter of initials.[20] We are also told that books could be bound by the nuns of St John's convent at Lübeck.[21]

Scriptoria appear to have belonged to the Cistercian monasteries of Løgum and of Ryd,[22] whereas the chapter of Hamburg charged a certain Karl with the copying of the Bible; in 1255 he finished the first of the three volumes.[23]

As is well known, the monastery of Neumünster was founded in the 1130s as a centre for the evangelization of Holstein. In this Christian island "in partibus infidelium" we may assume that future priests would receive at least part of their education. In the twelfth century a number of manuscripts were copied in the scriptorium of Neumünster, and their contents are remarkable. We find here the classical authors of the Latin golden age: Cicero, Lucan, Sallust, Josephus (in Latin translation) and Vergil as well as theological works.[24]

---

18 Today to be seen in the Landesmuseum, Schloss Gottorf, cf. Hirschfeld (1961), p. 321.
19 Czech National Library, Prague, mss. XIV.A.6 and XIV.A.8., cf. Truhlář (1906), nos. 2418 and 2420-2421.
20 Collijn (1939), p. 130.
21 Ibid., p. 150 (fol. 130 recto).
22 Royal Library, Copenhagen, ms. Gamle kongelige Samling 54 in 2° and 1978 in 4°.
23 Ibid., Gamle kongelige Samling 4 in 2°.
24 See Jørgensen (1926), pp. 12-13, 287-290, 295-296, 311-312, 317, 320-321, and 333-335.

In the second quarter of the fourteenth century the monastery was moved from Neumünster to Bordesholm between Neumünster and Kiel. At least in the fifteenth century a scriptorium worked at Bordesholm.[25]

The works copied at Neumünster show clearly the canons' concern about the purity of Latin which ongoing priests were to learn in the classical form of the golden age. It seems thus safe to see in Neumünster a representative of the so-called "Renaissance of the Twelfth Century".[26]

In 1784, the cathedral chapter of Hamburg sold a number of manuscripts, of which some were bought by the Royal Library in Copenhagen.[27] Several among them date from the eleventh and twelfth centuries and contain copies of classical authors like Vergil, Ovid and Lucan as well as commentaries on Cicero or Terence. Thus also this institution felt concerned about the purity of Latin and can, like Neumünster, be seen as a representative of the twelfth century Renaissance. Perhaps the manuscripts of the eleventh century were acquired after the last pagan revolt in 1066 when the evangelization could be taken up again. In spite of the chapter's classicist leaning, a work of contemporary literature was also to be found at Hamburg, viz. Gautier de Châtillon's *Alexandreis*.[28]

Book collections and learned studies

Research into chancery practice and charters has identified a number of scribes or drafters of charters.[29] When their eyes did not permit them this type of work any longer, their former employer would find them a prebend in a chapter, where their administrative experience and legal knowledge could be useful to the institution.[30]

Besides theology, law held a significant place in the libraries; the catalogue of books belonging to the chapter of Lübeck in 1297 is an obvious example.[31] Strangely enough, medical books are rare; we know, however, that in the fifteenth century, Segeberg was presented with a collection of medical treatises.[32]

---

25 See Jørgensen (1926), pp. 15-16, 20, 219-220, and 347-351.
26 For this concept, see Haskins (1927).
27 See Jørgensen (1926), pp. 1-2, 47-48, 258, 293, 304-309, 314-318, 332, and 347.
28 Royal Library, Copenhagen, ms. Gamle kongelige Samling 2146 in 4°.
29 See e.g. Skyum-Nielsen (1963), pp. 225-245; Skyum-Nielsen (1966), pp. 141-181; Eick (2008).
30 Eick (2008), pp. 86-87.
31 Published in the Urkundenbuch des Bistums Lübeck I no. 348.
32 Royal Library Copenhagen Gamle kongelige Samling 1654 in 4°.

In certain institutions teaching took place. Towards the end of the fourteenth century Thidericus Koller, professor of theology, taught at Lübeck, perhaps at the Blackfriars' monastery.[33] Also the bishop of the city and his chapter decided in the 1390s to engage a professor of theology, Bartholomäus Thorgelow, who was given a fee for his lectures.[34] Later, in 1461 an office as lector was created by the bishop of Schleswig. Every week he was to lecture on theology and sometimes deliver the sermon in the cathedral. Moreover, the bishop saw to it that a library was created.[35]

In the mentioned cases books were acquired according to a certain plan, they were copied in the scriptorium of the monastery (Neumünster, Segeberg) or commissioned outside the institution itself (chapter of Hamburg).

Many works came to the institution as gifts. King Valdemar IV of Denmark presented the chapter of Schleswig with an illuminated manuscript with the Apocalypse, which appears to have been lost,[36] and we know that in 1310 King Håkon V of Norway gave a sum to the Scandinavian Blackfriars. For this amount the provincial prior of Dacia acquired an illuminated manuscript of the Bible, possibly written at Paris. In 1514 it belonged to the Blackfriars of Schleswig.[37] Obviously, these were the more distinguished gifts, other books were presented to the institution by more modest individual benefactors.[38] Thus in 1350, the priest Hermann Hose left by his last will a number of books to the Blackfriars of Lübeck, all of them theological works as one might expect.[39]

Besides theology and law a few, not very numerous, manuscripts deal with historical events. Writings on the early history of the evangelization of Holstein are to be found in a manuscript formerly belonging to Segeberg, but today kept at Prague.[40]

A clear interest in the history of the crusades is shown by a codex from Neumünster, today housed in the Royal Library at Copenhagen.[41] Except for the *Planctus Origenis* its twelfth century part contains texts relating to the crusades, and the same is true for the part written in the fifteenth century.

From the surviving sermons we know that studies of theology were under-

---

33 Lübeckisches Urkundenbuch IV nos. 515 and 690 Anmerkung 1.
34 SHRU VI nos. 1130 (7.5.1394) and 1522 (24.4.1399).
35 Danske Magazin 6. R. I, (1913), pp. 307-319.
36 DD 4. R. I. no. 377.
37 Royal Library, Copenhagen, ms. Acc. 2001/100.
38 Schnabel (2009), pp. 130-134.
39 Lübeckisches Urkundenbuch II no. 997 (8.9.1350).
40 Czech National Library Prague, Adligatum 44.E.4.
41 Royal Library, Copenhagen, ms. Gamle kongelige Samling 2159 in 4°; Jørgensen (1926), pp. 381-382.

taken at for instance the Cistercian monastery of Løgum,⁴² but as the sermons are to be discussed in another paper, I shall leave this topic to my colleague. In spite of the slight number of surviving historical manuscripts, it is astonishing that before 1400 historical studies were made in at least three institutions: in the monastery of St John at Lübeck Abbot Arnold composed a history of Northern Germany ending with the recognition of Otto IV as emperor in 1209.⁴³ Toward the end of the fourteenth century some councillors of Lübeck commissioned a history of the town from Detmar, lecturer at the Greyfriars of Lübeck,⁴⁴ and in the second half of the thirteenth century annals were written at the Cistercian monastery of Ryd by Flensburg.⁴⁵ Although Detmar's commission was to write the history of Lübeck since 1350, which he continued to 1395, he enlarged it to a history of the world 1101-1395. However, as he does not belong to the "long thirteenth century", we shall concentrate on the works of Arnold and the annalist of Ryd.

Arnold of Lübeck and his Chronicle

Arnold had been educated at Braunschweig and in 1177 became the first abbot of St John's Benedictine monastery at Lübeck. He remained in office until his death between 1211 and 1214. The chronicle begins with Henry the Lion's pilgrimage in 1172-1173 and ends with the coronation of his son Otto IV as emperor on 4 October, 1209. Arnold's declared intention was to continue Helmold of Bosau,⁴⁶ whose *Chronica Slavorum* ended with the agreement between Henry the Lion and King Valdemar I of Denmark in 1171.

In Book I, Arnold narrates mainly Duke Henry's pilgrimage to Jerusalem, but also the election of Bishop Henry of Lübeck (I 13) as well as a miracle by Thomas Becket in his lifetime (I 14).

Book II describes Duke Henry's relations to the emperor until Henry's defeat in 1181, when the King of Denmark's navy helped Barbarossa's troops by its blockade of Lübeck from the sea. If this conflict forms the central theme of the book, also a minor conflict, viz. between Duke Henry and his vassal Count Adolf III of Holstein, is described as well. Initially, Adolf had been a loyal vassal

---

42 Riising (1969), pp. 50-54 and 467-471.
43 Lexikon des Mittelalters I, col. 1007-1008.
44 Lexikon des Mittelalters III, col. 737.
45 Edited in Danmarks Middelalderlige Annaler, pp. 149-209.
46 Arnoldi Chronica Slavorum, p. 295 (VII 20): "...volens continuare hoc dictamen operi Helmoldi sacerdotis, qui de statu terre nostre et regibus sive principibus multa premiserat, precipue, de vocatione vel subactione Sclavorum, que per nobilem ducem Heinricum facta est, memorie fidelium perennare..."

to his overlord, but in 1180 the rupture came. Adolf left Henry's party, in return Henry occupied Holstein (II 16). In the settlement of 1181, Henry had to cede Lübeck to Barbarossa; he lost his fiefs, but was allowed to keep his patrimony. He had to go into exile for three years, which he spent with his family-in-law in England. Moreover, Barbarossa confirmed the Counts Adolf of Holstein and Bernhard of Ratzeburg in their possessions (II 22).

In Book III, which deals with the years between 1181 and 1187, mainly North German events are described. Danish affairs play a certain role because of the submission of Pomerania in 1185 and King Knud's refusal to pay homage to Barbarossa (III 7). In this context, Arnold gives a very positive, even flattering description of contemporary Denmark (III 5). Obviously, important events in the German empire are also related. Arnold appears to have acquired a predilection for moments of strife: the struggle for imperial power in the Byzantine Empire following the Emperor's death in 1180 (III 8), a question of protocol opposing the abbot of Fulda and the archbishop of Cologne (III 9), which causes Arnold to condemn the vice of pride (*superbia*), especially among monks (III 10), Barbarossa's disagreement with the pope (III 11, III 17, and III 19), strife between Barbarossa's son and the Archbishop of Cologne (III 12), between the latter and Barbarossa (III 18).

Book IV deals entirely with the struggle for the throne in Jerusalem and the fall of the city in 1187, as well as the Third Crusade, from which Barbarossa was not to return.

In Book V events from 1191 to the death of Henry VI in 1197 are told.[47] Count Adolf III of Holstein had taken part in the Third Crusade, but in the meantime Henry the Lion had tried to restore his lost power. Against him stood Adolf of Holstein, whereas Denmark supported Duke Henry against Count Adolf.

Duke Henry died in 1195, and even if he did not conceal his conflicts with the emperor, Arnold wrote him a very positive obituary (V 24). The last chapters of the book narrate the crusade organized by Henry VI, in which Adolf III participated, distinguishing himself in action by Beirut (V 27-29). The very last chapter (V 30) describes the beginning of the evangelization of Livonia from 1186 to the turn of the century.

Book VI covers only a few years; the expansion in North Germany plays an important role, ending with the Danish conquest of Holstein. As a trend through the chapters runs the rivalry between the two presumptive kings of Germany, Philip (Henry VI's brother) and Otto, son of Henry the Lion. Also in the archdiocese of Mainz there was strife because of a double election after the death of Archbishop Conrad in 1200 (VI 3). The last chapters of the book

---

47 Nevertheless, the death of Archbishop Absalon of Lund in 1201 is mentioned in V 18.

describe the Fourth Crusade and the Latin conquest of Constantinople in 1204. Their major part consists of extracts of letters, of which the first describes the intrigues for the throne by members of the imperial family. For Arnold, the conquest was a positive fact, which took place because God allowed it to happen; thus the Roman Church ruled also on the Bosporus.

The seventh and last book informs us about the events since 1204, ending with the imperial coronation of Otto IV in 1209. Three ecclesiastical conflicts play a role in this book: the political involvement of the archbishops of Cologne and the succession to Bishop Isfrid of Ratzeburg, who died in 1204; this conflict was peacefully solved (VII 9); finally the election of the deposed Bishop of Schleswig, Valdemar, to the archbishopric of Bremen (VII 10-11). Inserted as chapter VII 8 we find the report by Barbarossa's envoy to Egypt, Syria and Palestine in 1175.

King Philip was murdered in 1208: according to Arnold he was a man of many virtues – friendly, humble, pious and with a certain intellectual culture (*litteratus*) (VII 12). Chapters 13-19 describe the unanimous election of Otto IV as King of Germany and his coronation as emperor. He showed himself to be conciliatory, as when he declared his intention to marry Philip's daughter, which the prelates present at Würzburg accepted.

In the last chapter, VII 20, Arnold declares his intention to continue Helmold's work; if an event deserves to be remembered, he will tell it both when it causes joy or sorrow. In a similar way God leads the faithful to salvation through success and adversity.

We may now ask whether or not a moral for the reader is to be found in Arnold's work. According to Bernd Ulrich Hucker, Arnold wrote a royal chronicle which stressed the task of Otto IV, viz. the evangelization of the heathen and the liberation of the Holy Land.[48] The same author finds that someone had commissioned Arnold to write his chronicle: Bishop Philip of Ratzeburg, to whom it was dedicated; Otto IV's brother Wilhelm of Lüneburg; possibly Count Adolf III of Holstein or even Otto IV himself.[49]

These are, of course, possibilities, but to my mind, no conclusive evidence in favour of any of these can be found in Arnold's work. This appears, however, to contain so much information which would be irrelevant if Arnold had wanted only to glorify the deeds of Henry the Lion, his sons, Barbarossa or Adolf III.

We have already seen that Arnold describes a considerable number of conflicts, sometimes with little relation to the principal trend of his narrative. But he also demonstrates the consequence of unity: the description of a flourishing

---

48 Hucker (1988), p. 108.
49 Ibid., p. 119.

Denmark after the restitution of the strong monarchy in 1157 is ample proof. The chapter in question (III 5) is rather a digression from the main narrative, and I thus propose to see it as an example of prosperity nourished by the absence of strife. Obviously, Arnold takes a keen interest in the events in Outremer (Syria, Palestine), which appears irrelevant for the evangelization of the heathen in the Baltic region. However, it makes sense if wee see them as different aspects of the propagation of the faith in general.

At the time when Arnold finished his work, Lübeck belonged to the Danish monarchy, and obviously, he had to be circumspect as an author and to keep the balance between pro-Danish and pro-German attitudes. If national unity had furthered Danish prosperity, the same could become true in Germany, now that Otto IV had been universally recognized. If this interpretation is correct, we understand better why Arnold ended his work with the imperial coronation of Otto IV.

The Annals of Ryd

The author of the Annals remains unknown, but the reference to charters in favour of the Cistercian monastery of Ryd near Flensburg indicates a connection with this institution. The author begins with the origin of the Danes, necessarily basing himself on Saxo's *Gesta Danorum* and the annals of Lund until the middle of the thirteenth century. This must mean that he knew only the earlier version of the annals which ended in 1255.[50] Moreover, the author appears to have used other yearbooks as well, mainly from sister monasteries, which like Ryd had been founded from Esrum.[51]

The author reveals himself as a staunch nationalist: with delight he informs us of the numerous times when the Germans had been obliged to pay tribute to the Danes.[52] Whereas Saxo did not discuss the origin of the Danes, who as a matter of course were seen as autochthonous, the author of the Annals gives us a different, sophisticated construction. At the time of Abraham's grandfather the Danes came from Götaland in Sweden and settled in the territory known as Denmark. The eponymous King Dan ruled over the islands between the Sound and the Great Belt. At the same time the inhabitants of Jutland feared the attack by a mighty king. In order to save themselves they constructed the fortification of the Kovirke (still to be seen near Schleswig) and asked Dan for help, promising to accept him as their ruler. The attack was unsuccessful, and in this way

---

50 Kristensen (1969), pp. 84-94.
51 Danmarks middelalderlige Annaler, p. 149 introduction.
52 Ibid., e.g. pp. 151 and 154.

Denmark was united under the rule of Dan.[53] The reference to the Kovirke, which appears to have been constructed c. 980,[54] is interesting; the author must have recognized the purpose for which it had been built and had perhaps even seen it himself.

Especially when the author speaks of events belonging to the last century before his own time, his national attitude becomes obvious. Thus the fortification of the Dannevirke was improved with a wall of bricks, because Valdemar I did not trust the Germans.[55] According to our author, Frederick Barbarossa had ceded the territories north of the Elbe to King Valdemar I by a chrysobull. The author sees this cession as an outcome of Valdemar's meeting with Barbarossa in 1181, but actually it was Frederick II who in 1214/1215 ceded the land north of the Elbe and the Elde to Valdemar II. This charter was authenticated by a chrysobull. The transaction was confirmed by Innocent III, but after King Abel's death in 1252, a German woman, daughter of the devil, destroyed the document, because she hated the Danes ("...has litteras...quedam mulier Teutonica, filia dyaboli, destruxit in odium Danorum...").[56] In this, however, the devil's daughter had little success, because in 1301 the charter was still kept in the original in the cathedral of Roskilde.[57]

Under the year 1223 the Annals tell us about the kidnapping of Valdemar II and his son by Count Heinrich of Mecklenburg. The author's comment could not be more venomous: "Note, my reader, that the Germans were never or rarely successful unless by treason or fraud which is in their nature..."[58] The numerous cases where Danes and Germans had been loyal to each other were not mentioned. Further, the author cannot or would not realize that the Danish position in the Baltic had become so dominating that it had to be curtailed in order to restore the political equilibrium of the region.

In 1237, Duke Abel of Schleswig married Mechtild, daughter of the Count of Holstein. According to the annals, King Valdemar was not very pleased with

---

53 Ibid., pp. 150-151.
54 Andersen (1996), pp. 8 and 13.
55 Danmarks middelalderlige Annaler, p. 166; see further Andersen (1996), pp. 6-7 and 12-13.
56 Danmarks middelalderlige Annaler, p. 167, l. 26-27: See DD 1. R. V no. 48 for the text of the chrysobull and no. 83 for the confirmation by Innocent III.
57 DD 2. R. V no.150.
58 „...Nota lector Teutonicos nunquam aut raro prevaluisse et triumphos duxisse nisi per proditionem et fraudem, quod habent ex natura..." Danmarks middelalderlige Annaler, p. 170 l. 40-42. Four years later, the troops from Dithmarsia behaved in a treacherous way according to our author, as during the battle of Bornhöved in 1227 they changed side, going over to the enemy of the Danish army, ibid., p. 171.

this union, because he feared a schism between Abel and his brothers.[59] After Valdemar's death in 1241, hostilities between King Erik IV and his brothers Abel and Christopher broke out, ending only with the murder of Erik in 1250. Our author did not hesitate to assign the responsibility for the conflict to the counts of Holstein.[60] In spite of his severe remarks on the Germans in general, he tells us without comment about Erik IV's marriage to the daughter of the Duke of Saxony in 1239.[61]

Under 1241 our author laments the state of Denmark after the death of Valdemar II. "His death meant that the crown fell from the head of the Danes"; the country suffered from civil war, during which former conquests were lost.[62]

Although the Annals describe the capture of Erik IV by Duke Abel as treason, they maintain that the king was murdered without his brother's knowledge.[63]

The author of the Latin annals which end with the year 1288 had a very negative view of the counts of Holstein, whom he saw as the instigators of civil war in Denmark. In order to counterbalance royal power, the dukes of Schleswig sought and found support in Holstein; for its counts, the creation of a buffer zone in Schleswig would be most welcome. Apparently, the author was aware of this situation, of which he disapproved. His final remark about the demolition of the castle of Gottorp, in spite of its role as the key and the lock of Denmark,[64] also points in the same direction. However, his very harsh words about the Germans in general must be taken with a grain of salt, as apparently he did not object to the Saxon marriages of Erik IV or of Duke Valdemar of Schleswig. To our author the "bad Germans" were those in the North, who could become a threat to Denmark.

Besides the Latin annals, three Danish yearbooks have survived, which were probably written at the monastery of Ryd. The first of these is a Danish version of the Latin annals with a continuation to 1314.[65]

As in the Latin text, we read about the strengthening of the Dannevirke, because Valdemar I did not trust the Germans (i.e. Frederick Barbarossa, whereas

---

59 Ibid., p. 171 l. 76-81.
60 „…bellum intestinum in Dacia inter reges et duces comitibus eos instigantibus, qui semper querunt mala Dacie…", ibid., p. 171 l. 79-81.
61 Ibid., pp. 171-172. Also the marriage of Duke Valdemar to the daughter of the Duke of Saxony in 1287 is related without comment, ibid., p. 176.
62 „…In cuius morte uere cecidit corona capitis Danorum…", ibid., p. 172. Again, under 1247, he laments the civil war, loc. cit.
63 Ibid., pp. 172-173.
64 „…quasi clauis et custodia totius Dacie…", ibid., p. 176 l. 35.
65 Ibid., pp. 176-209.

Henry the Lion had helped him).[66] Although the text informs us that the kidnapping of the kings in 1223 by Count Heinrich of Schwerin was made possible through the betrayal by their own servants, the negative verdict on the Germans in general is taken over from the Latin yearbook.[67] Further, according to the first Danish text, which here follows the Latin yearbook, the Danish defeat at Bornhöved was caused by the defection of the Dithmarsians during the battle to the anti-Danish party.[68] Also here the text expresses King Valdemar's misgivings about Abel's marriage to the daughter of the count of Holstein.[69] The murder of Erik IV is described but with the omission of the observation that it took place without the knowledge of Duke Abel,[70] and also the role of Gottorp as Denmark's key and lock is left out. In return we are told that in 1295, Duke Valdemar built Gottorp again.[71] The closing event of this yearbook is the crushing of the revolt of 1313 and the subsequent exile of the Abildgaard family.[72]

The second Danish version[73] ends in 1295 with the construction of Gottorp which had been demolished in 1288 in spite of its role as key and lock of Jutland (not Denmark).[74] It is a rather sloppy version of the Latin yearbook; when the latter tells us that after the death of King Abel a German woman destroyed Innocent III's confirmation of the imperial cession of the land north of the Elbe, the second Danish version calls her Abel.[75] As in the first Danish version the murder of Erik IV is mentioned without the piece of information that it happened without his brother's knowledge.[76]

The third Danish version[77] ends in the middle of the 1220s with the liberation of the kings, but before the battle of Bornhöved. This text is considerably shorter than the other three and must be seen as a summary. It is characteristic of this text that the anti-German aspect has been considerably weakened. The Dannevirke was strengthened as a defensive measure against Germany,[78]

---

66 Ibid., pp. 197-198.
67 Ibid., p. 202.
68 Ibid., p. 203.
69 Loc. cit.
70 Ibid., p. 205.
71 Ibid., p. 208.
72 Ibid., p. 209.
73 Ibid., pp. 209-236.
74 Ibid., p. 236 l. 30.
75 Ibid., p. 229; the version given in the first Danish text corresponds to the one in the Latin yearbook, ibid., p. 199.
76 Ibid., p. 234.
77 Ibid., pp. 237-253.
78 Ibid., p. 251 l. 60-63.

and a German woman destroyed Innocent III's confirmation of the imperial chrysobull,[79] but the kidnapping of the kings by Count Heinrich of Schwerin was possible only because the kings were betrayed by their own servants. Moreover, in this text we do not find the very negative judgement on the Germans in general.[80]

Our analysis has shown that the anti-German attitude is more pronounced in the Latin yearbook and in the first Danish version than in the subsequent Danish versions. This is probably due to the fact that the author observed how the duchy of Schleswig gradually detached itself from Denmark. We may add that he must also have been a witness to the advance of the German language in the southernmost part of the duchy. About 1200, Danish appears to have been spoken as far as Eckernförde, whereas the region between Eckernförde and the frontier (Der Dänische Wohld, i.e. the Danish forest) had not yet been fully colonized. When in the course of the thirteenth century this happened, it was the work of German settlers.[81] Thus already in the lifetime of our historian, the south-eastern part of Schleswig spoke German.

Conclusions

Unfortunately, our sources are not as informative as one could wish, but nevertheless they have shown us activities which allow us to qualify several monasteries as cultural centres. Embroideries have survived which were made in Preetz and Uetersen, scriptoria were active in Segeberg and Neumünster, where, at least at the latter place it appears to have worked in the spirit of the Twelfth Century Renaissance. Theology was an obvious field of study, but as another paper deals with this aspect, I have left it out here. In two monasteries, St John at Lübeck and Ryd by Flensburg, important historical studies were undertaken, and in both cases we have been able to identify the outlook of the author. Abbot Arnold of Lübeck regrets the many examples of strife in contemporary society; if only unity could prevail instead of conflict, society would flourish, as could be seen in contemporary Denmark. The recognition in 1209 of Otto IV as only king of Germany and emperor opened the possibility of a similar favourable development.

The annalist of Ryd is more pessimistic, as he witnesses the budding Germanization of Schleswig, hence his sweeping, exaggerated and unfair statements against the Northern Germans.

---

79 Ibid., p. 251 l. 70-73.
80 Ibid., p. 253 l. 26-33.
81 Unverhau (1990), pp. 51, 63 and 66.

These examples must suffice to show that the monasteries were cultural centres; it would not surprise me if the analysis of other sources containing music and art would add other monasteries to those treated in this paper.

Literature

Manuscript sources
Royal Library, Copenhagen, mss.
Gamle kongelige Samling 4 in 2°
Gamle kongelige Samling 54 in 2°
Gamle kongelige Samling 1654 in 4°
Gamle kongelige Samling 2146 in 4°
Gamle kongelige Samling 2159 in 4°
Acc. 2001/100

Printed sources
Arnoldi Chronica Slavorum, ex recensione I.M.Lappenbergii in usum scholarum ex Monumentis Germaniae Historicis recudi fecit Georgius Heinricus Pertz (Hannnover, 1868).
Danmarks Middelalderlige Annaler, ed. Erik Kroman (København, 1980).
Danske Magazin 6R.I. (København 1913), pp. 307-319.
DD: *Diplomatarium Danicum,* various editors (København, 1938 –).
Lübeckisches Urkundenbuch 1-11, ed. Verein für Lübeckische Geschichte und Altertumskunde (Lübeck, 1843-1905).
Meklenburgisches Urkundenbuch, ed. Verein für Meklenburgische Geschichte und Alterthumskunde (Schwerin, 1863 –).
SHRU: *Schleswig-Holsteinische Regesten und Urkunden,* ed. Landesarchiv Schleswig-Holstein (Kiel, 1886 –).
Urkundenbuch des Bistums Lübeck 1-5, ed. Landesarchiv Schleswig-Holstein (reprint Neumünster, 1994-1997).

Studies
Andersen, H. Hellmuth, *Zur Wehr des ganzen Reiches – das Danewerk*. Geschichte und Kultur Schleswig-Holsteins 2 (Neumünster, 1996).
Collijn, Isak, 'Rester av Heinrich Rantzaus Bibliotek på Breitenburg i National- og Universitetsbiblioteket i Prag I', *Nordisk Tidskrift för Bok- och Biblioteksväsen* 26 (1939), pp. 125-145.
Eick, Stefan, *Die Kanzlei und das Urkundenwesen der Grafen von Holstein-Schaumburg zwischen 1189 und 1290 unter besonderer Berücksichtigung materieller, prosopographischer und verwaltungspraktischer Aspekte,* (Kiel, 2008).
Haskins, Charles Homer, *The Renaissance of the Twelfth Century* (s.l., 1927).
Hirschfeld, Peter, *Die Kunstdenkmäler des Kreises Pinneberg,* bearb. von Wolfgang Teuchert

and Arnold Lühning; Die Kunstdenkmäler des Landes Schleswig-Holstein vol. 9 (München/Berlin, 1961).

Hucker, Bernd Ulrich, 'Die Chronik Arnolds von Lübeck als „Historia Regum"', *Deutsches Archiv für Erforschung des Mittelalters* 44 (1988), pp. 98-119.

Jørgensen, Ellen, *Catalogus codicum latinorum medii aevi Bibliothecae Regiae Hafniensis* (København, 1926).

Kristensen, Anne K.G., *Danmarks ældste annalistik* (København, 1969).

Lexikon des Mittelalters I-IX (München-Zürich, 1977-1999).

Lorenzen-Schmidt, Klaus-Joachim, and Ortwin Pelc, ed., *Das neue Schleswig-Holstein Lexikon* (Neumünster, 2006).

Riising, Anne, *Danmarks middelalderlige Prædiken* (København, 1969).

Schnabel, Kerstin 'Die Bibliothek des Benediktinerklosters Cismar', *Zeitschrift der Gesellschaft für Schleswig-Holsteinische Geschichte* 134 (2009), pp. 123-151.

Skyum-Nielsen, Niels, 'Den danske konges kancelli i 1250'erne', in *Festskrift til Astrid Friis på halvfjerdsårsdagen den 1. august 1963,* ed. Svend Ellehøj, Svend Gissel, and Knud Vohn (København, 1963), pp. 225-245.

Skyum-Nielsen, Niels, 'Kanslere og skrivere i Danmark 1250-1282', in *Middelalderstudier. Tilegnede Aksel E. Christensen på tresårsdagen 11. september 1966,* ed. Tage E. Christiansen, Svend Ellehøj and Erling Ladewig Petersen (København 1966), pp. 141-181.

Truhlář, Joseph, *Catalogus codicum manuscriptorum latinorum, qui in c.r. Bibliotheca publica atque Universitatis Pragensis asservantur* II (Prag, 1906).

Unverhau, Henning, *Untersuchungen zur historischen Entwicklung des Landes zwischen Schlei und Eider im Mittelalter* (Neumünster, 1990).

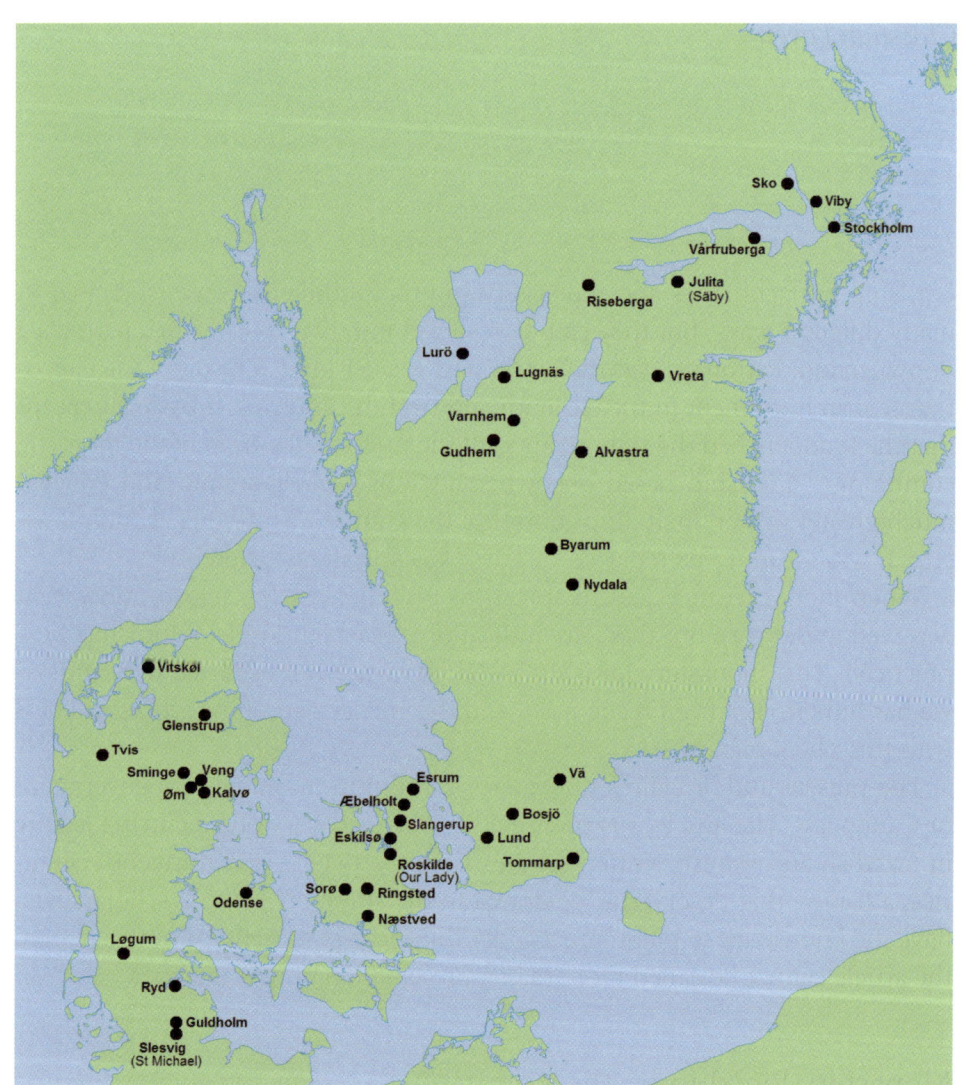

Monastic locations cited in the article.

Lordship over Monasteries in Twelfth and Thirteenth Century Sweden and Denmark

Christian Lovén

Lordship over churches and monasteries in the Middle Ages was exercised in many different ways, but they can be resolved into two basic forms: patronage or ownership. Patronage was the newer and weaker kind, a result of the Gregorian reform movement in the eleventh and twelfth centuries. It basically meant that the founders had the right to appoint the priest or the head of the monastic community.[1] Lordship based on ownership was the older kind and entailed much greater power, including control of the church institution's economic assets. It was meant to be replaced by patronage but in fact lived on.

When monasticism began to spread in Scandinavia, the reform movement was well under way, but there are indications that both kinds of lordship were practiced. That monastery lordship based on ownership occurred in Scandinavia has hitherto not been recognised, and the greater part of the article will deal with this phenomenon.

The present author claims no expertise in European monastery governance or Canon law. The article was prompted by the discovery of a recurring feature in Swedish and Danish written sources from the twelfth and thirteenth centuries, a feature that deserves to be drawn to the attention of those scholars who have the knowledge to put it into a wider European perspective. For this reason, the article cannot be called more than a presentation of new material.

Monastery lordship on the Continent

When Ulrich Stutz coined the word *Eigenkirche*, 'proprietary church', in 1895, he opened up a large scholarly field. Research was conducted all over Europe, but mainly in Germany. Stutz believed that lay ownership of churches was specific to German areas, reflecting an old custom of private ownership of pagan cult sites. Twentieth century research disproved this particular idea, and lay

---

1   Landau (1975), pp. 128–129 and *passim*.

ownership of churches has been de-dramatised, but the word *Eigenkirche* lives on.[2]

The lay ownership included monasteries, *Eigenklöster*, and Stutz's definition of this phenomenon was more consistent. One key to defining a proprietary monastery was that a lay person claimed *dominium*, but the most distinctive feature was that lordship was maintained through the founder's assuming the office of *advocatus* at the monastery, and making this office hereditary. The *advocatus* was responsible for the economy of the monastery, thus giving the founding family control. The land given to the monastery formed a *Sondervermögen*, a reserved part, of the founder's holdings.[3]

The conditions for this research field changed when Susan Wood published a substantial monograph, *The Proprietary Church in the Medieval West*, in 2006. It critically reassesses the source material. A major result is that the forms of lordship, and the vocabulary used, varied enormously. With regard to the monasteries, Wood points to lay abbacy as an important form of lordship, and she demonstrates that the title *advocatus* did not always indicate lordship. This work has in many ways made research easier, but the catch-words of earlier research have been undermined. The terminology must in every case be viewed in its context.

Scandinavian research

Proprietary churches have been studied, or sought after, in all the Scandinavian countries, with Iceland as the foremost example.[4] The research has been less concerned with monasteries. In Denmark, late medieval royal patronage rights over monasteries have been identified.[5] With regard to the twelfth and thirteenth centuries, the idea has mostly been rejected. In 1936, Hal Koch addressed the question of whether there were *Eigenklöster* in Denmark. He found that the absence of the word *dominium* and one single mention of an *advocatus* in the charters proves that there were not.[6] Koch's explanation was that monastic life spread in Denmark only after the reform movement had begun. In the same year, Erik Schalling arrived at the conclusion that some Danish monasteries lay under patronage, but the argumentation does not hold up well under

---

2   Stutz (1895); Plöchl (1953), 1 pp. 237–241; Olsen (1966), pp. 79–82; Landau (1982).
3   Stutz (1913); Rathgen (1928).
4   Koch (1936b) 2, pp. 35–58; Skovgaard-Petersen (1960); Smedberg (1973); Nyborg (1974).
5   Skyum-Nielsen (1957), p. 58; Dahlerup (1968), col. 139.
6   Koch (1936a), pp. 564–582; Koch (1936b), 2, pp. 66–68.

scrutiny.[7] In contrast to these results, Arne Odd Johnsen viewed *Eigenklöster* as common in Norway prior to 1153, when ownership of churches was forbidden in an agreement.[8] This was however a general conclusion, not supported by case studies.

Traditionally, Scandinavian research has had a rather innocent view of the relations between founder and monastery once the monastery had been established. Free monasteries (see below) have, more or less unconsciously, been considered the norm.

This changed with Thomas Hill's monograph *Könige, Fürsten und Klöster: Studien zu den dänischen Klostergründungen des 12. Jahrhunderts* (1992). In this valuable work, Hill identified a number of services that monasteries provided for their founders. They include burials, prayers and memorial masses, a saint's cult of a family member and hospitality or other economic obligations. A table summarises his results, where (X) marks a clear case, (x) a partial case and (–) that the monastery did not provide this service. Hill divided some monasteries into two periods.[9]

	St Knud Odense I	St Knud Odense II	Ringsted	Sorø I	Sorø II	Slangerup	Tvis	Guldholm	Næstved	Esrum I	Esrum II	Our Lady Roskilde	Øm	Løgum
Burials	x	–	X	X	X	–	–	–			X	–	X	X
Memorials	x	x	X	X	X		X	X	X		X		x	X
Cult	X	X	X	x	–	x	–	–	–	–	–	X	–	–
Hospitality				X	–	X		–	X	X	–	X	X	X

This table could be lengthened to include Swedish monasteries. The Cistercian monasteries Alvastra in Östergötland and Varnhem in Västergötland were burial sites for the two dynasties that alternated on the Swedish throne 1130–1250.[10] Descendants of the founders were buried at the nunneries of Vreta[11]

---

7   Schalling (1936); Hill (1992), pp. 24–26.
8   Johnsen (1951), p. 16 & *passim*; Johnsen (1965), pp. 24–26.
9   Hill (1992), p. 339.
10 See for instance Lagerquist (1996).
11 Ahnlund (1945).

in Östergötland, Riseberga[12] in Närke and Sko[13] in Uppland. Memorial masses have not been scrutinised for the present article but can be assumed to have been common. Sko and possibly Alvastra had saints of the founding families, and a late thirteenth century parallel was Stockholm's Franciscan convent.[14] Hospitality is only attested with certainty at Nydala Cistercian monastery in Småland (below), but thirteenth century visits that may have been based on hospitality obligations are known at Vreta[15], Gudhem[16], Riseberga[17] and Varnhem[18].

A weakness in Hill's investigation is that the legal basis for these demands on the monasteries is unclear. He doubts the validity of King Valdemar I calling himself the *advocatus* of Saint Knut's Cathedral priory in Odense in 1180 and when Duke Valdemar is stated as having patronage of Saint Mikael's Benedictine double monastery in Slesvig in the 1190s (below). Instead, he finds that charters of defence indicate patronage or lordship. This is however an unreliable basis, as charters of defence were issued by persons not associated with the monastery.[19] But the services provided by the monasteries, especially expensive ones like hospitality, are unlikely to have been delivered *pro bono*. Non-written or personal agreements may have existed that we cannot trace, but the need for such assumptions is reduced if a legal basis can be identified.

Patronage

There are a number of twelfth and thirteenth century cases where patronage is claimed over parish churches. But in only two instances, one Swedish and one Danish, is the word explicitly used concerning monasteries.

The *Säby/Julita* Cistercian monastery lay in Södermanland, Sweden. It was originally founded by nobles at Viby in Uppland in 1160 (below). Sometime between 1167 and 1185 the monastery moved to Säby with the aid of King Knut Eriksson. In one charter, the monks receive land at Säby in exchange for land

---

12 Ahnlund (1945), p. 331; Tunberg (1951), pp. 208–210.
13 Gardell (1937), pp. 185–186.
14 Lundén (1983), pp. 353–356 & 364–365. Alvastra will be treated in a forthcoming study.
15 DS 432 (1266).
16 DS 377 (1250) & DS 617 (1276). These visits were probably to the royal manor, not the nunnery.
17 DS 185 (1220).
18 DS 631 (1277) & DS 684 (1279).
19 Nyd. 6 = DS 119 (beginning of the thirteenth century); DS 492 (1264, see Sko below); DD 2:7, no. 65 (1313); DS 2994 (1333).

at Viby. The king has been included in their brotherhood and also proclaims himself to be their 'patron, founder and defender' (*ipsorum quoque patronum. fundatorem. defensorem exhibeo*).[20] In 1210 Knut's son, King Erik Knutsson, calls himself the monastery's *prouisor ac prolocutor atque defensor*, roughly 'provider, lawyer and defender'.[21] Only the word *defensor* is used in both charters, but there is a parallelism in the triple titles. Erik had obviously inherited the patronage from his father, but the different choice of words may mean that he was loosening the grip. Then again, the change of wording may be just another illustration of the inconsistent terminology.

The Danish case of the word patronage being used in connection with a monastery concerns *Saint Mikael's* and *Guldholm*, at Slesvig in south Jutland.

Saint Mikael's was a Benedictine double monastery. It may have been founded very early, even in the tenth century.[22] In 1191, Bishop Valdemar of Slesvig founded the Cistercian house Guldholm near the city. He moved the monks of Saint Mikael's there, which led to a conflict with the local Duke, also named Valdemar. The legal issues are primarily known from two contemporary charters written by Abbot Vilhelm of Æbelholt, who was one of two judges appointed by the Pope to solve the conflict.

In one charter, Vilhelm states that the judges' mission was to find out whether the Duke had patronage of Saint Mikael's, whether he had given his permission for the move of the monks and whether the Cistercians were willing to respect the patronage rights. The judges authorise the transfer made by the bishop, but with the correction that there are always to be some Cistercian monks at Saint Mikael's monastery. Vilhelm states that the Cistercians had offered the Duke the patronage rights over their monastery.[23]

In the second charter, Vilhelm states that should it become evident that the Duke had patronage rights over the Benedictine monastery and that he had not given his permission for the transformation (*mutationi*) of Saint Mikael's church, and considering that the Duke could not have patronage rights in the Cistercian monastery, then the Benedictines should get back all that had been taken from them. But the Cistercians would get everything if they were willing to preserve, in their monastery, all the rights that Saint Mikael's church had. The judges however found that this would be hard to control. The Cistercians had then 'with joy' offered the Duke the patronage rights over their monastery.[24]

---

20 DS 64.
21 DS 137.
22 Nyberg (2000), pp. 32–35 & pp. 88–89.
23 DD 1:3, pp. 489–490.
24 DD 1:3, p. 491.

The 'rights that Saint Mikael's church had' may either mean that Saint Mikael's holdings were to be a separate unit within the Cistercian monastery, or be a circumscription of the patronage right over Saint Mikael's. The offer by the Cistercians to come under a layman's patronage has been termed 'an uncanonical compromise'.²⁵ This explains why Vilhelm states that the monks offered it 'with joy' (*libentissime*), emphasising that the monks had not been forced into it. Brian Patrick McGuire has pointed out that the Benedictines at Saint Mikael's needed the Duke's patronage for their monastery to survive.²⁶ A transfer of the patronage to Guldholm meant that they had lost.

It should be noted that both Scandinavian instances of explicit monastery patronage concern Cistercian monks' houses. This may be surprising, considering the strong self-sufficiency of the Cistercians. However, Canon law allowed for monastery patronage as well as Cathedral patronage, and the Cistercians were not excluded.²⁷

There are but two cases of outright use of the word *patronus*, but there were a number of monasteries that must also be interpreted as lying under patronage (cf. Hill's table above and Veng below) although the word is never mentioned in the preserved charters. This may in part be explained by the unevenness of the sources, and the fact that nearly all preserved texts stem from ecclesiastical institutions may give rise to the suspicion that documents indicating patronage have been suppressed. But more important is the lesson from Susan Wood's research, that the terminology was not consistent. There were also a number of other terms centered on protection that can, with caution, be assumed to imply lordship.

Nydala in Småland, Sweden, was a Cistercian monastery founded in 1143 or 1144 by the bishop of Linköping, in cooperation with a local nobleman and the king.²⁸ In a charter issued in 1216–1220, a Linköping bishop calls himself its *fundator et protector*, and in another contemporary charter its *fundator* 'as his predecessors had been'.²⁹ The word *fundator* meant 'important benefactor' as well as 'founder'.³⁰

---

25 DRB 1:3, p. 340, note 2.
26 McGuire (1982), p. 102.
27 Landau (1975), pp. 186–194; Burton (1999), pp. 195–203; Könighaus (2004), pp. 128–135; cf. Rathgen (1928), pp. 10–13 and DD 1:6 no. 188 (1234) on lay advocacy over Cistercians.
28 Tollin (1998), p. 48.
29 Nyd. 12 & 13 = DS 165 & 166.
30 Glossarium mediæ et infimæ Latinitatis 3 (1884), p. 628; Dictionary of Medieval Latin 4 (1988), pp. 1029–1030; cf. Lovén (2010a), pp. 202–204, for Scandinavian cases.

That Nydala was under episcopal lordship is indicated by an agreement that can be dated to 1266. In exchange for the bishop's tithes from some parishes, the monks were to receive the bishop and his entourage from the first Sunday of Advent until Christmas Eve, should he choose to stay that long. In 1300, the duty was removed and some of the tithes withdrawn.[31] That this very burdensome hospitality, 3–4 weeks, was actually exacted is apparent from a bishop's charter issued at Nydala on 14 December 1287.[32] The burden may have been new in 1266, but it is more likely that the parish tithes were given as an alleviating of an old hospitality duty: a bishop's charter concerning Nydala was issued several years earlier during the stipulated period, on 23 December 1258.[33]

The nunnery of *Gudhem* in Västergötland, Sweden, was founded around 1160 and became Cistercian in the thirteenth century. In a charter of protection issued in 1266, King Valdemar Birgersson takes the monastery under his *protectionis & defensionis*.[34] These words are not in the form of titles, but it is likely that the king had patronage. The monastery had a long history of royal support and was founded on land belonging to the Crown (below). Valdemar had recently assumed full power, as his father, the *jarl* and regent Birger, had died earlier that year.

A division of what appears to have been patronage rights is known at *Næstved* on Zealand, Denmark. It was a Benedictine monks' monastery founded in 1135. That year, the local bishop confirms what the monastery has received from the founders Peder Bodilsen, his brothers and his mother. They had given the church in Næstved, which lay under their jurisdiction (*ius*), and land in Great Næstved and Little Næstved.[35] But in 1140, King Erik Lam gives the monks some incomes and states that Næstved church, through hereditary rights, lies under his protection (*hereditario iure sub mea tutela est*).[36] *Ius* and *tutela* are not synonyms, and it is possible that one implied ownership and the other patronage. However, patronage over a church could be split between different holders.[37] Apparently the lordship over the church had been divided earlier: Peder's mother Bodil was in some way related to the king.[38]

---

31 Schück (1959), pp. 278–279; DS 1316 & DS 1320.
32 DS 953.
33 Nyd. 35 = DS 452, no place of issue is given.
34 DS 524.
35 DD 1:2, no. 64.
36 DD 1:2, no. 78.
37 DS 557 (1272), concerning Kaga in Östergötland, Sweden; Rosén (1949), pp. 141–142.
38 Hermanson (2000), pp. 154–155.

Charters promising *protectionis, defensionis* and similar terms cannot however by themselves be taken as evidence of patronage. The Cistercian nunnery of *Sko* in Uppland, Sweden, is first mentioned in 1244 (below). Its founder was probably Knut Långe ('the tall'), a nobleman who was king 1230–1234, and it lay on his private land. In a charter issued in 1264, King Valdemar Birgersson and his father *jarl* Birger confirm two older charters concerning the nuns' right to some land, and they state that they take the nuns under their special protection and defence (*sub nostram protectionem specialiter suscepisse pariter et tutelam*).[39] However, they had no hereditary or royal claims here, as the monastery had been founded on another family's private property. In the 1260s there was a dispute concerning a will in which the monastery was to inherit the Sko estate (below). Most likely Valdemar's and Birger's special protection was a support during this conflict, not an expression of patronage.

Odense Cathedral chapter – the only clear Eigenkloster case in Scandinavia?

Odense Cathedral on Funen in Denmark had a chapter consisting of Benedictine monks.[40] It was originally founded in 1095 and became a Cathedral chapter in 1117. The Cathedral housed the remains of King Knut the Holy, killed here in 1086. The monastery was founded by Knut's brother, King Erik the Good, and later kings continued to support the monks and the cult.[41] In 1180, King Valdemar I issued a charter of protection in which he is said to hold *iure advocacie*.[42]

Hill points out that this term is lacking from royal charters of protection issued in 1174 and 1183, and he explains it as just another way to express protection.[43] In the light of the uncertainty let loose by Wood, this is a wise interpretation. However, there is no doubt that in most cases the expression had proprietary connotations, and it is unlikely that these connotations were not known in Denmark. In view of the material about to be treated below, it is worth noting that the oldest known papal charter of protection that mentions the estates belonging to the monastery was issued as late as 1226.[44] It begins with 'the site where the monastery lies'. It is quite possible that the site of the

---

39 DS 492.
40 Nyberg (2000), pp. 55–61.
41 Hill (1992), p. 105–125; Nyberg (2000), pp. 52–63
42 DD 1:3, no. 89.
43 Hill (1992), p. 119.
44 DD 1:6, no. 62.

monastery had originally been part of the royal manor of Odense.[45] There are no sources indicating how long before 1226 it was donated to the monastery. It cannot be ruled out that King Valdemar regarded Odense in the same way that his princely colleagues in the German areas looked upon their monasteries.

Monasteries on unfree ground

The starting point of the present investigation was a detail in a donors' list, discovered as late as in 1945, from *Vreta* nunnery in Östergötland, Sweden.[46] Vreta was probably Benedictine at the start but became Cistercian in the thirteenth century. The donors' list is a sixteenth century transcript in Swedish, done by the archivist and historian Rasmus Ludvigsson, of an original that can be dated to around 1170. The list has at least one erroneous genealogical statement inserted by Rasmus, marked by square brackets here, and the original was certainly in Latin, but the basic contents are reliable. In translation, the first half reads:

> King Inge of Sweden, [who was Queen Christine's (father), Saint King Erik of Sweden's wife,] with his Queen Helena first founded Vreta monastery, and gave to it these estates and farms, namely
>
> 4 attungs[47] of land in Little Vreta
> 2 attungs in Bro
> 9 attungs in Brunneby
> 4 attungs in Hucklum
> 2 attungs in Mällatorp
>
> King Magnus gave to it 6 attungs of land in Vreta, and for his brother Duke Ragvald's soul 3 attungs in Brunneby, and the same Duke Ragvald had given it for his brother Duke Johan's soul 3 attungs in Vadeby.
> (The list continues with later donations.)

The list has one mystifying feature which has not received any attention. The original donation, made by King Inge and Queen Helena around 1100, did not include Vreta itself. They gave some land in Little Vreta, which must have been a hamlet nearby, and in several other hamlets. But the monastery did not receive land in Vreta itself until King Magnus Henriksson, who reigned for a short pe-

---

45 Bøggild Johannsen & Johannsen (1995), p. 94.
46 Ahnlund (1945); Gillingstam (1948); Lovén (2010a).
47 An *attung*, 'an eighth', was the usual land evaluation unit in south east Sweden. An ordinary farm in the twelfth century consisted of one attung.

riod around 1160, gave six attungs here. Magnus was Inge's and Helena's son's daughter's son. According to this source, Vreta lay on unfree ground for six decades.

Had Vreta been an isolated case, it could be explained as a misinterpretation by Rasmus, but a closer scrutiny shows that a number of Swedish and Danish monasteries appear to have lain on unfree ground for years or decades after their foundation. Furthermore, in most cases it is clear that they had estates elsewhere, which means that the monastery site had not been withheld for economic reasons.

The source material is diverse and demands careful consideration. Donor lists are scarce. Charters where the monastery site was donated although the nuns or monks were already in place are more common. They are by themselves not reliable, as a donation could be repeated by the next king or by the heirs of the original founder.[48] The context of each such charter must be reviewed.

A third type of source is charters of protection, papal or episcopal. They often only refer to the holdings in a general way, but many enumerate the monastery's estates individually by name. In contemporary papal charters of protection for Continental monasteries, the holdings are listed according to type, to location or to donor.[49] In the Scandinavian material, enumerations according to location were common, but there are echoes of *Ex dono* enumerations. However, the lists always start with the monastery site. One example is a papal charter for Sorø (Denmark) issued in 1165.[50] The list begins with 'the place itself (*locum ipsum*) where the monastery is situated, with all its appurtenances (*adiacensiis et pertinentiis*) and the monastery itself (*claustrum ipsum*) with all its appurtenances'.

If a charter of protection that enumerates the estates does *not* include the monastery site, an explanation is required, but this problem has never been addressed. Probably the unconscious assumption has been that the core of the monastery was incontestable and did not have to be mentioned in the charters. But this explanation is in conflict with the fact that the monastery site is actually mentioned regularly in the detailed charters of protection. Furthermore, the few protection charters that lack the monastery site among the holdings are old – they are never preceded by charters including the monastery site among the holdings. The clearest case of this is Esrum, which will be treated in more depth below. A papal charter of protection was issued in 1151 and mentions several estates but not the monastery site. The monks probably received the site

---

48 Rosén (1949), pp. 28–29; cf. Esmark (2004).
49 Lohrmann (1982), pp. 74–88.
50 DD 1:3 no. 138.

in 1153, and there is a series of protection charters issued in 1158–1211 where Esrum or 'the place where the monastery is situated' is mentioned first.[51]

The charters of protection are not always as useful as at Esrum. In many cases, the monastery 'with its rightful possessions' is protected, but the estates are not mentioned by name. This formula does not show whether the monastery site had been handed over. The Sorø charter above begins by mentioning 'the place itself', followed by 'the monastery itself', making what appears as an unnecessary repetition. But as 'the monastery' could be mentioned in charters of protection when the monastery site was apparently still in other hands (cf. Eskilsø below), this is no repetition. The monastery and the site were different things. Finally there are a few protection charters in which only a few holdings are mentioned but not the monastery site, although earlier sources show that the monastery had much more land than this.[52] These must be assumed to have been issued to protect contested land, not the monastery as a whole.

We should differ between short and long periods on unfree ground, and between different reasons for the founders to keep the monastery site. In several cases, the founders held on to the land for only a few months or years before it was given to the monastery. This may be termed *delayed surrendering*. These delays should in fact be interpreted as a service to the newly arrived monks or nuns, because ownership of land meant responsibilities as well as an income.[53] When the new foundation had achieved stability, it could assume full control. Even in cases where the time lag between foundation and land transfer was several years, it is sometimes clear that the original plan was to hand over the land.

When the founders withheld ownership for decades, it was no longer a service to the monastery. The reason must have been to keep some form of lordship. In practice, the period on unfree ground sometimes lasted for only a few years, but if it is obvious that the founders only let go of the monastery site unwillingly, these cases are not equivalent to delayed surrenders.

A third possibility was for the founders to hold on to a part of the monastery site. If it was a manor, this meant that the monastery and the, for instance royal, manor coexisted and held different parts of the site. Such cohabitation of different power centres would not be surprising, as it was the rule in towns. There is at least one fairly clear case of split ownership. The nunnery of *Gudhem* in Västergötland, Sweden, is mentioned for the first time in a papal charter of protection issued in 1168–1177. The Pope confirms what the monastery had

---

51 DD 1:2 no. 126 (1158); DD 1:3 no. 76–77 (1178); no. 117 (1184); no. 160 (1189); DD 1:5 no. 5–6 (1211).
52 DD 1:5 no. 219 (Esrum 1223); DS 281 (Vårfruberga 1233).
53 Tollin (1999), pp. 59–61.

received in Gudhem from the king and his predecessors.[54] But in 1216, King Johan Sverkersson donated his possessions in Gudhem to the nuns.[55] This might be explained as a confirmation of the gifts of previous kings, a type of repeated transaction known from other cases.[56] However, nothing in the wording of the charter suggests this, and the gift was made in memory of the king's parents. A more plausible explanation is that the nuns received Gudhem in portions. Even after this gift there was a royal presence here: Gudhem was a royal administrative centre, mentioned both in the older (1240s) and later (1290s) provincial law.[57]

These cohabitations have not been scrutinised for this article, but they are worth considering. For instance, the Vreta donation around 1160 consisted of six attungs, but normally a hamlet had eight attungs.

Delayed surrender of the monastery grounds

Viby, a Cistercian house in Uppland, Sweden, was founded in 1160.[58] In 1164–67, the noblewoman Doter gave Viby 'to the monks that serve God there'.[59] The charter, issued by the entire local power elite including the king, states that Doter had been in conflict with her son Gere over this gift, and it was resolved by her giving Gere her patrimony in exchange for Viby, which she then gave to the monks. The reason for the conflict must have been that the monastery had been founded on her husband's land, and subsequently the husband had died. She had no right to Viby, as it was the children who inherited. The conflict may originally have been between her husband and Gere, opposing the diminishing of his inheritance. It is impossible to say whether her husband had given Viby to the monks and Gere had reclaimed it or whether the monks only came into possession through Doter's donation. This was at most a case of involuntary delay.

Some years later, the monastery moved to *Säby* (later known as *Julita*) in Södermanland at the initiative of King Knut Eriksson. In one document, the king, in exchange for Viby and other estates, gives Säby to 'the monks that had previously lived in Viby'.[60] They had obviously moved to Säby before they acquired ownership. Swedish twelfth century charters regularly lack a dating,

---

54 DS 72.
55 DS 161.
56 Rosén (1949), pp. 28–29.
57 Lundahl (1961), pp. 9–12 & 73.
58 ADM, pp. 83 & 145 under its later name Saba (Säby); a later annalist has 1159 (ASM, p. 276).
59 DS 51, *religiosis ibidem* (i.e. in Viby) *uiris deo seruentibus*.
60 DS 64 (1167–1185), *monachis qui prius morabantur in wiby*.

which makes it impossible to say for how long this unfree state lasted, but the exchange of land must have been planned all along.

Riseberga nunnery in Närke, Sweden, was founded by *jarl* (Earl) Birger Brosa sometime between the 1170s and 1202. Like Vreta, it probably began as Benedictine but later became Cistercian. In what was in the fifteenth century termed the monastery's 'principal charter', the jarl gives to the nuns (*sororibus*) eight attungs in Riseberga.[61] The wording implies that the nuns were already in place.[62] This was probably a case of delayed surrendering.

The Cistercian abbey of *Tvis* in northern Zealand, Denmark, was founded in 1162.[63] In a charter issued the following year, but only known from a late translation, Duke Buris Henriksen hands over the Tvis estate to 'the beloved brethren in Tvis'.[64]

The foundation of the Premonstratentian abbey of *Vä* in Skåne is known through three charters, the two oldest of which were probably issued in 1170.[65] They show how the founding involved the transfer of a complicated set of rights, held by a bishop from another see, by the archbishop and by the king and queen. What is important in the present context is that in one of the charters, the archbishop gives 'the church of Saint Mary with all its belongings' to the brethren at Saint Mary's. The monks were already in place.

Æbelholt on Sjælland, Denmark, was a Victorine canons' house that moved there from Eskilsø in 1175. After the move, the land was withheld for around four years (see Eskilsø and Æbelholt below).

These cases of delayed surrendering of the monastery plot are of little consequence in the discussion of lordship. Their importance lies in their showing that transfer of the monastery grounds was not automatic at the moment of foundation, and that even Cistercian monks were willing to settle at places they did not yet own.

Monasteries on unfree ground for an extended period

Vreta nunnery (above) lay on unfree ground from its foundation ca 1100 until around 1160, for six decades. This is the longest clearly discernible period in the source material, but there are indications of at least one that may have been even longer and several others persisting for decades.

---

61 DS 823.
62 Conradi Mattsson (1998), p. 213, observed this; cf. Ahnlund (1945), p. 307.
63 Green-Pedersen (1981), p. 48.
64 DD 1:2, no. 152.
65 Skyum-Nielsen (1951). On the dating see Nyberg (2007), pp. 379–382 & Lovén (2010b), pp. 17–18 with note 44.

Vårfruberga nunnery in Södermanland, Sweden, was founded around the middle of the twelfth century by an otherwise unknown *jarl* Siward and his daughter Ingeborg.[66] This was yet another case of probably Benedictine nuns turning Cistercian in the thirteenth century. A land register from 1257, known from a sixteenth century copy, mentions a large number of land acquisitions from the foundation onwards.[67]

It is clear from the land register and some charters that the original name of the monastery was *Sätuna*. The location of Sätuna is unknown, but must have been in the same parish as the later sites, because the earliest donations lay here.[68] Apparently, the monastery moved twice. The first move is implied in an episcopal charter of protection from 1233, which includes 'Saint Peter's church where [the nuns] now serve as [the Lord's] soldiers'.[69] This church is probably identical with Fogdö parish church which, according to a nineteenth century topographical work, was dedicated to Saint Peter.[70] That it functioned as a monastery church is shown by a charter issued in 1252, when the name 'Fogdö monastery' is used.[71] It has been suggested that Sätuna was the original name of the location where Fogdö parish church lies.[72] However, the use of the word 'now' (*nunc*) in 1233 indicates that a move had taken place. A second move, two kilometres to the north, was done around 1289, and after that the nunnery changed its name to Vårfruberga.[73]

The monastery apparently lay at Sätuna from the middle of the twelfth century until not long before 1233. The place name Sätuna was typical for an early manor and was therefore not a constructed monastery's name that might be forgotten, but it is not mentioned in the land register or in the charter of protection from 1233. Siward and his daughter gave other land, as did later donors. It should be stressed that the land register includes estates that the nuns had alienated before 1257.[74] Had the monastery received Sätuna, it ought to have been mentioned in the register.

This is the only instance where the sources imply that the monastery plot was never acquired. It is tempting to see the move from Sätuna as a reaction to the unwillingness of the heirs of the founders to part with the site.

---

66 An attempt at identifying Siward is made in Bengtsson & Lovén (2012), pp. 30–33.
67 Ossiannilsson (1945); Ståhle (1948).
68 A possible location is suggested by Calissendorf (1989), p. 6.
69 DS 281, *ecclesiam beati petri in qua nunc domino militatis*.
70 Indebetou 1877 p. 74.
71 DS 390.
72 Oral comment by Sigurd Rahmqvist.
73 Annell (1983), pp. 84–85.
74 Ossiannilsson (1945), pp. 84–85, notes 6, 8, 17 & 18.

Sko in Uppland, Sweden, was a Cistercian nunnery and the latest foundation treated in this article. Here, the sources concerning ownership are clearly contradictive. Sko is first mentioned in 1244, and according to the seventeenth century historian Johannes Messenius it was founded in 1225 by Knut Långe ('the tall'), who was king 1231–1234.[75] The word 'founded' is misleading in this case, for it is clear that the nuns at Sko had moved from *Byarum* in Småland, much further south in Sweden. The age of Byarum is unknown: it is first mentioned in 1208–1216, but there is an indication that it existed in the second half of the twelfth century. According to a sixteenth century chronicle, the nuns moved to Sko during an episcopacy that lasted 1232–1255.[76] This source is more reliable than Messenius.[77] Knut Långe died in 1234, making 1232–1234 the likely time for the establishing of the nunnery at Sko.

The monastery church at Sko is a sumptuous brick building that can stylistically be dated to the middle of the thirteenth century.[78] However, there are indications that it was not initially built for a monastery.[79] This fits well with observations made at the Romanesque church ruin at *Flastad*, one kilometre to the west. Several traits point to this being the original nunnery. In two charters, Flastad is mentioned as a part of the Sko estate (below). On the southern side of the church there is an enclosure that does not look like an ordinary church yard, and excavations have revealed traces of wooden buildings here.[80] According to Messenius, the nuns moved 'nearer to the water' after a fire in 1297, and Sko lies by the lake shore. However, the move to the brick church probably took place in 1275 at the latest.[81]

From a series of documents concerning a testament, it is clear that the nuns owned neither Flastad nor Sko in 1260, long after the foundation. That year, the nobleman Karl Ulfsson died, and Sko was among his possessions. He was in some unknown way related to the monastery's founder Knut Långe.[82] It is therefore possible that he had inherited the estate through some reversion, i.e. a parent inheriting from a dead child.[83] In 1269, Karl's relatives confirmed his

---

75 Hall (1909), p. 2.
76 Härenstam (1946), p. 221–226.
77 Norman (1940).
78 Tuulse (1967).
79 Pointed out by Gunnar Redelius in a lecture in 1998. Redelius has later changed his opinion, but the idea has great merit.
80 Fredricson-Hoberg (1969).
81 Hall (1909), pp. 2 & 9.
82 Gillingstam (1973); Rosén (1940), p. 76.
83 Another possibility is that the estate had been seized by the Crown when Knut Långe's sons rebelled and were killed in 1248 and 1251 – the seized property may have been

testament, and here it is stated that Karl had bequeathed *mansionem de sco* with all its appurtenances to the nuns.[84] One of the relatives objected, and two of the charters issued during the ensuing strife make it clear that *mansio* Flastad was part of the Sko domain.[85] Regardless of when the nuns moved from Flastad to Sko, they owned neither site until 1260.

These sources indicate that the nunnery lay on unfree ground for at least 16 and perhaps as long as 35 years. This result is contradicted by a papal charter of protection, issued in 1244. Here the nuns and the site where they serve God, with all its estates (*locum in quo diuino estis obsequio mancipate cum omnibus bonis*) are protected.[86] But the estates are not mentioned by name, and the documentation surrounding Karl's testament provides strong evidence for Sko not being owned by the nuns before 1260. Three alternative solutions to this conflict between the sources are possible. One is that the original founding family had in fact given the monastery site at the time of foundation but that it had been reclaimed in connection with Karl's inheriting Sko. Another is based on the fact that in 1244, the *locus* must have been Flastad. Could the move to Sko have taken place before 1260, entailing that the nuns gave up ownership of Flastad in return for getting to use a much more imposing church? Such a surrender of the site had a parallel at Saint Mikael's in Slesvig in the 1190s (below). The third alternative is to give in to the terminological uncertainties demonstrated by Wood and assume that the nuns had some kind of ownership in 1244 but Karl had another kind in 1260. The present author would prefer alternative number two, as it is in line with the rest of the material presented here and has a parallel.

The Benedictine monastery of *Veng* in Jylland, Denmark, is only known in connection with its reformation into a Cistercian house in 1165/1166. The Cistercian monks had earlier lived at *Sminge* for a short while. After three years at Veng they moved to *Kalvø* before finally settling at *Øm* in 1172. The early history is known from a chronicle from Øm, the earlier part of which was probably written in 1207.[87]

According to the chronicle, the transferral of Veng to the Cistercians was made by King Valdemar after he had consulted with some bishops. A cited papal charter states that Veng had been founded by Valdemar's predecessors.

---

given to Karl Ulfsson's father Ulf Fasi, who was *jarl* (earl) at the time. This is however contradicted by the presence of other relatives who were not children of Ulf Fasi in the following strife.
84 DS 538.
85 DS 563, 569, 598 & 624.
86 DS 315.
87 SMHD 2, pp. 158–264, especially pp. 158–176, with Gertz' comments pp. 154–157. Danish translation Øm klosters krönike (1968).

The architecture of the monastery church and the lack of any information on its foundation make it likely that Veng was founded already around 1100 or in the first quarter of the twelfth century.[88]

There are indications that the Benedictine monastery lay on unfree ground for its entire existence, and a royal charter, cited in the chronicle, states that it had tenants, making it a parallel to Vreta. The chronicle relates a contest over the Veng estate. When the Cistercians were about to move again, to Kalvø, they gave the king two thirds of Veng in exchange for other land. A noblewoman Margareta, the sister of the monastery's *fundator* Count Erik, had persecuted the Cistercians during their three years at Veng. After they moved to Kalvø, she wanted to found a nunnery at Veng and sought to acquire the land from the king. The monks were opposed to her plans and managed to get a promise from the king that they could exchange back the two thirds of Veng. But as Margareta was a relative, the king did not want to cause her sorrow while she was alive. Finally, we get a clarifying piece of information: after Margareta's death, the king would give the monks the third of Veng that she had promised him.

The text shows that the Veng estate was divided: two thirds had been given to the Cistercians, while Margareta held one third. With some certainty, her brother Count Erik had been the original owner of the two thirds. He is termed *fundator* in the chronicle, which could mean 'important donor' as well as 'original founder'. The numbers indicate an inheritance where a daughter's share was half of a son's share, although this principle did not become law until 1170/1171.[89] This implies that the Veng estate had been undivided until the death of some close relative of Margareta and Erik, plausibly their father or mother. The siblings were probably getting old in the 1160s: Erik was dead by 1168, and the king awaited Margareta's death before returning the estate to the monks. The parent who owned all of Veng had perhaps died in the 1130s or so, and it is possible that he or she had been the original founder. As both Erik and Margareta are unknown from other sources, this founder is anonymous.

It is unclear at what time Erik gave his share to the monks. It may have been soon after he inherited it, but it is more likely that the estate changed hands with the arrival of the Cistercians. This would mean that Veng, like Vreta, lay on unfree ground for perhaps six decades.

There was however another element in the Veng transformation that did not involve ownership. The chronicle says that it was King Valdemar who decided

---

88 Nyberg (2000), pp. 109–113.
89 Gelting (2005); cf. Christensen (1969), p. 405. Several scholars, for instance Green Pedersen (1964), p. 194 and Hill (1992), p. 293, offer a different and more complicated interpretation.

that the monastery should be transferred to the Cistercians and that it had been founded by his predecessors. This means that Veng was a royal foundation.[90] Valdemar held some kind of patronage. But this has to be reconciled with Count Erik and his sister Margareta owning the estate. That the chronicle states that Margareta was a relative of the king is perhaps of interest but provides no ready explanation. A plausible interpretation is that Veng was founded through a joint effort, like Nydala and Vä (both above). There is no reason to doubt the statement that it had been founded by the king's predecessors, but Margareta's and Erik's mother or father can be assumed to have taken part. This would explain why ownership of the Veng estate and some other kind of lordship were in different hands.

Esrum in northern Zealand, Denmark, was an important Cistercian house. Annals give 1153 as the foundation year. This is confirmed by a charter given by Archbishop Eskil in 1158 where he states that he had brought monks from Clairvaux to Esrum: Eskil returned from a journey to Burgundy in 1152–1153.[91]

What happened in 1153 was the transformation of an older, probably Benedictine, monastery. The Pope had already issued a charter of protection for Esrum in 1151.[92] That the monastery had a pre-history is also apparent in a papal protection charter issued in 1228, where it is stated that the monastery had received land before it became Cistercian.[93] This prehistory has sometimes been doubted.[94] There are however several parallels, and in more recent research it is accepted.[95]

The original monastery never owned Esrum itself. The papal protection charter of 1151 mentions four landholdings, but nothing is said of Esrum. In a charter issued in 1151–1157, King Svend Grate confirms Eskil's transfer of Esrum to the brethren. The king states that Esrum pertains to royal authority (*iuri*) 'through royal decession and accession' and that Eskil had received it from King Erik Lam (1137–1146) as a *precarium*. This word is well known from Continental sources. It means that Eskil held Esrum as a loan from King Erik Lam, who could reclaim it whenever he wanted to.[96] King Svend's statement makes sense: when the king who had given the *precarium* died, it automatically

---

90 Nyberg (2000), pp. 112–113.
91 McGuire (1973), p. 125, note 16.
92 DD 1:2, no. 106. Most charters concerning Esrum are known only from the monastery's fifteenth century register.
93 DD 1:6, no. 76.
94 Skyum-Nielsen (1971), p. 120; McGuire (1973), pp. 125 & 132–133.
95 McGuire (1997), pp. 22–23; Nyberg (2006), p. 18.
96 Numerous instances of *precaria* are treated in Rosenwein (1989).

reverted to the Crown.⁹⁷ The charter goes on to state that King Svend confirms the transfer although the royal Majesty (*regalis majestatis*) hardly could tolerate such a donation, no matter that the forms had been lawful. The meaning of this is clear. Archbishop Eskil held Esrum as a *precarium*, a weak form of possession, from King Erik Lam. Disregarding the legal limitation, Eskil gave Esrum to the monks. This apparently happened in connection with the arrival of the Cistercians in 1153, as Esrum itself is not mentioned in the papal charter of 1151. Upon hearing of the unlawful donation, King Svend grudgingly gave his consent. In a charter of protection issued in 1158, Eskil claims that he had received Esrum from King Erik in exchange for inherited land, but this must be regarded as a rationalisation.⁹⁸

Eskil was the original founder of Esrum: the estates mentioned in 1151 are said to be his gifts. He was bishop of Roskilde, the see in which Esrum lay, in 1134–1137. It is likely that planning for the monastery was undertaken at this time, and he probably received the necessary *precarium* early in the time span 1137–1146. Esrum lay on unfree ground for about 15 years, its whole Benedictine existence.

Finally two Danish monasteries will be treated where, as at Vårfruberga, the sources are less clear.

Eskilsø on Zealand, Denmark, was a house of Victorine canons. It was probably founded by a bishop of Roskilde and may have existed in the 1130s, as the Roskilde Bishop Asser (1139–1158) took his vows here according to Lund Cathedral's memorial book. But the bishop may have become a member late in life, and it is only safe to assume that Eskilsø existed in 1158 at the latest.⁹⁹ Under its great Abbot Vilhelm, the monastery moved to Æbelholt around 1175.

There are two drafts, written by Vilhelm, for episcopal charters of protection for the monastery. They are problematic, because it is unknown whether they were ever issued, but as they were drafted by the abbot, they surely do not understate the land possessions. In a draft from 1171, the monastery church and the island (Eskilsø means Eskil's Island) on which it lies are taken into protection, but in the actual list of land holdings, Eskilsø is not mentioned.¹⁰⁰ In another draft from 1178, after the move to Æbelholt, the words are put into

---

97 Fenger (2000), pp. 264–265, claims that Esrum was King Svend's private property, inherited from King Erik. It is however unexplained how he could have inherited it from his cousin, and the phrase *regum decessione et successione* is centered on the royal office.
98 DD 1:2, no. 126.
99 Nyberg (2000), pp. 164–165.
100 DD 1:3, no. 20 with note 1.

Bishop Absalon's mouth that 'we have decided' that the island Eskilsø belongs to the monastery.[101] Absalon was bishop in Roskilde from 1158. In 1177 he became archbishop, but he kept the Roskilde bishopric. The decision that Eskilsø belonged to the Victorines was taken some time between 1158 and 1178, and in view of the content of the 1171 draft, a date nearer to 1178 is more likely. The wording in the 1178 draft implies that the ownership was contested and that the Bishop had passed judgement. But the background was hardly an inheritance struggle, because such a lawsuit would not have been handled by a bishop. It is more likely that the land had belonged to the bishops and cathedral of Roskilde.

Eskilsø apparently lay on unfree ground for twenty years or more. If Bishop Asser was a monk here before he assumed office in 1139, the unfree period lasted for at least four decades.

The move to Æbelholt was made in 1175, but the canons did not become owners of the new site immediately. The draft from 1178 does not include Æbelholt in the list of holdings. A draft for a papal charter of protection from the same year maintains this silence.[102] A real papal charter of protection, issued in 1180–1181, mentions Æbelholt first among the estates, as do a number of later charters.[103] This was probably a case of delayed surrendering, although the fact that the monastery was an old establishment at this time makes it unclear why the canons should not have been able to assume full responsibility from the start.

Bosjö in Skåne, in medieval Denmark, was a Benedictine nunnery. Its foundation can be glimpsed through a papal charter of protection issued in 1182. The text is only known from partial transcripts but can be reconstructed.[104] The Pope confirms the possession of the entire island where the monastery lies, some estates and mills 'and all the estates that Thord, the founder of your monastery, owned, and half the fishery in Ringsjön lake for as long as Thord might live (*uixerit*), and all of it after his death'.

That Thord is called *fundator* might mean that he was a secondary benefactor, someone who had donated land to an already existing monastery, but as he is the only person mentioned in the charter, he in all probability was the original founder. As usual in a charter of protection, the monastery site is mentioned first among the estates. But nothing indicates that this site, i.e. the island, was included in Thord's donation. What he had given lay elsewhere. He had given half

---

101 DD 1:3, no. 78.
102 DD 1:3, no. 78–79.
103 DD 1:3, no. 95, no. 203; DD 1:5 no. 138; DD 1:7 no. 75.
104 DD 1:3, no. 101.

the fishery for as long as he lived, which has been taken as proof that he was still alive when the papal charter was written.[105] It is more likely that the wording was taken from his original foundation charter.[106] Thord has been identified as a *praefectus* in Lund in the 1170s or, more plausibly, as a *conversus* (lay brother) at Bosjö whose son died in 1160–1200.[107] Tore Nyberg has pointed out that no members of the Bosjö community are mentioned in the Lund necrology, which went out of use around 1170, but a number of them are mentioned in the new obituary book *Liber daticus Lundensis*, begun in 1146. The earliest entries concerning deceased at Bosjö have been paleographically dated to 1160–1200.[108] This would mean that the nunnery was founded in the 1150s at the earliest.

To summarise, Bosjö was probably founded in the 1160s and received estates in the neighbourhood. The monastery site itself was donated, presumably by the heirs, after the founder had died. Bosjö lay on unfree ground for a maximum of two decades. That the monastery estate was not given by the founder shows that this was not a case of delayed surrendering.

If the identification of the founder Thord with a lay brother is correct, it is of great interest. In a similar situation in for instance Germany, the founder would have assumed the much more elevated position of *advocatus*.

Non-monastic parallels

Outside the monastic world, there are some Scandinavian parallels. All eight *fylkeskirker*, district churches, of Trøndelag in Norway apparently lay on unfree ground on royal manors. They had incomes from other estates. This unfree state lasted throughout the Middle Ages.[109] In Iceland, only 52 out of 87 *maldagi*, deeds listing a church's endowments, issued before 1300 include the farm where the church was built.[110]

Saint Mary's church in the town Östra Aros (present day Uppsala) in Uppland, Sweden, was probably founded in the 1150s, but in 1231 the king gave the church the plot where it lay.[111] That it had lain on unfree ground until then is confirmed by a papal charter of protection, issued in 1221, where a number of estates are named, none of them situated in Östra Aros.[112] Like the *fylke*

---

105 Clemensson (1956), pp. 103–105.
106 Cf. DS 214 (1222) & DS 455 (1259).
107 Hermansson (2000), p. 239; Nyberg (2000), p. 207.
108 Nyberg (2000), p. 207.
109 Sandnes (1969).
110 Skovgaard-Petersen (1960), p. 247.
111 DS 259; Carlsson & Lovén in print.
112 Westman (1914), no. 1.

churches of Norway, this was no ordinary parish church. It was one of three deanery churches in Uppland, had no parishioners, but instead received an income of one penny from every farmer in the deanery.[113]

Among ordinary parish churches, this kind of lordship may have been common. There are however few early sources. A list of the holdings of Vallentuna parish church in Uppland, Sweden, was compiled in 1200, and it mentions no land in the village (or manor) of Vallentuna. Another list was written a century later, and now all of Vallentuna had become a very large vicarage.[114] A search through Danish material would probably provide more examples. The number of confirmed cases would rise if one sees ownership of the church plot as the legal base when parish churches are treated as property.[115]

The importance of owning the monastery grounds

According to early Canon law, ownership of the church plot gave the right of patronage. Around 1190, instead the donation of the piece of land where the church stood was considered a basis for patronage rights.[116] This elegant adjustment shows how seriously the canonists took the question of ownership, and of course the concept "patronage" was itself a modification of the older forms of lordship.

In a general sense, the ownership aspect is confirmed in the Norwegian pamphlet 'A speech against the bishops', written around 1200 and arguing the case of King Sverre against the emancipation of the Church. A passage from Canon Law is cited where the abbot is to be elected by the monks and 'the Lord of the estate' (*possessionis dominus*). The regulation is then translated into Norwegian as 'the abbot is to be appointed with the approval of the Lord of the estate on which the monastery is built'.[117] The translation emphasises the importance of who owned the monastery grounds.

So far, the cases where monasteries lay on land they did not own have been identified through donors' lists, late land transferrals and letters of protection. This is an inert source material, as it is never actually stated that ownership was important. And in the Vreta donor's list, the gift of Vreta itself is not highlighted. But in one account of monastic strife, the importance of ownership is clearly

---

113 Lovén (2009).
114 Ferm (1991), pp. 392–395; oral comment by Sigurd Rahmqvist.
115 Several Danish cases are identified by Ebbe Nyborg (1974), Appendix A.
116 Landau (1975), pp. 9 & 17–19.
117 Gunnes (1971), p. 213, "lafwardr er ifuir eighn þeire er sa stadr er vp gor af"; Landau (1975), p. 186.

expressed. It concerns Saint Mikael's in Slesvig, which has already been treated as one of the two cases where monastery patronage is explicitly expressed.

In the contemporary judgements that were passed concerning the takeover of Saint Mikael's by the newly founded Cistercians at Guldholm, the patronage rights over Saint Mikael's were central. But in a narrative written in 1289, another aspect is in focus. The author was a monk at Ryd, where Guldholm had moved at that time, who claimed that it was based on old documents and writings.[118] He does not mention the patronage rights. Instead, the Benedictines 'surrendered the site into the hands of the bishop' (*resignauerunt locum in manum episcopi*). As Hill has pointed out, this was a gift act.[119] It should be emphasised that this happened well before the monastery was abandoned. What was given was the monastery plot itself, the *locus*, and to the author of the narrative it meant the control of the monastery. The lordship based on ownership belonged to the Benedictine monks themselves, while the patronage belonged to Duke Valdemar. This matches our picture of parish church patronage, but the active divesting of the land makes Saint Mikael's unique.

A division of rights can also be glimpsed at Næstved in 1135–1140 and at Veng in the 1160s, and in the Sorø charter of protection issued in 1165, a similar division is implied. Ownership of the site was one form of lordship, patronage another.[120]

The lack of context

The conclusion that the monasteries on unfree ground were part of the *Eigenkloster* customs is inevitable. But there are a number of important questions that have not been treated in this article.

Considering the extreme variations pointed out by Susan Wood, it seems unlikely that monasteries on unfree ground existed solely in Scandinavia. In the literature consulted, no Continental or British cases have surfaced where the author states that a monastery had ownership of estates elsewhere but not of the monastery site itself. Likewise, a search through a number of German monastery cartularies has been fruitless: in every case, the monastery site was included in the original foundation. However, one English parallel has emerged. Waltham (Essex) was founded around 1060 as a college of secular canons, i.e. not a monastery proper although the charters use that word, and was transformed into a house of Augustinian regular canons in 1177. From a late twelfth

---

118 SMD 2, pp. 146–151.
119 Hill (1992), p. 169.
120 Cf. Bolvig (1977) for an interesting parallel.

century narrative and a number of charters, it is apparent that Waltham was not owned by the canons even in the middle of the twelfth century. The church had received a number of estates in the early eleventh century and at the college's foundation, but Waltham itself is not mentioned among them. Instead, Waltham along with 'the service of the canons and their men' was transferred between members of the royal family several times in the first half of the twelfth century.[121] A wide scrutiny of monasteric charters would probably reveal that the practice existed in other areas but that it was overshadowed by more prominent expressions of lordship.

Another fallacy is that only a few of these unfree monasteries can be found in Hill's list of Danish monasteries providing services for their founders. The reason for this could be twofold. The sources are fragmentary and, for instance, estates mentioned in charters of protection may have been given with counter-claims. More interesting as a topic of discussion is that there was a difference between having the right of lordship and actually using this right.

A third problem is that "ownership" was a far from clear cut concept in the Middle Ages.[122] Wood stresses that this was a world "where loans may be permanent and gifts temporary, one shading into the other; and where more than one *dominium* or different degrees of *potestas* can coexist in the same thing".[123] But something did change hands in the estate transferral charters, something important enough to be mirrored in charters of protection. It would therefore be going too far to deny the importance of ownership as expressed in charters, but in every case there may have been shadings that we now have difficulty discerning.

Tentative conclusions

Given the reservations on the lack of context, the material shows that Scandinavia was not untouched by the European *Eigenkloster* practices. However, there were differences. One single *advocatus* and no known lay abbots in the period treated here sets Scandinavia apart. Instead, there was what appears as a set custom: the founder gave land but at the same time withheld the monastery site itself. Clear cases are Vreta, Veng and Esrum, probable cases Vårfruberga, Sko, Eskilsø and Bosjö. In some cases where it is apparent that the monastery lay on unfree ground, we have no information on its owning estates elsewhere. But the

---

121 The Foundation of Waltham Abbey, pp. XX–XXIV, pp. 11–12 with note 31, pp. 15–17, pp. 46–53.
122 For Denmark see Fenger, Knudsen & Reinholdt (1982) and Schalling (1936).
123 Wood (2006), p. 754.

probable explanation in these cases is a lack of sources: there are no indications of monasteries totally lacking land holdings.

It seems reasonable to interpret this Scandinavian system as a more primitive form of lordship than the Continental practice of reserving a governing position in the monastery for oneself and one's heirs.

It should be pointed out that there were monasteries that were free from lay authority right from the start, in Scandinavia as well as on the Continent.[124] Vä (above) is one case. Skyum-Nielsen noted the prominence of the word *libertas* in the Vä foundation documents of 1170. He considered whether this had bearing on the *Eigenkloster* question, but leaning heavily on Koch's finding that there was no such thing in Denmark, Skyum-Nielsen dismissed the idea.[125] In view of the present material, this conclusion must be reconsidered. The Vä documents made the new monastery freeholding, while a number of monasteries were not, motivating the word *libertas*.[126]

Another conclusion is that ownership and patronage could be treated as different rights and be in separate hands. This is in line with our general picture of parish church patronage, where we always assume that the church owned the plot where it lay. But at Saint Mikael's and perhaps at Sko/Flastad, ownership of the site was yielded by the monastery. At Veng, both rights were apparently in different lay hands.

That Scandinavia imported *Eigenkirchen* customs along with the rest of the church and monastery concepts is hardly surprising. However, it is interesting if a monastery lordship model was applied that differed from those common on the Continent.

Where the sources allow us to see when the unfree period ended, it mostly happened in the second half of the twelfth century. At Vårfruberga it appears to have lasted well into the thirteenth century, when the nuns moved away, and Sko shows that the system could be freshly implemented in the thirteenth century. In the theme of this conference volume, the long thirteenth century stretching back into the twelfth, a conclusion would be that during this period the monasteries achieved a basic freedom from lay influence.

---

124 Wood (2006), pp. 834–850.
125 Skyum-Nielsen (1951), p. 13.
126 Cf. Wood (2006), p. 839.

Literature

Sources

ADM = *Annales Danici medii ævi*, ed. Ellen Jørgensen, Selskabet for udgivelse af kilder til dansk historie (København, 1920).

ASM = *Annales Suecici medii aevi: Svensk medeltidsannalistik*, ed. & comm. Göte Paulsson, Bibliotheca historica Lundensis 32 (Lund, 1974).

DD = *Diplomatarium Danicum* 1:1–, Det danske sprog- og litteraturselskab (København, 1938–).

DRB = *Danmarks riges breve* 1:1–, Det danske sprog- og litteraturselskab (København, 1938–).

DS = *Diplomatarium Suecanum*, ed. Johan Gustaf Liljegren, Bror Emil Hildebrand et al. (Stockholm, 1829–). [All DS-documents can be accessed at http://sok.riksarkivet.se/sdhk]

The Foundation of Waltham Abbey, ed. & comm. William Stubbs (Oxford & London, 1861).

Nyd. = *Diplomata Novevallensia: The Nydala charters 1172–1280*, ed. & transl. Claes Gejrot, Acta Universitatis Stockholmiensis, Studia Latina Stockholmiensia 37 (Stockholm, 1994).

Ossiannilsson [Dovring], Folke, *Fogdö (Vårfruberga) klosters jordebok*, Vetenskapssocieteten i Lund, Årsbok 1945 (Lund, 1945).

SMD = *Scriptores Minores Historiae Danicae Medii Aevi* 2, ed. Martin Clarentius Gertz (København, 1918–1922).

Westman, Knut B., 'De äldsta kända påvebrefven för Östra Aros', *Kyrkohistorisk årsskrift* 13 (1914), pp. 468–471.

Øm klosters krønike, transl. Jørgen Olrik (Århus, 1968).

Studies

Ahnlund, Nils, 'Vreta klosters äldsta donatorer', *[Svensk] Historisk Tidskrift* 2:8 (1945), pp. 301–351.

Annell, Gunnar, 'Bidrag till Vårfruberga klosters äldsta historia', *Kyrkohistorisk årsskrift* 83 (1983), pp. 78–90.

Bengtsson, Herman & Christian Lovén, 'Spår av den längre Erikslegenden', *Fornvännen* 107 (2012), pp. 24–40.

Bolvig, Axel, 'Stridighederne omkring Brede kirke 1250–1350', *[Dansk] Historisk Tidsskrift* 13:4 (1977), pp. 85–95.

Burton, Janet, *The Monastic Order in Yorkshire, 1069–1215* (Cambridge, 1999).

Bøggild Johannsen, Birgitte & Hugo Johannsen, *Danmarks kirker: Odense amt, 1 h. 2–4* (København, 1995).

Calissendorff, Karin, 'Ortnamn på Fogdölandet', *Årsskrift för Fogdöns hembygdsförening* [2] (1989), pp. 4–11.

Carlsson, Ronnie & Christian Lovén, 'En ombildning, två flyttningar och en problemlösande nygrundning. Uppsalas sockenkyrkor under medeltiden', in print in *forthcoming*.

Christensen, Carl Andreas, 'Falsterlistens tal og talforhold samt deres tolkning', *[Dansk] Historisk Tidsskrift* 12:4 (1969), pp. 401–421.

Clemensson, Gustav, 'Bosjö klosters historia', in *Archivistica et mediævistica: Ernesto Nygren oblata*, ed. Ingvar Andersson, Sven Tunberg, Sten Engström & Jan Liedgren (Stockholm, 1956), pp. 102–113.

Conradi Mattsson, Agneta, *Riseberga kloster – förutsättningar och framväxt*, Vetenskapliga skrifter utgivna av Örebro läns museum 2 (Örebro, 1998).

Dahlerup, Troels, 'Patronatsrätt, Danmark', in *Kulturhistoriskt lexikon för nordisk medeltid* 13 (Malmö et al., 1968), cols. 138–139.

Dictionary of Medieval Latin from British sources, ed. Ronald Edward Latham & David R. Howlett 1– (London, 1975–).

Esmark, Kim, 'Godsgaver, *calumniae* og retsantropologi', in *Ett annat 1100-tal*, red. Peter Carelli, Lars Hermanson & Hanne Sanders (Lund, Göteborg & Stockholm, 2004), pp. 143–180.

Fenger, Ole, Bodil Møller Knudsen & Helle Reinholdt, *"I være have": Om ret til hus og jord i middelalderbyen* (Århus, 1982).

Fenger, Ole, 'Kongelev og krongods' *[Dansk] Historisk Tidsskrift* 100 (2000), pp. 257–284.

Ferm, Olle, 'De uppländska sockenkyrkornas jordinnehav', in *Kyrka och socken i medeltidens Sverige*, ed. Olle Ferm, Studier till Det medeltida Sverige 5 (Stockholm, 1991), pp. 379–400.

Fredricson-Hoberg, Birgitta, *Rapport: Beskrivning över fynd och byggnadsarkeologiska förhållanden vid Flasta mur* (unpublished report in Antikvarisk-Topografiska Arkivet, Riksantikvarieämbetet, Stockholm, 1969).

Gardell, Sölve, *Gravmonument från Sveriges medeltid*, 1, Text (Göteborg, 1937).

Gelting, Michael, 'Pope Alexander III and Danish Laws of Inheritance', in *How Nordic are the Nordic medieval laws?*, ed. Ditlev Tamm & Helle Vogt, (Medieval Legal History 1) (København, 2005), pp. 86–115.

Gillingstam, Hans, 'Ett nytt bidrag till kunskapen om Vreta klosters äldsta historia', *[Svensk] Historisk Tidskrift* 2:11 (1948), pp. 26–29.

Gillingstam, Hans, 'Holmger Knutsson', *Svenskt biografiskt lexikon* 19 (Stockholm, 1971–1973), pp. 251–252.

Glossarium mediæ et infimæ Latinitatis, ed. Charles du Fresne, sieur du Cange, new ed. Léopold Favre, G. A. Louis Henschel & Johann Christoph Adelung, 1–10 (Niort, 1883–1887).

Green-Pedersen, Svend E., 'Øm klosters grundlæggelse og dets forhold til bisp Sven af Århus', *Århus stifts årbøger* 57 (1964), pp.173–246.

Green-Pedersen, Svend E., 'De danske cistersienserklostres grundlæggelse og den politiske maktkamp i det 12. årh.', in *Middelalder, metode og medier: Festskrift til Niels Skyum-Nielsen* (København, 1981), pp. 41–65.

Gunnes, Erik, *Kongens ære. Kongemakt og kirke i 'En tale mot biskoperne'* (Oslo, 1971).

Hall, Frithiof, 'Skokloster', *Fornvännen* 4 (1909), pp. 1–38.

Hermanson, Lars, *Släkt, vänner och makt* (Göteborg, 2000).

Hill, Thomas, *Könige, Fürsten und Klöster: Studien zu den dänischen Klostergründungen des 12. Jahrhunderts*, Kieler Werkstücke, Reihe A 4 (Frankfurt am Main et al., 1992).

Härenstam, Curt, *Finnveden under medeltiden* (Lund, 1946).

Indebetou, Harald Otto, *Södermanlands minnen från äldsta till närvarande tider* 1 (Stockholm, 1877).

Johnsen, Arne Odd, 'Kongen og de patronatsrettslige bestemmelser av 1153', *Norsk teologisk tidsskrift* 52:1 (1951), pp. 1–37.

Johnsen, Arne Odd, *Om pave Eugenius III's vernebrev for Munkeliv kloster av 7. januar 1146*, Avhandlinger utgitt av Det Norske Videnskaps-Akademi i Oslo, 2, Hist.-Filos. Klasse, Ny Serie 7 (Oslo, 1965).

Koch, Hal, 'De ældste danske klostres stilling i kirke og samfund indtil 1221', *[Dansk] Historisk Tidsskrift* 10:3 (1936a), pp. 511–582.

Koch, Hal, *Danmarks kirke i den begyndende højmiddelalder* 1–2 (København, 1936b)

Könighaus, Waldemar P., *Die Zisterzienserabtei Leubus in Schlesien von ihrer Gründung bis zum Ende der 15. Jahrhunderts* (Wiesbaden, 2004).

Lagerqvist, Lars O., *Sveriges regenter från forntid till nutid*, 2nd ed., (Stockholm, 1996).

Landau, Peter, *Jus patronatus. Studien zur Entwicklung des Patronats im Dekretalenrecht und der Kanonistik des 12. und 13. Jahrhunderts* (Köln, 1975).

Landau, Peter, 'Eigenkirchenwesen', in *Theologische Realenzyklopädie* 9 (Berlin & New York, 1982), pp. 399–404.

Lovén, Christian, 'Upplands tidiga prosterier – argument i en kunglig prestigekamp', *Hikuin* 36 (2009), pp. 71–84.

Lovén, Christian, 'Vreta år 1162, donatorslängden och årboken', in *Fokus Vreta kloster*, ed. Göran Tagesson, Elisabet Regner, Birgitta Alinder & Lars Ladell (Stockholm, 2010a), pp. 199–218.

Lovén, Christian, 'Biskopssätets historiska bakgrund', in *Uppsala domkyrka 2: Domkyrkan i Gamla Uppsala: Nuvarande domkyrkans omgivningar*, Sveriges kyrkor 228 (Uppsala, 2010b), pp. 11–23.

Lundahl, Ivar, *Det medeltida Västergötland*, Nomina Germanica: Arkiv för germansk namnforskning 12, (Uppsala/København, 1961).

Lundén, Tryggve, *Sveriges missionärer, helgon och kyrkogrundare* (Storuman, 1983).

McGuire, Brian Patrick, 'Property and Politics at Esrum Abbey: 1151–1251', *Mediaeval Scandinavia* 6 (Odense, 1973), pp. 122–150.

McGuire, Brian Patrick, *The Cistercians in Denmark: Their Attitudes, Roles, and Functions in Medieval Society* (Kalamazoo, 1982).

McGuire, Brian Patrick, 'Esrum kloster – forhistorien og grundlæggelsen', in *Bogen om Esrum Kloster*, Årbog for Frederiksborg Amts Historiske Samfund, 1996–1997 (Frederiksborg, 1997), pp. 13–29.

Norman, Hugo, 'Rimkrönikan om Linköpings biskopar', *Kyrkohistorisk årsskrift* 40 (1940), pp. 128–174.

Nyberg, Tore, *Monasticism in North-Western Europe, 800–1200* (Aldershot et al., 2000).

Nyberg, Tore, 'De benediktinske klostergrundlæggelser i Norden', in *Tidlige klostre i Norden før 1200*, ed. Lars Bisgaard & Tore Nyberg (Odense, 2006), pp. 13–30.

Nyberg, Tore, 'Kong Niels. Skitse til en biografi', *[Dansk] Historisk Tidsskrift* 107 (2007), pp. 353–388.

Nyborg, Ebbe, *Egenkirke, patronatsret og inkorporation* (unpublished thesis, University of Århus, 1974).

Olsen, Olaf, *Hørg, hov og kirke* (København, 1966).

Plöchl, Willibald M., *Geschichte des Kirchenrechts* 1 (Wien & München, 1953).

Rathgen, Georg, 'Untersuchungen über die eigenkirchlichen Elemente der Kloster- und Stiftsvogtei vornemlich nach thüringischen Urkunden bis zum Beginn des XIII. Jahrhunderts', *Zeitschrift der Savigny-Stiftung für Rechtsgeschichte, Kanonische Abteilung* 17 (1928), pp. 1–152.

Rosén, Jerker, 'De sekulära domkapitlens tillkomst', *Svensk teologisk kvartalsskrift* 16 (1940), pp. 60–81
Rosén, Jerker, *Kronoavsöndringar under äldre medeltid* (Lund, 1949).
Rosenwein, Barbara, *To Be the Neighbor of Saint Peter: The Social Meaning of Cluny's Property, 909-1049* (Ithaca, 1989).
Sandnes, Jørn, 'Fylkeskirkerne i Trøndelag i middelalderen', *Årbok for Trøndelag* 3 (1969), pp. 116–136.
Schalling, Erik, *Kyrkogodset i Skåne, Halland och Blekinge under dansk tid*, Statens offentliga utredningar 1936:28, Ecklesiastikdepartementet (Stockholm, 1936).
Schück, Herman, *Ecclesia Lincopensis: Studier om Linköpingskyrkan under medeltiden och Gustav Vasa*, Acta universitatis Stockholmensis / Stockholm Studies in History 4 (Stockholm, 1959).
Skovgaard-Petersen, Inge, 'Islandsk egenkirkevæsen', *Skandia* 26 (1960), pp. 230–296.
Skyum-Nielsen, Niels, 'De ældste privilegier for klostret i Væ', *Scandia* 17 (1951), pp. 1–27.
Skyum-Nielsen, Niels, *Kvinde og slave*, Danmarkshistorien uden retouche 3 (København, 1971).
Smedberg, Gunnar, *Nordens första kyrkor*, Bibliotheca theologiae practicae 32 (Uppsala, 1973).
Stutz, Ulrich, *Die Eigenkirche als Element des mittelalterlich-germanischen Kirchenrechtes* (Berlin, 1895).
Stutz, Ulrich, 'Eigenkirche, Eigenkloster', *Realenzyklopedie für protestantische Theologie und Kirche*, 3rd ed., 23 (Leipzig, 1913), pp. 364–377.
Ståhle, Carl Ivar, 'Om vår äldsta jordebok (Vårfruberga klosters godsförteckning)', *Namn och bygd* 36 (1948), pp. 81–140.
Tollin, Clas, 'Nydala klosters grundläggning och jordegendomar under äldre tid', in *Nydala kloster: Andligt centrum och maktfaktor i det medeltida Småland*, ed. Lars Aldén, Växjö stiftshistoriska sällskap, Meddelande 20 (Växjö, 1998).
Tollin, Clas, *Rågångar, gränshallar och ägoområden. Rekonstruktion av fastighetsstruktur och bebyggelseutveckling i mellersta Småland under äldre medeltid*, Meddelande 101, Kulturgeografiska institutionen, Stockholms universitet (Stockholm, 1999).
Tunberg, Sven, 'Folkungarna', *Svensk tidskrift* 38 (1951), pp. 203–212.
Tuulse, Armin, *Skoklosters kyrka*, Upplands kyrkor 125 (Uppsala, 1967).
Wood, Susan, *The Proprietary Church in the Medieval West* (Oxford, 2006).

Monastic locations cited in the article.

Male Monastic Recruitment among the Cistercians in Medieval Sweden, c. 1143–1450

Catharina Andersson

The *Ordo Cisterciensis* was the first monastic order to establish itself in medieval Sweden. The monasteries were affiliated with Clairvaux, and the first monks were sent to this faraway northern region by Clairvaux' well-known Abbot Bernard in the mid-twelfth century. In 1143, Alvastra and Nydala abbeys were established, and thereafter a number of monasteries were founded in rapid succession. In the middle of the thirteenth century, a total of twelve Cistercian monasteries and female convents were established by or had converted to the Cistercians.[1]

During the twelfth century, the abbots and monks were primarily of French origin, but also of German and English descent. After this period of settlement, the abbots normally seem to have been native Scandinavians, and it has been suggested that they generally were recruited from the region where the monastery was located.[2] The abbots active in each Swedish Cistercian monastery have earlier been listed by Edvard Ortved, and more recently by James France.[3]

Apart from this general assumption about the Cistercian abbots, as well as the origin of the pioneer monks who can be linked to the earliest time of the order in Scandinavia, monastic recruitment has not, at a general level, been very much discussed in a Swedish context. No fundamental investigation of the origin of the monks has been carried out, and the social background of the monks who inhabited the monasteries has not been the subject of exhaustive study. Still, as elsewhere in Europe, studies on monastic conditions, for instance the recruitment process and the genealogical background of the monks, can achieve a more thorough understanding not only of the monastic orders, but also of the surrounding society.

---

1 For a brief summary of the foundations of the Swedish Cistercian monasteries, see Berntsson (2003); Andersson (2006).
2 France (1992), pp. 117–119.
3 Ortved (1933), France (1992).

The present article focuses on male Cistercian recruitment in Sweden between the years 1143–1450. The aim is to identify the social background of the monks, and to analyze the results in relation to ambient social, economic and cultural structures. These prerequisites might also help us to understand why certain men, at different periods in life, chose to enter a monastery. Thus, the aim of this contribution is to improve our understanding of monastic culture as well as its relations to society. However, as a result of the scarsity of sources, a reliable investigation of the social background of the monks is not conducted without difficulty. Separate individuals are rarely mentioned in the charters, and if they occur, the only information normally provided is the name of the monk – at least his first name – and his position in the monastery, but usually there is no further information on his family background. Therefore, the sources do not allow establishing social stratifications or statistics, and general questions such as "from which social groups were the monks generally recruited?" are more difficult to answer. This paucity of reliable source information explains, at least partly, why the issue has not previously been given much attention in investigations of Swedish monasticism.[4]

King's head, probably the head of Christ. Detail from the northern portal to the nave in Roma Church, Gotland.

---

4   When the Swedish Cistercians have previously been studied within the historical field, most attention has been paid to their agrarian activities and holdings of land; see for example Stensland (1945); Winroth (1987); Holmström (1990). Different families and persons have also been connected to certain monasteries in a political context; see for example Nyberg (2000). The tradition of *gift-giving*, especially the tradition to give daughters as gifts to the female convents, has been analysed in Andersson (2006).

Nevertheless, some personal information can occasionally be gained from the Swedish charters. Even though social stratifications or statistical analyses are not possible, the sparse information available on some monks can still be used as a point of departure in improving our understanding of the social structures of monasticism, and for comparisons with other European regions. The sources also allow us to put forward hypotheses regarding social recruitment in the Swedish monasteries, hypotheses that might be evaluated in a wider social context and discussed from economic, social and/or ideological perspectives.

The empirical basis for the analysis consists primarily of preserved charters connected to the Cistercian monasteries in medieval Sweden up to and including the year 1450, recorded in the database *Svenskt Diplomatariums huvudkartotek* (SDHK) at the Swedish National Archives (Riksarkivet, RA).[5] Two groups of entrants will be given special attention. First, *children*, i.e. either *child oblates* who were given to the monastery with the intention that they would live their entire lives in the monastery, or, children who, for various reasons, were put in the monastery for only a limited period. Second, *adult entrants*, i.e. choir monks who left the secular world and took the monastic vow as grown-up men. Certainly, the monasteries were also inhabited by other groups of men. The *conversi* were men who had made a less extensive vow and whose main task was to perform a large part of the manual labour within the monastery. These men were not ordained priests, neither did they learn to read and write, or to speak Latin. The monasteries were also inhabited by elderly men, for whom the monastery functioned as a sort of retirement home after a long secular life, whereas others sought the monastic life just before their anticipated death and entered *ad succurendum*.[6] However, the *conversi* and the elderly entrants will not on this occasion be taken into account.

Children

Ever since the beginning of the sixth century, when the monastic rule which bears the name of Benedict of Nursia was written down, child oblation was a natural part of monastic recruitment.[7] Young boys were offered to God, given

---

5   http://www.nad.riksarkivet.se/sdhk. The database contains transcribed, full text charters up to and including the year 1378 and the time period 1401–1420, whereas the charters from the period 1379–1400 as well as after 1421 are presented in shorter summaries (*regests*).
6   On elderly entrants, see Lynch (1976), pp. 27–36; on *conversi*, see Lekai (1977), pp. 334–346; Alfonso (1991), pp. 10–19.
7   RB 58.

to the monasteries as a gift by their parents, and were then raised and expected to live inside the community throughout their life. In the eleventh century this custom was well established. Many of the monks had usually lived their lives in the monastery since childhood, a practice well "sanctioned by religious sentiment, custom, and considerations of family pride and self-interest."[8]

In the eleventh and twelfth century, in the era of reform, views on child oblation changed. Personal and inner salvation became increasingly important. Consequently, reformed orders such as the Cistercians and Carthusians formally forbade child novices – "not only could nurturing and educating children be distracting, but the oblation of children was a family decision, not an individual one, and thus did not involve the personal interior change that adult conversion could foster".[9] In 1134, the Cistercian general chapter stated that no boy younger than sixteen was to be educated in the monastery, or to be received as a novice. Thus, in the twelfth century the admission of child oblates declined, a phenomenon which also affected the older Benedictine houses. However, even if the practice was criticized and banned, child oblation continued to occur. Religious houses continuously accepted young boys, as showed by recurrent sanctions which the General Chapter imposed on Cistercian abbots who regularly neglected the statutes and welcomed children into their communities. Nevertheless, over time the reception of child oblation became less important for monastic recruitment.[10]

Only rarely were boys, or young men, given to the Swedish Cistercian houses, if we are to trust extant charters. A few examples are preserved where sons were given to a monastery by their parents, even though not earlier than the fourteenth century. As will be seen, in some of these cases it is uncertain whether the boy was given to the monastery as an *oblate*, or if he was sent to the monastery only for a limited period, for instance to get an education and/or to be brought up by the monks. Despite these different motives, both variations can be used as a starting point for a subsequent discussion on the social background of the monks.

Child Oblates in Swedish monasteries?
In 1348, Sven, a goldsmith in the town of Söderköping, in the province of Östergötland, and his wife declared that they gave their son *Olof* to Alvastra abbey as a novice. At the same time the parents also donated ½ *attung* of estate

---

8   Lynch (1976), p. 37. On child oblation, see de Jong (1996).
9   Newman (1996), pp. 22–24, at p. 24; see also Lynch (1976), pp. 37–39.
10 Lynch (1976), p. 37–39; Newman (1996), pp. 22–24.

to the monastery – a relatively modest donation – on condition that Olof did not leave the monastery until he had formally been professed.[11] In spite of the fact that the Cistercians normally are associated with the rural aristocracy and feudal structures, we here have an example of monastic recruitment from an urban burgher.

Our second case, the young novice Sune, on the other hand, descended from the group of secular aristocrats whose fundamental power-base was holdings of land and estates. In 1363, Sune's father Elof Bengtsson gave Alvastra abbey an estate in connection with his son's entrance into the monastery, in which Sune had promised to take the monastic vow. Elof Bengtsson was most likely, in the second generation, a descendant of Birger jarl's brother Elof, who was thus Sune's great-grandfather (Birger jarl's sons Valdemar Birgersson and Magnus Birgersson eventually became Swedish kings). Even though not very much is known of Sune's father – he was apparently not dubbed a knight and did not belong to the nobility – Sune obviously descended from a family that a few generations back belonged to the upper strata of the nobility. Sune and his father were also, however distantly, through marriages and kinship related to knights as well as members of the Council of the Realm (*riksråd*), Law-Speakers (*lagmän*) and a *drots*, i.e. the highest responsibility for the administration of royal justice. Further, Sune's paternal uncle, Lars Boberg, was canon in the diocese of Västerås – for a short time also deputy bishop, although never ordained.[12]

Elof's decision to let his son Sune take the habit is thus an example of how an aristocratic family, distantly related to the upper strata of the nobility, but themselves somewhat lower on the social ladder, saw monasticism as a conceivable alternative for a young son. Moreover, some years before he gave his son to the monastery, Elof had already bequeathed property and money to Alvastra, and his family had already some generations earlier established a close and mutually beneficial relationship with the monastery through donations and burial sites.[13] This family tradition might have been one reason for the decision to let Sune

---

11 SDHK 5599. Normally land was valued in *marklands*, where one *markland* has been estimated to be equivalent to approximately twelve hectares. Concurrently the measure *attung* was used (especially in the eastern parts of Sweden) which was equivalent to ½ *markland* (Myrdal (1986), p. 36; Dovring (1947), p. 188–192.
12 SDHK 8309; ÄSF 1957–1989, pp. 23, 26–27; Ekström (1939), pp. 86–87. Sune's paternal aunt Helga was in her first marriage the wife of Sune Jonsson (Båt), and in her second marriage of Magnus Knutsson (Blå), both of whom were knights, law-speakers and members of the Council of the Realm. The law-speakers, *lagman* [sing.], held the highest secular office of the province and, according to the law code of Uppland from 1296, also elected the King. See Lindkvist (2007).
13 SDHK 887; 7615.

enter the monastery – it was not uncommon that entrant children were given to a monastery with which the family had already established close and personal bonds through different kinds of earlier donations.

Olof and Sune were most likely received in the monastery as oblates, as future monastic vows are indicated in both cases. However, since the boys' age is unknown – they might be young men – it is difficult to determine whether the reception of the boys infringed against the Cistercian statutes, which stipulated the prohibition against child oblates. Still, the fact that in both cases the sons' own desires and decisions are mentioned might indicate that they had reached a certain age.

Other Children in Cistercian monasteries

The primary reason for Olof Lang and his wife Gyrid Gjurdsdotter placing their son *Håkan* in a monastery seems, on the other hand, to have been concern for his education, rather than his being given as an offering to God. In 1407 Abbot Jöns of Nydala monastery accepted Håkan as a pupil in the monastery, and the monastery received a mill with adherent meadows and fields from the parents. One condition, however, accompanied the gift: The abbot should accept their son "and give him knowledge of books and help him to school until he grows to manhood, because we cannot offer him a better inheritance."[14] The text reveals the parents' care and concern for their son, and is in a way also touching for a modern reader – in a time when estate was the common base for influence and social positioning, the parents valued and chose education as the best inheritance they could give their son.

Håkan's parents, Olof and Gyrid, are also known from other charters. They both gave their consent when Gyrid's brother Peter in 1399 donated landed property to Nydala. In 1406, Olof bequeathed the family farm to Nydala for the sake of his, his wife's, his childrens' and parents' souls. The will also stated that Olof's family retained possession of the donated farm as long as they lived. After that, Olof and his wife were to be buried in the monastery. Four years later, a final charter was drawn up by the Nydala Abbot Jöns, in which Olof's will is confirmed, with the additional remark that the monks, to the best of their abilities, should hold masses and prayers for Olof and his wife.[15] Neither Olof, nor his brother in-law Peter, is mentioned with any particular title in any of the charters mentioned. Nor are the donations to Nydala remarkably large – even

---

14 SDHK 16861: *ok læta kenna hanom book ok hielpa hanom til skola alt til thes han vardhir moghande man, for thy wi kunnom hanom ekke bætre boosloth giwa.*
15 RPB (II) 3001; SDHK 16721; SDHK 17514.

though a mill was a valuable property and did not necessarily represent a modest donation. Nevertheless, the family did in all probability belong to the local aristocracy (or the more prosperous farmers), i. e. they acted principally within a geographically local environment, without any or with only limited relationships with the national elite.

It is likewise unknown whether Håkan eventually took the habit and remained in the monastery as an adult, or if he left it for the world. The parents' intention seemed however only to secure his education "until he grows to manhood". There is also another indication that Håkan lived his adult life as a layman. In 1424, the district judge of the hundred of Mark in the province of Västergötland certified that Håkan's father and siblings had assigned part of their possessions to Håkan. This development seems somewhat unlikely (although not entirely unreasonable) if he was a monk.[16] Either way, the case with Håkan is still of interest when the monk's origin is under discussion, as it reveals a local family's close bonds with, and even its willingness to give a son to, the monastery – if only for a limited time.

A second case where a boy was raised in the monastery concerns *Johan Erlandsson*. However, in this case, we know for certain that he lived his adult life as a layman. In 1327, Johan made his will and chose Alvastra abbey as burial place for himself and his wife. At the same time he bequeathed to the monastery money, grain, and various personal property in addition to a farm, a *curia*. It also appears that Johan was brought up in the monastery, with "the respected monks, who have raised me since childhood, and in everything honestly and praiseworthily have treated and fostered me with love".[17] Johan's family background remains, however, unknown to us, but we can notice that his own legacy to the monastery was fairly large.[18]

---

16 SDHK 20199. The ban on personal property in the monastery seems, in certain cases, to have been negotiable. It was not uncommon that a person donated property to a convent, whereby the yield should go to a certain nun in the communion as long as she lived, and only after her death accrue to the convent (Andersson 2006, pp. 220–231). A similar example from a male house concerns Folke, who in previous research has been identified as a monk in Nydala abbey. In 1376 he bought back his hereditary estate and, on the same occasion, received his sisters' shares – the latter with the explicit condition that it would become part of the monastery's property only after Folke's death (SDHK 10819; Ortved 1933, p. 188). Hundred [härad] was an administrative entity.

17 SDHK 3454: *reuerendi domini monachi me ab infancia nutriuerant et in omnibus honeste et laudabiliter pertractauerant ac dilexerant.*

18 The latin term *curia* has in earlier research been interpreted as a relatively large farm – normally not less than one markland – see Andersson (2006), pp. 89–93, and literature referred to there.

A final example of a local family's desire to have a son in a monastery is provided by the case of Nanne Kärling, from the first half of the fifteenth century. It was Nanne's family's intention and wish that their son should become a monk. However, Nanne was of another opinion and his family's ambition was never carried out. This fact does not necessarily make his case less interesting, since we have quite a lot of information about the Kärling family. We thus get an indication of which social circles a monastic life was a conceivable and eligible option when a son's future life was under discussion.

Nanne Kärling originated from an aristocratic family in the province of Västergötland. His father, Torbjörn Kärling, held the post as district judge (*häradshövding*) in the hundred of Vartofta. Torbjörn Kärling never succeeded in advancing to the higher nobility, but remained part of the local elite and gradually enlarged his possessions. Nanne's social origin can thus be described as deriving from the local aristocracy.[19]

Nanne had two siblings, an older brother and an older sister. When he was thirteen, in 1435 or 1436, his parents decided that their third son, Nanne, should become a monk. He was then placed in the abbey of Varnhem.[20] This decision has in previous research been explained on the basis of pure strategic and economic motives. According to this opinion, the parents' aim was to keep the family possessions as intact as possible – as a monk Nanne would have no rights of inheritance. Thereby Nanne's older brother would have an economic foundation for further social advancement into the nobility.[21] It must be remembered, however, that a person never entered the monastery empty-handed, *manu vacua* – a gift, normally landed property, to the monastery was expected.[22] To this must be added that close personal bonds to ecclesiastical institutions also could be of significance in terms of social strategies and positioning.[23]

However, irrespective of the parents' motives, Nanne did not share their ambitions. Quite soon after he arrived in Varnhem, he escaped from the abbey. He was then transferred to Alvastra monastery, and then again sent back to Varnhem. The ensuing case, in which he sought to be released from the monastic life, is rather well documented. It ended with his official return to secular life, although it was beset by inheritance disputes, since his relatives claimed he had

---

19 Nordmark (1942), pp.129–133.
20 SDHK 24962.
21 Nordmark (1942), p. 134.
22 Lynch (1975), pp. 431–434; see also Andersson (2006), esp. pp. 235–240, where it is suggested that the donation a daughter brought with her into the nunnery corresponded to the share of the inheritance that she had been entitled to as a secular woman.
23 Andersson (2006); Andersson (2010), pp. 262–266, 270.

lost his rights of inheritance – despite the fact that he was placed in the monastery against his will and never took the monastic vow.[24]

The absence of children
Is it possible then, to make any general conclusions regarding child oblates or young sons in a Swedish monastic context? Obviously it did occur, even if preserved charters are extremely few. Moreover, several of the examples we do have information on concern cases where the child was most likely placed in the monastery only for a limited period. Based on these grounds it is difficult to draw any other conclusion than that child oblation was not very common in male Cistercian houses in medieval Sweden. Normally, a gift of land or property followed the boy into the monastery.[25] This gift would in turn have required a charter to be drawn up, in order to secure the monastery's legal right to the donated possession. If boys, or young sons, were given to the monastic houses as oblates to a large extent and on a fairly regular basis, i.e. if the practice was predominant, there is reason to believe that these charters would have been preserved to a greater extent than actually is the case. A contrast can be noted with the female houses, from which several Swedish charters drawn up in connection with an aristocratic daughter's entrance into a nunnery have been preserved.[26]

Thus, considering the small number of charters, general conclusions regarding the social background of the sons that were in fact given to the monasteries are not possible. Yet, we can note that most of the charters we do have do not represent the upper layers of the nobility, despite the above-mentioned Sune, whose family bonds to the nobility after all were fairly distant. This situation cannot be taken as evidence that child oblation did not occur among the highest elite. Nevertheless, *if* it did, perhaps it is more likely that it was primarily a phenomenon in early times – up to the thirteenth century, a period from which we do not have many extant charters at all – when the elite manifested relations with the Cistercian monasteries and nunneries with donations, and generally was very active as protectors of the monasteries.[27] This conclusion, however, remains speculative.

---

24 Nordmark, (1942), pp. 135–153; Salonen 2002.
25 Lynch (1975), pp. 431–434; Lynch (1976), p. 49.
26 Andersson (2006).
27 For a brief review of the Cistercian monasteries, their foundations and first donators and protectors, see Nilsson (1998), pp. 120–131; on their role in a broader political context, see Nyberg (2000).

Besides the absence of entrance charters, the lack of evidence for child oblates should also be understood in connection with the fact that the General Chapter's prohibition against accepting children as novices was already in effect by the time the first monasteries were established in Sweden. There are also other possible explanations – economic, demographic and social – for the small number of child oblates found in the sources, and why monasticism was not necessarily an option for the aristocratic family when the son's future was under discussion. Before we take these other explanations into consideration, however, we need to scrutinize the social background of the other monks in the community.

Adult Entrants

Joseph Lynch, who has thoroughly investigated the status of entrants into monastic houses, pointed out that adult entrants "probably never constituted a majority of the religious" in the different communities during the eleventh and early twelfth century. This is probably due to the large number of child oblates. However, in connection with the decline of child oblation in the eleventh and twelfth century, the proportion of adult entrants increased. Consequently, in the Cistercian houses, adult entrants must have constituted a larger part of the monks than had been the case in the older monasteries.[28]

Considering the relative silence on child oblates, one can assume that adult entrants constituted a majority of the monastic religious also in the Swedish male monasteries. It is not a matter of course, however, that the choir monks constituted the majority of the adult entrants, as the monastery was also inhabited by *conversi* and eldery entrants. Still, seen from a religious and ideological point of view, it was this group of adult entrants – choir monks – who formed the core of the monastery, and it is this group that will be in focus in the following discussion.

The information on these men's personal background is, in both a European and a Swedish context, sparse, and an exhaustive analysis of their genealogical background can evidently not be carried out. However, Martha Newman emphasizes two types of written sources which, on a general level, reveal information on the background of the Cistercian monks who entered as adults. First, there are letters written by monks and abbots for the purpose of "encouraging conversion" and, second, there are biographical details on saints in different *vitas*, as well as on certain monks in the historical writing that was produced in the monasteries. Of course these sources call for a critical approach and must be

---

28 Lynch (1976), pp. 36–40, at p. 36; Bouchard (1987), p. 54; Newman (1996), pp. 16, 23.

used with caution by the historian, since they were normally written for a special purpose. There are, for example, many Cistercian stories of how knights left the secular world and took the habit, which does not necessarily correspond to actual and contemporary conditions. Rather, these narratives were an essential part in the creation of the order's self-image, and played an important role in the effort to recruit young unmarried knights to the order.[29]

Still, according to Newman and other scholars, the men who entered the Cistercian monasteries normally originated from the aristocratic milieu. They were knights and priests, as well as monks who came from other monastic orders.[30] Not least the clerics were well represented in Cistercian houses and could, according to letters and biographical texts, outnumber the former knights. Also, the Cistercians actively encouraged priests to leave the secular world and convert to monasticism, and Newman points out that "[m]any of these men still came from knightly families and had been raised in a military milieu, but they had been trained in letters rather than swordplay".[31]

The Swedish sources, however, include neither *vitas* on certain monks nor historical writings or other narrative texts on different monastic houses. Instead the historian is obliged to use the charters. However, as was the case with children, charters were only rarely drawn up in connection with male adult entrants, which would have revealed genealogical information on the entrant. Similarly, a clear gender difference can be noted also among the adult entrants.[32] The difference between the sexes in this respect is so large that it cannot be explained solely by a random preservation of entrance charters. Rather it must be explained by contemporary circumstances – it was obviously more common that a charter was drawn up when women entered a monastic house than was the case with male entrants. This fact can be due to the fact that a man who sought monastic life could, in contrast to both women and children, bring other gifts to the monastery, gifts that did not demand a written manifestation. If the entrant was an ordained priest, he was of course needed in the monastery and brought with him theological knowledge for the benefit of the monks. The man entering could also bring valuable books to the monastery, and some men, most likely normally of lower social rank, could offer manual labour, i.e. they could be received in the monastery as *conversi*. None of these gifts required a written, legal manifestation, as was the case when land and real estate was transferred to the monastery.

---

29 Newman (1996), p. 24–27.
30 Newman (1996), p. 16; Lawrence (2001, 1984) p. 181; Bouchard (1987), pp. 77–78.
31 Newman (1996), p. 27.
32 Andersson (2006).

However, monks also appear in other types of charters than "entrance-charters". If we broaden the investigation to include all preserved charters linked to the various houses, occasionally some information about the monks' lay family conditions and previous activities emerges. What, then, do these sources disclose about the family backgrounds of the monks?

Social Background I: Abbots
Despite the fact that the abbots are relatively often mentioned in the sources, further information on their individual background is almost non-existent. Occasionally, we do get a glimpse of a family relative, information that still does not necessarily bring us much further in our aim to map out the family structure. One example is *Rudolf*, abbot in Julita abbey 1433–1454. Thanks to a letter preserved through the *Apostolic Penitentiary*, we know that he had a relative, the Franciscan priest-brother Olavus Johannis, who was invited to Julita by Abbot Rudolf, and spent some time at the abbey.[33] Still, since no further information is given about this relative of Rudolf, not much more can be concluded on Rudolf's social background, besides the fact that he came from a family with more than one ordained priest.

Another case where we get a brief glimpse of an abbot's relative concerns *Birger*, abbot in Alvastra at the beginning of the fourteenth century. In 1321, Bo Polen donated a farm to Nydala monastery for his and other unnamed persons' souls. Bo and his "beloved brother" (*dilecti fratris mei*), Abbot Birger in Alvastra, affixed their seals on the charter. Bo is also known from another monastic donation. In 1326, he donated a plot of forest to Nydala and Gudhem monastery (the latter a female convent in the province of Västergötland), a charter also sealed by Abbot Birger.[34] Apart from these donations, not very much is known about Bo. However, a namesake is mentioned in a charter from 1292, in which the former king Waldemar gives his servant Bo Polen a farm as a reward for faithful service.[35] This may be the very same man who later gave gifts to different monasteries, but it remains speculation.

There are also, however, other indications, perhaps more substantial, that Abbot Birger and his brother Bo were, if not a part of the upper nobility themselves, at the very least located within its wider circles. At least two wills have survived in which Abbot Birger personally seems to have received legacies. Asmund Lang is not known from other charters, but does not seem to have lived under too mod-

---

33 APS Poen. no 56; Collmar (1977), pp. 608–609.
34 SDHK 3084; SDHK 3399.
35 SDHK 1718.

est conditions. According to his will, Alvastra monastery gets a *curia*, and among other beneficiaries, Birger personally receives a red horse. Further, the Swedish dukes confirmed the will and affixed their seals on it, which also indicates that Asmund was connected with the upper strata of society.[36] The second will in which Birger personally seems to have received a legacy is with certainty drawn up by a man from the nobility, namely Håkan Jonsson Läma. Håkan was a knight, member of the Council of the Realm (*riksråd*) and held the title *marsk*, i.e. he was the king's supreme military commander.[37] In his will dated 1327, Håkan chose to be buried in Alvastra, and for this reason he bequeathed a *curia* to the monastery. Certain conditions however accompanied the gift. Apart from the request that Håkan should be remembered annually by the monks, the *curia* was to be entrusted to Abbot Birger, as long as he lived – a wording that can be interpreted to mean that the income from the curia should accrue to Birger personally.[38] In other words, both these wills indicate close personal bonds between Abbot Birger and at least one, perhaps two, members of the secular nobility.

Social background II: Choir-monks
In most cases where we catch a glimpse of a monk's relatives, however, they do not belong to the upper strata of society. Sometime between 1292 and 1312, the parish priest Johannes in Lommaryd (province of Småland), made his will. He too chose to be buried in Alvastra. Among the beneficiaries one of his relatives, and a namesake, is included, namely *domino iohanni congnato nostro, de aluastrum*, who received some books.[39] The assumption that the latter Johannes was part of the monastic community in Alvastra is strengthened by a passage later in the text. The priest Johannes chose, among others, *fratrem iohannem monachum, de aluastrum* as executor. The monk Johannes seems to have been chosen for personal reasons – he is neither entitled abbot, nor prior (a prior named Ragvald is on the other hand mentioned in the will, most likely from Alvastra monastery), which might have motivated his choice as executor. Hence, in all probability there were family ties between the priest Johannes and his namesake, the monk Johannes in Alvastra. If this assumption is correct, the monk Johannes can also be expected to have been an ordained priest, in accordance with the title *domino*.[40] We thus have a little information on the social back-

---

36 SDHK 2337.
37 ÄSF 1957–1989, p. 78b.
38 SDHK 3474: *birgero abbati ad dies suos committatur.* See also Ortved (1933), s. 87.
39 SDHK 1534.
40 See also Ortved (1933), p. 84.

ground of Johannes in Alvastra abbey. He originated from a family that at least had an ordained priest in its circle, not however to be found among the higher ecclesiastical posts but in a local parish environment.

Three further examples of choir-monks will be given, all from the fourteenth century and Nydala monastery. *Mats Esgersson* is known as subprior (*suppriore*) in Nydala 1369. Mats had a relative named Björn Johansson, who donated an estate to Nydala monastery, with the condition that the estate should accrue to Mats as long as he lived.[41] Other family names are also mentioned in connection with Björn's donation, however no one known from the upper strata in society. Rather, most likely Björn's family, accordingly also Mats's (at least partly), derived from the lower aristocracy or local peasantry.

The second example concerns the monk *Nicolaus Ebbonis*. We know him from a diploma drawn up by Pope Clement VI, dated 21st of October 1352.[42] In this diploma, the pope provides certain exemptions, among others one concerning the Nydala monk Nicolaus. It appears that Nicolaus was the illegitimate son of a priest and an unmarried woman, and could therefore, according to the statutes, not become a monk in a Cistercian abbey – which he nevertheless apparently already was.[43] Furthermore, the monks had also provided for him to go abroad to study in Paris. Nicolaus is described as a well-read man, with a virtuous living and good in speech and manners. And indeed the pope accommodated the monks, and gave them an exemption to appoint Nicolaus to whichever position they liked, including the office of abbot. We know that Nicolaus subsequently served as monk in Nydala – he is also mentioned in a diploma issued by Pope Innocent VI in 1360.[44] On this occasion it is reiterated that Nicolaus may be appointed as abbot with full legal authority, since he had great knowledge of theology and canon law. We have no certain knowledge of his subsequent activities, but it has been suggested that it is the same monk "N" who is mentioned in a testament drawn up by the parish priest Ulf in 1371.[45] In this testament Nydala abbey is the primary beneficiary, and "N. former abbot in Roma" (i.e. a daughter house of Nydala), is appointed as executor. However, whatever the future held in store for Nicolaus, the point here is to draw attention to his background – Nicolaus was an illegitimate son of a priest.

---

41 SDHK 9453; RPB 2067; Ortved (1933), p. 181. Björn is described as Mats' "maternal uncle" by Ortved, and as "second cousin" in the RPB-regest.
42 SDHK 6470.
43 A resolution passed in 1308 by the General Chapter prescribed that only a legitimate child could become a monk (Ortved 1933, s. 178).
44 SDHK 7687.
45 France (1992), p. 502; SDHK 9994.

Mathias was active as monk in Nydala about the same time as Nicolaus. In the year 1353, Mathias' father Esger from Knutstorp in the province of Småland wrote his will. Among the witnesses, we find his two sons; Joar, choir-priest (*coralis*) in Linköping and his brother Mathias, monk in Nydala, probably an ordained priest-monk (*domini Mathie, monachi monasterii prefati*).[46] Not much is known about Mathias's father, besides his decision to choose Nydala abbey as his burial-place, and in connection with this decision to bequeath a gift to the monks. He seems not to be known from other charters. However, the size of the gift may give us some indications of Esger's assets. The estate he transferred to the monastery was estimated at a value of 30 *mark penningar*, which indicates that the property in question was not remarkably large, although some cattle also were included in the gift. Therefore, and in view of the fact that Esger does not seem to appear in other sources, a reasonable assumption is that Mathias, as well as his father Esger, belonged to the local aristocracy, or perhaps to the wealthier groups of peasants.

Ordained priest-monks
Some of the monks previously mentioned were possibly ordained. Before some concluding remarks are offered on the social background of the monks in Swedish Cistercian communities, some attention will be given to a few more of those monks whom we know with certainty were ordained. Besides the abbot, a post always held by an ordained priest, the community consisted of several ordained monks. Some of them were ordained after they had entered the monastery – a tradition which over time became increasingly frequent within the monastic tradition – whereas others had held various ecclesiastical posts outside the monastery before taking the monastic vow.

Olaus Petri was a priest and monk living in Alvastra abbey in the fourteenth century. We are familiar with his activities before he took the habit in 1340, thanks to a charter drawn up 1361.[47] In this letter, it appears that Olaus had been asked to write down the properties that belonged to the prebend he had previously held as parish priest in Kungslena in the diocese of Skara. Apart from working as a parish priest before he became a monk, he had also been one of the canons in the Skara diocese, in the province of Västergötland. We can conclude that Olaus had been in Alvastra for over 20 years when this compilation of the properties was written down. Thus, one cannot take for granted that his entrance in Alvastra was an act of retirement. Rather it seems that Olaus took the habit as an adult, but not yet elderly, man.

---

46 SDHK 6566.
47 SDHK 8008.

Olaus had apparently been able to study and eventually become a priest, and must therefore have come from a family with some material assets. He had also transferred some properties of his own to the prebend he had held as a parish priest. Apart from this information, nothing further is known about his background, though an educated guess might be that he originated from the local aristocracy or the upper ranks of prosperous peasants.

Thanks to a similar inquiry for information addressed to another monastery, this time from the cathedral dean in Strängnäs to Julita abbey in the province of Södermanland, we have some knowledge of another monk who apparently had worked as a priest outside the abbey before taking the habit, namely *Torsten Andreasson*, monk and priest in Julita abbey. In a letter written in February 1414, the abbot of Julita answers the dean's questions about the rights and obligations connected to the post as dean of the cathedral, a post which apparently earlier was held by Torsten, to whom the question was initially addressed.[48]

We have some additional information about Torsten's previous activities and genealogy. He descended from a local aristocratic family in the province of Södermanland – his parents were probably Anders Torstensson and Cecilia Eriksdotter. On his mother's side, a younger cousin of Torsten would later reach the ecclesiastical elite, namely Nicolaus Ragvaldi, archbishop in Uppsala between 1438 and 1448. Also Torsten entered an ecclesiastical career, albeit lower down in the church hierarchy. He was enrolled at the University of Prague in 1373, probably already as an ordained priest. He is then known as parish priest in Vingåker parish in Södermanland between 1381 and 1391, and thereafter as cathedral dean in Strängnäs between 1394 and 1396. In February 1400, he transferred property to his brother, an event that has been interpreted by earlier research as evidence that Torsten was already professed as monk at this time, or that the assignment took place in connection with his entrance. If so, he lived his life in the abbey for at least 14 years or longer. He died sometime before 12 March 1427.[49]

So, we know for certain that Torsten originated from the lower aristocracy. He probably wore the habit for at least 14 years, maybe longer. It may be that he sought the monastic life at the approach of old age, but we cannot say so for sure – a reasonable assumption might be that he was born in the 1350s – he was then possibly approaching the age of 50 when entering Julita.

It can also be concluded from less detailed charters that a monk had been ordained as a priest, simply by the way he is addressed. This is the case with

---

48 SDHK 18449.
49 Åsbrink and Westman (1935), p. 142; Ljung (1963), pp. 52–53; Collmar (1977), pp. 131–132; SDHK 15343; SDHK 18449; RPB II: 3062.

Rudolf, a monk in Alvastra monastery at the beginning of the fifteenth century. In June 1419, the Abbot Henry in the Danish monastery of Esrum issued a receipt confirming that Rudolf, *sacerdotis in Aluastrom professi*, in his capacity as Julita monastery's envoy had handed over money to Henry.[50] Rudolf was in other words priest and professed monk. Also, this is true for *Anders*, monk in Varnhem monastery in the first half of the fifteenth century. He is known to posterity as he left the monastery and apostatized. He thereafter turned to the *Apostolic Penitentiary* and requested absolution, as well as dispensation with a view to moving to another monastery. In the letter drawn up by the cardinal priest of Santa Croce in Gerusalemme, Dominicus, Anders' request is approved, and he is entitled *presbyter monachus professus*, i.e. as a priest and professed monk.[51] However, in none of these examples do we know whether Rudolf or Anders had held any ecclesiastical post in the secular world before taking the habit – they can also very well have been ordained within the monastic enclosure.

Hence, in addition to the abbots, whom we safely can assume were ordained priests, occasionally also other priest-monks appear in the charters. It is true that they are rare, but the general absence of these priest-monks in the sources must nevertheless not, as in the case with the children, be interpreted as meaning that they were rare in reality. In contrast, the Cistercian structure demanded that ordained priests perform different spiritual tasks and rituals inside the monastery.[52] The silence in the sources must rather be explained by the fact that the monastery in most cases was represented by the abbot or prior when an official document was to be drawn up. In addition, an entering priest did in all probability not necessarily bring estate with him as a gift to monastery when he was taken up into the community – this being so, no charter needed to be drawn up.

Concluding remarks

What can then be concluded from this sparse, but still extant, information about certain monks' personal circumstances and social background? One of the most noticeable aspects regarding these men is the almost complete absence of monks

---

50 SDHK 19301. Possibly the very same Rudolf mentioned above who, if this assumption is correct, later advanced to the post as abbot in Julita abbey. According to Edvard Ortved, Abbot R in Julita is the same R that later became abbot of Alvastra – in that case, he might very well have returned to his original abbey (Ortved 1933, p. 282; Collmar 1977, pp. 608–609).
51 SDHK 42084.
52 On Cistercian liturgy, see Johansson (1964).

or child oblates from society's uppermost layer, i.e. the aristocratic elite. Only rarely are knights, law speakers or other nobles found within the monk's or child's family circles. When they appear, it is at a major genealogical distance from the monk/child – as in the case of Sune Elofsson, whose great-grandfather Elof was the brother of Birger jarl; i.e. the family relation goes three generations back.

Thus, in no case has it been proven that a knight's son was given to a monastery or served in it as an adult. It has rather been the "lower" social layers that appear in the charters. We must, of course, constantly remind ourselves that many charters have been lost. Neither do charters reveal information on all men who served in the monasteries: it is mainly the monastic leaders that are named in the texts, whereas the majority of the other monks remain unknown to us. Therefore, the existence of monks of noble birth in the monasteries cannot be completely ruled out. It does, however, appear reasonable that the total convergence of the sources we nevertheless have – the lack of the higher layers of the aristocracy, and the domination of lower, locally situated social groups – allows us to establish a fairly plausible hypothesis, namely that entry into a male monastic institution was primarily a matter for the local, lower aristocracy, as well as local, wealthier farmers.

If this interpretation is correct, does it differ from European conditions? At first sight, this might be the case. When the social origins of Cistercian monks are discussed in a wider European context, it is often observed, as mentioned above, that these men derived from the aristocratic milieu, i.e. they were sons and men from the knightly families. Apparently, this seems not to have been the case in Sweden. However, I would argue that the difference between the Swedish and European monasteries that at first seems apparent is partly illusory. Despite the fact that European monks often derived from an aristocratic, knightly milieu, these knightly backgrounds did not necessarily represent the upper strata of the nobility. In her study on Burgundian nobility and church, Constance Bouchard observes that the monastic leaders in the region in general "tended to be noble but of the middle or lower nobility. They were not burghers' or peasants' sons, but neither were they sons of great dukes or counts. At Cluny, for example, the abbots were routinely the sons of castellans and knights".[53] Further, when she comments on the Cistercian abbots in particular, she concludes that they "were always of the lower levels of the nobility, at least those whose origins are known".[54]

In other words, a *knight* did not necessarily represent the same social level in a European context as it did in medieval Sweden. In contrast to the Burgundian

---

53 Bouchard (1987), p. 77.
54 Bouchard (1987), p. 78.

region, a Swedish knight, a *dominus*, did in most cases belong to the upper layer of the nobles. He was normally part of, or had close bonds to, the national elite. I would therefore argue that there is a fundamental similarity between Swedish and European recruitment to the Cistercian male communities. They both primarily attracted the *lower aristocratic layers*, rather than its nobility – in Sweden perhaps also the wealthier groups of peasants. Consequently, to a large extent the recruitment is assumed to be *local* in nature (which, as mentioned in the introduction, has previously also been suggested by James France regarding the Scandinavian abbots). Hence, what at first appears to be a substantial difference between the Swedish and European conditions when the Cistercians' social background is discussed – the absence of knights among the Swedish monks – on a closer examination turns out to be a fact that actually connects Sweden with a wider European context, namely that the Cistercian monks generally were recruited from the lower aristocratic layers. In these Swedish lower layers though, the prevalence of knights was exceptional.

Even if the upper layers of the nobility did not seem to include monasticism as an alternative when their sons' futures were planned, other groups of men found their way into the monastic life. The adult men for whom this study has been able to obtain information have in the majority of the cases proved to be priests. In two cases we know for certain that these priest-monks had served as priests in the secular world, before taking the monastic vow – Olaus Petri had served as a parish priest as well as canon in the diocese of Skara, and Torsten Andreasson ended his pre-monastic career as cathedral dean in the diocese of Strängnäs.

The presence of priest monks accords of course very well with the Cistercian culture, whose activities required a number of ordained priests within the abbey. Let us for a moment return to the previously noted gender differences regarding charters drawn up in connection with a person's entrance into the monastery, i.e., the absence of charters connected to male entrants. Ordained priests were likely to join the monastery with their theological knowledge and status, or they brought books and other liturgical items for the benefit of the monastery. I therefore suggest that most of the adult men who chose a monastic life – probably often of local (aristocratic) origin – to a large extent were already ordained priests, or at least theologically trained. If not, another gift to the monastery would have been expected – not least properties and estate. In turn, this type of transfer should have left more traces in the charters. The assumption that it was to a great extent priests who found their way to the Cistercian Order, is also consistent with Newman's observation that among the Cistercian monks on the European Continent, many had had a previous career as priests in secular society. Moreover, these ordained priest monks could very well outnumber the non-ordained monks.

Demographic and economic aspects

How, then, can we explain that a large part of the aristocracy seems to have been uninterested in placing their sons in monasteries, or in becoming a part of the monastic culture themselves? Why do we not find sons of knights in the monastic sources?

The explanation for this phenomenon is of course not unambiguous, and several causes are possible. One might be connected to the laws of inheritance. In Sweden primogeniture was never established. All sons, not only the first born, had rights of inheritance. Of course, one may assume that Swedish families too sought to keep the property as intact as possible. Nevertheless, the absence of primogeniture meant that a large group of aristocratic sons in need of alternative lives, for instance within the monastic field, never arose. The Nanne Kärling case can be taken as an example of how the inheritance could not be negotiated to its detriment, regardless of the intentions of the family. In Europe the situation was different. Newman discusses for example how Cistercian stories of making monks out of knights – an important part in the construction of the order's self-image – had such young, unmarried nobles, who could not expect to receive part of the family inheritance, among its audience.[55]

It is also worth noting that medieval Sweden was a relatively small country, with a limited group of noble families. Naturally this situation affected the base for monastic recruitment from the upper strata of the population. And, *if* an ecclesiastical career was under consideration, there were other alternatives for the nobility that could lead to both political and cultural influence in society, i.e. within the bishoprics, or perhaps the cathedral chapter. Moreover, these alternatives did not require as extensive personal sacrifices as were the case when a man took the monastic vow.

One can also reflect on the lower aristocracy's strong presence in the sources from another economic perspective. Most of the cases date from the second half of the fourteenth century, or the beginning of the fifteenth. Certainly, this fact does not say anything about the social structure regarding earlier recruitment – it is not unlikely that the lower aristocracy inhabited the monasteries on a large scale also in earlier periods, even if one can assume that the further back we go in time, the greater is the chance of finding nobles among the monks. Still, it is reasonable also to take contemporary economic circumstances into consideration when the recruitment of these monks is considered. The second half of the fourteenth century was a time of the agrarian crisis, which lasted until the middle of the fifteenth century. The crisis meant that the aristocracy was exposed to strong economic pressures, which in particular affected the local aristocracy.

---

55 Newman (1996), p. 25.

It is well known that many people within this group did not manage to uphold their economic base, and moved down the social ladder. This change has been demonstrated by Lars-Olof Larsson, among others, in his study of the Värend region in the province of Småland, i.e., the same province in which we find Nydala abbey.[56] Hence, the monastery may very well have emerged as a more useful option for this lower aristocracy than it had previously been, as regards the future of their male family members.

Children in monasteries
The absence of child oblates in the Swedish monasteries corresponds well with Cistercian ideals that a decision to devote one's life to God should be based on a genuine personal conviction. The fact that child oblation was prohibited by the General Chapter almost a decade before the first Cistercian abbeys were founded in Sweden, was perhaps one main reason why child oblation never seems to have established itself more broadly in the Swedish male monasteries. A prohibition is likely to have a greater impact if it does not infringe an already long-established tradition, as was the case in other European regions with an older monastic tradition.

Yet, the prohibition did not, as we have seen, prevent families from placing a son in a monastery for a limited time. Although the examples are few, this practice shows similarities with the medieval tradition of *fostering*. This practice, to give away a child to be raised with other relatives or kin-groups, was rather common among aristocratic families in medieval Scandinavia. The meaning of such an arrangement was not merely that the child would be nourished, fostered and educated by a relative. It was also a way to create and maintain social bonds between more distant relations and kin-groups.[57] Therefore, it is reasonable to assume that the tradition of letting a child from a certain age be fostered by others – a tradition that was well established by the time of the monks' arrival – was transferred and incorporated quite naturally into the monasteries. By giving a son to a monastery, albeit for a limited time, valuable social bonds could also be created with a respected and prestigious monastic institution. In other words, when Håkan's and Johan's parents sent their sons to be educated and brought up by the monks, they probably also established valuable and prestigious relationships between their families and the monasteries.[58]

---

56 Norborg (1964).
57 See Gurevitj (1968), pp. 135–136; Miller (1986); Lahtinen 2009, pp. 119–125.
58 See also Andersson (2006).

Conflicting masculine ideals

Finally, a reflection should be offered regarding the fact that the nobility, the knights, as a general rule are absent among the Cistercians, and that the aristocracy did not give sons to the monastery to the same extent as daughters. I would argue that the absence of the nobility in the male monasteries is also an expression of a cultural conflict between parts of monasticism and lay aristocrats. This point will be exemplified by a final case, namely that of Klemens Tyrgilsson.

The monk Klemens Tyrgilsson was, in this context, something as unusual as a fourteenth century son of a knight. Thus, Klemens was of noble birth, and both his father and his brother were knights. Furthermore, he had a maternal uncle who, besides the title of knight, was both a Law-Speaker and a member of the Council of the Realm.[59] However, Klemens did not choose the Cistercians when he decided to make his monastic vows. Instead he chose the Order of St. John, and served in its priory in Eskilstuna – a decision, I would argue, which is symptomatic for his time and culture. The monastic and the secular aristocratic life were in many ways each other's opposites. Still, if the nobility nonetheless chose a monastic career, like Klemens, it is not unreasonable to assume that it was more natural to enter an order culturally closer to the knightly milieu, namely the Order of St. John. The monks of St. John initially served sick and poor pilgrims in Jerusalem, but in the twelfth century they increasingly developed into a military order with close bonds to the crusades.[60] The Cistercians on the other hand, despite a military rhetoric during the order's earliest times, focused rather on agrarian activities in their daily lives.[61]

These cultural conflicts between the secular nobility and part of the monastic culture can also be described in terms of contemporary ideals and perceptions of manliness.[62] In medieval society, as in other periods, different masculinities appeared side by side. Ideals of manliness connected to traditional monasticism and the secular aristocracy did not only differ; they were in many respects in direct contradiction to each other. From this point of view, it was undoubtedly a larger break to hand over a son to monastic life than it was to do so with a daughter. R W Swanson points out that "[r]eligious women still fitted into the traditional trinity of female life-styles (virgins, married, widows), but religious

---

59 Raneke (2001), p. 569.
60 Lawrence (2001), pp. 212–213.
61 See also Andersson (2010), pp. 272–273.
62 During the past decades study of medieval masculinities has developed into a well-established research field, where not least different ecclesiastical masculinities have been studied. See for example Lees (1994); Hadley (1999); Karras (2003); Thibodeaux (2010).

men became extraneous to contemporary gender constructions".[63] Furthermore, Bouchard states that "...entering the ecclesiastical life was not equivalent to entering a life of ease and dignity. Novices in the monastery or new members of the cathedral chapter indeed generally lost some of their dignity of position: from being noble sons with a flock of attendants to obey them, they became ecclesiastics whose first duty was obedience to their superiors".[64]

There were thus significant differences between the life of an aristocrat and the life of a monk. The aristocrat's right to self-determination and guardianship over himself and others – children, women, servants and tenants – stood in sharp contrast to the monk's life primarily based on humility and obedience. The thought of equality between the monks was also essential according to the Rule of St. Benedict – "[a] man born free is not to be given higher rank than a slave who becomes a monk".[65] Another essential attribute when it comes to how a secular aristocratic masculinity and identity was constructed, was the basic right to own and dispose of property. This was not only a right, but an absolute condition of power and influence for a secular aristocratic man in society, which of course contrasted sharply to the monk's vow of poverty. The ban on weapons within the monastic enclosure is yet another thing that profoundly contrasts to one of the most important attributes in constructing masculinity within the aristocratic world, namely the right to bear arms.[66]

Swedish monastic recruitment – a matter for the local aristocracy
Despite these contradictory ideals between monastic and secular masculinities, the monastic orders were of course, in different ways, of great importance and interest for the entire aristocratic group. However, this interest could be manifested in various ways. In this article, the intention has been to show that when support for different monasteries was intended, or family strategies were drawn up, taking the habit, or placing a son in a monastery, was not the primary choice for the knightly families or other distinguished members of the nobility in medieval Sweden. Perhaps it was not a choice at all, at least as long as it did not concern an ordained family member. Recruitment to the Cistercian monasteries in medieval Sweden was rather, as elsewhere in Europe, primarily an issue for the groups in society whose activities were based in a local environment. The men who found their way to the Cistercian communities thus originated from

---

63 Swanson (1999), p. 167.
64 Bouchard (1987), p. 60.
65 RB 2:18.
66 Ney (2002), s. 25.

the lower aristocracy and, perhaps, also from the group of wealthier farmers who could afford an entrance donation, or let their sons be trained to become a priest.

Charters referred to in the article
presented by year and person of interest

Date	Charter/regest	Name (abbey)
1268–10–27	SDHK 887	Sune (Alvastra abbey)
1359–11–07	SDHK 7615	Sune (Alvastra abbey)
1363–05–06	SDHK 8309	Sune (Alvastra abbey)
1292–00–00	SDHK 1534	Johannes (Alvastra abbey)
1296–09–21	SDHK 1718	Birger, abbott (Alvastra abbey)
1310–02–26	SDHK 2337	Birger, abbott (Alvastra abbey)
1321–04–12	SDHK 3084	Birger, abbott (Alvastra abbey)
1326–06–09	SDHK 3399	Birger, abbott (Alvastra abbey)
1327–04–22	SDHK 3474	Birger, abbott (Alvastra abbey)
1327–00–00	SDHK 3454	Johan Erlandsson (Alvastra abbey)
1348–04–25	SDHK 5599	Olof (Alvastra abbey)
1352–10–21	SDHK 6470	Nicolaus Ebbonis (Nydala abbey, *abbott in Roma abbey?*)
1360–01–02	SDHK 7687	Nicolaus Ebbonis (Nydala abbey, *abbott in Roma abbey?*)
1371–08–16	SDHK 9994	Nicolaus Ebbonis (Nydala abbey, *abbott in Roma abbey?*)
1353–05–22	SDHK 6566	Mathias (Nydala abbey)
1361–08–16	SDHK 8008	Olaus Petri (Alvastra abbey)
1369–06–11	SDHK 9453	Mats Esgersson (Nydala abbey)
1384–12–13	RPB 2067	Mats Esgersson (Nydala abbey)

1399–08–15	RPB 3001	Håkan (Nydala abbey)
1406–06–24	SDHK 16721	Håkan (Nydala abbey)
1407–04–10	SDHK 16861	Håkan (Nydala abbey)
1410–06–24	SDHK 17514	Håkan (Nydala abbey)
1424–01–29	SDHK 20199	Håkan (Nydala abbey)
1414–12–14	SDHK 18449	Torsten Andreasson (Julita abbey)
1400–02–06	SDHK 15343	Torsten Andreasson (Julita abbey)
1400–02–06	RPB 3062	Torsten Andreasson (Julita abbey)
1419–06–24	SDHK 19301	Rudolf (Alvastra abbey, the same Rudolf as in 1455–09–07?)
1446–06–16	SDHK 24962	Nanne Kärling (Varnhem abbey, Alvastra Abbey)
1450–12–10	SDHK 42084	Anders (Varnhem abbey)
1455–09–07	APS Poen. no 56	Rudolf, abbott (Julita abbey, the same Rudolf as in 1419–06–24?)

Literature

Sources

APS: Poen., *Auctoritate Papae. The Church Province of Uppsala and the Apostolic Penitentiary 1410–1526*, ed. Sara Risberg, introd. by Kirsi Salonen (Stockholm, 2008).
RB: *RB 1980. The Rule of St. Benedict. In Latin and English with Notes and Thematic Index*, ed. Timothy Fry (Collegeville, 1980).
RPB: *Svenska Riks-Archivets Pergamentsbrev I-III* (Stockholm 1866–1872).
SDHK: *Svenskt Diplomatariums Huvudkartotek över medeltidsbreven*, http://www.nad.riksarkivet.se/sdhk.

Studies

Alfonso Isabel, 'Cistercians and Feudalism', *Past & Present* 133 (1991), pp. 3–30.
Andersson, Catharina, *Kloster och aristokrati. Nunnor, munkar och gåvor i det svenska samhället till 1300-talets mitt* (Göteborg, 2006).
Andersson, Catharina, 'Vreta kloster ur ett gåvoperspektiv', in *Fokus Vreta kloster. 17 nya rön om Sveriges äldsta kloster*, ed. Göran Tagesson, Elisabet Regner, Birgitta Alinder, Lars Ladell (Stockholm, 2010), pp. 257–259.
Berntsson, Martin, *Klostren och reformationen. Upplösningen av kloster och konvent i Sverige 1523–1596* (Skellefteå, 2003).

Bouchard, Constance Brittain, *Sword, Miter, and Cloister. Nobility and the Church in Burgundy, 980–1198* (Ithaca, 1987).
Collmar, Magnus, *Strängnäs stifts herdaminne*, Del 1: Medeltiden (Nyköping, 1977).
Dovring, Folke, *Attungen och marklandet. Studier över agrara förhållanden i medeltidens Sverige* (Lund, 1947).
Ekström, Gunnar, *Västerås Stifts herdaminne*, vol. I. Medeltiden och reformationstiden. 1. Västerås stad (Falun, 1939).
France, James, *The Cistercians in Scandinavia* (Kalamazoo, 1992).
Gurevitj, Aaron, 'Wealth and Gift-Bestowal among the Ancient Scandinavians', *Scandinavica* 5 (1968), pp. 126–138.
Hadley D. M. (ed.), *Masculinity in Medieval Europe* (London, 1999).
Holmström, Marie and Claes Tollin, 'Alvastra klosters äldsta godsinnehav. Framväxt och rumslig struktur samt jämförelser med kontinentala förhållanden', in *I den Heliga Birgittas fotspår*, ed. Göran Dahlbäck (Stockholm, 1990), pp. 301-327.
Johansson, Hilding, *Ritus Cisterciensis. Studier i de svenska cistercienslostrens liturgi* (Lund, 1964).
de Jong, Mayke, *In Samuel's Image. Child Oblation in the early Medieval West* (Leiden, 1996).
Karras, Ruth Mazo, *From Boys to Men. Formations of Masculinity in Late Medieval Europe* (Philadelphia, 2003).
Lahtinen, Anu, *Anpassning, förhandling, motstånd. Kvinnliga aktörer i släkten Fleming 1470–1620* (Helsingfors, 2009).
Larsson, Lars-Olof, *Det medeltida Värend. Studier i det småländska gränslandets historia fram till 1500-talets mitt* (Lund, 1964).
Lawrence, C. H., *Medieval Monasticism. Forms of Religious Life in Western Europe in the Middle Ages* (Harlow, 2001 [1984]).
Lees, Clare A. (ed.), *Medieval Masculinities. Regarding Men in the Middle Ages* (Minneapolis, 1994).
Lekai, Louis J., *The Cistercians. Ideal and Reality* (Kent, 1977).
Lindkvist, Thomas, 'The *Lagmän* (Law-Speakers) as Regional Elite in Medieval Västergötland', in *Les élites nordiques et l'Europe occidentale, XIIe-XVe siècle*, ed. Tuomas Lehtonen & Élisabeth Mornet (Paris 2007), pp. 67-78.
Ljung, Sven, "Prelatskolan' på Fjällskäfte gård. Till ärkebiskop Nicolaus Ragvaldis biografi', *Personhistorisk Tidskrift* 61 (1963), pp. 41–53.
Lynch, Joseph H, 'Monastic Recruitment in the Eleventh and Twelfth Centuries: Some Social and Economic Considerations', *American Benedictine Review* 26 (1975), pp. 425–447.
Lynch, Joseph H, *Simonical Entry into Religious Life from 1000 to 1260. A Social, Economic and Legal study* (Columbus, 1976).
Miller, William Ian, 'Gift, Sale, Payment, Raid: Case Studies in the Negotiation and Classification of Exchange in Medieval Iceland', *Speculum* 61 (1986), pp. 18–50.
Myrdal, Janken, *Medeltidens åkerbruk. Agrarteknik i Sverige ca 1000 till 1520* (Stockholm, 1986).
Newman, Martha G, *The Boundaries of Charity. Cistercian Culture and Ecclesiastical Reform, 1098-1180* (Stanford, 1996).
Ney, Agneta, 'Myter, ideologi och ogifta kvinnor. Mö-traditionen i fornnordisk myt och verklighet', in *Makalösa kvinnor. Könsöverskridare i myt och verklighet*, ed. Eva Borgström

(Göteborg, 2002), pp. 25–61.
Nilsson, Bertil, *Sveriges kyrkohistoria. Missionstid och tidig medeltid* (Stockholm, 1998).
Nordmark, Marie-Lousie, 'Nanne Kärling, munk och frälseman. Studier kring en medeltida arvsprocess', *Kyrkohistorisk Årsskrift* 42 (1942), pp. 124–153.
Nyberg, Tore, *Monasticism in North-Western Europe, 800-1200* (Aldershot, 2000).
Raneke, Jan, *Svenska medeltidsvapen* II (Nora, 2001).
Ortved, Edvard, *Cistercieordenen og dens klostre i Norden,* del II: Sveriges klostre (København, 1933).
Salonen, Kirsi, 'Fallet Nanne Kärling. Att kombinera biografiska uppgifter ur olika arkiv', in *Ny väg till medeltidsbreven,* ed. Claes Gejrot, Roger Andersson, and Kerstin Abukhanfusa (Stockholm, 2002), pp. 99-106.
Stensland, Per G., *Julita klosters godspolitik* (Stockholm, 1945).
Swanson, R. N., 'Angels Incarnate: Clergy and Masculinity from Gregorian reform to Reformation', in *Masculinity in Medieval Europe,* ed. D. M. Hadley (London, 1999), pp. 160–177.
Thibodeaux, Fennifer D., *Negotiating Clerical Identities. Priests, Monks and Masculinity in the Middle Ages* (Basingstoke, 2010).
Winroth, Anders, 'Den världsliga grundvalen för Gudsberga kloster. Ett senmedeltida klosters ekonomiska förhållanden', *Bebyggelsehistorisk tidskrift* 13 (1987), pp. 97-112.
Åsbrink, Gustav, and Knut B. Westman, *Svea Rikes ärkebiskopar från 1164 till nuvarande tid* (Stockholm, 1935).
ÄSF: Äldre svenska frälsesläkter. Ättartavlor, published by Riddarhusdirektionen, ed. Folke Wernstedt, Hans Gillingstam, Pontus Möller (Stockholm, 1957–1989).

Monastic locations cited in the article.

Networks, Contacts, and Change in Alvastra Abbey, c. 1185-1350

Elisabet Regner

Among the archaeological finds from Alvastra abbey, the first Cistercian settlement in Sweden, are pilgrim badges from Spain, German stoneware, French ivory carvings, Norwegian coins and seals owned by Swedish nobility. These small finds, fragmented and often overlooked in monastic research, speak volumes of a monastic institution not only deeply enmeshed with its region but with contacts across Europe.

Recent monastic research has focussed on regional differences and interactions between the Cistercians and secular society.[1] This research has shown that while there is great uniformity in Cistercian art and architecture – seen by the Cistercians themselves as the outward expression of the Order – there are also regional variations.[2] On a political level, there is a new understanding of not only the ties to royal founders, but also the importance of donors from local society.[3] Today, it seems clear that the abbeys of the order were deeply dependent on local society for survival and growth. There has also been a renewed interest in social relations within the abbeys, deriving inspiration from sociological research on so-called total institutions.[4] This paper will focus on the abbey of Alvastra in the province of Östergötland in Sweden, and attempt to trace patterns of continuity and change with particular focus on its relations to secular society.

An underlying question also concerns structures of long-term change within the Cistercian order in Sweden. Traditionally, the study of the Cistercians has emphasized the importance of the order in the twelfth century. The theme of this volume is the idea of a long thirteenth century, and the relevance of a long-term perspective. In this paper, I will deal with several kinds of change in the material culture of Alvastra in an attempt to define points of change.

---

1 For instance Bouchard (1991); Jamroziak & Burton ed. (2006); Jamroziak (2005), (2011).
2 Untermann (2001); Mohn (2006); Rüffer (2008).
3 Andersson (2006); Rasmussen (2006)
4 Füser (2000); Cassidy-Welch (2001)

On continuity and change

The theme of continuity and change has for a long time been at the heart of monastic research. Jean Louis Lekai's 1977 study of the Cistercians was very influential in emphasizing a conflict between ideals and reality as a driving force in monastic change.[5] This perspective has also been used to study the Swedish Cistercians.[6] One of the distinguishing features of the Cistercian Order was its great coherence both in religious practices and in architectural form. Within Cistercian studies much effort has been invested into defining what constitutes this similarity and coherence, how it was upheld and what its most important characteristics were.[7] Similarity has been interpreted as a result of adherence to a monastic ideal, while changes are seen as the result of a conflict between that ideal and social reality.

In Sweden, the earliest excavations of monastic sites were made in the first half of the nineteenth century, and larger excavations continued to be made up to the 1950s.[8] These excavations were to a large part focussed either on finding royal burials or on clearing the remains of the central abbey buildings and turning them into ruin parks. Studies of the abbey architecture were generally oriented to the establishment and earliest period of the abbeys and the similarities with Cistercian architecture in continental Europe.[9] The rest of the archaeological material, burials and small finds, was rarely comprehensively published apart from the royal burials.[10] In recent years, there has been a resurgence of interest in monastic archaeology in general, both through new, large-scale excavations and through re-examination of older material.[11] This research has concentrated both on more traditional themes such as royal burials but has also explored newer themes such as power structures, change and the relationship to secular society.

The archaeological material provides a view from within the abbey, clues to life inside the monastic walls. Burials, coins, ceramics and architecture are well suited to illuminate the themes of culture contacts and change. Material culture is an active part both in social relations and change.[12] It is used both intention-

---

5 Lekai (1977).
6 Parikh (1991)
7 Curman (1912); Aubert (1947); Dimier (1949); Auberger (1986); Untermann (2001)
8 For example Hildebrand (1898), Curman & Lundberg (1935), Frödin (1942), Schnell (1964),
9 Curman (1912); Curman & Lundberg (1935); Swartling (1967a,b), (1969).
10 For instance Fürst (1920, 1928); Roth (1973a,b); Svanberg (1987).
11 Menander & Tagesson (2005); Tagesson & Regner et al. (2010); Borgehammar & Wienberg (ed.) (2012).
12 Shanks & Tilley (1987).

ally and unintentionally to enforce, negotiate or subvert power-relations. As an example, the thirteenth century Cistercian concept, *forma ordinis*, the form of material things that distinguished the Cistercians from others, shows that the Cistercians themselves used material culture intentionally to create unity within the order and to define themselves in relation to others. The activities of the Cistercians grew out of their interpretation of central religious symbols. However, they still shared ingrained ideas and customs with secular society and these changed over time. The Cistercians are best understood as a product of that society, not as a separate entity. The relationship between secular culture and monastic culture should be seen as an ongoing reciprocal process of mutual change that occurs through action and social relations. The aim of this study is to trace that process at the abbey of Alvastra.

Thirty years of archaeology[13]

In the early nineteenth century, antiquarian Leonard Räf conducted excavations at Alvastra Abbey during which the tombstone of Saint Birgitta's husband Ulf Gudmarsson was discovered. Later in the same century, the ruins of the abbey church were restored and the interior of the ruins cleared of rubble, down to the presumed medieval floor level. However, more large-scale excavations were still to come.

During the 1910's, the archaeologist Otto Frödin was conducting excavations of both stone-age and medieval remains in the vicinity of the abbey. These excavations were only concluded after his death in 1953. During over thirty years of excavation, the whole of the central abbey building complex was excavated. This article is based on the archaeological material recovered during this excavation.[14]

As a prehistoric archaeologist, Frödin used stratigraphic field methods that were advanced for his time. The site was excavated in a grid, creating profiles that cut through the cultural layers. All layers were documented, and any features recorded both in scale drawings and through tower photography. Field journals listed any important observations not contained in other forms of documentation. More than 50,000 small finds were meticulously recovered, and specimens of organic materials were collected of which some are still kept in the original test-tubes. The excavations at Alvastra abbey were one of the first

---

13 See Regner (2005) for a general overview of excavations at the site and methods used.
14 The documentation – field journals, scale drawings and photographs - is kept at the archives of the Swedish National Heritage Board (Antikvarisk-Topografiska Arkivet). The small finds are in the Swedish History Museum (Historiska museet) in Stockholm.

Excavations underway at Alvastra Abbey in 1922. The stratigraphy of the site was recorded through profiles running north-south and east-west across the site (Photo H. Faith-Ell 1922, © Riksantikvarieämbetet/ATA).

At Alvastra, burials were excavated in the church, sacristy, north cloister and chapter house as well as outside the church. These burials were found in the nave before the high altar, probably buried in the space left free between the monks' choir stalls (Photo 1927, © Riksantikvarieämbetet/ATA).

Pilgrims' badges from several different pilgrimage sites were found at Alvastra, for instance this badge from Aachen (Photo Gabriel Hildebrandt 2011, © SHMM).

Fragment of an ivory crozier, originally depicting the coronation of Mary, probably made in France in the mid-14th century (Photo Christer Åhlin 2008, © SHMM).

instances in which medieval remains in Sweden were excavated and recorded in this way. Frödin himself published a handful of articles concerning the excavations, but his death in 1953 meant that there was never any comprehensive publication. The small finds were catalogued at the Museum of National Antiquities, and the documentation from the excavation was in time filed at the National Heritage Board. The architecture of the abbey was published in 1969 by Ingrid Swartling.[15]

Frödin also excavated a handful of medieval remains outside the abbey buildings proper, closer to the shores of lake Vättern. One building should probably be interpreted as a crypt church dating to around 1100, possibly with baptismal wells, and surrounded by a very large cemetery, while another building might have been used for parchment production.[16]

While there are source-critical problems associated with older archaeological materials compared to current stratigraphic methods, the archaeological material recovered by Frödin does represent an almost untapped source of information concerning life in the abbey.

A network of friends and benefactors

The monastic community was positioned in a network of power relations involving members of secular society. The majority of the Swedish abbeys was founded by members of the royal family. In the case of Alvastra, the founder was King Sverker the Elder and his Queen Ulvhilde.[17] By providing the original grants of land that made the establishment of an abbey possible, the founder played a crucial role in the history of the abbey.

Lars Hermanson has shown that the social and political position of the elite in early-medieval Nordic society was to a large extent based on a horizontal network of relations within a bilateral kinship system centred on the individual.[18] The members of a particular social network frequently acted as witnesses in transactions involving other members, and so the networks are visible through the witness lists in different kinds of documents.

The wills and deeds from Alvastra reveal that only a small group of documents was witnessed and/or sealed by the abbey of Alvastra or its abbot. During the thirteenth and early fourteenth centuries, these wills/deeds were all issued by individuals who were either connected to the area around the abbey, or re-

---

15 Swartling (1969)
16 Frödin (1918), (1919), (1921), (1933); Ersgård (2006); Holmström (2006), (2012).
17 France (1992), p. 27.
18 Hermanson (2000).

lated to the Sverker and Folkunga families (or both). It would also seem that the small number of wills containing a *pitancia* or gift of extra food to the abbey was to a large extent issued by the same persons or their family members. This network was centred on members of the Ama family.[19]

The Ama family was related by blood and marriage to both the older royal dynasty of the Sverker family, and the royal line of the Folkunga family. During at least three generations the men of the Ama family were knighted and they maintained close relationships with the kings of the Folkunga dynasty. At least one son went into the church and became a member of the cathedral chapter of Linköping in the province of Östergötland. Several members of the Ama family chose to be buried at Alvastra Abbey.[20]

The close ties between Alvastra Abbey and the Ama family probably affected the abbey in several ways. It gave it an important link to the royal family, and the abbey received exempt status during this time. However, the continuing ties to the higher levels of the nobility do not exclude the possibility that bonds with the lower nobility played a significant, perhaps even decisive, role for the abbey.[21] The number of donations to Alvastra remained fairly constant from the middle of the thirteenth to the middle of the fourteenth century, when secular support seems to have decreased. At this time, there are also indications that recruitment to the abbey may have widened also to include the burgher class.[22] This development coincides not only with the Black Death and the establishment of the Birgittine convent of Vadstena, but also with the disappearance of the Ama family. After the middle of the fourteenth century no single family would predominate among the abbey's donors in the same way.

The Ama family is an example of how long-term power structures were established and continued through the thirteenth century. Why, then, was it so important for the knightly class to maintain family-based social relations with the abbey? The social network that constituted their primary basis of power was by its nature unstable – an individual could form new alliances with other branches of his or her family. Donations to an abbey were made to an institution that was supposed to last forever. The institution was stable, permanent. Therefore, by forming a lasting relationship with an abbey the family could in a sense create some stability in its networks, which became more like institutions themselves. Kim Esmark has argued that recurring donations from the

---

19 See Regner (2005) for a more detailed discussion of donations to the abbey.
20 The Ama family has been described by Gillingstam (1957-1989); Fritz (1988).
21 See Andersson's contribution in this volume.
22 In 1348, Sven goldsmith in Söderköping and his wife make a donation to Alvastra at the entry of their son Sven. SDHK 5599.

same family to Sorø abbey was not only a result of family consciousness but, in fact, a way to create and maintain that consciousness.[23] By becoming part of the social networks of the nobility the abbey in turn became part of the structure of medieval society. This way of building power broke down in the middle of the fourteenth century, resulting in a decrease in donations to Alvastra Abbey. This development would in turn deeply affect life in the abbey and is an important aspect of the interpretation of the material culture of Alvastra.

Burying the dead

In medieval society, the dead were much more present than today in the minds of the living.[24] Nowhere was this truer than within the monastic culture. The Cistercians encountered the dead in all parts of their world. They read masses for them in church, they tripped over tombstones in the cloister and the food on the refectory table was paid for by the donations of the deceased. The Cistercians were originally restrictive concerning the burial of lay people within the abbey churches, but they nevertheless became important burial places.[25] In the abbeys, prayers and masses for the dead and anniversaries of the death of donors occupied an extensive amount of time. Burial was also at the core of the reciprocal relationship established with donors.

The medieval burial can be seen as a tripartite rite of passage, meant to guide the individual from life through separation from the living to transition to the afterlife. These rites ideally began in the home with confession and absolution before death and the preparation of the dead body, which was probably a task that was frequently performed by the female relatives of the deceased. The rites continued with burial in the cemetery. However, in the medieval world the remembrance of the dead continued long after the burial of the body with masses and prayers. As a part of these memorial practices, tombs, gravestones and other markers were used to give the grave a patent form.[26] All these stages can be studied archaeologically.

At Alvastra, burials were excavated in the church, the north cloister and the chapter house. Test-trenches showed that there were also burials to the west, north and east of the church. In particular in the abbey church and the chapter house, there were up to four layers of burials and large quantities of bones disturbed by later burials.

---

23 Esmark (2006).
24 Ariès (1977).
25 Johansson (1964).
26 Gilchrist & Sloane (2005).

It is clear from wills and from the archaeological material that individuals from secular society were buried at Alvastra from the earliest times. The seals found in the abbey church show that from the fourteenth century onwards there was a significant number of lay people of varying social status buried in the abbey church.[27] Linda Rasmussen has argued that older research has under-emphasized the occurrence of monastic benefaction in lower levels of society.[28] At Alvastra, the seal matrices indicate that at least during the later Middle Ages, burial in the monastic church was possible for individuals of the lower nobility and the burgher class as well. There is also a matrix belonging to a priest in a nearby parish church.

During the period between the 1100s and 1350, the dead were buried in both the chapter house and the church. In the later Middle Ages the chapter house continued to be used sporadically for burials, but not to the same extent as the church, where the number of burials increased. This development also occurred in the surrounding society and in other Cistercian abbeys, indicating a broader shift in burial practices that affected the abbey as well.[29] It seems likely that individuals from secular society were a driving force behind the shift towards more burials in the church.

The chapter house is often seen as a burial place exclusively for the abbots of the abbey. At Alvastra, this was probably never the case. During the excavations, more than 60 burials were recorded in the chapter house, among them several burials of children. In fact, such burials were also found in other places such as the north cloister walk, the nave, the choir and the north transept. While osteological analyses are required to discuss changes in burial practices based on age and/or sex, it is possible that the frequency of burials of children has varied over time.

Burial was not only a matter of the body, but also of giving the grave a manifest form. Limestone cists had been used in the chapter-house, the sacristy and the church, but they were more common in the church where they occurred in the transepts and the nave. The cists were therefore in all likelihood for persons with a special relationship with the abbey. The cists were still in use in the early part of the 1300s, but after 1350 new cists were no longer being built. At Alvastra, there are no fragments of tombstones from the late twelfth/thirteenth century, only fragments of gothic tombstones. It is likely that from the fourteenth century on tombstones along with chapels and altars were erected to commemorate the dead. Megan Cassidy-Welch has interpreted the presence of

---

27 Regner (2004).
28 Rasmussen (2006).
29 Andrén (2000).

tombstones in the Yorkshire abbeys as attempts to curtail the presence of the dead and to control them by assigning them specific sites in the church and abbey buildings.[30] At the same time, the dead were thereby in a very distinct way represented within monastic space.

The attempt to control the dead through the use of space coincided with a significant change in the general burial practices in the abbey, a change fostered by secular society. The attempts of the abbey to link the dead and their memory to certain sites within the abbey may then be seen as an expression of a conflict between old and new practices.

Constructing the Abbey

The architecture of the abbey regulated the movements of the monks and lay brothers for most of their adult life. Cistercian architecture exhibits great conformity across time and space, a conformity that must be viewed as the result of an active choice to use or discard certain architectural forms, reflecting Cistercian ideas about self and the identity of the order.[31] It was primarily an architecture of stone, a material that has qualities other building materials do not possess: its permanence signifies continuity and stability of form and function across time. It may therefore also stand for stability and permanence within the monastic community and the Cistercian Order. Changes in architectural form may therefore also signal changes in the self-perception of a particular abbey.

Before the establishment of a Cistercian community certain buildings had to be provided, namely an oratory, a refectory, a dormitory, a hospice and a gate-house. These buildings could be of irregular form and were in general built of wood. At Alvastra, the earliest buildings have not yet been identified. According to Ann-Cathrine Bonnier, Frödin found remains of three wooden buildings under the western range.[32] However, if this was the case they were either not recorded or Frödins interpretation may have been incorrect. The documentation shows that there were post-holes both in the cloister and under the western range but they do not necessarily belong to houses or even to the earliest phase of the abbey. It is therefore quite likely that the permanent stone buildings were not erected directly on top of earlier buildings. However, they may still have been very close - the area immediately to the west of the western range has not been excavated.

The architecture and building history of the abbey has been discussed by sev-

---

30 Cassidy-Welch (2001).
31 See for instance Unternann (2001).
32 Bonnier (2012), p. 22.

eral authors and the general view is as follows.[33] The abbey church at Alvastra had the usual cruciform plan used in most of the abbeys within the Order, with a presbytery flanked by four chapels. It was consecrated in 1185. The church was vaulted with a barrel vault running the length of the nave. The floor of the church was completely gone at the time of the excavations. The sacristy was placed adjacent to the south transept and had a lower floor level. It was provided with an altar as late as the first half of the fourteenth century. The earliest burials in both the church and the sacristy can be dated to the period before c. 1250. The eastern range came into use in the thirteenth century. The south range as a whole has not been dated, but it appears likely that it was erected during the course of the thirteenth century. The western range as a whole may have been a part of the original abbey buildings, but it is also possible that this range was not erected until the fifteenth century. These buildings were all constructed of ashlars. At the heart of the abbey lay the cloister and the cloister garth. It is difficult to draw any definitive conclusions concerning the cloister from the excavations. It is likely that at least the northern half of the cloister garth at Alvastra was built as part of the first permanent abbey buildings. It is not impossible that the southern part was not built until much later, a parallel to the development in Denmark.[34]

The earliest buildings at Alvastra were all part of the central claustral buildings, representing strong iconographic ties to the Cistercian Order. In other Swedish abbeys of the order – Vreta, Varnhem, Gudhem, Julita – the same pattern may be discerned. In the early years resources were invested primarily in the church and the east, south and west ranges. An important distinction must however be made between the nunneries and the monasteries. The nunneries seem on the whole to have invested primarily in the eastern range, with its strong connections to institutionalisation and the expression of Cistercian identity (the chapter house). Other buildings continued to be less well regulated. This would in turn indicate a gender-based difference in the relationship with the Cistercian Order.[35]

At Alvastra, a fire in 1312 was followed by extensive building work both within the claustral buildings and in adjacent buildings. In the area east of the eastern range, there were at least five houses erected during the fourteenth and fifteenth centuries. Four of these were built of stone. In contrast to the adjacent cloister buildings, these houses were built alternately of limestone and granite,

---

33 Swartling (1969); Regner (2005); Bonnier (2012).
34 Krongaard Kristensen (2000).
35 Swartling (1967a, b), (1969). Edenheim & Lidén (1978); Curman & Lundberg (1935); Schnell (1964); Edenheim & Rosell (1982); Regner (2005).

they may have been plastered and they were provided with coloured glass windows.[36] These buildings have been interpreted by Frödin and Swartling as the guesthouse, infirmary and abbot's house, while Johanna Bergqvist has recently suggested that all the buildings may have constituted an infirmary complex.[37] However, it has been shown that in English abbeys the uses of these types of building complexes could be quite interchangeable - many grand infirmary buildings were also used as abbots' lodgings and guest-houses.[38]

The outer form and interior plan of these houses have close parallels in secular buildings, in particular town residences. They do not use elements from Cistercian architecture to express a Cistercian identity; instead the use of elements from secular architecture expresses a new sense of proximity to secular society. The houses were, however, placed in accordance with a "Cistercian plan", indicating that a secular element was in a sense incorporated into the structure of the abbey. This development coincides in time with the breakdown in the social network of the abbey, and may have been a response to changes in the relationship between the abbey and secular society. By incorporating these secular houses into the permanent structure of the abbey this new relationship was made manifest and presented as natural, everlasting and legitimate.

Money, trade and consumption

The stone architecture of the abbey was well suited to create stability and continuity within the abbey. The objects that the individual handled during a lifetime within the abbey walls – the cup he drank from, the quill he held in his hand – were susceptible to more rapid changes that would be noticed by the individual. While monastic artefact assemblages exhibit several distinguishing traits, such as liturgical objects, writing equipment, ornate metalwork and the like, the main part is to a large extent of the same artefact types that may be found in secular society. It is difficult to find "typically Cistercian" traits in the artefacts. The Cistercians were using artefacts available in the surrounding society, and the artefacts from abbey excavations may be used to study contacts between the abbey and this surrounding society.

The use of coins, or rather the existence of a common currency, has been emphasised as an important difference between the medieval and the prehistoric

---

36 Swartling (1969); Regner (2005).
37 Frödin (1942); Swartling (1969); Bergqvist (2013), pp. 428-433.
38 Hall (2004).

economy.³⁹ When Alvastra Abbey was founded in 1143 there was no national currency, but rather several monetary regions with their own separate currencies.⁴⁰ In Alvastra coins were used at a fairly early stage, but the general breakthrough of a money-based economy seems to have occurred some 50 years later than in the surrounding society.⁴¹ Some 1450 coins were retrieved during the excavations at Alvastra abbey, and the main part of this material is medieval.⁴² During the period 1140–1350 domestic currency, particularly coins which were minted and/or circulated in the surrounding region of eastern Götaland, dominated the currency used in Alvastra. A small number of coins was minted outside this region and international currency was scarce. This fact would appear to indicate that during this time the monastery was an integral part of the regional monetary system. This situation changed during the second half of the fourteenth century. After the 1360s, international currency became more common at Alvastra. The coin material indicates that increasing international contacts were primarily directed towards the northern German and Baltic area, and that a large number of towns and regions controlled by the Hansa were represented. A comparison with coin material from towns and parish churches shows that even though international currency seems to have circulated widely, there are in general fewer mints represented. Heterogeneous assemblages of coins comparable to the material from Alvastra are in general found only in larger religious institutions such as the convent of Vadstena or the cathedral of Linköping. In Alvastra, increasing contacts with the German area are visible also through the occurrence of pilgrims' badges from Aachen and Wilsnack, which are exceptionally rare finds in Scandinavia.⁴³ However, a study of pilgrimage in Lübeck wills shows Wilsnack in particular as one of the most popular pilgrimage sites in the fifteenth and early sixteenth centuries.⁴⁴

Changes in the international contacts of the abbey are visible in the ceramic material as well. During the period between *c.* 1140 and the 1350s, pottery consumption was limited, the abbey primarily using small amounts of imported ceramics intended for the table. It is possible that wooden tableware was also used, but which has not survived until the present day. It is likely

---

39 Klackenberg (1992).
40 Jonsson (1995).
41 Klackenberg (1992), p. 94, 96.
42 See Malmer (1982) for chronological and chorological analysis. The coin attributions in the following text were made by Nils Ludvig Rasmusson and compiled by Brita Malmer. The archival material kept in the Royal Coin Cabinet in Stockholm. See also Regner (2005).
43 Andersson (1989).
44 Selch Jensen (2003).

that the tableware at Alvastra was less varied and the consumption of food was less ritualised. From the mid-fourteenth century onwards, German stoneware dominated the pottery used in the abbey. This would mirror the development in the larger medieval trading towns such as Stockholm,[45] and in all likelihood nearby Söderköping.

An interesting future area of research is the question of which types of food was consumed. There is a large osteological material from Alvastra that has not yet been studied. However, roe deer is present in the assemblage indicating that food consumption may at some point in time have been quite exclusive.

Among the more elite finds at Alvastra are fragments of fourteenth century ivory carvings. One fragment comes from a devotional image, probably a diptych or a triptych. Three fragments probably come from a crozier. One of these is a seated Virgin Mary possibly originally part of a scene depicting the coronation of the Virgin. Both fragments have traces of paint and gilding, and are probably of French manufacture. Interestingly, there is a will from 1318 in which Lars Ulfsson (Ama) and his wife Ingrid Anundsdotter donate an ivory piece for their altar.[46] It is tempting to connect this donation with the above fragment, but the date of the donation may be too early. In this case several or at least two ivory pieces would have been owned by the abbey.

Conclusion

As a starting point for understanding monastic culture in Scandinavia the theme in this paper, a "long" thirteenth century, certainly seems appropriate in looking at the archaeology of Alvastra. The archaeological material does not indicate that the thirteenth century was a period of diminishing importance and declining secular support. Instead, I would argue that the thirteenth century was a time of great stability, a continuation of conditions of life in the abbey established in the twelfth century. The abbey was supported by a network of friends, great investments were made in central but also traditional abbey buildings, trade and consumption was local rather than interregional. The archaeological material, however, points to the middle of the fourteenth century as a time of deep change. Several if not all of the changes discussed here may be interpreted as part of a transformation of the relationship between the abbey and secular society at this time.

By opening the abbey to lay persons and making them a part of the Cistercian brotherhood, the monks adapted a traditional structure to changing circum-

---

45 Gaimster (2002).
46 SDHK 2907.

stances. At the same time, the very relationship with the laity changed. The position and authority of the Cistercians stemmed in large part from their distance and isolation from lay society. This position was undermined when the distance between the abbey and secular society diminished.

Literature

Andersson, Lars, *Pilgrimsmärken och vallfart. Medeltida pilgrimskultur i Skandinavien* (Stockholm, 1989).

Andersson, Catharina, *Kloster och aristokrati: nunnor, munkar och gåvor i det svenska samhället till 1300-talets mitt* (Göteborg, 2006).

Andrén, Anders, 'Ad sanctos - de dödas plats under medeltiden', *Hikuin* 27 (2000), pp. 7-26.

Ariès, Philippe, *L'homme devant la mort* (Paris, 1977).

Auberger, Jean-Baptiste, *L'unanimité cistercienne primitive: mythe ou réalité?* (Achel, 1986).

Aubert, Marcel, *L'architecture cistercienne en France* (Paris, 1947).

Bergqvist, Johanna, *Läkare och läkande. Läkekonstens professionalisering i Sverige under medeltid och renässans* (Lund, 2013).

Bonnier, Ann Catherine, 'Alvastra kloster och kyrkobyggandet i Östergötland', in *Munkar och magnater vid Vättern: studier från forskningsprojektet "Det medeltida Alvastra"* ed. Lars Ersgård (Lund, 2012), pp. 7-88.

Borgehammar, Stephan & Jes Wienberg (ed.), *Locus Celebris: Dalby kyrka, kloster och gård* (Göteborg, 2012).

Bouchard, Constance Brittain, *Holy entrepreneurs: Cistercians, knights, and economic exchange in twelfth-century Burgundy* (Ithaca, N.Y., 1991).

Cassidy-Welch, Megan, *Monastic spaces and their meanings: thirteenth-century English Cistercian monasteries* (Turnhout, 2001).

Curman, Sigurd & Erik Lundberg, *Östergötland. Bd 2, Vreta klosters kyrka* (Stockholm, 1935).

Curman, Sigurd, *Bidrag till kännedomen om Cistercienserordens byggnadskonst 1: Kyrkoplanen* (Stockholm 1912).

Dimier, Marie-Anselme, *Recueil de plans d'églises cisterciennes* (Grignan & Paris, 1949).

Edenheim, Ralph & Ingrid Rosell, *Varnhems klosterkyrka: Valle härad, Västergötland* (Stockholm, 1982).

Edenheim, Ralph & Hans A. Lidén, *Julita kloster* (Stockholm, 1978).

Ersgård, Lars, 'Dödens berg och Guds hus: förfäderskult, kristnande och kloster i Alvastra i den tidiga medeltidens Östergötland', in *Helgonets boning: studier från forskningsprojektet "Det medeltida Alvastra"* ed. Lars Ersgård (Lund, 2006) pp. 23-140.

Ersgård, Lars (ed.), *Helgonets boning: studier från forskningsprojektet "Det medeltida Alvastra"* (Lund, 2006).

Ersgård, Lars (ed.), *Munkar och magnater vid Vättern: studier från forskningsprojektet "Det medeltida Alvastra"* (Lund, 2012).

Esmark, Kim, 'Religious patronage and family consciousness: Sorø abbey and the 'Hvide family', c. 1150-1250' in *Religious and laity in Western Europe, 1000-1400: interaction, negotiation, and power,* ed. Emilia Jamroziak & Janet E. Burton (Turnhout, 2006).

France, James, *The Cistercians in Scandinavia* (Kalamazoo, Mich., 1992).
Fritz, Birgitta, 'Riddaren Lars Ulfsson (Ama)', in *Medeltid*, ed. Gösta Vogel-Rödin (Skövde, 1988), pp. 77-87.
Frödin, Otto, 'Alvastra under medeltiden: undersökningarna år 1917', *Meddelanden från Östergötlands och Linköpings stads museum* (1918), pp. 43-114.
Frödin, Otto, 'Från det medeltida Alvastra: undersökningarna 1918', *Fornvännen* (1919), pp. 43-68.
Frödin, Otto, 'Från det medeltida Alvastra: undersökningarna år 1919', *Fornvännen* (1920), pp. 169-197.
Frödin, Otto, 'Alvastra under medeltiden: undersökningarna år 1920', *Meddelanden från Östergötlands och Linköpings stads museum* (1921), pp. 74-84.
Frödin, Otto, 'Den äldsta klosterkyrkan i Alvastra', *Fornvännen* (1933), pp. 168-181.
Frödin, Otto, 'Alvastra kloster, inför ett 800-årsminne', *Svenska Turistföreningens Årsskrift* (1942), pp. 137-164.
Fürst, Carl M., *När de döda vittna* (Stockholm, 1920).
Fürst, Carl M., *Birger Jarls grav i Varnhems klosterkyrka* (Stockholm, 1928).
Füser, Thomas, *Mönche im Konflikt: zum Spannungsfeld von Norm, Devianz und Sanktion bei den Cisterziensern und Cluniazensern (12. bis frühes 14. Jahrhundert)* (Münster, 2000).
Gaimster, David R. M., 'Keramik i Stockholm 1250-1600: inflytande från Hansans handel, kultur och teknik', *Upptaget. Arkeologi i Stockholm inför 2000-talet. Sankt Eriks Årsbok* (2002), pp. [189]-210.
Gilchrist, Roberta & Barney Sloane, *Requiem: the medieval monastic cemetery in Britain* (London, 2005).
Gillingstam, Hans, 'Ama', in *Äldre svenska frälsesläkter. Attartavlor* ed. Folke Wernstedt (Stockholm, 1957-1989), pp. 107-110.
Hall, Jackie, 'East of the Cloister. Infirmaries, Abbots lodgings and other Chambers', in *Perspectives for an Architecture of Solitude. Essays on Cistercians, Art and Architeture in Honour of Peter Fergusson*, ed. Terryl N. Kinder (Turnhout, 2004), pp. 199-211.
Hermanson, Lars, *Släkt, vänner och makt: en studie av elitens politiska kultur i 1100-talets Danmark* (Göteborg, 2000).
Hildebrand, Hans, 'Sko kloster och dess kyrka', *Upplands fornminnesförenings tidskrift* (1898).
Holmström, Marie, 'Makten och Himmelriket: kontinentala kontakter och föränderliga förbindelser i det medeltida Alvastra och Linköpings stift', in *Helgonets boning: studier från forskningsprojektet "Det medeltida Alvastra"* ed. Lars Ersgård (Lund, 2006), pp. 141-240.
Holmström, Marie, 'Kontinental ideologi i monastisk regi: cistercienserna och "Sverkerskapellet" vid Alvastra kloster i ny belysning', in *Munkar och magnater vid Vättern: studier från forskningsprojektet "Det medeltida Alvastra"*, ed. Lars Ersgård (Lund, 2012), pp. 151-262.
Jamroziak, Emilia & Janet E. Burton (ed.), *Religious and laity in Western Europe, 1000-1400: interaction, negotiation, and power* (Turnhout, 2006).
Jamroziak, Emilia, *Survival and success on medieval borders: Cistercian houses in medieval Scotland and Pomerania from the twelfth to the late fourteenth century* (Turnhout, 2011).
Johansson, Hilding, *Ritus Cisterciensis: studier i de svenska cistercienklostrens liturgi* (Lund, 1964).
Jonsson, Kenneth, 'Från utländsk metall till inhemskt mynt', in *Myntningen i Sverige 995-1995*, ed. Kenneth Jonsson, Ulf Nordlind & Ian Wiséhn (Stockholm, 1995), pp. 43-61.

Klackenberg, Henrik, *Moneta nostra: monetarisering i medeltidens Sverige* (Stockholm, 1992).
Krongaard Kristensen, Hans, 'Korsgangsmotivet ved danske klostre', in *Aspekter af dansk klostervæsen i middelalderen,* ed. Inger-Lise Kolstrup (Aarhus, 2000), pp. 47-76.
Lekai, Louis J., *The Cistercians: ideals and reality* (Kent, Ohio, 1977).
Malmer, Brita, 'Numismatik och bebyggelsehistoria i Sverige – aspekter på den medeltida myntmassans korologi och kronologi', *Bebyggelsehistorisk Tidskrift 3* (1982), pp. 137-147.
Menander, Hanna & Göran Tagesson, 'Monastisk kultur i urban miljö: ett arkeologiskt perspektiv på östgötsk klosterforskning', in *Diocesis Lincopensis. 2, Medeltida internationella influenser: några uttryck för en framväxande östgötsk delaktighet i den västeuropeiska kultursfären,* ed. Kjell O. U. Lejon (Skellefteå, 2005).
Mohn, Claudia, *Mittelalterliche Klosteranlagen der Zisterzienserinnen: Architektur der Frauenklöster im mitteldeutschen Raum* (Petersberg, 2006).
Parikh, Kristin, *Kvinnoklostren på Östgötaslätten under medeltiden* (Lund, 1991).
Rasmussen, Linda, 'Monastic Benefactors in England and Denmark: Social Background and Gender Distribution', in *Religious and laity in Western Europe, 1000-1400: interaction, negotiation, and power,* ed. Emilia Jamroziak & Janet E. Burton, (Turnhout, 2006), pp. 77-93.
Regner, Elisabet, 'Sigillstampar och gravar från Alvastra kloster', *Fornvännen* (2004), pp. 193-200.
Regner, Elisabet, *Den reformerade världen. Alvastra kloster från medeltid till modern tid* (Stockholm, 2005).
Roth, Stig, *Gudhems klosterruin: grävningsberättelse avseende planform och murverk, altaren, stendekor och gravar* (Stockholm, 1973).
Rüffer, Jens, *Die Zisterzienser und ihre Klöster: leben und bauen für Gott* (Darmstadt, 2008).
Schnell, Ivar, *Fogdö kyrka och Vårfruberga kloster* (Nyköping, 1964).
Selch Jensen, Carsten, 'Stellvertretende Pilgerfahrten in lübischen Testamenten', in *Pilgerreisen im Mittelalter,* ed. Niels-Knud Liebgott et al. (Odense, 2003), pp. 22-51.
Shanks, Michael & Christopher Tilley, *Re-constructing archaeology: theory and practice* (Cambridge, 1987).
Svanberg, Jan, *Furstebilder från Folkungatid* (Skara, 1987).
Swartling, Ingrid, *Nydala abbey: an outline of its architecture from foundation to dissolution* (Stockholm, 1967).
Swartling, Ingrid, *Roma abbey church in the Middle Ages* (Stockholm, 1967).
Swartling, Ingrid, *Alvastra abbey: the first Cistercian settlement in Sweden* (Stockholm, 1969).
Tagesson, Göran & Elisabet Regner (ed.), *Fokus Vreta kloster: 17 nya rön om Sveriges äldsta kloster* (Stockholm, 2010).
Untermann, Matthias, *Forma ordinis: die mittelalterliche Baukunst der Zisterzienser* (München, 2001).

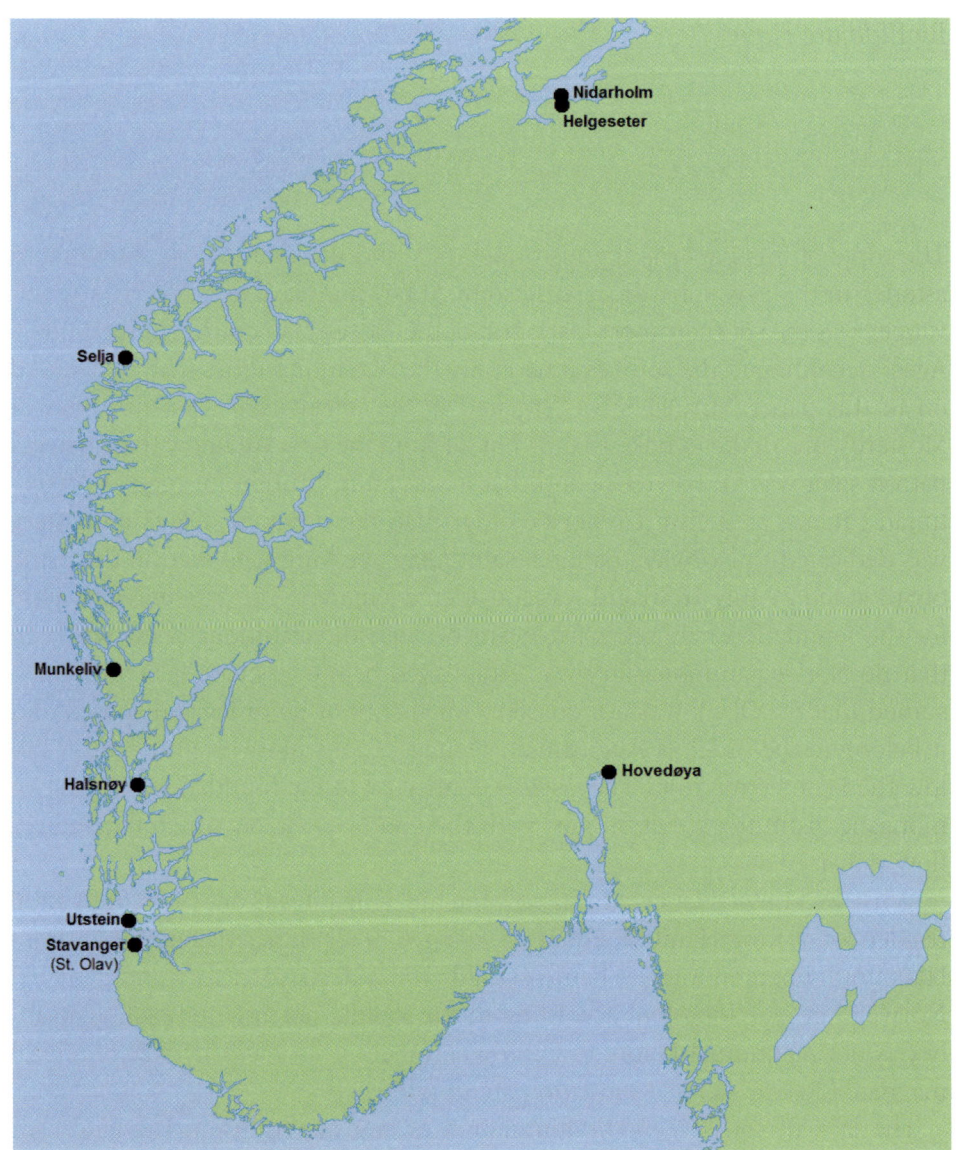

Monastic locations cited in the article.

Augustinian Canons and Benedictine Monks in the Medieval Stavanger Diocese

By Eldbjørg Haug

The topic of this paper is the historiography and the foundation of two monasteries in the Stavanger diocese, Utstein Abbey and St. Olav's Monastery. Stavanger was the southernmost bishopric of the Norwegian church in the Middle Ages. According to the sources it had only the two monasteries that are focused on in this paper. St. Olav's was situated in Stavanger itself, Utstein Abbey at Mosterøy, one of the Ryfylke islands not far from the city. We know that Utstein's patron saint was St. Lawrence and that it was an institution for regular Augustinian canons; as such it cannot be older than the order. St. Olav's monastery was dedicated to Norway's national saint Olav, the king who died in the battle of Stiklestad 29 July 1030 and was considered a martyr. This *terminus ante quem* for the foundation may seem irrelevant because the traditional view has been that no Norwegian monastery was established before c. 1100. It is further assumed that St. Olav's was a monastery for men, but its order is disputed; did it belong to the order of Augustinian regular canons like Utstein or did it follow the Benedictine rule? The issue is connected to the foundations of the two monastic institutions. Let us start with the younger one on which the sources flow richer:

What we know of Utstein's early ownership is that it was one of the four royal residences of King Harald Fairhair (c. 875 – c. 932). It is situated not far from Hafrsfjord where in a naval battle Harald won a decisive victory and gathered Norway into one kingdom according to the skaldic poem *Hrafnsmál*.[1] The abbey is not mentioned before c. 1280 when it received a gift by will of a local magnate.[2] Records of its foundation are unknown.

The lack of sources on the foundation of any monastery in the Stavanger church transforms the research on their earliest history to case studies in his-

---

1   *Hrafnsmál* ("raven's song") is a fragmentary skaldic poem that is preserved in *Heimskringla*. It is considered to be authored by the Norwegian skald Þorbjörn Hornklofi. Haug (2005c), pp. 55-63.
2   DN I:70.

torical method and new approaches in an attempt to extend the source material and interpret the existing evidence in new ways. Three men should be mentioned as pioneers in this discussion: Chr. C.A. Lange (1810-1861) was the first critical scholar on Norwegian monasteries including Utstein Abbey. Ludvig Ludvigsen Daae (1834-1910) was a great empiricist. He used new evidence and contextualised his finds by bringing the convent of St. Olav into the discussion. Asgaut Steinnes (1892-1973) was one of the founding fathers of the Norwegian agrarian school and used the retrogressive method on the cameral evidence of Utstein supported by letters and documents.[3] To these three scholars should be added architect Gerhard Fischer (1890-1977) who had a dominant position within medieval archaeology in the 20th century and performed the last restoring and the only limited excavation of Utstein.

Let us start with Asgaut Steinnes's research. In 1962 he published his analysis of monastic landed property in Rogaland, the modern county in which both Utstein Abbey and St. Olav's monastery are situated. Steinnes's point of departure was *Bergen Fundas*, the first narrative on the history of Bergen. It was probably written towards 1560 by one of the scriveners at the royal castle of Bergenhus. The anonymous writer had rich access to the royal archives, and used the documents in his narrative.[4] *Bergen Fundas* tells that when the minor Magnus Erlingsson was anointed and crowned in Bergen in 1164 as Norwegian king his father Erling Skakke ("the tilted") promised to found Halsnøy Abbey in honour of his son and in praise and honour of St. Augustine.[5] Halsnøy Abbey was among the richest monasteries in Norway in the Middle Ages. It was situated on an island in the mouth of the Hardangerfjord which is part of the coastal district of Sunnhordland in the Bergen diocese.

The statement of *Bergen Fundas* is significant for many reasons. We have preserved only a few foundation letters for Norwegian monasteries, and also the letter concerning Halsnøy Abbey is lost. Its archive was probably kept at the royal castle after the Reformation, similar to monasteries in Oslo diocese whose archives were kept at the royal castle of the region.[6] Although *Bergen Fundas* is a narrative that was written 400 years after the presumed foundation of Halsnøy there is reason to believe that it was mostly based on documentary sources.

---

3   Lange (1856); Daa (1899); Steinnes (1962).
4   Storm (1898), pp. 426-427.
5   *Wdi samme Cronnelse loffuede Erlanndt skacke, Konngenns Fader, adt opbygge sinn Sønn till en Heider [till Bønnehalld] Halssnø Closter. Oc Sancto Augustino till Loff och Erre.* Bergen Fundas (1957), p. 34.
6   Cfr. Tank (1916), preface.

In this case the anonymous author has seen and read the foundation letter of Halsnøy Abbey.

Another significant feature of the narrative is that it mentions St. Augustine in connection with the foundation. Halsnøy Abbey belonged to the Order of the Augustinian Canons Regular like Utstein and many monasteries in the province. Men of this order played a major role in the organisation of the Norwegian church. Three archbishops of the twelfth and early thirteenth century had studied at the school of St. Victor in Paris, two of them as canons regular. Two more bishops in the province were Victorines (Hamar and Skálholt). The church province of Nidaros was in fact founded by a Victorine, the Papal Legate Nicholas Breakspear who had been the abbot of St. Rufus, the southernmost Victorine abbey, before he was created cardinal bishop of Albano in 1149/1150.[7] The actual archbishop in 1164, Øystein Erlendsson, who anointed and crowned the minor Magnus Erlingsson, had studied at St. Victor's. Øystein was elected as the second archbishop of Nidaros in 1157, but probably due to the conflict between Pope Adrian IV and the emperor the archbishop elect spent several years with the Victorines. It was thus Pope Alexander III who presented him with the pallium in 1161. Archbishop Øystein definitely had a part in the foundation of Halsnøy Abbey as he anointed and crowned King Magnus Erlingsson.

Our question is the relevance of this abbey's foundation to the monasteries within the Stavanger church.

The Retrogressive Analysis of the Monasteries

Medieval cadasters from Rogaland have not been preserved. In the post-Reformation cameral evidence nothing is left of St. Olav's former lands, while Utstein's properties and the domain of the monastery itself formed a royal fief. By analysing this material Steinnes deduced that the abbey's most central properties were concentrated in the Stavanger peninsula, situated south of Utstein.[8] It consisted of twelve farmsteads, five of them wholly owned properties, while the ownership was shared with the bishop of Stavanger in four farms and there were additional owners in two.[9] Steinnes considered that the twelve properties originally had belonged to St. Olav's monastery. His reason was that the properties were situated closer to Stavanger than to Mosterøy.

---

7   Johnsen (1943-46); Johnsen (1945). To Johnsen's pioneer work should be added Bergquist (2003), pp. 41-48.
8   Steinnes gives an overview of the cameral sources (1962), p. 8-9. More on Utstein as a secularized fief in Weidling (2005), pp. 291-315.
9   Map in Haug (2005c), p. 113.

But the fief of Utstein also had other lands. In an area from the river Hå in Jæren in the south to Åmøy in the northern shipping lane the majority of farms were divided up between the abbeys of Halsnøy and Utstein. For a historian who is familiar with the medieval Norwegian property system such a division points with certainty to one large donation from one major property owner in former times. Historians of the Norwegian agrarian school moreover consider that the gift has been given at a point when both monasteries were quite new and thus identical to their founding property; no-one has questioned this point of view with regard to Steinnes' analysis. But he concluded that the donation had been given to Halsnøy Abbey and *St. Olav's monastery* in Stavanger.

While I agree with Steinnes concerning the divided properties of Halsnøy and Utstein originating from one donor, his construction of St. Olav's as the recipient contradicts the methodological principle of simplicity ("Occam's razor"); why could not Utstein Abbey be the other receiver? Moreover, Steinnes did not take notice of a particular feature of the fief's properties: they were not divided in two equal halves. A review of the properties of the post-Reformation fief shows that when the two abbeys were the main owners of each farmstead, Halsnøy owned 2/3 while Utstein owned 1/3.[10] There are, however, records of farms fully owned by Utstein Abbey. Those in the very surroundings of the abbey probably was a part of the royal estate as far back as the time of Harald Fairhair, while St. Olav's sole ownership of properties on the Stavanger peninsula was a part of its foundation.

More objections arise. Although the post-Reformation fief was named Utstein it was not necessarily identical with the properties of the abbey 300 years earlier.[11] To this should be added that within a radius of less than 10 km and Utstein as the centre there were twelve churches, eight of them made of stone. Nowhere else in Norway but in Bergen were the churches more densely located in the High Middle Ages. The priests of these churches had the opportunity to form a clerical brotherhood at Utstein, which may have existed for a while as one of the royal proprietary monasteries in Norway before it became an abbey.[12]

---

10 Haug (2009), p. 458, note 18. Norway's topography prohibits the large manors seen elsewhere in Europe. A medieval landowner had only the right to the rent of his landed properties. The rent could thus be divided between several owners.
11 Weidling (2003), pp. 349-380.
12 See the chapter on the Order of the Regular Augustinians in Haug (2005c); Lovén in this volume.

Did Magnus the Lawmender found Utstein?

Steinnes concluded in accordance with a traditional theory that Utstein Abbey was founded by King Magnus IV Haakonsson the Lawmender (1263-1280). The view can be summarised in this way: Magnus received the region surrounding Stavanger as a part of his duchy and kingdom when in 1257 he became a duke and in the same year succeeded his older brother to become a king and co-regent with his father. The abbey was presumably established when in March 1264 Magnus heard of his father's death on Orkney and became the sole king of Norway. He no longer had need for a residence in Stavanger or a royal estate at Utstein and apparently gave both properties to the Church.[13]

In his will of 1277 King Magnus mentions properties as well as funds that he had already given to various ecclesiastical institutions. If Utstein Abbey had been founded by him it should have been mentioned in this connection. Moreover, he bequeathed money to several monasteries, but not Utstein.[14] King Magnus was a very pious king, so the omission is suggestive. A foundation by him was rather late for an abbey of the Canons regular of the Augustinian Order; in the Norwegian province they were active in the latter half of the 12th century with some late foundations in Iceland in 1295 and -96. Why had medievalists arrived at this result concerning Utstein?

Chr. C.A. Lange was the first to date the foundation of Utstein Abbey, as well as the other monasteries in mainland Norway. He did so according to a methodological principle: he based his research exclusively on the oldest written source which positively mentioned a monastery and excluded the evidence from ruins etc.[15] He thus assumed that Utstein Abbey had been founded somewhat earlier than the first written source, i.e. the above-mentioned will from around 1280.[16] From this followed that Magnus the Lawmender had founded the abbey.

With regard to the archaeological evidence the buildings at Utstein are relatively well preserved in contrast to all other medieval monasteries in Norway. The ruins of most of them have been systematically analysed by archaeologists, but an excavation at Utstein would endanger the remaining monastic complex. The abbey has been restored several times, though. When Gerhard Fischer restored the buildings c. 1960 he carried out a limited excavation and uncovered remnants from a wall within the present church. He dated the present church to c. 1260 and identified the fragments of the wall as originating from the church

---

13 Lexow (1987), p. 157.
14 DN IV:3; Regesta Norvegica II:171; revised and extended version in http://www.dokpro.uio.no/perl/middelalder/regest_vise_tekst.prl?b=1330&s=n&str=.
15 Lange (1856), p. 7.
16 DN I:70. A discussion of the testament in Haug (2006), pp. 7-22.

of the former royal complex. On this basis he supported the interpretation of a foundation by King Magnus IV.[17]

Nobody has denied that the church of this monastic installation is from the second part of the 13th century or that the uncovered fragments of a wall are from the first stone church at the site. But there are older elements in the complex. A typical arrangement in a monastery of the Middle Ages comprised a church with a cloister yard nestling against its nave. The square courtyard was walled with dormitory on the east wing, kitchen and refectory on the south, offices and storehouses on the west. The oldest part of the monastic complex at Utstein, the east wall adjoining the church, can be interpreted as Romanesque rather than Gothic, which in Norway points to an establishment before 1240. A new ^{14}C dating from this wall shows that it is older than Fischer's dating to the 1260s.[18] By comparing the remnants of the excavated old church with the measures of the church ruin at Halsnøy Abbey Øystein Ekroll put forward the hypothesis that both ruins seem to have had the same proportions of their walls as King Salomon's temple in Jerusalem, i.e. 3 : 1.[19] Moreover, the baptismal font of soapstone in the present-day church clearly points to an origin in the 12th century.[20] There are thus several indications of Utstein Abbey being founded in that century.[21]

To the archaeological evidence should be added a critical reflection by Lange. He was not as sure as later historians concerning the age of Utstein Abbey and stated in an overlooked footnote that his theory on the foundation was based on his methodology of relying only on written evidence. "Nothing contradicted that Utstein Abbey was established at the same time as the other convents for canons regular in Norway, i.e. the second half of the 12th century."[22] We should add that there is no evidence for the manor of Utstein ever being used by King Magnus the Lawmender as his residence.[23]

---

17 Fischer (1965), p. 5.
18 Hommedal (2001).
19 Ekroll (2005), pp. 231-232; Ekroll and Haug (2008), p. 180.
20 Reidar Kjellberg found the font to be carved by the Master of Bore. Asgaut Steinnes inspired him to a conjecture of the font being moved to Utstein Abbey from St. Olav's church in Stavanger (Kjellberg (1954), p. 79, p. 82). This is doubtful, in view of the distance between the two monasteries. And why was the heavy font moved when St Olav's Church was still in use? (DN IV:16).
21 I am indebted to Brian Patrick McGuire for having led me to this theory (Haug (2005c), pp. 104-125).
22 Lange (1856), p. 378, note 1.
23 Ekroll and Haug (2008), p. 176.

The Theory of St. Olav as an Abbey

Lange had denied the existence of St. Olav's as a convent in Stavanger. Although it was explicitly mentioned as a monastery in Bishop Alf Thorgardsson's will (1478) Lange put it in a category of "doubtful monasteries".[24] The first objection to this came from Ludvig Daae. He pointed out that the abovementioned will on which Lange had based his dating of Utstein Abbey also leaves a large donation to St. Olav's Church and its altar dedicated to St. Mary. This church must therefore have been the church of the monastery. Daae was sceptical with regard to a foundation of a monastery for canons regular as late as the 1260s. This was the golden age of the preachers and not least the Franciscan friars in Norway. But he seemingly did not wish to challenge Lange's result concerning the establishment of Utstein Abbey. He assumed therefore that St. Olav's church had belonged to a convent of Augustinian Canons Regular that had moved to Utstein and formed the core of the new Augustinian abbey that Magnus the Lawmender had established. According to this interpretation St. Olav's had originally been a monastery for Augustinian canons. Daae suggested that Eirik Ivarsson established St. Olav's Abbey while he was bishop in Stavanger (c. 1170 – 1188). He had been a Canon Regular at St. Victor in Paris before he became bishop and later archbishop (1188 – 1205).[25] Recent research indicates that he was the head of the royal church at Finnøy, perhaps also archdeacon of Shetland, and had received the consecration as a bishop before he received the Stavanger church. The question has been raised whether he had been an abbot at one of the Augustinian foundations, but nothing definitive can be said on this issue.[26]

Daae's suggestion that the community of St. Olav was transferred to Utstein when King Magnus the Lawmender founded the abbey could be supported by documents showing that Stavanger properties close to the church belonged to Utstein in the late Middle Ages. And already in 1295 two canons from that abbey celebrated Mass at the altar of St. Olav's Church.[27] Their celebration might indicate that Utstein Abbey now had the responsibility for the liturgical functions and that the monastery had been dissolved.[28] Steinnes could thus explain the composition of the Utstein fief: the original property of the Augustinian convent St. Olav in Stavanger formed the main part of Utstein Abbey's property

---

24 Primary sources that mention the monastery: Bugge (ed.), Henrik Kalteisens kopibog (1899), pp. 191-192; DN IV:987; DN XV:695; Norske Rigs-Registranter 2, p. 223.
25 Daae (1899), p. 9.
26 Sandaaker (1984), p. 63; Haug (2005), p. 131-132; Haug (2009), p. 459, note 20.
27 DN IV:16; cf. *Regesta Norvegica* 2:789.
28 DN II:134; DN IV:536, 537. Lange (1856), p. 388; Steinnes (1962), p. 7.

complex.²⁹ Daae's and Steinnes's observations concerning the properties have been generally accepted, but *when* they were transferred to Utstein Abbey is still an open question.

Edvard Bull found new evidence in one of Reginald of Durham's best known narratives regarding a young boy of noble birth who had attended a cloister school in Stavanger c. 1160. While a student he caught a severe illness that was miraculously healed when he visited the shrine of St. Cuthbert in Durham.³⁰ This narrative without doubt referred to the school at St. Olav's with the implication that the monastic institution had to be founded at an earlier stage than Halsnøy Abbey. Bishop Eirik Ivarsson could not have been the founder of the monastery. Bull believed it to be likely that St. Olav was founded as a Benedictine monastery. He emphasized that the Benedictines were dominant in Winchester to which the Stavanger church had a special relation; its cathedral had received a precious relic from Winchester, an arm-bone of St. Swithun who was the patron saint of the cathedral.³¹ Stavanger's first permanent Bishop Reinald (before 1125-1135) was a Benedictine monk and may have belonged to a monastery in Winchester.³²

The bishop could not, however, establish a monastery in Stavanger by himself. The organisation required a major foundation, which points to it being established by the king or a local magnate; descendants of Erling Skjalgsson of Sola (before 995-1027) have been mentioned.³³ Erling was married to King Olav Tryggvasson's sister and collaborated with him in being the real ruler of the West Coast of Norway. He was not so close to King Olav Haraldsson and was killed by him on Christmas Eve 1027. Sola was his residence, situated not far from Stavanger.

The terms in the evidence that refers to St. Olav's monastery in Stavanger indicate a Benedictine foundation. In a letter of 1171 Pope Alexander III explicitly refers to an Estonian brother Nicholas in the monastery as *monachus*; at the request of the Estonian Bishop Fulko the monk is asked to join King Valdemar the Great's crusade to Estonia as a missionary.³⁴ Fulko belonged to the Benedictine Order. The usual Latin terms for Augustinian canons were *canonici*, *fratres* and *clerici*, whilst *monachi* was kept for the Benedictines and the monastic orders. It is therefore probable that also the Stavanger monk Nicholas was Benedictine.³⁵ *Monachus* is also the term that Reginald of Durham used in the narrative on St.

---

29   Steiness (1962), pp. 14-15; 18-20.
30   Reginaldi monachi Dunelmensis (1835), p. 249.
31   Bull (1910), pp. 3-5; Bull (1912), pp. 210-217.
32   Brøgger (1915), pp. 39-40, 174-176; Kolsrud (1925), p. 41.
33   Steiness (1962), pp. 25-28.
34   DN XVII:4; Daae (1899), p. 9; Brøgger (1915); Helle (1975), p. 110; Nenseter (2002), p. 34; Bisgaard and Nyberg (2006), pp. 18-19.
35   Dickinson (1950), pp. 198-201; Nenseter (2002), p. 34.

Cuthbert's miracles. We can therefore assume that when Pope Alexander III, who was connected to the same reform movement as the regular canons, called Nicholas "monk" St. Olav's at this point in time had not been converted into a convent of regular Augustinian canons.

Another term is Reginald of Durham's reference to St. Olav's as *coenobium*, a rather old-fashioned concept that was hardly used for an Augustinian convent. The explanation of the terms *monachus* and *coenobium* substantiates Bull's theory that St. Olav monastery originally belonged to the Benedictine Order.[36]

There were no great discrepancies between convents of this or that order, but the affiliation of St. Olav continued to puzzle, due to the orthodox view on the foundation of Utstein. Daae's old theory was revived when Arne Odd Johnsen in his seminal doctoral thesis challenged Bull's interpretation. He was of the opinion that Cardinal Nicholas Brekespeare founded St. Olav's as a convent for Canons Regular of the Augustinian Order when he arrived in Norway to establish the church province in 1152. The cardinal had himself been the abbot of the Victorine St. Rufus Abbey from c. 1140. Although there are few sources on Nicholas Brekespeare's whereabouts while in Norway Johnsen established an itinerary for the cardinal legate, based on assumptions and conjectures.[37]

Johnsen never considered the orthodox view on Utstein Abbey as founded by Magnus the Lawmender nor raised as an issue why St. Olav and not Utstein was established at this juncture. His conjecture has neither been critically researched nor extensively referred to, but it fits with his general view of the Augustinian Canons as instrumental in forming the Norwegian church province.[38]

The new research on Utstein Abbey has sought to rectify this view: the abbey was founded in the same period as the other institutions that belonged to the order of the Augustininan canons regular. And King Magnus IV Håkonsson should be excluded as its founder.[39]

The Benedictine Role in the Institutionalisation of the Church

Bull dated the establishment of the St. Olav monastery to around 1130, which seems to be the latest possibility for a Benedictine foundation in Norway. In

---

36 Reginaldi monachi Dunelmensis (1835), p. 249.
37 Johnsen (1945), pp. 117-118.
38 Fischer (1965); Helle (1975), p. 99; Lexow (1987), pp. 155-168; Helle (1995), pp. 43-44, 119, 169.
39 Ekroll (2005); Haug (2005a); Eide (2006); Haug (2006); Ekroll and Haug (2008); Haug (2008b); Haug (2008a); Helle (2008); Ekroll (2009); Haug (2009); Ekroll (2009); Helle (2009), pp. 685-697; Haug (2010); Haug (2012).

the 1140s the Cistercians dominated in establishing monasteries.[40] It is hardly likely that a new Benedictine monastery was founded in competition with the new orders, and St. Olav was probably established before the Cistercians had a foothold in Norway.

By comparing the situation of the earliest church of Stavanger with the other episcopal sees in Norway the impression is, though, that St. Olav monastery is older than the permanent see which was established around 1125 at the latest. Let us take a closer look at the oldest monasteries which were established at the first three episcopal sees in Norway: Selja, Nidaros, and Oslo.

The monastery of Selja has traditionally been regarded as the oldest. It should, however, be observed that there are two sources on the establishment of Nidarholm monastery outside of Trondheim which seemingly are opposed to each other, one of them giving a date for the foundation of c. 1030, the other the first decades of the 1100s. According to Matthew of Paris the monastery at Nidarholm was founded by Cnut the Great when he was acclaimed as king at Øyratinget outside of Nidaros in 1028. Mathew Paris went to Norway to reform Nidarholm monastery. His evidence cannot be mere guesswork; he had probably access to the monastery's archive where the foundation was recorded in some way or other. In this way he may have been informed about Cnut the Great's deed. The Norwegian historian Theodricus Monachus (late 12th century) gave another version, writing that the crusader Sigurd Ullstreng from Trøndelag built the monastery in honour of St. Benedict and the martyr Lawrence "on a fairly small island near the bishop's town Nidaros".[41] These two pieces of information can be reconciled. The conventional explanation is that Cnut the Great's monastic establishment was abandoned when Danish rule collapsed in 1035. One then disregards that the relic of St. Olav was transferred to St. Clement's Church in Nidaros by 1031. This cannot have happened without the approval of the actual king. There is reason to believe that Cnut the Great and his son Svein Alfivasson supported the sanctifying of their earlier enemy. The cult of St. Olav came quickly into existence and needed an institution at Nidaros to serve the pilgrims.[42] Benedictine monks could contribute to the preparation of a liturgy and take care of the liturgical functions at St. Olav's shrine; after a while

---

40 In contrast to Denmark and Sweden this order played no political role in Norway. Skovgaard-Petersen et al. (1977), p. 316.
41 Theodrici Monachi, cap. 31 in Monumenta Historica Norvegiæ (1880), p. 62. Christopher McLees excluded the possibility of an earlier wooden monastery complex at Nidarholm, assuming that stave church architecture should then have been used; McLees (1993).
42 Lange (1856); Mortensen and Mundal (2003), pp. 353-384; Townend (2005), p. 251, pp. 258-266.

a community of priests probably was established closer to the actual sacred relic. The growth of the community of regular Augustinian canons in Helgeseter monastery may be seen in this light.[43] Moreover, Norwegian monasteries were hardly likely to have been built in stone from the start. Sigurd Ullstreng may therefore have founded such a monastery at Nidarholm. My understanding of the evidence is that Nidarholm was the first attested monastery founded in Scandinavia.

The monastery church at Selja was dedicated to St. Alban, but the most important saints were the Holy men of Selja and St. Sunniva. It is thus reasonable to believe that St. Alban's already existed when according to the legend the relics of the men of Selja and St. Sunniva were discovered by Olav Tryggvason. The holy site presumably dates from the early 11th century. King Olav Kyrre ("the still" 1170 – 1193) established a permanent episcopal see there for all Gulatingslagen, the West Coast of Norway. The monastery is another example of an early monastic foundation connected to an episcopal see. The dating of the remains of the monastery has given an approximate foundation date towards 1100, but it is reasonable to believe that the first buildings were made of wood. The ruin of the stone church shows that it was the church of a bishop; King Olav Kyrre was probably the first builder.[44] The cult of saints was an important element for an episcopal see at the somewhat uninviting location of Selja, and when the see was moved to Bergen in 1170, it was necessary to translate the relic of St. Sunniva.

The third episcopal see, Oslo, was also founded at the shrine of a Norwegian saint, St. Hallvard (martyred ca. 1040). The oldest male monastery in Oslo was situated at Hovedøen in the Oslofjord, a short boat trip from the town in the centre of Viken. A Cistercian monastery was established there in the 1140s. The ruins of the monastery are, however, untypical for the order and imply that originally it was a Benedictine monastery. Its church was dedicated to St. Edmund as well as, like all Cistercian churches, to St. Mary. The dedication to an Anglo-Saxon saint signifies a greater age.[45]

We take note of the first episcopal sees all being established at the shrines of domestic saints – St. Olav, the Holy Men of Selja and St. Sunniva, and St. Hallvard. It is interesting that Benedictine monasteries were established close to

---

43 Helgeseter is first mentioned in connection with Archbishop Øystein Erlendsson in 1183 and considered as founded by him. Another idea is that the foundation was a slower process, and that Helgeseter started as a daughter of the Benedictine monastery at Nidarholm.
44 Nybø (2000); Nybø (2001a); Nybø (2001b).
45 Johnsen (1974), pp. 37-49.

all of them; there has probably been a need for clerics to perform the liturgical functions connected to the holy sites. When a bishop celebrated Mass at the sanctuary, there was a need of priests who normally belonged to a chapter. In the missionary period the priest of the actual monastic community could perform the same functions. Taking into consideration that there was a significant Anglo-Saxon influence on the organisation of the first Norwegian church and that the Benedictine monasteries in Wessex functioned as chapters of the cathedrals from the tenth century this may have been a model for the first collegiate churches in Norway. When Tore Nyberg studied the early church in Odense in Denmark, he found that it was modelled on the Winchester church-reform. An important element was the worship of St. Knud.[46] We should still have in mind that there were several priests in the cathedrals; it was time-consuming to build up a chapter. Moreover, the Church had to recruit priests from Norway in order to have a well-functioning organisation.[47]

St. Olav Abbey and the Influence from Winchester

What about the Stavanger church in this context? My hypothesis is that St. Olav's was established as a small monastic community before the permanent episcopal see was established and functioned as a regular first chapter of the cathedral. This hypothesis is two-fold. First, we have to substantiate that there was a relationship between the Stavanger chapter and St. Olav's monastery based in common tasks and practical duties. Second, we have to substantiate that the monastery has an older history than the episcopal see.

The relationship between the two institutions is seen in two verdicts from the *officialis* in Stavanger that are both written in Old Norse. The first one states that his court was in session in the same "room as the members of the chapter used when they had their daily meals" (*stofunni sem korsbrœdunner œta j daghligha*). This dining hall is further explained in a second letter connected to the court of the *officialis*. Its session was in *refectorio brœdranna* ("the refectory of the friars").[48] In English this term means the dining hall of any ecclesiastical institution, which is not particularly interesting, but in Old Norse I have found

---

46 Taranger (1890); Aethelwold and Symons (1953); Nyberg (2000), pp. 52-63.
47 When King Olav Kyrre complained to Pope Gregory VII in 1078 regarding the lack of priests in Norway, the pope recommended him to send some young men from good families for an education under the wings of St. Peter and St. Paul. DN VI:1; Oksholen (2012), p. 52.
48 DN IV:335 (7.7.1348), 340 (21.10.1348); Lange (1856), p. 391; Haug (2005c), p. 158.

"refectory" only in the context of monasteries. Its use in the letter indicates that the court was in session in the dining hall of a monastic institution, indicating St. Olav's monastery.

Another indication of a relationship between chapter and monastery was seen in 1236. In an agreement an abbot at St. Olav's in Stavanger and a prior *eiusdem loci* were among those who sealed the document.[49] The common interpretation has been that the convent at St. Olav's by then was so large that it had two leaders. While I in 2005 raised as a possibility that the prior had his title as the leader of Utstein before it became an abbey and that *eiusdem loci* referred to the Stavanger diocese, I now consider that the prior belonged to St. Olav's, but had his title "prior" as the leader of the *chapter*; the chapter consisted of both regular canons from the monastery and secular ones.[50]

The secularisation of the chapter was a process occurring during the better part of the 13th century, but the reallocation of its properties caused conflict.[51] The indications of a close relationship between monastery and chapter allow us to dig further into why two canons from Utstein Abbey celebrated Mass in St. Olav's church in 1295, as mentioned above. The reason was a severe conflict between the Stavanger bishop and his chapter which turned into a canonical process and fostered a rich variety of procedural documents. The abbot of Utstein was involved in the process in being authorised to summon the bishop before the ecclesiastical court, and instructed to absolve all clerics who might have been excommunicated to enable them to testify in the lawsuit.[52] The abbot belonged in other words to a neutral body. Several canons had been excommunicated by the bishop, and it is reasonable to believe that those that ordinarily celebrated Mass in St. Olav's church were prevented from doing so by the ban. The monks from Utstein were asked by their superior to celebrate Mass in this church because they were neutral in the conflict, not because the monastery had ceased to exist.

Although the evidence of a regular chapter connected to St. Olav's monastery in Stavanger is circumstantial, there are many parallels in other Scandinavian countries to such an organisation. Which rule the community followed after c. 1200 is impossible to decide from the meagre evidence – but is not of great significance to this article.

The second question is whether the monastery had an older history than the permanent Stavanger see. I consider this to be a probable assumption which is

---

49 Bugge (1899), p. 192.
50 Haug (2005c), pp. 119-120; Haug (2009), p. 166.
51 Haug (2012), pp. 133-134.
52 DN IV:17, 47. Haug (2012), pp. 122, 128.

based in the local cult of St. Swithun. In Scandinavia there is only one example of a church having this Anglo-Saxon saint as its patron, namely Stavanger Cathedral. Swithun was a bishop in Winchester (d. 2 July 863) whose cult began with the translation of his relics into the Old Minster on 15 July 971. Although the reliquary was guarded by sacristans it should not be excluded that there were many opportunities for some bones to go missing. The first recorded dispersal, and the most important one, was when Bishop Ælfheah was elevated to the archbishopric of Canterbury in 1006 and when he moved took with him the head of St. Swithun. By the twelfth century, many English churches claimed to possess relics of St. Swithun.[53] Concerning the relic in Stavanger there is no record on how it was achieved, but the prevailing opinion is that Bishop Reinald brought the saint's arm-bone when he became the first permanent bishop sometime between 1112 and 1125.[54]

The English historian Christopher Hohler challenged this view. His project was the age of the old Romanesque basilica of Stavanger. The basilica was severely damaged by a fire in 1272, but some pillars still remain. By comparing details in the capitals of these pillars with three Anglo-Norman churches Hohler established that the best and apparently the only parallels to the cathedral of Stavanger are the cathedrals of Norwich, Castle Acre, and Ely. The building of Castle Acre started in 1089, Norwich started in 1086, while the building of Ely started in 1081.[55] He moreover pointed out that the translations of relics from Anglo-Saxon saints became rare after the Conquest. St. Swithun's shrine is not known to have been opened between 1093 and 1150. Hohler thus tried to maintain that the Romanesque basilica in Stavanger was consecrated perhaps as late as 1150. He would therefore date the translation of the Swithun relic in Stavanger to the later opening of the shrine and connect it to a gift from the Stavanger bishop Jon Birgersson when he became the first archbishop of Nidaros (1152-1157).[56] His deduction against Reinald translating the relic is a valid argument *e silentio*; a translation or *furta sacra* of such a big relic would have been recorded. But also a translation in 1150 should have been recorded. A translation as late as 1152 is highly improbable. In 1150 there was another archbishop elect than the Stavanger bishop, but he died while he was in Rome to collect the pallium.

To date a stone church from the Middle Ages precisely is difficult if there is no other evidence than the building itself, and to date remains of such a church

---

53 Lapidge (2003), pp. 37-38.
54 The latest to discuss and support this theory is Lapidge (2003), pp. 38-48.
55 Hohler (1964), p. 116. Norwich was dedicated to St. Swithun; see Lapidge (2003), p. 44, fig. 3.
56 Hohler (1964), p. 94.

is even more difficult. However, we can take into consideration that the builder always started with the choir of the church. The reason is that when the main altar in the choir was consecrated it was possible to celebrate Mass and use the church, even if there was still building work to be done. The decorated capitals of the cathedral's pillars, performed by highly skilled masons, presumably were among the last elements to be finished. There is, however, more evidence. Underneath the choir of the present cathedral an archaeological excavation has uncovered a layer of charcoal from a fire; that layer covered holes from pillars of a construction. The ^{14}C test of the charcoal indicated that it burnt down towards the end of the 11th century.[57] Archaeologists have been reluctant to connect the findings with a church beneath the present cathedral, but the fact that Erling Skjalgsson's priest erected a memorial stone to him in its churchyard is another indication of a church at this place as early as in the 1020s. Christopher Hohler has noted the archaeological excavation, and in a later article he developed his theories on the Stavanger basilica further and dated it to c. 1105.[58]

Any altar to be consecrated was in need of a saint's relic. A translation of the relic of St. Swithun from Winchester to Stavanger after the opening of his shrine in 1093 thus fits better than 1150, as the altar of the basilica in Stavanger may have been finished towards the end of the 11th century.[59]

There is another possibility. A manuscript from the middle of the thirteenth century says that Cnut the great transferred a relic of St. Swithun to "Dacia", which has been understood as Denmark.[60] As far as we know St. Swithun was not cultivated in Denmark. We have no clues concerning which Danish church was supposed to have received the relic of Swithun. In the Anglo-Saxon evidence Danes often seem to be a synonym for Vikings in the early Middle Ages, and Dacia/Dania in some cases refers to the whole sphere of Viking activity. It should not be excluded that Dacia in this case hints at Cnut's Anglo-Danish empire, which also included Norway: Cnut was acclaimed as

---

57 Rolfsen (1968). Today there are better methods to analyse the profile of carbon with the atomic weight 14 than when the test was made in 1968, but to my knowledge no new analysis has been performed.
58 Hohler (1967), pp. 7-52. Hohler does not state why he uses "1105" rather than "1100". His reasons may be that the Norwegian churches became a part of the Lund province in 1103, and that there was a change of kings in this year.
59 Marit Nybø suggests in her doctoral thesis that Olav Kyrre started to build the churches of Selja monastery and Stavanger as churches for the bishop in addition to the well-known Christ Church of Bergen. For more on this, see Nybø (2001a) and Nybø (2001b).
60 *Nes solum ibi ob sanctum sui merita diuina fiebant miracula, immo in Dacia quo pars reliquiarium eius a rege Cnutone est translata...* Lapidge (2003), p. 702.

Norway's king in 1028 after Olav Haraldsson fled to Swedish territory, and continued as such with his son Svein as a puppet king after Olav's fall at Stiklestad in 1030. A possible explanation is that his gift of a Swithun relic to *Dacia* referred to the one in Stavanger. Cnut had an ally in the magnate Erling Skjalgsson, the possible founder of a wooden church beneath the present Stavanger cathedral.

This interpretation is weak if based on the late manuscript alone; the remark may well be a late interpolation. Moreover, Dacia may refer to Cnut's English territory. However, there are other indications of a rather early cult of St. Swithun in Norway. The Norwegian church was the only one outside Winchester that commemorated all three Swithun masses.[61] The masses point to an early dating of the relic in Stavanger.

Another indication is the relic itself. An arm-bone is a large relic, different from a knuckle of a toe, a finger, a hand, or a foot that could more easily go missing when the reliquary was damaged or opened. Lapidge finds it hard to believe that when Archbishop Ælfheah of Canterbury took Swithun's head with him to his new cathedral he had the permission of the monks of the Old Minster. "... then his act must count as one of the great *furta sacra* of the English Middle Ages."[62] I agree in this; such a precious relic could not be removed by anybody. The arm-bone of St. Swithun in Stavanger was of course not of the same importance, but it is hard to believe that Bishop Reinald was allowed to remove it; it demanded a man of power to remove such a large relic.

And there were other powerful Norwegians in England in the late 10th and early 11th century. It is worth mentioning that Olav Tryggvasson was baptised by Bishop Ælfheah and that King Ethelred was his godfather.[63] He probably received many relics of Anglo-Saxon saints when he went on to Norway to

---

61 St. Swithun had three feasts: the day of translation 15 July, his deposition 2 July, which was the most important one, and his day of ordination 30 October. 2 July was called *Sviptunsvaka* or *syftesok* in Norway, while 15 July was called *Sviptunsvaka siðari*. This feast is seldom mentioned in English calendars, probably because it coincided with *divisio apostolorum*. According to Michael Lapidge 30 October was only celebrated in Winchester (he also mentions that four English calendars have this entry, perhaps a misprint). Lapidge (2003), pp. 2, 28. However, a letter of *Munkelivs Brevbog* p. 83 (also published as DN XII:81) dates a transaction to *Svitunar messa um haustit* ("Swithun's Mass in autumn"). It would have been easier to date the event to the mass-day of the two apostles or All saints' day if Swithun Mass in autumn had not been commonly known in Bergen in the 1330s.

62 Lapidge (2003), p. 40.

63 Birkeli (1995), pp. 108-109; Borgehammar and Wienberg (2012), p. 2, pp. 81-82, p. 143.

Christianise the people. We remember that he and Erling Skjalgsson were close. A precious relic for Stavanger is quite possible.

Another indication of high age is the dedication of the basilica in Stavanger to an Anglo-Saxon saint while the nearby monastery was dedicated to St. Olav. After Olav Haraldsson's martyrdom a relic from him was very attractive, but only a few were distributed. That it was achieved by the monastery, not the basilica, points to a later foundation of St. Olav's than St. Swithun's. The saint had the fame of possessing miraculous powers and the relic in Stavanger probably saw many pilgrims in the hope of salvation and cure. The sanctuary needed clerics to care for the pilgrims, hear their confessions and absolve them, perform the liturgical service of the saint as well as celebrate Mass. In this context I see Benedictine monks, perhaps from Winchester, who could constitute the core of a monastic community that developed into St. Olav's monastery.

This article has discussed the historiography of the foundation of Utstein Abbey and St. Olav's Monastery in Stavanger diocese. Written evidence of the foundation is non-existent, and it has been necessary to use all data of social life from multiple disciplines. Chr. C.A. Lange started the critical examination of the written evidence on monasteries. Ludvig Daae extended the research by including more evidence from the Stavanger church, and Edv. Bull widened the scope by using the miracles of St. Cuthbert. Arne Odd Johnson's doctoral thesis represented a turning point in the understanding of the Augustinian influence in the new province during its first decades. Asgaut Steinnes extended the evidence considerably when he analysed retrospectively the properties of monasteries in Rogaland. Scholars have extended our understanding of the stone architecture of the medieval churches and archaeologists have produced new evidence by the ^{14}C analyses. Christopher Hohler initiated a discussion on liturgy and the cult of St. Swithun. Although I disagree in some results, my predecessors' scholarly works are building blocks in reaching new insights.

In an attempt to sift facts and fiction I have found substantiated that the post-Reformation fief Utstein consisted of properties both from the abbey as well as from St. Olav monastery. Utstein and Halsnøy shared rather a lot of the properties that were divided between the two in the relationship 1 : 2. There is a general agreement that the church at Utstein was built in the latter part of the 13th century, but no evidence supports the suggestion that King Magnus the Lawmender founded the monastic community; the archaeological evidence points to an earlier foundation. This article has supported the position that Utstein Abbey was established at the same time as the other convents for canons regular of the Augustinian Order in Norway, i.e. the second half of the 12th century. This was the golden age of the order. The regular canons were important in shaping the Norwegian church province that was established in 1152-1153 by the legation of Cardinal Nicholas Brekespeare, himself a Victorine canon. Three Norwegian archbishops and several bishops were students or canons at St. Victor's in Paris.

In the missionary church the connection to Wessex and Winchester was equally important to institutionalise a domestic church, but we have far less documentation than from the Augustinian heyday. That St. Olav's monastery in Stavanger was founded as an Augustine convent at the same time as Halsnøy Abbey cannot be confirmed. The monastery had a school that was well established around 1160. The meagre evidence without exception indicates that St. Olav's was a Benedictine foundation up to at least 1171. We should not exclude the possibility that the community was identical with a regular chapter according to the model from Winchester and *Regularis concordia* up to the middle of the 13th century. It should, however, be emphasized that there was no competition between Benedictines and Augustinian canons, and St. Olav's may have been modernised, or reformed, according to the rule of Augustine; the tenure of the Victorine Eirik Ivarsson as bishop of Stavanger (c. 1170 – 1188) could be an appropriate period.

Documents from the conflict between the bishop of Stavanger and the chapter in the 1290s cannot prove that St. Olav's monastery had been merged with Utstein Abbey at this stage. It is more probable that the monks, or perhaps the secular canons, had been banned in the conflict. Documents support the thesis that the monastic complex was used by the Stavanger chapter in the Late Middle Ages.

The seed of the monastery may have been the priesthood that served the precious relic of St. Swithun. I have suggested that the relic was translated in the period when the relationship to Winchester was most intense, but new evidence may demolish the synthesis that I have presented.

Bibliography

Sources

Aethelwold, *Regularis concordia Anglicae nationis monachorum Sanctimonialiumque*, ed. Thomas Symons (London, 1953).

Akershusregisteret af 1622: Fortegnelse optaget af Gregers Krabbe og Mogens Hæg paa Akershus slot over de derværende breve, ed. G. Tank (Kristiania, 1916).

Bergens Fundas, ed. Mikjel Sørlie (Bergen, 1957).

DN: *Diplomatarium Norvegicum*, various editors (Oslo, 1849-2011) (online version: http://www.dokpro.uio.no/dipl_norv/diplom_field_eng.html).

Erkebiskop Henrik Kalteisens Kopibog, ed. Alexander Bugge (Christiania, 1899).

Norske Rigs-registranter: Tildeels i Udvaalg, various editors (Christiania, 1861-1891).

Regesta Norvegica, various editors (Oslo, 1898-2010).
Reginaldi monachi Dunelmensis, 'Libellus de admirandis beati Cuthberti virtutibus', ed. The Surtees Society (London, 1835).
Theodrici Monachi 'Historia de antiquitate regum Norwagiensium', in *Monumenta historica Norvegiæ: Latinske kildeskrifter til Norges historie i middelalderen*, ed. Gustav Storm (Kristiania, 1880); pp. 1-68.
Vita Griffini Filii Conani: The Medieval Latin Life of Gruffudd ap Cynan, ed. Paul Russell (Cardiff, 2005).

Studies

Bergquist, Anders, 'The Papal Legate Nicholas Breakspear's Scandinavian Mission', in *Adrian IV The English Pope (1154-1159): Studies and Texts*, edited by Brenda Bolton and Anne J. Duggan (Aldershot, 2003), pp. 41-48.
Birkeli, Fridtjov, *Tolv vintrer hadde kristendommen vært i landet* (Stavanger, 1995).
Bisgaard, Lars, and Tore Nyberg, ed., *Tidlige klostre i Norden* (Odense, 2006).
Brooke, Christopher, *The Age of the Cloister: The Story of Monastic Life in the Middle Ages* (Thrupp, 2003).
Brøgger, A. W., *Stavangers historie i middelalderen* (Stavanger, 1915).
Bull, Edv., 'Et kloster i Stavanger', *Stavanger Museums Årskrift* (1910), pp. 3-5.
Bull, Edv., *Folk og kirke i middelalderen: Studier til Norges historie* (Kristiania, 1912).
Daae, Ludvig, 'Om Stavanger stift i middelalderen', *Historisk tidsskrift (Kristiania)* 3 rk. V (1899), pp. 219-336.
Dickinson, J. C., *The Origins of the Austin Canons and their Introduction into England* (London, 1950).
Eide, Ole Egil, 'Om Utsteinklosterets bygningshistorie', *Collegium Medievale* 19 (2006), pp. 164-176.
Ekroll, Øystein, 'Bygning og bruk', in *Utstein Kloster og Klosterøys historie*, ed. Eldbjørg Haug (Rennesøy, 2005), pp. 215-261.
Ekroll, Øystein, 'Om Utstein kloster - replikk', *Collegium Medievale* 22 (2009).
Ekroll, Øystein, and Eldbjørg Haug, 'Om Utstein klosters bygningshistorie (English Summary)', *Collegium Medievale* 20/2007 (2008), pp. 353-363.
Fischer, Gerhard, *Utstein kloster, kongsgård - kloster - herregård* (Stavanger, 1965).
Gjerløw, Lilli, *Adoratio Crucis: The Regularis Concordia and the Decreta Lanfranci: Manuscript Studies in the Early Medieval Church of Norway* (Oslo, 1961).
Haug, Eldbjørg, 'Noen refleksjoner etter arbeidet med Utstein klosters historie', in *Den kirkehistoriske utfordring*, edited by Steinar Imsen (Trondheim, 2005a), pp. 91-114.
Haug, Eldbjørg, 'Nye perspektiver på Stavanger-privilegiet 1093 - 1450', in *Det Norske Videnskaps-Akademi Årbok* 2004 (2005b), pp. 325 - 45.
Haug, Eldbjørg, ed. *Utstein kloster og Klosterøys historie* (Rennesøy, 2005c).
Haug, Eldbjørg, 'Den første abbeden på Utstein og Arnbjørn av Heimnes', *Ætt og heim* (2006), pp. 7-22.
Haug, Eldbjørg, 'Askell Jonsson, bishop of Stavanger c. 1190 - 1254', *International Encyclopaedia for the Middle Ages-Online. A Supplement to LexMA-Online* (2008a), www.brepolis.net.
Haug, Eldbjørg, 'Challenges in the Research of Norwegian Monastic History', *American Benedictine Review* 59 (2008b), pp. 64-96.

Haug, Eldbjørg, 'Fra Stavanger-kirkens tidligste historie', *Historisk tidsskrift (Oslo)* 88, no. 3 (2009), pp. 453-483, 554.

Haug, Eldbjørg, 'Stavanger-privilegiet, Stavangers romanske domkirke og klostersamfunnet på Utstein: Replikk til Knut Helle', *Historisk tidsskrift (Oslo)* 89, no. 2 (2010), pp. 263-271.

Haug, Eldbjørg,'The Conflict in the Stavanger Church around 1300 and the Intervention of Håkon Magnusson', in *Law and Power in the Middle Ages: Proceedings from the Fourth Carlsberg Academy Conference on Medieval Legal History*, edited by Per Andersen, Mia Münster-Swendsen and Helle Vogt (København, 2012 [2008]), pp. 105-138.

Helle, Knut, *Stavanger fra våg til by* (Stavanger, 1975).

Helle, Knut, *Under kirke og kongemakt: 1130 - 1350* (Oslo, 1995).

Helle, Knut, 'Stavanger by og Utstein kloster', *Historisk tidsskrift (Oslo)* 87, no. 4 (2008).

Helle, Knut, 'Stavanger som by og kirkelig sentrum: Svar til Eldbjørg Haug', *Historisk tidsskrift (Oslo)* 88, no. 4 (2009), pp. 685-97.

Hohler, Christopher, 'The Cathedral of St. Swithun at Stavanger in the Twelfth Century', *The Journal of the British Archeological Association* 3rd series 27 (1964), pp. 92-118.

Hommedal, Alf Tore, 'Utstein Klosters restaureringshistorie: Presentasjon av restaureringane med dokumentasjons-materialet for desse', (Bergen, 2001).

Johnsen, Arne Odd, *Studier vedrørende kardinal Nicolaus Brekespears legasjon til Norden* (Oslo, 1945).

Johnsen, Arne Odd, 'Omkring grunnleggingen av klostret på Hovedøya', in *Oslo bispedømme 900 år*, ed. Fridtjov Birkeli, Arne Odd Johnsen and Einar Molland (Oslo, 1974), pp. 37-49.

Kjellberg, Reidar, 'Døpefonter fra middelalderen i Rogaland', *Stavanger Museum Årbok* 1954 (Stavanger, 1954), pp. 77-90.

Kolsrud, Oluf, 'Stavanger bispestol', In *Stavanger 1125 – 1425 – 1925*, ed. Jan Petersen (Stavanger, 1925).

Lange, Chr.C.A., *De norske Klostres Historie i Middelalderen*, 2nd ed. (Christiania, 1847).

Lapidge, Michael, *The Cult of St Swithun* Vol. 4.ii Winchester Studies (Oxford, 2003).

Lexow, Jan Hendrich, 'Utstein kloster i middelalderen', *Årbok* 1987 (Foreningen til norske fortidsminnesmerkers bevaring, 1987), pp. 155-168.

Lidén, Hans-Emil, 'Utstein klosters bygningshistorie nok en gang', *Collegium Medievale* 22 (2009).

McLees, Christopher, 'Nidarholm ved Nidaros - Klosterkompleksets utformning i nytt lys', in *Kloster og by: Omkring Olavsklosteret, premonstratenserordenen og klostervesenet i middelalderen*, ed. Jan G. Eriksson and Kari Schei (Tønsberg, 1993), pp. 23-43.

Monumenta historica Norvegiæ: Latinske kildeskrifter til Norges historie i middelalderen, ed. Gustav Storm (Kristiania, 1880).

Mortensen, Lars Boje, and Else Mundal, 'Erkebispesetet i Nidaros - arnestad og verkstad for olavslitteraturen', in *Ecclesia Nidrosiensis 1153-1537: Søkelys på Nidaroskirkens og Nidarosprovinsens historie*, ed. Steinar Imsen (Trondheim, 2003), pp. 353-384.

Nenseter, Olav, *Augustinerordenen. Å lære andre gjennom ord og eksempel: Religiøse ordener i middelalderens Norge* (Oslo, 2003).

Nyberg, Tore, *Monasticism in North-Western Europe 800 - 1200* (Aldershot, 2000).

Nybø, Marit, *Albanuskirken på Selja: Klosterkirke eller bispekirke?* Bergen: Universitetet i Bergen, Det historisk-filosofisk fakultet, 2000.

Nybø, Marit, 'Albanuskirken - bispekirken på Selja', Årbok for Bergen Museum 2000 (Bergen, 2001a), pp. 4-9.
Nybø, Marit, 'Albanuskirken på Selja: Nye resultater - nye perspektiver', in Norske kirker (Oslo, 2001b), pp. 111-124.
Sandaaker, Odd, 'Biskopen av Finnøy', Historisk tidsskrift (Bergen) 63 (1984), pp. 315-327.
Skovgaard-Petersen, Inge, Aksel E. Christensen, and Helge Paludan (ed.), Danmarks historie: Tiden indtil 1340 (København, 1977).
Steinnes, Asgaut, 'Klostergods i Rogaland', Ætt og heim (1962), pp. 7-30.
Storm, Gustav, 'Om skriftet "Bergens Fundats" og dets forfatter', Historisk tidsskrift (Oslo) 3. rk. 4 (1898), pp. 418-427.
Taranger, Absalon, Den angelsaksiske kirkes indflydelse paa den norske (Kristiania, 1890).
Townend, Matthew, "Knutr and the Cult of St. Óláfr: Poetry and Patronage in Eleventh-Century Norway and England", Viking and Medieval Scandinavia 1 (2005); pp. 251-79.
Weidling, Tor, 'Klosteret som verdslig len 1537-1664', in Utstein kloster og Klosterøys historie, ed. Eldbjørg Haug (Rennesøy, 2005), pp. 291-315.

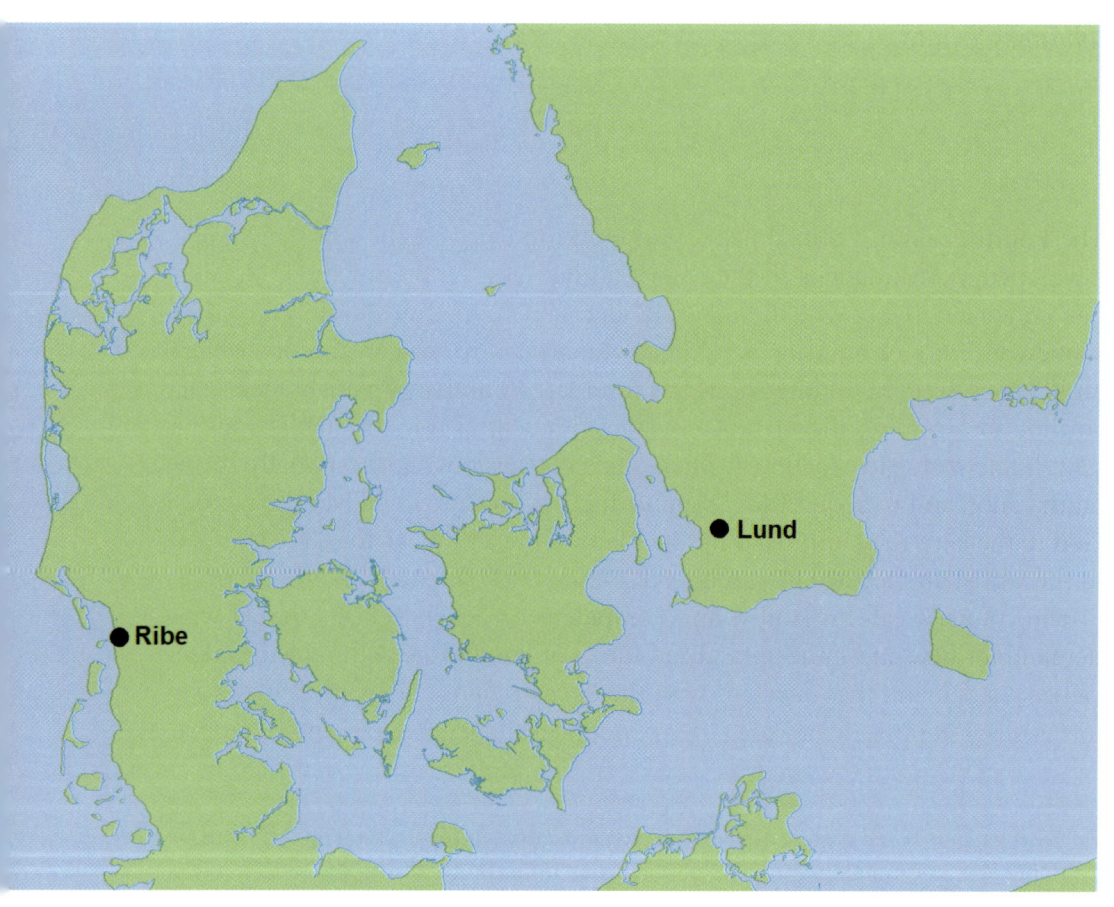
Monastic locations cited in the article.

Dominican Experts in Medieval Scandinavia: The Order of Preachers and the Dissemination of Knowledge in Northern Societies[1]

Johannes Schütz

The Fourth Lateran Council had a profound influence on the way Christianity developed in Scandinavia in the Later Middle Ages. As Brian Patrick McGuire has convincingly shown, the conciliar decisions aimed at developing a new framework for pastoral care, which in Denmark led to the construction of new and bigger church buildings designed for a large number of parishioners.[2] According to McGuire, the Mendicants played a central role in establishing this new framework.[3] In reaction to the conciliar decisions, and especially to the tenth canon and its request for "suitable men" who were to deliver the word of God to the laity, they improved the standard of preaching, giving a great impact to the Christian message in Scandinavia.

The council's call for skilled and competent preachers reflects the growing demand for new and more specialized forms of knowledge within medieval societies – a demand that dovetails with the development of new institutions and forms of social power in a wide range of political and legal, social and economic,

---

1 This paper is based on research I conducted in relation to my doctoral project, with the DFG Research training group "Expert cultures from the twelfth to the sixteenth century" at the Georg-August-Universität Göttingen. My upcoming dissertation focuses on the relationship between the education, preaching and cure of Souls of the Dominican order in Scandinavia. Grateful thanks are due to the following people for their help: First and foremost Nikolas Helm, Benjamin Müsegades and Matthias Roick, who read the whole paper and gave indispensable advice; secondly, I would like to thank all members of the Research group for their critical assessments and comments.
2 McGuire (2008), pp. 166-185.
3 McGuire (2008), p. 176: „Hvor tit almindelige sognepræster faktisk prædikede, er imidlertid umuligt at sige. Samtidig er det uomtvisteligt, at tilstedeværelsen af dominikaner- og franciskanerklostre i de allerfleste danske købstæder betød, at prædikenens standard blev højnet. […] Franciskanernes og dominikanernes ihærdige og synlige arbejdsindsats i det danske kirkelandskab har givet det kristne budskab stor gennemslagskraft."

cultural and religious contexts. As Frank Rexroth has suggested, these processes of specialization and institutionalization are best captured in the figure of the expert.[4]

In this essay, I will argue that the evolution and expansion of the Dominican order played an important part in the formation of medieval expert cultures. As qualified preachers and confessors, the Dominicans became experts on religious guidance. However, their expertise depended on a series of factors, such as the situation of the church at the beginning of the thirteenth century, the Dominicans' design of a new educational system, the reactions of the laity's religious demands and the promotion through the papacy. In what follows, I will briefly describe some of these factors. Then I will turn to the Dominicans' preaching activities in Scandinavia and focus on Mathias Ripensis, a Dominican lector who lived around 1300, and examine his sermons in the light of the rise of an expert culture.

The Lateran Council and the early beginning of the Dominican Order

At the beginning of the thirteenth century, the Church came increasingly under pressure. Among other things, Pope Innocent had to react to religious movements such as the Cathars, the Humiliati and the Waldensians. The appearance of heterodox ideas and beliefs indicates that the Latin Church after the Gregorian reform was not capable of spreading their world view throughout society. Hence, the Fourth Lateran Council was intended to reform the church's pastoral communication. The attendees stated that prelates and bishops seemed to neglect the pastoral communication with their flock due to insufficient knowledge and personal inability. The tenth decree of the Fourth Lateran Council alleges the decay of public preaching:

"It often happens that bishops by themselves are not sufficient to minister the word of God to the people, especially in large and scattered dioceses, whether this is because of their many occupations or bodily infirmities or because of incursions of the enemy or for other reasons – let us not say for lack of knowledge, which in bishops is to be altogether condemned and is not to be tolerated in the future. We therefore decree by this general constitution that bishops are to appoint suitable men to carry out with profit this duty of sacred preaching, men who are powerful in word and deed and who will visit with care the peoples entrusted to them in place of the bishops, since these by themselves are unable to do it, and will build them up by word and example".[5]

---

4   Rexroth (2008); Rexroth (2012).
5   Decrees of the ecumenical councils (1990), pp. 239-240: *Unde cum saepe contingat, quod*

The attendees of the Council asked the bishops to appoint suitable men (*viros idoneos*), who were to deliver the word of God to the laity. Preaching ought to be improved and bishops had to provide the pastoral renovation by hiring experts on the propagation of a Christian world view. Furthermore, in Canon 21, called 'Omnis utriusque sexus', the Council obliged the laity to confess annually to their own priest, who was to be educated adequately. The confessor was expected to act like an experienced physician, looking cautiously for the reasons of spiritual disease and selecting the right means to cure the souls.[6] Pastoral service was to be improved not only by changing the preaching activity but also by demanding a complete confession every Easter; experienced and qualified men were to fulfil these demands.[7] The church thus aimed at gaining more control over the laity's religiosity and at fighting heretical offspring.[8]

The Dominicans were seen as being precisely these qualified preachers and confessors, who could provide new forms of pastoral service. To medieval Churchmen the Dominicans seemed to be the appropriate propagators and defenders of orthodoxy the Roman curia was longing for in its fight against heresy and deviance.[9] Hence, I suggest that the Dominicans can be appropriately described as experts in pastoral care.

An 'expert' is not only a person with a special kind of knowledge, but also someone with a particular role in society. This role is connected to the expert's social background. One does not become an expert by accumulating knowledge, by reading and studying but one has to be appointed *as* an expert by

---

episcopi propter occupationes multiplices vel invaletudines corporales aut hostiles incursus seu occasiones alias – ne dicamus defectum scientiae, quod in eis est reprobandum omnino nec de caetero tolerandum – per se ipsos non sufficiunt ministrae populo verbum Dei, maxime per amplas dioceses et difussas, generali constitutione sancimus, ut episcopi viros idoneos ad sanctae praedicationis officium salubriter exequendum assumant, potentes in opere et sermone, qui plebes sibi commissas vice ipsorum, cum per se idem nequiverint, sollicite visitantes, eas verbo aedificent et exemplo [...].

6   Decrees of the ecumenical councils (1990), p. 245: *Omnis utriusque sexus fidelis, postquam ad annos discretionis peruenerit, omnia sua solus peccata confiteatur fideliter, saltem semel in anno, proprio sacerdoti, et iniunctam sibi poenitentiam studeat pro uiribus adimplere, suscipiens reuerenter ad minus in Pascha eucharistiae sacramentum, nisi forte de consilio proprii sacerdotis ob aliquam rationabilem causam ad tempus ab eius perceptione duxerit abstinendum [...].*

7   Decrees of the ecumenical councils (1990), p. 245: *Sacerdos autem sit discretus et cautus, ut more periti medici superinfundat vinum et oleum vulneribus sauciati, diligenter inquirens et peccatoris circumstantias et peccati, quibus prudenter intelligat, quale debeat ei praebere consilium et cuiusmodi remedium adhibere, diversis experimentis utendo ad sanandum aegrotum.*

8   Bériou (1983); Ohst (1995); Tanner (2000), pp. 112-125.
9   Oberste (1999), pp. 245-254; Bériou (2006), pp. 51-59, Stansbury (2010), pp. 23-25.

other members of society. Without society, the expert is nothing but a scholar in an ivory tower.[10] By applying this definition, I will be able to analyse the way Dominicans worked in medieval society and emerged as propagators and controllers of a socially constructed reality. Thus, the history of the education and pastoral care of the Order of Preachers will be set in its social context.

This approach demands that one studies the social integration of the Friars Preachers with care. Unfortunately, Scandinavian sources report only laconically about the Friars' arrival and the perception of their contemporaries. However, the increasing integration of the Dominican order into Scandinavian societies and the donations of Nordic people bear witness to the confidence in Dominican expertise.[11] More generally, the German provost Burchard of Ursberg, an eyewitness of the Order's expansion from the very beginning, describes the impact of Dominican expansion in his chronicle, although he criticised the papal effort to intervene in imperial issues:

"Others, namely the Predicatores, are believed to have succeeded the Humiliati. The Humiliati, who did not have the authority and affirmation of the prelates, used their sickle to harvest an alien crop by preaching to the laity, trying to guide the latters' lives as well as hearing confessions and withdrawing priests from their offices. [...] Even though they were crude and ignorant, they performed manual labour with vigour and eagerness and preached accordingly. [...] But these [sc. the predicatores, J.S.] studied and read the holy scripture untiringly, wrote a lot of books and listened attentively to the lectures of their masters, and thus equipped with bow and arrow as well as all weapons of the brave they were able to attack and stand up for the defence of holy mother church".[12]

Burchard thinks the Dominicans to be similar to the Humiliati. The religious movement of the Humiliati was first condemned as heretical but was later brought back within the pale of the church by Pope Innocent III.[13] Burchard,

---

10 Berger/Luckmann (1966), pp. 122-146; Schützeichel (2007), pp. 549-550; Rexroth (2012).
11 Gallén (1946), pp. 80-81; Jakobsen (2008), pp. 158-165.
12 Chronik Burchards von Ursberg (2007), pp. 282-284: *Alii, videlicet Predicatores, in locum Humiliatorum successisse creduntur. Humiliati quippe nulla habita auctoritate aut licentia prelatorum, mittentes falcem in messem alienam, populis predicabant et vitam eorum plerumque regere satagebant et confessiones audire et ministeriis sacerdotum derogare.* [...] *Ille quippe rudes et illiterati cum essent, operibus manuum instabant et predicabant* [...]. *Isti vero studio et lectioni sacre scripture iugiter insistentes tantum in scribendo libros opus faciebant et eos diligentissime a magistris suis audiebant, ut cum sagittis et arcu et omni armatura fortium possent ingredi et stare pro defensione sancte matris ecclesie* [...].
13 Bolton (1994); Andrews (1999).

however, is also able to state the decisive difference between both movements. Unlike the Humiliati, the Order of Preachers emphasized intense study as one main point of religious life. Burchard gives an account of these studies, which consisted of close reading of the bible, extensive copying and writing of theological texts as well as paying close attention to the lectures held by their own schoolmasters. According to Burchard of Ursberg, this intense way of studying had made the Dominicans defenders of the Latin Church in the thirteenth century.

Some years later, in 1273, Bishop Bruno von Schauenburg complains about the Mendicant influence on the laity's behaviour. In his 'Relatio de statu Ecclesiae in regno Alemanniae' he reports that the friars were preaching without interruption. On Sundays and the greater feast days the cities' parishioners avoided visiting the regular masses of the parish priests. Instead, they went into mendicant churches where they found incessant pastoral service from dawn till the third hour.[14] Especially the new art of preaching and the innovative sermons seemed to impress medieval observers. Bruno states quite critically that modern and short sermons were the reason for the friar's success.[15] The frequency and mode of Dominican preaching apparently attracted the lay people. Only a few years after the order's foundation, the Dominicans were engaged as experts on pastoral care.

The popes, too, valued the Dominicans as important agents of knowledge and thought them able to renew the pastoral communication of the church. They recommended the Order of Preachers to bishops and kings and pointed out to them the ability of the Preachers: Qualified through academic studies and experienced in pastoral communication, they met current demands and communicated that the current problems of the Latin Church would be solved.[16] As experts on religious service, they were ordered by the popes to

---

14 Bruno von Holstein-Schauenburg, (1904-1906), p. 591: *Sunt alia vero, in quibus clerum et ecclesias seculares conventuales seu parrochiales adeo contingit offendi […] Ipsas conventuales et parrochiales ecclesias in diebus dominicis et festivis non contingit a populo frequentari et hoc maxime in civitatibus et oppidis, ubi Predicatores et Minores domicilia sua habent. Solent enim dicti fratres primo diluculo dicere missas usque ad horam terciam non cessando, preter unam autem, quam dicunt sollempniter in conventu, legendo breviter continuant pluras missas.*

15 Ibidem: *[…] et quoniam gaudent brevitate moderni, populus querit pocius missas illas, conventualibus et parrocialibus ecclesiis pretermissis.*

16 Monumenta Diplomatica (1966), Nr. 143, 144, 147-151, 156, 164. All these letters were directed to *universis ecclesiarum praelatis* and recommend the Dominicans with the words: *Cum qui recipit prophetam in nomine prophete mercedem prophete accipiat, universitati vestre viros praedicatores ecclesie sancte pernecessarios pro eo quod ministrant pabulum*

advance new patterns of pastoral care. The papal support had strong influence on the Dominican expansion in Europe. Within half a century, the order spread to all European kingdoms and reached the remote areas of medieval Scandinavia. Around 1222 the first Dominican convent was founded in the city of Lund and some years later – in 1228 – the Province of Dacia was confirmed by the chapter general. In the following years the order expanded considerably. By the year 1303 there were about 30 convents located in this Dominican province.[17]

The Dominican system of studies

From its very beginning, the Dominican order focussed on bringing about social change effected by preaching and rooted in study and education. The relevance of the order to ecclesiastical reformation was to be measured by their effects on the communication between church and laity. The prologue to the Dominican Constitutions claimed that the Friars Preachers would achieve an impact on society by two means: improved preaching activity based on an effective educational organisation.[18] Thus, the Constitutions of the Friars Preachers demanded a course of studies for every Dominican, due to the belief that only learned preachers would be able to fight heretics and instruct lay people regarding the patterns and rules of the Christian religion. The Friars were to study ardently to become well-educated preachers. The founders of the order were conscious of the social relevance of their knowledge. Since they were distributing their knowledge to lay members, they considered themselves to be an important part of society. The Dominicans obliged themselves to communicate the knowledge gained by intensive studies to the rest of society.

This goal guided the Dominican order in creating a functional system of studies. Each friar was educated according to his abilities, and by no means every-

---

verbi Die merito commendamus, ut ex hoc mercedem vobis incomparabilem comparetis. Barone (1998), esp. pp. 88-90.

17 Gallén (1946), pp. 12-29, 33-43, 80-81; Jakobsen (2008), pp. 30-38; Jakobsen (2011). Freed agrees that the friars' success and rapid expansion bear witness to the confidence in their pastoral service. Freed (1977), pp. 32-43, esp. p. 34: "In exchange for the burghers' material support, the friars offered the townspeople spiritual leadership. Unfortunately, it is nearly impossible to document this most important aspect of the friars' activity; but the rapid spread of the mendicant orders in the 13th century and the popularity of such preachers as Berthold of Regensburg testify to the friars' success."

18 Thomas (1968), p. 311: [...] *cum ordo noster specialiter ob predicationem et animarum salutem ab initio noscatur institutus fuisse, et studium nostrum ad hoc principaliter ardenterque summo opere debeat intendere, ut proximorum animabus possimus utiles esse.*

one went through the full course. Basically, studies were organized on three different levels: convent schools (*scholae convetuales*), provincial schools (*studia provincialia*), and houses of general studies (*studia generalia*).[19]

Every priory had to provide the education for the young friars in theology and rhetorical skills.[20] These schools were modelled on the example of university courses, but provided a curriculum tailored to the Dominican purpose. Strong emphasis was put on the normative elements of the Christian creed: In the second half of the thirteenth century, the provincial prior Augustinus de Dacia wrote a handbook for the Scandinavian convent schools. In the prologue to this 'Rotulus pugillaris', Augustinus demands the firm handling of pastoral knowledge. A Dominican Friar should know the fundamental definitions and concepts of the Christian religion and he was to learn the doctrine of virtues and vices, commandments and sins, sacraments and means of grace.[21] The handbook of Augustinus introduced the young Dominican to the aim, subject and methods of theology, i.e. the way of expounding Holy Scripture according to the system of the four levels of meaning. By adopting the exegetical technique of the universities, the friar was enabled to obtain religious knowledge of the Bible, which he was supposed to break down into more accessible form for his lay audience.

In addition, the Dominican convent lectors instructed their pupils in the art of preaching and the technique of hearing confession. Rhetoric was used to form structure and achieve a persuasive sermon. Different levels of practicing

---

19 Berg (1977); Le scuole degli ordini mendicanti (1978); Mulchahey (1998); Studio e Studia (2002).
20 Boyle (1981); Mulchahey (1997); Mulchahey (2002).
21 Walz (1955), p. 136-137: *Ad laudem Iesu Christi pro instructione iuvenum fratrum ordinis Praedicatorum et aliorum qui pro tempore ob salutem animarum praedicationi et confessionum auditioni sunt exponendi ea quae communia sunt et in sacra theologia magis neccessaria simplicibus ad sciendum in unum quasi rotulum pugillarem breviter collecta redegi.* [...] *Moneo vero iterum atque iterum ne aliqui fratres dicti ordinis Daciae ad praedicta officia praedicationis et confessionis assumantur priusquam de his quae hic conscripta sunt et aliis quae in constitutionibus praefati ordinis ponuntur ad memorata officia pertinentia diligenter examinati fuerint et approbati. Habet autem hic rotulus quindecim tractatus. In primo tractatur de introductoriis scientiae theologiae. In secundo de fide, symbolis et fidei articulis. In tertio de angelis et animabus. In quarto de gratia et eius differentiis. In quinto de virtutibus theologicis, cardinalibus et allis. In sexto de donis et operibus misericordiae. In septimo de beatitudinibus et contemplatione. In octavo de oratione et specialiter de oratione dominica. In nono de praeceptis et plagis. In decimo de votis, iuramentis et ignorantia. In undecimo de peccatis et eorum speciebus et differentiis in generali. In duodecimo de quibusdam peccatis in speciali. In decimo tertio de sacramentis. In quarto decimo de distinctione temporum. In quinto decimo de antichristo et ultimo iudicio.*

the preaching abilities led the young friar to his first sermon from the pulpit. At least, the schools taught the legal and dogmatic fundamentals of penance and introduced the methods of counselling and judging in the *forum internum* to the Dominican student. The new genre of *Summae confessorum* was adopted and utilized as means of forming trained confessors.[22]

By studying these different stocks of knowledge and particular skills in disseminating the religious knowledge, the Dominicans were most suitable to cope with the task of renewing the orthodox cure of souls. The Friars Preachers were promoted to the role of experts due to their particular combination of different areas of knowledge: They were trained not only in theology and scriptural exegesis but also in the art of preaching and the practices of hearing confessions. Therefore, the papal curia regarded the Dominicans as the experts of the council's decrees and promoted their expansion, aiming to supersede the heretical competitors.

This was, however, the syllabus of the convent schools, where the elite of the Order educated the *fratres communes*. The Order aimed at a qualified system of education and ordered every convent to have a lector.[23] At least four years of studying were required to become such a lector.[24] The prerequisite for the lectors-to-be was to complete a course of studies at a Dominican school of higher education, so called *studia particularia* and *studia generalia*. Different houses of study existed and integrated the particular fields of medieval theology and philosophy. Thus, the future lectors had to become acquainted with Aristotelian logic, natural philosophy and the Sentences of Peter Lombard before they were allowed to study the Holy Scripture. The study of the Bible according to scientific rules, that is by using means of arguing in the scholastic forms of teaching, *lectio* and *disputatio*, made these lectors the erudite elite of the Order, which was to hand down its knowledge to the rank and file friars in the convent schools. After completing their studies at one of the general houses of study the lectors returned to their home provinces to teach the friars there.[25]

---

22 Boyle (1981), pp. 249-254; Mulchahey (1998), pp. 193-203.
23 Thomas (1968), p. 358: *Conventus citra numerum duodecorum et sine licentia generalis capituli et sine priore et doctore non mittantur.* In the following years, the word *doctor* was replaced by the word *lector.*
24 Ibidem, p. 363: *Nullus fiat publicus doctor, nisi per quatuor annos ad minus theologiam audierit*
25 Berg (1977), pp. 58-84, 118-121; Mulchahey (1998), pp. 351-378; Senner (2005), pp. 151-175.

The Dominican preaching activity in Scandinavia

One of these Dominican lectors was Mathias Ripensis. Only a few sources mention this Friar Preacher, thus, he rarely ever emerges from under the shadow of history. Mathias was a Dane or at least a Scandinavian, because in his sermon collection he referred to a Scandinavian language being his mother tongue.[26] He was probably lector in the Danish convent of Ribe, whose necrology mentions him as *lector Mathias*. This document, however, does not give any hints concerning his biography.[27] The Dominican historiographer Laurentius Pignon (d. 1449) listed Mathias Ripensis in his catalogue of Dominican writers and ascribed two sermon collections to him. One, *sermones de tempore*, is still extant in several manuscripts in the University library of Uppsala; the other collection, *sermones de sanctis*, is lost.[28] The latest entry in this catalogue probably dates from 1323, which led Henrik Schück as well as Anne Riising to assume that Mathias lived around the year 1300.[29] Mathias Ripensis was part of the Dominican system of studies, first as a student and afterwards as a lector in thirteenth century Ribe.

The sermons of Mathias Ripensis bear witness to the deep impact that scholarly education had on the way Dominicans structured their sermons and thus give an account of the prerequisites of the Dominican success. The academic commitment tied the Order of Preachers closely to the nascent universities. Therefore, the Dominican sermons were influenced by university developments both in homiletic theory and in scriptural exegesis. The 'erudite sermon' of the thirteenth century was mainly influenced by the new methods of medieval theology. Biblical exegesis, based on the hermeneutical, semantic and historical criticism of the page, together with the awareness of rhetorical skills shaped the new theory of preaching.[30] Therefore, the stock of knowledge a Dominican was supposed to possess was built on two different pillars: the formal structure and the thematic composition of sermons. A Dominican was to know what he was supposed to preach and how he should preach. Furthermore, the Dominican stock of knowledge encompassed dogmatic, natural, historical and normative knowledge as well as rhetorical and exegetical skills.[31] This body of knowledge was taught at the Dominican convent schools; every Friar Preacher had to be

---

26 MS Uppsala, Universitetsbiblioteket, C. 343, fol. 35r: *legitur de sancto georgio qui in lingua nostra iurian vocatur*. Riising (1969), p. 48.
27 Nogle Brudstykker af et Nekrologium (1853-1856), p. 494.
28 Laurentius Pignon (1936), p. 32; Lehmann (1962), p. 304.
29 Schück (1891), p. 164; Riising (1969), p. 48.
30 Oberste (1999), pp. 245-254; Bériou (2006); Schütz (2012), pp. 253-256.
31 Humbert de Romanis, De eruditione praedicatorum, pp. 400-403: *Multiplex autem est scientia, quae eis est necessaria.*

able to interpret the Bible according to theological methods and was supposed to be able to communicate Christian religion according to the rules of rhetoric.

By looking at the formal aspects of Mathias' sermons the dependencies on rhetorical issues become obvious.[32] The formal composition of the sermon was deeply rooted in rhetorical practice reaching back to classical antiquity.[33] Both preaching and oration had the same goal: to *persuade* the audience. The authors of medieval preaching manuals adopted the old theory of oration to construct the medieval sermon. Analogous to classical speeches, Mathias Ripensis composes his sermons following the traditional sections such as exordium, narration, confirmation and epilogue. He structures his sermons according to elements like theme, prologue, division, confirmation and conclusion. Furthermore, the invention of the arguments was covered by the theory of preaching. Christian *topoi* were defined and elaborated, which served as the main source of persuasive arguments for the sermons. The most important source was, of course, the Bible. In the majority of cases, Mathias uses scriptural quotations to prove assumptions in his argumentation. In addition, he refers to natural science by using *similitudines* to explain difficult theological concepts. He also uses exempla for legitimizing and advising with historical references. Another example of the relationship between rhetoric and preaching is the *modus argumentativus*. Mathias Ripensis only rarely argues with complete logical syllogisms. Instead, his confirmation is based on shortened syllogisms, the so-called enthymeme.[34] This common rhetorical mode of arguing, which did not need logical completeness, was the main form of confirmation used by Mathias Ripensis.[35] The art of preaching borrowed its techniques in some aspects from the classical *ars rhetorica* and the formal construction of medieval sermons depended on rhetorical patterns and ideals.

The study of the Bible and especially the technique of scriptural exegesis influenced the construction of sermons as well. The exegesis of the bible, following the four senses or levels of meaning of the Scripture, was used to hand down biblical knowledge to lay people.[36] Furthermore, the moral sense was more important to preaching than the other three, because by emphasizing the moral sense of the Bible, the main goal of preaching was to be achieved – the instruction of laymen in the normative patterns of Christian religion. The

---

32 In the following, I would like to give a rough outline of some findings of my doctoral thesis, which is to be published under the tittle "Hinter der Wirklichkeit. Der Dominikanerorden in der mittelalterlichen Gesellschaft Skandinaviens" in 2014.
33 Murphy (1990), pp. 303-326; Morenzoni (1995), pp. 200-222; Kühne (2005).
34 Lausberg (1990), pp. 198-200.
35 For instance: MS Uppsala, Universitetsbiblioteket, C. 343, fol. 44v-46r.
36 Smalley (1983), pp. 242-244, 254-257; Bataillon (1992); Meier (1996), p. 60-61.

preachers wanted lay people to follow Christian rules and norms. Scriptural exegesis unlocked the moral sense of the Bible and deduced moral guidelines. The Dominican education of laymen was aimed at providing the Scandinavian people with patterns of conduct within a Christian worldview.

Dominican experts disseminating knowledge

To give an example of how the Dominican sermons intended to disseminate different elements of knowledge, I would like to choose one particular topic of Mathias' sermons. The behavior expected of all groups of society in respect to their socio-economic status was publicly communicated and the Dominicans tried to teach the poor or the rich in what way they had to behave in their social context.[37] I will show how poverty and prosperity were reflected in Dominican sermons from Scandinavia and, thus, I will exemplify the Dominican preaching activity with regard to particular content.

Like almost all European preachers, Mathias Ripensis picks out the story of Lazarus and the rich man in the Gospel of Luke as an occasion to preach about the impact of social disparity.[38] The story is about an unnamed rich man and a poor beggar named Lazarus. The rich man lives in luxury and is not willing to share his wealth with Lazarus, who desires "to be fed with the crumbs which fell from the rich man's table". [Luke 16.21] Both have to face the consequences of their behaviour after death – the rich man is buried in hell and has to suffer torture. Lazarus, however, is carried into Abraham's bosom by angels. Seeing this, the rich man begs for mercy, but Abraham says: *Fili recordare quia recepisti bona in vita tua, etc.* – "Son, remember that thou in thy lifetime receivedst thy good things, and likewise Lazarus evil things: but now he is comforted, and thou art tormented." [Luke 16, 25]. This biblical verse is the starting point of Mathias's sermon. After naming the pericope of the day, Mathias recounts the scriptural parable and then unfolds his admonition.[39] According to his sermon, the misery of the rich man is caused by three things. First of all, he has set his mind on gathering worldly treasures. Mathias teaches that people should aim at achieving the heavenly treasure and scorn the worldly, because they could only get one of the two. Thus, the rich man separates himself from God. His greed leads to the loss of his eternal life.[40]

---

37 Little (1978); Lesnick (1989), pp. 99-136; Schmidt (1992); Oberste (2001); Oberste (2002); Ertl (2006).
38 Hanska (1997), pp. 28-63.
39 MS Uppsala, Universitetsbiblioteket, C. 343, fol. 88v-89v.
40 MS Uppsala, Universitetsbiblioteket, C. 343, fol. 88v-89r: *Fili recordare quia rece[pisti]*

Secondly, the rich man, Mathias continues, did not behave as was expected of him. He points out that he remained in mortal sin throughout his whole life because the reception of temporal prosperity was mostly connected to improper behaviour. And third, the preacher claims that either unjust acquisition or inequitable retention or abuse lead the owner of temporal prosperity to mortal sin.[41] Before explaining this threefold misconduct, Mathias reminds his audience that mortal sin would drag humans down to eternal death.[42] He points out that the rich man did not acquire his wealth in an unjust manner, because this would have included harming or robbing somebody. But he received, as Mathias emphasizes, all these good things from God. However, he committed a sin by keeping his wealth to himself and by not sharing it with the poor. Mathias sees only one solution to living with worldly wealth – the rich man would have had to share his property. Because he did not he was buried in hell and was to experience eternal torture.[43]

In an earlier sermon, Mathias exemplifies this code of conduct. He uses an *exemplum*, which deals with the emperor Theodosius I, also known as Theodosius the Great. Mathias shows in what way a rich man ought to behave. This example, probably taken from the Golden Legend, reports that the emperor gave all his treasures to the poor. His wife objects to this behavior, but Theodosius defends his deed by referring to his trust in God and claims that real treasures do not consist of money. Rather, if he took this treasury, which he had received from God to give away as alms, he would receive a proper treasure in heaven. Later, when Theodosius goes through his palace, he sees a marble plate on the ground floor with a cross on it. The plate is elevated and the emperor finds a treasure of infinite measure beneath. Mathias directs his criticism against the av-

---

    bo[na] in vi[ta] tua etc. luc. xvi[.25] Inspicientibus seriem ewangelium apperet status istorum duorum de quibus hec agitur diffire quam ad tria s. quam ad vitam quia alius dives alius pauper. Quantum ad mortem quia alius portatus ab angelis in sinum abrahe. Alius sepultus in inferni quam ad statum post mortem quia alius erat in consolatione alius in tormento quia ipse prius totam consolationem suam receperat et hoc est quod dicitur in verbis propositis. Fili recordare. Ubi tria ad memoriam reducuntur. isti misero divici primo ad quid deus eum fecerat cum dicitur fili. Secundo multiplicia bona quae a deo receperat. Recordare [...] quasi dicat omnia recepisti in vita tua et ideo nihil remanet tibi post mortem in vita s. quae est transitoria. Vita autem [dei] eterna.

41 MS Uppsala, Universitetsbiblioteket, C. 343, fol. 89r: *Notandum quod circa divicias temporaliter peccatur scilicet iniusta aquisione. Iniqua intentione et malo usu sine mala expensione.*

42 Ibidem: *peccatum mortale est quod detinet et trahit hominem ad eternam mortem.*

43 MS Uppsala, Universitetsbiblioteket, C. 343, fol. 89r-89v.

aricious stating that temporal wealth ought to be used to help people in need.[44]

Mathias provides his audience with two examples, one for the right and one for the wrong use of money. The rich man in the Bible does not acknowledge what he is supposed to do. He does not donate to Lazarus and in consequence he has no merits to expect. Theodosius, instead, gives the whole empire's wealth to the poor and receives infinite prosperity. The knowledge of history serves both to exemplify and to legitimize the stipulated code of conduct. By referring to the humble poor, the rich man and the emperor Theodosius, Mathias provides his audience with alleged historical facts[45] which show the benefit of proper, and the danger of improper, behaviour. Christian norms are exemplified by individual events in history to provide Christians with guidelines to a life in accordance with religious norms.

Another important concern of the preachers was the giving of alms. Giving alms were a central element of Christian charity and can be seen as a necessary part of a process aiming towards social balance. A couple of biblical examples prefigured and justified the obligation of distribuing money to the poor. In the Middle Ages social circumstances also made it necessary to give alms because poverty and social disparity were two of the most essential problems.[46] Thus, Dominican preachers were supposed to instruct lay people in the theory and practice of giving alms.

In the margin of one folio of Codex 356 of the University Library of Uppsala, which contains one version of Mathias Ripensis, one section is marked as *de elymosina*.[47] In this section, Mathias explains the preconditions, practices and consequences of giving alms. In fact, Mathias writes, humans were not supposed to sin. But if they committed sins nevertheless, they could gain help by a divine medicine, *divina medicina*, to fight this spiritual disease. Giving alms was, in fact, such a divine medicine, Mathias emphasizes. By giving alms, humans were able to gain redemption as reward. The inner attitude, however, was as important as the external practice. It was not possible to maintain sin-

---

44 MS Uppsala, Universitetsbiblioteket, C. 343, fol. 51r: *legitur de theodosio imperatore christianissimo quod cum thesauros palacii daret pauperibus. Arguebatur ab uxore. Respondit Confido in domine quod fisco nostro non deerit pecunia. Si de hiis quae nobis deus contulerit elemosinas faciendo. thesauros nobis acquiramus in celo et cum transiret per palacium imperiale vidit in pavimento tabulam marmoream in qua crux erat scripta quam elevari fecisset invenit infinitum thesaurum.*

45 The Parables of the bible and Legends of Saints are of course not necessarily historical facts, but in the medieval tradition the literal sense of Scripture provided historical information. Melville (1982).

46 Oexle (1991); Schubert (1992).

47 MS Uppsala, Universitetsbiblioteket, C. 356, fol. 36v.

ful behaviour and redeem oneself with money. Contrition and confession were defined as the prerequisites for the satisfactory impact of almsgiving. Using a medical metaphor, Mathias points out to his audience the proper way of being absolved. But giving alms was only one way of doing penance.[48] To those lost in sinfulness and thus in danger of eternal condemnation, the Church offered redemption through obedience: A contrite confession of one's sins to a priest was the prerequisite for reintegration into society; and an obedient fulfillment of the confessor's decision was used to discipline the laiety and to subject them to the ecclesiastical definition of reality.[49]

Experts on religion are obliged to fulfil a particular task in human societies: They are to construct, conceptualize and systematize a symbolic universe. This symbolic universe provides human practice and social systems with meaningful explanations of origin, condition and future. By doing this, social universes are to explain and legitimize institutional orders and to construct a common reality.[50] The religious experts see to the dissemination of religious knowledge and the internalization of the common worldview by every member of society; they have to oversee their socialization to secure the maintenance of a socially shared symbolic universe from generation to generation. "As monopolistic combination of full-time experts in a religious definition of reality",[51] the Latin Church and its footmen were the effective holders of the "monopoly over all ultimate definitions of reality in [..] society"[52] and so they controlled the 'inhabitants' of the symbolic universe and fought open heresy. The Dominican expert thus tried to harmonize the subjective with a socially constructed reality. By connecting the anthropological theology of sin with the ecclesiastical practice of penance, Mathias establishes a meaningful relationship between individual behaviour and religiously defined reality.

Mathias' general message can be summed up the following way: Keeping money could be dangerous for human beings, because it quickly led into sin. This attitude towards worldly property leads Mathias to argue that the rich should share their property with the poor. Theodosius was only one extreme example of acting this way but it demonstrated the significance of charitability. As the general remarks on the giving of alms demonstrate, it was seen as a proper means of sharing one's wealth with society and thus of receiving redemption of sins in return. By underlining this crucial point, Mathias provides a guideline of

---

48 The latest works on the history of penance: Ohst (1995); Firey (2008).
49 Tentler (1974); Tentler (1977); Ertl (2006), pp. 253-305.
50 Berger/Luckmann (1966), pp. 122-146.
51 Ibidem, p. 140.
52 Ibidem, p. 138.

moral behavior for all groups of society. His rules are not restricted to a particular stratum of society, but could be followed by everyone. Regarding the giving of alms, a difference was made with respect to a person's economic status and how much they would be required to give. This it was the duty of the Friars to teach in each particular case.

The sermons of Mathias Ripensis were meant as a useful guide to preaching according to the ecclesiastical year. The guidelines of moral behaviour were only outlined in general remarks and not connected to a particular social or regional context. Thus, Mathias Ripensis gives an account of the means adequate for every Christian to achieve salvation. But first, he had to educate the laity regarding the dogmatic background. Sin, and especially the deadly sins of luxury and avarice, are mentioned, explained and illustrated. The Dogmatic knowledge of the Christian religion, i.e. the socially constructed reality, is to be handed down to the ordinary parishioners by the medieval experts on religion. Even though the theological doctrine was not named explicitly in any instance it had to be communicated to the audience. For a proper understanding of his sermons one had to know that sin was a transgression of the divine law, that there were different kinds of sinful behaviour, and a particular concatenation and hierarchy of sins, and that sin would be punished by eternal torment.[53] Furthermore, the consequences of sin as well as the impact of virtuous conduct are shown.

By using the biblical example of Lazarus and the rich man as well as the example of Theodosius, Mathias illustrates the Christian dogmas and legitimizes the Christian norms. Abstract theological doctrines and moral behavioural guidelines are explained by referring to historical cases and borrowing from scientific language. Thus, the example leads to a better comprehension of the code of rules and gives lay people guidelines to act in accordance with. Mathias handed down the code of correct conduct to the Scandinavian people. Either they were able to live without sin – which was virtually impossible – or they were to use the divine medicine to cure their souls. Sin was not necessarily punished by damnation because honest penance (consisting of contrition, confession and satisfaction) was the remedy leading out of the state of sin. After satisfaction – in the case of avarice by giving alms – every Christian had a new chance to live according to Christian rules. In fact, preaching about confession and penance was the main concern of Mathias, who thus tried to teach moral behaviour within a Christian reality and to normalize the life of the Scandinavian people.[54] The confessor controlled and punished the transgression of Christian rules and by doing penance the sinner was given the op-

---

53 Casagrande/Vecchio (2002); Newhauser (2005); Newhauser (2009).
54 MS Uppsala, Universitetsbiblioteket, C. 343, fol. 42v, 48, 53v, 71v.

portunity to reintegrate into society. Thus, Mathias refers his audience to the Dominican confessor and strengthens the Dominicans' position as experts on pastoral service. Their responsibility was not only to disseminate the Christian worldview but also to monitor the adherence to the definition of reality as well as to persecute apostasy.

Conclusion

The decisions made by the Fourth Lateran Council in 1215 had a crucial impact on the expansion and the evolution of the Dominican Order and the concept of expert cultures seems to be a suitable approach for a detailed and new description of the Friars' success: The Dominican Order was as a community of experts on the cure of souls. The Friars Preachers founded a system of education which provided a particular curriculum in theology, rhetoric and secular arts. Furthermore, they applied this knowledge in their preaching activities and their sermons were shaped by rhetorical skills and scriptural exegesis. However, the knowledge disseminated to society varied. The Dominicans intended to hand down the soteriological knowledge, which laypeople needed to know for their everyday life as Christians. The Dominican stock of knowledge came into practice in the pastoral activities of the friars – mainly in preaching to the laity and in hearing confession. The Dominicans applied their knowledge in sermons, which led to a novel rendition of the Gospel. The Dominicans took up contemporary theoretical considerations that had developed a new foundation of pastoral theology. Preaching and hearing confession were to be the focus of pastoral care. Through didactical explanations of a moral nature in the sermons all members of medieval society were shown the path to a meaningful life in the world. In trying to change the behaviour of the Scandinavian people Mathias Ripensis aimed at educating the Scandinavian laity to follow the Christian rules and, thus, aimed at influencing social order in the north. Confession served to establish a direct relationship between priests and the faithful in order to control individual comprehension of faith. Ultimately, the goal was to advance the spread of orthodox perceptions of Christian religion and to fight heretical assaults against the official doctrine of the church. In the name of the popes, the Dominican preachers tried to homogenise the Christian worldview and sought to eradicate deviant models of Christian reality.

In consequence, the commitment to studying and applying their education in preaching advanced the dissemination of knowledge. The Dominican Friars were trained experts on pastoral care, able to preach and hear confession. In the course of the thirteenth century, the clerical elite discovered in the Dominicans the suitable men and doctors of souls that decrees 10 and 21 were asking for. The papacy promoted the Order of Preachers, which in consequence spread over the whole of Europe to different social realities. The way, however, in which society accepted the Dominican effort and followed Christian rules, is in need of further study.

Literature

Manuscript sources
MS Uppsala, Universitetsbiblioteket, C. 343.
MS Uppsala, Universitetsbiblioteket, C. 356.

Printed sources
Burchard of Ursberg, 'Chronik', in *Ausgewählte Quellen zur deutschen Geschichte des Mittelalters*, Vol. 18b, ed. Matthias Becher et al. (Darmstadt, 2007), pp. 101-311.
Bruno of Holstein-Schauenburg, 'Relatio de statu Ecclesiae in regno Alemanniae', in *Monumenta Germaniae Historica. Leges, Constitutiones et acta publica imperatorum et regum*, Vol. 3, ed. Jacob Schwalm (Hannover/Leipzig, 1904-1906), pp. 589-594.
Decrees of the ecumenical councils, Vol. 1: Nicaea to Lateran V, ed. Norman P. Tanner (London, 1990).
Humbert of Romans, De eruditione praedicatorum, in duos tractatus divisus, in quo de modo prompte cudendi sermones ad omne hominum et negotiorum genus pertractus, in *Maxima bibliotheca veterum patrum*, Vol. 25 (Lyon, 1677), pp. 456-567.
Laurentius Pignon, *Catalogus fratrum spectabilium Ordinis fratrum Praedicatorum*, ed. G. G. Meerssemann (Roma, 1936).
Monumenta Diplomatica S. Dominici, ed. Raymond J. Loenertz and Vladimir J. Koudelka (Roma, 1966).
'Nogle Brudstykker af et Nekrologium fra Dominikaner-Klosteret i Ribe', ed. J. Kinch, *Kirkehistoriske Samlinger* 2 (1853-1856), pp. 490-500.
'Rotulus pugillaris', ed. Angelus Walz, *Classica et Mediaevalia* 16 (1955), pp. 136-194.
Thomas, Antoninus Hendrik, *De oudste Constituties van de Dominicanen. Vorgeschiedenis Tekst, Bronnen, Onstaan en Ontwikkeling (1225-1237)* (Leuven, 1965).

Studies
Andrews, Frances, *The Early Humiliati* (New York, 2006).
Barone, Giulia, 'Il Papato e i Domenicani nel Duecento', in *Il Papato duecentesco e gli ordini mendicanti. Atti del 25. Convegno internazionale* (Spoleto, 1998), pp. 81-103.
Bataillon, Louis Jacques, 'Early Scholastic and Mendicant Preaching as Exegesis of Scripture,' in *Ad litteram. Authoritative Texts and their Medieval Readers*, ed. Mark D. Jordan (Notre Dame, 1992), pp. 165–198.
Berg, Dieter, *Armut und Wissenschaft. Beiträge zur Geschichte des Studienwesens der Bettelorden im 13. Jahrhundert* (Düsseldorf, 1977).
Berger, Peter L., and Thomas Luckmann, *The Social Construction of Reality: A Treatise in the Sociology of Knowledge* (Garden City, NY, 1966).

Bériou, Nicole, 'Autour de Latran IV (1215). La naissance de la confession moderne et sa diffusion', in *Pratiques de la confession. Des Pères du désert à Vatican II; quinze études d'histoire,* ed. Groupe de la Bussiere, (Paris, 1983), pp. 73–92.

Bériou, Nicole, 'Prédication et Communication du message religieux. Le tournant du XIIIe siècle', in *Annoncer l'Evangile (XVe-XVIIe siècle). Permanences et mutations de la predication,* ed. Matthieu Arnold (Paris, 2006), pp. 41–60.

Bolton, Brenda, 'Innocent III and the Humiliati', in *Innocent III. Vicar of Christ or Lord of the World?,* ed. James M. Powell, 2nd ed. (Washington, D.C., 1994), pp. 114–120.

Boyle, Leonard E., 'Notes on the Education of the Fratres Communes in the Dominican Order in the Thirteenth Century', in *Pastoral Care, Clerical Education and Canon Law, 1200-1400.* ed. Leonard E. Boyle (London, 1981), pp. 249–267.

Casagrande, Carla, and Silvana Vecchio, *Histoire des péchés capitaux au Moyen Âge* (Paris, 2002).

d'Avray, David L., *The Preaching of the Friars. Sermons Diffused from Paris before 1300* (Oxford, 1988).

Ertl, Thomas, *Religion und Disziplin. Selbstdeutung und Weltordnung im frühen deutschen Franziskanertum* (Berlin, 2006).

Firey, Abigail (ed.), *A New History of Penance* (Leiden, 2008).

Freed, John B., *The Friars and German Society in the Thirteenth Century* (Cambridge, 1977).

Gallén, Jarl, *La Province de Dacie de l'Ordre des frères prêcheurs. 1. Histoire générale jusqu'au grand schism* (Helsingfors, 1946).

Hanska, Jussi, *"And the Rich Man also died; and He was buried in Hell". The Social Ethos in Mendicant Sermons* (Helsinki, 1997).

Jakobsen, Johnny Grandjean Gøgsig, *Prædikebrødrenes samfundsrolle i middelalderens Danmark* (Odense, 2008).

Jakobsen, Johnny Grandjean Gøgsig, 'Venerunt fratres predicatores. Notes on Datings of the First Dominican Convent Foundations in Scandinavia', *Collegium medieval* 24 (2011), pp. 5-22.

Kühne, Udo, 'Die Lehre vom Predigtaufbau in frühen Artes praedicandi', *Mittellateinisches Jahrbuch* 40 (2005), pp. 171–190.

Lausberg, Heinrich, *Handbuch der literarischen Rhetorik. Eine Grundlegung der Literaturwissenschaft,* 3rd ed. (Stuttgart, 1990).

Lehmann, Paul, 'Skandinaviens Anteil an der lateinischen Literatur und Wissenschaft des Mittelalters. Erstes Stück', in *Erforschung des Mittelalters. Ausgewählte Abhandlungen und Aufsätze,* ed. Paul Lehmann, Vol. 5 (Stuttgart, 1962), pp. 275–429.

Le scuole degli ordini mendicanti (secoli XIII - XIV) (Todi, 1978).

Lesnick, Daniel R., *Preaching in Medieval Florence. The Social World of Franciscan and Dominican Spirituality* (Athens, 1989).

Little, Lester K., *Religious Poverty and the Profit Economy in Medieval Europe* (London, 1978).

McGuire, Brian Patrick, *Da himmelen kom nærmere. Fortællinger om Danmarks kristning 700-1300* (Frederiksberg, 2008).

Meier, Christel, 'Wendepunkte in der Allegorie im Mittelalter: Von der Schrifthermeneutik zur Lebenspraktik', in *Neue Richtungen in der hoch- und spätmittelalterlichen Bibelexegese,* eds. Robert E. Lerner and Elisabeth Müller-Luckner (München, 1996), pp. 39–64.

Melville, Gert, 'Wozu Geschichte schreiben? Stellung und Funktion der Historie im Mittelalter', in *Formen der Geschichtsschreibung. Traditionen der Geschichtsschreibung und ihrer Reflexion. Fallstudien, systematische Rekonstruktionen, Diskussion und Kritik*, ed. Reinhard Koselleck (München, 1982), pp. 86–146.

Morenzoni, Franco, *Des écoles aux paroisses. Thomas de Chobham et la promotion de la prédication au début du XIIIe siècle* (Paris, 1995).

Mulchahey, Marian Michèle, 'More Notes on the Education of the Fratres Communes in the Dominican Order: Elias de Ferreriis of Salagnac's Libellus de doctrina fratrum', in *A Distinct voice. Medieval Studies in Honor of Leonard E. Boyle, O.P.*, ed. Jacqueline Brown (Notre Dame, 1997), pp. 328–369.

Mulchahey, Marian Michèle, *"First the bow is bent in study …". Dominican Education before 1350* (Toronto, 1998).

Mulchahey, Marian Michèle, 'The R le of the Conventual Schola in Early Dominican Education', in *Studio e studia: Le scuole degli ordini mendicanti tra XIII e XIV secolo*, Atti del 29. Convegno internazionale (Spoleto, 2002), pp. 119–150.

Murphy, James J., *Rhetoric in the Middle Ages. A History of Rhetorical Theory from Saint Augustine to the Renaissance* (Berkeley, 1990).

Newhauser, Richard (ed.), *In the Garden of Evil. The Vices and Culture in the Middle Ages* (Toronto, 2005).

Newhauser, Richard, 'The Capital Vices as Medieval Anthropology', in *Laster im Mittelalter. Vices in the Middle Ages*, ed. Christoph Flüeler (Berlin/New York, 2009), pp. 105–123.

Oberste, Jörg, 'Predigt und Gesellschaft um 1200. Praktische Moraltheologie und pastorale Neuorientierung im Umfeld der Pariser Universität am Vorabend der Mendikanten', in *Die Bettelorden im Aufbau. Beiträge zu Institutionalisierungsprozessen im mittelalterlichen Religiosentum*, eds. Gert Melville and Jörg Oberste (Münster, 1999), pp. 245–294.

Oberste, Jörg, 'Bonus negotiator Christus - malus negotiator dyabolus. Kaufmann und Kommerz in der Bildersprache hochmittelalterlicher Prediger', in *Institutionalität und Symbolisierung. Verstetigungen kultureller Ordnungsmuster in Vergangenheit und Gegenwart*, ed. Gert Melville (Köln, 2001), pp. 425–450.

Oberste, Jörg, 'Gesellschaft und Individuum in der Seelsorge der Mendikanten. Die Predigten Humberts de Romanis (†1277) an städtische Oberschichten', in *Das Eigene und das Ganze. Zum Individuellen im mittelalterlichen Religiosentum*, eds. Gert Melville and Markus Schürer (Münster, 2002), pp. 497–527.

Oexle, Otto Gerhard, 'Armut, Armutsbegriff und Armenfürsorge im Mittelalter', in *Soziale Sicherheit und soziale Disziplinierung. Beiträge zu einer historischen Theorie der Sozialpolitik*, eds. Christoph Sachße and Florian Tennstedt, 6th ed. (Frankfurt a. M, 1991), pp. 73–100.

Ohst, Martin, *Pflichtbeichte. Untersuchungen zum Bußwesen im hohen und späten Mittelalter* (Tübingen, 1995).

Rexroth, Frank, *Expertenweisheit. Die Kritik an den Studierten und die Utopie einer geheilten Gesellschaft im späten Mittelalter* (Basel, 2008).

Rexroth, Frank, 'Systemvertrauen und Expertenskepsis. Die Utopie vom maßgeschneiderten Wissen in den Kulturen des 12. bis 16. Jahrhunderts', in *Wissen, maßgeschneidert. Experten und Expertenkulturen im Europa der Vormoderne*, eds. Björn Reich, Frank Rexroth, Matthias Roick (München, 2012), pp. 12-44.

Riising, Anne, *Danmarks middelalderlige prædiken* (Odense, 1969).

Schmidt, Hans-Joachim, 'Allegorie und Empirie. Interpretation und Normung sozialer Realität in Predigten des 13. Jahrhunderts', in *Die deutsche Predigt im Mittelalter,* eds. Volker Mertens and Hans-Jochen Schiewer (Tübingen, 1992), pp. 301–330.

Schubert, Ernst, 'Gestalt und Gestaltwandel des Almosens im Mittelalter', in *Festschrift Alfred Wendehorst,* ed. Jürgen Schneider, 2 Vols. (Neustadt, Aisch, 1992), pp. 241–262.

Schück, Henrik, 'Svenska Medeltidsförfattare', *Samlaren* 12 (1891), pp. 154–170.

Schütz, Johannes, 'Gelehrte Predigt als dominikanische Innovation. Anmerkungen zur Studienorganisation und Predigtpraxis des Dominikanerordens im 13. Jahrhundert', in *Innovation in Klöstern und Orden des Hohen Mittelalters. Aspekte und Pragmatik eines Begriffs,* eds. Mirko Breitenstein, Stefan Burkhardt, Julia Dücker (Berlin, 2012), pp. 247-262.

Schützeichel, Rainer, 'Laien, Experten, Professionen', in *Handbuch Wissenssoziologie und Wissensforschung,* ed. Rainer Schützeichel (Konstanz, 2007), pp. 546-578.

Senner, Walter, 'Gli studia generalia nell'ordine dei Predicatori nel duecento', *Archivum Franciscanum historicum* 98 (2005), pp. 175-199.

Smalley, Beryl, *The Study of the Bible in the Middle Ages* (Oxford, 1983).

Studio e studia: Le scuole degli ordini mendicanti tra XIII e XIV secolo (Spoleto, 2002).

Stansbury, Ronald J., 'Preaching and Pastoral Care in the Middle Ages', in *A Companion to Pastoral Care in the Late Middle Ages (1200 - 1500),* ed. Ronald J. Stansbury (Leiden, 2010), pp. 23–39.

Tanner, Norman P., 'Pastoral Care. The Fourth Lateran Council 1215', in *A History of Pastoral Care,* ed. Gillian Rosemary Evans (London/New York, 2000), pp. 112–125.

Tentler, Thomas N., 'The Summa of Confessors as an Instrument of Social Control', in *The Pursuit of Holiness,* eds. Charles Edward Trinkaus and Heiko Oberman (Leiden, 1974), pp. 103-126.

Tentler, Thomas N., *Sin and Confession on the Eve of the Reformation* (Princeton, 1977).

Monastic locations cited in the article.

Who ordered the Dominicans? Initiators behind Dominican Convent Foundations in Northern Europe, c. 1216-1350

Johnny Grandjean Gøgsig Jakobsen

When the Spanish canon regular Dominic Guzman in the beginning of the thirteenth century got the idea to develop a new monastic order of 'Friars Preachers', he could hardly have chosen a more difficult time to do so. At the Fourth Lateran Council in 1215, it was proclaimed that the world by now had all the monastic orders it needed, and that no more orders were to be allowed. Nevertheless, the very next year, Pope Honorius III gave his permission for the foundation of Dominic's order, the *Order of Preachers*. He apparently saw a need for it, and so did many others.

To some extent, one could claim that "Black became the new White" of the thirteenth century, in the sense that the black friars of the Dominican Order in some ways replaced the white monks of the Cistercians as the new monastic vogue of the time. It was after witnessing how Cistercian preachers failed to counter heresy in southern France that Dominic got the idea of establishing a new society of mobile elite preachers, themselves living as they were preaching. Along with the contemporaneously established Order of Friars Minor (the Franciscans), the Dominican Order differed from the preceding monastic orders of Cistercians, Benedictines and Augustinians on a few major issues, first and foremost that they were to live as 'mendicants', without the steady income of any temporal possessions, and in addition to this they were to interact as much as possible with people outside the monasteries, in order to help them become better Christians. For the Friars Preachers this task was to be implemented through preaching.

The Friars Preachers, together with their Franciscan colleagues of the Friars Minor, soon spread throughout Europe, and before the middle of the fourteenth century almost every city and town within the Western Church had seen the foundation of at least one mendicant convent. The mendicant orders were without financial means of their own, and most town magistrates maintained strict regulations as to who was allowed inside the walls. Therefore such an extensive urban expansion had to rely on local support - but who would want to call in the friars and help them get established? *Who ordered the Dominicans*, so to speak?

Before searching for the foundation initiators, it is worth establishing just where and when the individual convents were founded, since taking Europe as a whole we can identify a certain pattern, dividing Dominican convent foundations of the time in question into four sub-periods. A first group of foundations from the initial year of 1216 and the following six years was initiated by the Dominican Order itself, clearly focusing on the university cities of Europe – Paris, Bologna and Oxford. From England, we have the tale that when the first Friars Preachers arrived in 1221, they were offered lodgings in both Canterbury and London by the archbishop and king respectively, but they humbly declined and rushed on to Oxford, as they had been told to do by their superiors.[1] The reason for this deliberate policy was that universities constituted a vital pool of recruitment for the order, especially in its early years. For instance, the first known Scandinavian friars were not recruited in Scandinavia, but at the universities in Bologna and Paris,[2] and this prominent role of the universities in attracting new brethren was still apparent in fourteenth-century England, as good families allegedly hesitated to send their sons to Oxford for fear that they would be 'seduced' by the recruiting professors of the mendicants, hereby joining the orders and skipping the careers originally planned for them.[3] The mendicant orders needed benefactors with money, power and land to support the foundations, but the main initiative for this early series of convents seem to have come from the Order of Preachers itself. The same can be said for a few other early foundations in the 1220s in some of the biggest cities of Europe, such as Cologne and Bruges, to which the first friars appear to have been sent on the initiative of the order itself in the hope that someone local would support them at arrival.[4] Again, this was undoubtedly due to these cities' important role as communication centres for almost all traffic between Northern and Western Europe.

After this initial Dominican settlement in the learned centres of Europe, the following three series of foundations all seem to have attracted a much more active involvement from outside the order. A second wave took place in the period 1220-1250, in which the majority of all secular-ecclesiastical centres of Northern Europe saw the foundation of a Dominican convent. These include cities which were episcopal seats with cathedrals and cathedral chapters, but to some extent also non-episcopal residences with some major role in the diocese,

---

1 Hinnebusch (1951), p. 20.
2 *Historia ordinis predicatorum in Dacia*; Jakobsen (2011).
3 Lawrence (1994), p. 127.
4 Knoll, *Geschichte Köln OP* (Cologne); De Pue (1981), pp. 13-14 (Bruges).

often with a chapter of canons secular living there. This second series is without comparison the largest and most important period in Dominican convent-foundation history. I will get back to the possible reasons and initiators behind it. A third and smaller series can be identified for the period around 1240-1275, where a number of larger cities without any particular ecclesiastical function, but with major commercial importance, were also added to the Dominican list of residences. Finally in the period 1275-1350, a number of smaller towns with little importance, ecclesiastical or commercial, acquired Dominican houses. Both the big and the small 'non-ecclesiastical' cities and towns were much more likely to receive a convent of Franciscan friars, which in general outnumbered the Dominican convents by about 50%, but some of these 'potentially-Franciscan-places-of-residence' for some reason or another instead became Dominican.

With only a very few exceptions, all Dominican convent foundations were urban; either within the town district itself or just outside the city wall in the surrounding suburbs. The reason for this urban choice of settlement was twofold. Firstly, the friars were meant to be heard and seen by as many people as possible, and thus it was the obvious choice to have them live where most people were living. Secondly, as mendicant friars without any rental income of their own, both Dominicans and Franciscans were dependent on the collection of everyday alms from as many people as possible. Once again, this aim was best achieved in urban societies, although the friars soon realized that they had to supplement the urban quest for alms with recurrent preaching-and-begging campaigns into the countryside, the so-called *terminario*.

The medieval town was, however, not necessarily the easiest place to get into, especially for an ecclesiastical institution. Many town magistrates were reluctant to let such institutions inside the city walls, as land owned by the Church generally did not pay municipal taxes. The already existing churches and monasteries were not certain to welcome new colleagues and competitors either, and finally there was the practical question of finding a building site big enough for a whole priory complex within a crowded urban space. Thus, the Dominican Order needed help from outside to get inside. The friars were not just passively let inside the city gates out of simple Christian hospitality, in most cases the convent foundations were actively endorsed and promoted by local supporters: but *who* and *why*?

Ecclesiastical initiators

One of the most important groups of friends for the Order of Preachers was the bishops. First of all, a positive attitude was needed from the local bishop in order to get permission for a monastic foundation in the first place. Without it, it may not have been completely impossible, but it certainly would be extremely difficult to have a convent established. This is seen in the first attempt to found a Dominican convent in Scandinavia, namely in Sigtuna, where the local provost visiting Rome in 1220 invited two Scandinavian friars to follow him back home and start a convent in Sigtuna - but as this initiative was not welcomed by his superior, Archbishop Olov Basatömir of Uppsala, the plans had to be abandoned.[5] A similar lack of episcopal enthusiasm met the first Friars Preachers in Moravia, where Bishop Robert in 1222 declined a Dominican offer to establish a convent in the diocesan centre of Olomouc (Olmütz). When the friars returned in 1227 with a firm recommendation letter from the pope, the bishop did not dare other than to grant them access to his town, but apart from that he did nothing to promote the foundation. Had it not been for eager support from the local Premonstratensian abbot and his brother at the Olomouc cathedral chapter, the Olomouc convent could easily have died out as soon as the one in Sigtuna.[6]

Most North-European bishops, however, not only accepted Dominican entries into their dioceses, they seem to have warmly welcomed the friars and helped them get established. The Danish Archbishop Anders Sunesen himself gave the Friars Preachers a house in central Lund next to the cathedral, which was eventually developed into a priory with its own church.[7] Even in Sweden, things changed significantly in favour of the Dominican Order when Archbishop Olov of Uppsala died and was replaced by Jarler in 1236, who not only endorsed the founding of Dominican convents in five Swedish dioceses, but in addition himself chose to be buried in the Dominican priory church in Sigtuna.[8] Numerous similar accounts with active episcopal involvement are preserved from especially North-Eastern Europe and the British Isles. In Poland, the support and even initiative of the bishops were one of the basic factors behind the rise of the first Dominican convents, notably in Cracow, Wroclaw, Kamien, Gdansk and Sandomierz.[9] In Prague, the first Dominican foundation of Bohemia was strongly helped into life by Bishop Pelhrim of Prague in 1224,[10] the first Friars Preachers to settle in Hungary in the early 1220s were eagerly supported by the energetic Bishop Robert of Esztergom,[11] and Bishop Nicolaus of Riga seems to have been the prime initiator behind the Dominican convent foundation in Riga in 1234.[12]

---

5   *Historia ordinis predicatorum in Dacia*; Jakobsen (2011), pp. 7-9.
6   Koudelka (1956), pp. 139-140.
7   *Historia ordinis predicatorum in Dacia*; Jakobsen (2011), pp. 9-15.
8   Gallén (1946), pp. 38-41.
9   Kłoczowski (1981), pp. 75-76.
10 Koudelka (1956), p. 137.
11 Kłoczowski (1981), p. 74.
12 Walther-Wittenheim (1938), pp. 6-7.

It was the bishop of Glasgow, who together with the cathedral chapter initiated the foundation of a local Dominican convent in 1246,[13] and further south his English colleagues in Lichfield, Winchester, Lincoln and Carlisle are known for similar initiatives.[14] At the very arrival of the first Friars Preachers in Ireland in 1224, Archbishop Luke Netterville of Armagh founded a convent for them in Drogheda, and in a similar way the archbishop of Cashel, David McKelly, had a Dominican convent founded by his archiepiscopal see in 1243 – the latter perhaps not all that surprising, as he himself was a Friar Preacher.[15]

The Friars Preachers were not just welcomed by the bishops, they were sometimes even invited by them. Such explicit invitations are preserved from, among others, Archbishop Albert of Magdeburg (1225), Bishop Hugues of Liège (1229) and Archbishop Juhel of Reims (1246).[16] The founding initiative was indeed expected to come from the bishops. This is indicated by the wording in the general chapter acts of the Dominican Order from 1245, where a number of named provinces are permitted the foundation of one or two new convents, *"...if the bishop asks for it and the provincial chapter allows it"*[17] – not the other way around. One particularly progressive bishop was the Polish Iwo Odrowaz of Cracow, who in 1220 allegedly sent a group of secular priests to St. Dominic himself in Bologna, asking him to admit them into his order and return them as Friars Preachers to form a convent in Cracow.[18]

Even in places with no extant written records on the Dominican foundation, it is possible to deduce a positive and active episcopal involvement, as in Denmark, where the Friars Preachers were given the former cathedral church in Århus to build their priory around c. 1240. Such a valuable donation partly reflects that a new cathedral had been taken into use shortly before, thus making the old cathedral superfluous, but it must also reflect a very supportive attitude from the bishop towards the new Dominican foundation.[19] A secular parish church was also given to the friars in Viborg; the priory in Roskilde was built in a quarter of the town owned by the bishop; and the entire town of Åhus – where the Friars Preachers settled early – was almost exclusively owned by the archbishop of Lund.[20]

---

13 Foggie (2003), pp. 14-15.
14 Jarrett (1921), pp. 3-4.
15 O'Sullivan (2009), pp. 16-19 and 37.
16 Freed (1977), p. 139 (Magdeburg); Simons (1987), p. 115 (Liège); Brett (1984), p. 13 (Reims).
17 DD 1:7 no. 197 (DOPD 1245 4/6).
18 Kłoczowski (1981), p. 73.
19 Søvsø (2004), p. 97.
20 Jakobsen (2008), pp. 140-141.

Thus, it was obviously no coincidence that the main Dominican convent foundations in the second quarter of the thirteenth century took place in cathedral cities and other major ecclesiastical centres, quite in the same way as recent research has pointed to the bishops of the eleventh century as the initiators behind Benedictine foundations in the Danish episcopal cities of Slesvig, Ribe, Roskilde and Lund.[21] With the foundation of a Dominican convent in Strängnäs in 1268, the Order of Preachers was represented in 17 of 21 dioceses in Scandinavia, in 14 cases in the very diocesan centre, and then almost always with a priory location in the immediate vicinity of the cathedral chapter. In addition, by the mid-thirteenth century, Dominican convents had been established in supplementary secular-ecclesiastical centres such as Haderslev, Åhus, Skänninge, Sigtuna and Visby; for the first of these, the foundation seems to coincide with the formation of a local secular collegiate chapter of canons subject to the bishop of Slesvig around 1250.[22]

The main exception in Northern Europe from the rule of early Dominican preference for cathedral cities is found in Brittany, where only four of the duchy's nine diocesan centres received a mendicant convent, and of which only the one in Nantes was Dominican. The reason for this situation does, however, not appear to be any episcopal dislike for mendicant and Dominican friars. On the contrary, the bishop of Tréguier is known to have initiated a Dominican foundation in Morlaix as early as 1236, and if anything, the Breton bishops refrained from calling mendicants to the cathedral towns out of consideration for the friars, since these towns by the thirteenth century was no longer of any financial or demographical importance in Brittany.[23] Together with Jarl Gallén I will suggest a similar explanation for the decision to have the Swedish archiepiscopal see of Uppsala served by a Dominican convent in nearby Sigtuna,[24] perhaps also for the foundation in Skänninge instead of Linköping.

But why would the bishops welcome these intruders, who would inevitably form a competing and alternative institution to the cathedral chapters - and to a large part were even placed outside episcopal jurisdiction? In Southern and Central Europe, an obvious and often articulated explanation was the fear of heresy, as the whole Dominican Order from the beginning was directed against the Cathars and other heretic movements, as stated by John Freed for the friars in Germany: "There can be little doubt that the bishops' concern about the

---

21 Nyberg (2006), p. 19.
22 Jakobsen (2010).
23 Martin (1975), pp. 19 and 25.
24 Gallén (1946), p. 39.

growth of heresy inspired them to patronize the friars."[25] But in thirteenth-century Northern Europe, one had to look very hard to find anything looking even remotely like heresy, and even if some North-European bishops actually did look very hard and claimed to find heresy, and then indeed with Dominican assistance,[26] their main incentive for bringing in the Friars Preachers must have been something else.

I believe that the main reason for such an outspoken episcopal favour for Dominican convents in this period was closely related to two of the canons (10 and 11) set by the Fourth Lateran Council in 1215, which obliged the bishops to 1) form schools for the secular clergy in all dioceses to improve theological understanding among parish priests and in this way secure a better administration of the Sacraments; and 2) to promote much more preaching to the laity in the dioceses. This was quite a challenging task placed on the bishops, because theological experts and quality preachers were hardly present anywhere outside the university cities and the top abbeys. Even the canons and bishops themselves were usually specialized in canon law, not in theology, and interest in and skills for preaching were – at best – limited to a very few. The introduction of the Friars Preachers must have come as a God-given answer to many bishops in this respect, as the friars were especially trained in both theology and effective communication.

This thesis is supported by some of the extant episcopal invitations to the Order, for instance in the case of Bishop Hugues of Liège, who explicitly wanted the friars to come to his bishopric to teach his clergy in theology, to spread the word of God all over the diocese, to take confessions and to generally promote and preserve the Divine Office.[27] Similar expectations were expressed in a circular forwarded by Bishop Konrad of Metz in 1221 for his entire diocese, in which he expressed hope that the newly arrived Friars Preachers would not only educate the believers through preaching, but also teach the clergy through theological lectures, and in a request by Archbishop Juhel of Reims in 1246, where he asked Pope Innocent IV for a Dominican convent to be founded next to the archiepiscopal centre, so that the friars could instruct the secular clergy.[28] Whether this pious episcopal ambition was fulfilled is less clear. We do not really have much concrete evidence of any local Dominican teaching of the canons at the cathedral chapters – and none whatsoever of Dominican teachers directly allocated to the cathedral schools. But we do have a solid stream of

---

25 Freed (1977), p. 139.
26 Such as in the case of the Stedingers. Freed (1977), pp. 146-147.
27 Simons (1987), p. 115.
28 Brett (1984), p. 13 (Metz); Simons (1987), p. 115 (Reims).

evidence that no other social group in medieval society felt as connected to the Friars Preachers as the cathedral canonry: both by donations and as a recruitment pool, as well as in recorded social contact in general. In Denmark, for instance, canons secular constituted around 40% of all registered donors for the Dominican convents in the thirteenth and fourteenth centuries.[29]

In some cases, it was even the canons themselves, not the bishops or anyone else, who took the initiative to a call for Friars Preachers. The case of Provost Gaudfred of Sigtuna has already been mentioned, and in 1224 his colleague Willem van Le Plouich of Lille wrote a thank-you letter to the Dominican prior provincial of Francia and the convent in Paris, because they had consented to establish a convent in his home town. After just three months, the foundation in Lille had been implemented, the cathedral chapter had donated a building plot for the project, and the local count – the provost's brother, as it happened – had accepted financing the whole enterprise.[30] In Dublin, it was even a cathedral chapter of canons regular who gave the Dominicans a site for their priory in 1224.[31] Certainly, there are examples of cathedral chapters where the canons immediately fell into rancorous dispute with their Dominican neighbours, such as in Bergen, where the parties never became friends,[32] but in by far the majority of chapter cities with Dominican convents in Northern Europe, we have multiple evidence of exceptionally good relations between the two groups.

Thus, it would appear as if Friars Preachers were meant to help promote the teaching at the cathedral schools, probably not as teachers themselves as much as consultants for the canons and the bishops, and therefore it was best to have them living close by the cathedral chapters. But also the task of preaching was of great importance for the bishops when they called in the Dominicans. This is for instance stated by the Polish Bishop Michael of Włocławek, who, unable to personally discharge his duties as preacher and pastor, ceded that duty to the Friars Preachers, granting them extensive privileges in his diocese.[33] Similar motives were, as already mentioned, explicitly stated in the invitational letters of the bishops in Liège and Metz. Furthermore, some reformist bishops, still struggling to introduce the ideas of the Gregorian Reform movement, may have seen the Dominican convents as potential allies in the fight for ecclesiastical independence from lay authorities.[34]

---

29 Jakobsen (2008), pp. 160 and 163.
30 Simons (1988), pp. 68-70.
31 Mould (1957), pp. 31-32.
32 Undset (1987), p. 30; Jakobsen (2008), pp. 153-154.
33 Kłoczowski (1981), pp. 75-76.
34 Kłoczowski (1981), p. 77.

It is a somewhat disputed issue to what extent secular bishops and parish priests of the Middle Ages preached for laypeople, and the practice probably varied quite a lot between regions and individual clergy. But apparently, even if popes and bishops of the high and late Middle Ages recurrently emphasized the importance of preaching God's word to the laity, it never seems to have become a central part of the pastoral duties of the parish priests. Besides a shortage in both the quantity and quality of secular preachers, it could seem as if most secular priests concentrated their efforts on celebrating Mass and the Divine Office, and administering the sacraments.[35] Especially in the rural districts, it was most likely mendicant preachers, sent out from the urban priories on *terminario* in the countryside, who were the first ones to consistently explain basic Christian ideas and values to the ordinary peasant population. One may even with Brian Patrick McGuire suggest that it was not until the efforts of the mendicant friars in the thirteenth century that Christianization of the Danes was truly completed – a task which King Harald Bluetooth had taken credit for 300 years earlier.[36] Many bishops throughout Europe therefore endorsed the access of mendicant friars to the parish pulpits, like the bishop of Cambrai, who in 1277 encouraged the diocese priests to allow Dominican preachers into their churches to give sermons "… on various important issues in the Gospels and to teach people about Faith."[37] In many parishes, this call was warmly met by the rural vicars, although this response is often only indirectly shown in the sources. As in Denmark, where the pope in 1268 during a politically-caused conflict between the two big mendicant orders had to castigate the Danish Dominicans for harassing their Franciscan colleagues, among other things by trying to hinder the Friars Minor from preaching in the parish churches, although being called to do so by the parish priests; the Dominicans allegedly had even tried to get vicars who had made these invitations removed from office.[38] Indeed, if the parish priest was not eager enough to open his church doors, he might risk trouble with the parishioners, as seen with the people of Colyton parish in England, who in 1301 wrote to the bishop in Exeter complaining that their present vicar, unlike his predecessor, did not invite friars to come and teach them about how to save their souls.[39] When a frustrated secular priest of Cologne approached a visiting cardinal in the 1220s, the cardinal only vented his anger on the priest, who was

---

35 Moorman (1945), pp. 77-78; Riising (1969), pp. 32-35; Freed (1977), p. 48; d'Avray (1985), pp. 14-15; Taylor (1992), p. 21; Jakobsen (2008), pp. 40-44.
36 McGuire (2008), pp. 173-176.
37 Simons (1987), pp. 193-194.
38 DD 2:2 no. 127 (DOPD 1268 29/11).
39 d'Avray (1985), p. 40.

responsible for 9,000 souls in his parish, but nevertheless too arrogant in his own pride to appreciate any help offered him for the tremendous task of leading his parishioners to salvation: "Since this complaint only shows that you are unworthy of your responsibility, I hereby deprive you of your pastoral office."[40] For the average parish vicar, though, it would seem as if such recurring visits of mendicant friars were only too welcome. The intellectual stimuli in the rural parishes of medieval Northern Europe for a semi-learned man probably left something to be desired, and the visiting friars must have offered a pleasant break in the everyday life of the priest.

In some cases and regions, the need within the secular church for outside help with regard to preaching and pastoral care was even more apparent. In Hungary, Tartar attacks on the city of Buda in 1241-42 had allegedly diminished the numbers of secular priests significantly, and the massive royal support for a Dominican foundation in Buda afterwards may therefore be linked to an acute need for assistance.[41] Sometimes the pastoral expectations directed at the Friars Preachers seem to have been of a more specific nature. In Ireland, the Anglo-Norman episcopacy may have seen an advantage in promoting the Friars Preachers of the thirteenth century as a possible means to 'anglicise' the Irish church with Dominican friars – in principle controlled from England through the province of Anglia – as an alternative to the numerous ancient Celtic monasteries on the island.[42] Later on, around 1500, the bishop of Dunkeld in Scotland, on the other hand, invited both Franciscan and Dominican friars to come and preach in his bishopric at least once a year, since the diocese counted numerous people of Gaelic origin, whom the friars apparently were expected to stand a better chance of reaching through preaching than the Scots-speaking secular clergy.[43] Likewise, Friars Preachers in North-Eastern Europe and Scandinavia seem to have been especially connected to German-speaking minorities.[44] Another specific task for the Friars Preachers was related to the crusades. Dominican foundations in Pomerania and Prussia were almost exclusively initiated by the Teutonic Order with the explicit wish that the friars should promote the Christianization of the defeated pagans, and preach in favour of new soldiers and funding for further crusades.[45] For instance the Polish convents in San-

---

40 Freed (1977), p. 89.
41 Gyürky (1981), p. 130.
42 O'Sullivan (2009), pp. 16-19.
43 Foggie (2003), p. 26.
44 E.g. Machilek (1974), p. 70; Grzibkowski (1983), p. 138; Jakobsen (2008), pp. 172-173.
45 Carstenn (1937), pp. 18-21; Kłoczowski (1981), p. 85; Nyberg (1999), p. 172; Radzimiński (1999), p. 157.

domierz, Płock and Gdańsk, all founded in the mid-1220s, may very well have formed a base for missionary activity in these regions. Certainly, the foundations in the Prussian towns of Chełmno and Elblag in the 1230s coincided with conquests of the Teutonic Order. Furthermore, three out of four Prussian dioceses created by the efforts of the Teutonic Knights were manned with Dominican bishops.[46] Also in the northern Netherlands, there seems to be a correspondence in the timing of Dominican convent foundations, e.g. in Leeuwarden (1240s) and Winsum (1275), and contemporary efforts by the Church and lay authorities to call for crusades against the Stedingers in the marshlands along the Frisian coast and the Muslims in The Holy Land.[47] I myself see similar signs of a possible relation between Dominican convent foundations in Sweden and the Swedish crusades into Finland.

Finally, one could argue that some bishops may have been personally attracted to the whole Dominican idea, and by promoting the establishing of a Dominican convent found a way to strengthen their own position and ecclesiastical-political aims against conservative groups among the canons and lay authorities. This seems to be the case with the learned Bishop Iwo Odrowaz of Cracow, who led a reformist wing in the Polish church in the 1220s, and initiated the foundation of both Dominican, Cistercian and Premonstratensian convents in his diocese, actively endorsed the Order of Preachers to get established in Poland, and himself chose to be buried in the first Polish Dominican church in Cracow; he even seems to have been the main initiator for his own biological brother, Jacek Odrowaz (St. Hyacinth), to join the order.[48] Also the Swedish Archbishop Jarler of Uppsala felt quite connected to the Friars Preachers. He was one of the first Swedes known to have studied in Paris, where he undoubtedly became familiar with the Dominicans at the university. It was during his time as archbishop (1236-1255), when he fought to implement the Gregorian church reform in Sweden, that both Friars Preachers and Friars Minor were introduced into the Swedish church province. Like Bishop Iwo, Archbishop Jarler was buried in the first Dominican church of his province, in this case in Sigtuna.[49] Likewise, the Danish Bishop Gunner of Viborg has been suggested by several scholars as the likely initiator behind the Dominican convent foundation in Viborg. Although no special interest can be documented from this Cistercian bishop in the Friars Preachers, the convent in Viborg was established during his episcopacy (1222-1251) around a former parish church, and Gunner seems to

---

46 Kłoczowski (1981), p. 85.
47 Brada (1982), pp. 4-5 and 8.
48 Kłoczowski (2000), p. 41; Madej-Anderson (2007), pp. 33-35.
49 Gallén (1946), 41.

have highly appreciated the ideals within monastic and pastoral life which the Order of Preachers represented, such as austere life, learning, and preaching. Furthermore, Fr. Salomon, the first Dominican friar in Denmark, was present in the retinue of Cardinal Legate Gregorius when he consecrated Gunner as bishop in 1222.[50]

Royal and princely initiators

Thus, national and regional leaders of the secular church actively supported the foundation of Dominican convents. But also lay sovereigns played an important part in this matter. Kings and princes all over Europe soon proved very favourable to the Order of Preachers, helping and even initiating new convent foundations.

The king of England was largely supportive of all Dominican foundations within his reign, giving them donations and privileges, along with access to various kinds of necessary building material.[51] One English convent received special royal attention, that of King's Langley in Hertfordshire, which was founded by Edward II and enlarged by Edward III, and practically ended up being a 'private chapel' of the royal family, which all royal estates as well as other Dominican convents in England were obliged to support in different ways.[52] King Alexander II was the prime initiator behind the first series of Dominican convent foundations in Scotland, and especially one friar, Fr. Clement, earned royal favour, as he was made bishop of Dunblane as early as 1233, and on the old king's wish given a seat in the governing council for the young king Alexander III in 1249.[53] Whereas the first Dominican convent foundations in Ireland were initiated by the archbishops, the lay rulers soon took over. First the Anglo-Normans, led by Earl William Marshal of Pembroke, who financed the Dominican Black Abbey in Kilkenny in 1225, to be followed by the Celtic-Irish princely families from the second half of the thirteenth century.[54]

In Flanders, it was the counts – or rather, the countesses Johanna and her daughter-in-law Margareta – who eagerly stood behind the foundation of six out of seven Dominican houses in the Flemish county during the thirteenth century.[55] The first Dominican convents founded in Holland around the mid-

---

50 Nielsen (1974), p. 17.
51 Hinnebusch (1951), passim.
52 Jarrett (1921), pp. 3-8.
53 Foggie (2003), p. 14.
54 O'Sullivan (2009), pp. 16 et passim.
55 Simons (1987), p. 115.

dle of the thirteenth century, in Haarlem and Utrecht, seem to have been supported by Count Willem II of Holland, whereas his mother is thought to have initiated the convent in Zierikzee.[56] Count Adolph IV of Holstein founded the Dominican convent in Hamburg,[57] and it may have been Duke Abel of Slesvig, who gave the Dominican friars a site for their priory in Slesvig around 1239,[58] just as Duke Heinrich II of Mecklenburg did in Wismar in 1293.[59] Margrave Otto III 'the Pious' of Brandenburg was a keen friend of the Friars Preachers and founded several Dominican convents, including the one in Strausberg in 1254, where he himself was buried in 1267.[60] While some regents supported one mendicant order, others preferred the other. In Bohemia, the Franciscan Friars Minor experienced a significant growth during the reign of King Wenzel I (1230-1253), whereas his successor Premysl Otokar II (1253-1278) seems to have preferred the Dominican Friars Preachers.[61] In the Dominican province of Polonia, mendicant convents became so popular that practically every princely court in the province decided to have one in its vicinity, and several Dominican houses in towns which otherwise would be considered too small for the foundation policy of the Dominican Order had especially close relationships to locally based princely houses. An example of this is Prince Mieszko II of Opole and Mazovia, who died in 1246 and had chosen the Dominican church in Racibórz as burial place.[62] Something similar was behind the Dominican convent in the small town of Röbel, halfway between Rostock and Berlin, where the convent in Rostock owned a house for the use of its friars, who became closely related to the local princely house of Werle. In 1298, Prince Nicolaus I of Werle endorsed the order to establish an actual convent in Röbel, which he provided with the necessary buildings and privileges, for the friars to serve the neighbouring princely castle as well as bringing urban-social prestige to the town.[63]

Several members of these ruling families throughout Northern Europe were buried in Dominican churches funded by themselves, priory churches which in this sense partly served as princely family chapels. This is perhaps especially evident for princely foundations in Poland, Germany, the Netherlands and Ireland. It has even been suggested that Dominican expansion in thirteenth-century Ireland partly owned its success to the priories' potential role as burial

---

56 Jongkees (1942), pp. 48-49.
57 Jensen (1874), pp. 120-121.
58 Radtke (1974), p. 58.
59 Kleiminger (1938), pp. 10-11.
60 Friske & Wittkopp (2007).
61 Machilek (1974), p. 69.
62 Kłoczowski (1981), p. 81.
63 Vorberg (1913), p. 2.

places for the Anglo-Norman aristocracy, constituting an attractive alternative to the old Celtic-Irish monasteries.[64] When the newly married royal couple King Valdemar of Sweden and Queen Sophie lost their first-born child Erik in 1261 shortly after his birth, it was decided that he should be buried with the Friars Preachers in Sigtuna.[65] Most likely this was a wish of his mother, whose Danish family – she was the daughter of King Erik IV Plovpenning of Denmark – until then had maintained close relations with the Order of Preachers. Even after her husband was deposed from the Swedish throne in 1275, she herself showed great affection for the order by helping with the foundation of a Dominican nunnery in Skänninge in 1281. Her sisters Agnes and Jutta had previously founded a Dominican nunnery in Roskilde in 1263.

In Scandinavia, royal participation in male Dominican foundations of the thirteenth century is a bit more difficult to identify than elsewhere. All three Nordic crowns made frequent use of Dominican advisers, diplomats and personal confessors, but it is in fact only for the convent in Oslo that any written sources speak of royal foundation, namely by King Håkon Håkonsson, who allegedly gave a church in Oslo dedicated to St. Olav to the friars around 1240.[66] Indication of royal involvement is also given in the small Danish town of Holbæk, where a Dominican convent was established in 1275, and the priory church, consecrated in 1323, is said to have been built by King Christopher II.[67] He had, however, only been crowned king a few years earlier, replacing his brother Erik, after Christopher himself for several years had been a princely vassal for his brother with residence at the castle in Holbæk; thus, it is more likely in his role as local lord than as king that he financed the church. If the Scandinavian kings were generally more reluctant than their Continental and British colleagues to support Dominican convent foundations in the thirteenth century, this situation changed significantly in the late Middle Ages, during which King Magnus Eriksson gave an urban site in the new Swedish capital of Stockholm for the construction of a priory when he was crowned in 1336;[68] Queen Margrete of Scandinavia stood behind the foundation in Vyborg in Karelia on the border to Russia in 1392;[69] and King Christopher III added a Dominican convent to the Franciscan and Carmelite foundations in Helsingør in 1441.[70] In some of these

---

64 O'Sullivan (2009), p. 37.
65 Scriptores Rerum Suecicarum III no. 1, p. 5 (DOPD 1261).
66 *Håkonar saga Håkonarsonar* ch. 333 (DOPD 1240).
67 Annales Danici, p. 210 (DOPD 1323 15/8); Jakobsen (2003); Jakobsen (2012), pp. 21-22.
68 Gallén (1946), p. 137; Hallerdt (2006), pp. 7-9.
69 DD 4:4 no. 531 (DOPD 1392 23/2).
70 Kirkehistoriske Samlinger 4. ser. I, pp. 59-60 (DOPD 1441 3/3).

late medieval cases, the sources provide us with the official royal justifications for promoting new Dominican convents, which may also have been valid for earlier times: to increase the Divine Office and religious devotion, and to let the friars attract God's grace and good will on the entire nation. In Karelia, it was also to bring comfort and salvation to poor Christian souls living there under continuous attacks from Russians and 'other pagans'.

There were several possible princely motives for promoting Dominican convents within their reigns. The perhaps most obvious one was in this way to establish a strong ecclesiastical institution independent of the bishops. Certainly in Denmark, Dominican friars and the entire network of their order were used by the kings as ecclesiastical allies against the bishops during 'the archiepiscopal strife' 1254-1274,[71] but this alliance does not seem to be based on any preceding royal attachment in Denmark to Dominican convent foundations. Rather it appears as if the mendicant orders in general, and the Friars Preachers in particular, were considered 'the new thing' by lay sovereigns all over thirteenth-century Europe. With distinct bitterness this situation was described by the Benedictine monk Matthew Paris around 1250: "They are regular visitors at the courts of kings and princes, where they serve as consultants, chancellors, ministers and marriage brokers. (...) Whereas those who serve the kings used to wear soft garments, they are now dressed in rough clothes." Within the Western Church, new emphasis was put upon personal devotion and confession among laypeople as well as clergy, and during the thirteenth century, all ruling families had to engage somehow in a more active apostolic life, usually by attaching personal preachers and confessors to their houses. The Order of Preachers soon took a significant share of this new 'private-ecclesiastical' market among the lay elite. A European ideal in this regard was set during the long reigns of kings Henry III of England (1216-1272) and Louis IX of France (1226-1270), who both showed special preference for the Dominicans – not just as courtly priests, but as advisers, commissioners and diplomats as well.[72]

Due to their linguistic skills and international network, not to mention their positive relations with the Roman Curia, high-ranking friars within almost every kingdom, duchy and county in Northern Europe were put to good use by royal and princely rulers. King Håkon Håkonsson of Norway on several occasions used friars as royal envoys. In 1256, he sent two Friars Preachers, Fr. Simon and Fr. Sigurd, as diplomatic officials to King Christopher I of Denmark to determine how the Danish king intended to respond to a series of Norwegian attacks on his country. The friars were received at the Danish court, only to

---

71 Gallén (1946), 30-32.
72 Lawrence (1994), pp. 166-180 (citation Paris, p. 166).

learn that Christopher was quite angry about the ravaging.[73] In 1256-58, Fr. Simon 'the Preacher' was once again out travelling in the diplomatic service of the Norwegian throne, this time as part of the retinue which accompanied Princess Kristina to her wedding in Spain.[74] Whether it was as diplomat or confessor – or both – that Fr. Simon accompanied King Håkon to the Scottish Isles in 1263 is not known, but he died during the campaign and was buried with the Cistercians in Saddell Abbey on Kintyre, where the monks "...laid a cloth over his grave and called him a holy man."[75] The Fr. Nicolaus, who in 1260-61 served as Norwegian messenger and diplomat in Denmark and Saxony in connection with arranging a marriage between King Håkon's son Magnus and the Danish Princess Ingeborg, was probably also a Dominican, although this is not explicitly stated.[76] Often the friars in royal service held quite prominent positions in the order. It was no less than the prior provincial himself, Fr. Absalon, who in 1257 was sent by King Christopher I of Denmark from Denmark to Tønsberg in Norway with an offer from the Danish king to meet with King Håkon to negotiate a peace between the two.[77] Absalon and five other high-ranking Danish friars were excommunicated by a papal legate in 1267 for their alliance with the king of Denmark against archbishop and legate in the above-mentioned archiepiscopal strife,[78] indicating a strong position at the king's court, and Fr. Absalon's successor as prior provincial of Dacia, Fr. Augustine, was listed among the many notabilities present at the royal meeting of three Scandinavian kings in Horsaberg in 1276.[79] Friars Preachers also found their way to the court of the Swedish rulers. In 1363, King Magnus Eriksson of Norway-Sweden supported Fr. Godskalk Falkdal, who served both as personal confessor to the king and as papal penitentiary in Avignon, for the episcopal see in Linköping.[80] In 1334, the same king sent another of his Dominican confessors, Fr. Johannes, as one of two royal envoys to King Philippe VI of France,[81] and in 1255, Earl Birger of Sweden had sent two Dominican messengers to King Henry III of England to instigate negotiations for a political alliance between the two kingdoms. The English king replied by sending two Dominican envoys of his own back to

---

73 *Hákonar saga Hákonarsonar* ch. 239 (DOPD 1256 24/8).
74 *Hákonar saga Hákonarsonar* ch. 290 and 296 (DOPD 1256-57 and 1258 autumn).
75 *Hákonar saga Hákonarsonar* ch. 320 (DOPD 1263).
76 *Hákonar saga Hákonarsonar* ch. 304-305 (DOPD 1260 summer and 1258 autumn.
77 *Hákonar saga Hákonarsonar* ch. 291 (DOPD 1257).
78 DD 2:2 no. 86 (DOPD 1267 10/9); Gallén (1946), pp. 72-73.
79 *Magnúss saga lagabætiss*, pp. 333-334 (DOPD 1276 26/6).
80 Acta Pontificum Svecica 1. ser. I no. 654 (DOPD 1363 1/9).
81 Regesta Norvegica IV no. 1034 (DOPD 1334 12/2).

Sweden.⁸² This was no rare phenomenon, as Friars Preachers from abroad on several occasions visited the high-medieval Scandinavian courts on behalf of their lay sovereigns. In 1264, for instance, two Dominican friars from Scotland were sent as diplomats to negotiate peace to the king of Norway on behalf of the Scottish king, for which their travel expenses were paid by the king's sheriffs in Perth and Inverness.⁸³ And in 1318, Prior Hason of the Dominican convent in Hamburg was one of three envoys sent by the city council of Hamburg to Tønsberg to negotiate with King Håkon Magnusson of Norway about Norwegian trading privileges for the Hamburg merchants.⁸⁴ Dominican friars were also used as official lay diplomats within the kingdom. The Friars Preachers in Dublin were on several occasions used as negotiators between the English authorities and Irish rebels around the country,⁸⁵ and in 1235, Fr. Robert Archer was sent to the court of King Henry III in England on behalf of the Anglo-Norman justice of peace in Ireland, Maurice Fitzgerald, who had brought the wrath of his sovereign upon him. The Irish-Dominican envoy apparently made a very good impression on the king, who afterwards suggested him to the papal curia as archbishop of Armagh.⁸⁶

Thus, for lay rulers Friars Preachers constituted a useful ecclesiastical alternative and supplement to the secular church of the bishops, offering independent, skilful and eloquent confessors, advisers and diplomats. Besides that, the friars helped filling a need which the regents shared with the bishops, that is to promote and strengthen Christian understanding and behaviour in their realms, a task for which the Crown was equally responsible as the Church. Furthermore, the order also provided a physical advantage in the form of the priories, which not only offered distinguished burial places for the ruling families, but also brought significant prestige to the towns and cities (see the section on 'Bourgeois initiators') and even constituted an appreciated part of the urban defence system. In numerous instances, especially on the Continent, mendicant priories were located out by the city wall, into which the priory walls and buildings were deliberately built to help increase the city's military strength.⁸⁷ In Bohemia, the significant number of Dominican convent foundations during the reign of Premysl Otokar II (margrave of Moravia 1247-1253, king of Bohemia 1253-1278)

---

82 DS 1:427 (DOPD 1255 22/7).
83 DN 19:278, 19: 283 (DOPD 1264).
84 DN 6:97 (DOPD 1318 22/7).
85 O'Sullivan (2009), p. 187.
86 O'Sullivan (2009), pp. 20-21.
87 Stüdeli (1969), pp. 68-83 and 132; Berger (1995), p. 312; Schenkluhn (2000), pp. 232-233.

even seems to have been deliberately integrated as part of the fortification plans for new princely/royal town foundations.[88]

Noble initiators

Where kings and princes led, the nobility often soon followed, and this is also the case in regard to Dominican foundation history. From the second half of the thirteenth century and a century onwards, noble initiators played an increasing part in mendicant convent foundations, especially for the Friars Minor, but to some extent also for the Friars Preachers. One very typical example of this, with numerous parallels all over Northern Europe is from the small town of Jablonné (Gabel) in Bohemia, which had been founded in 1245 by the noble family Marquard (Markwartinger). It was the local lord, Gallus Marquard von Lemberk, or rather his wife Zdislava, who decided that the young town as one of its first institutions should have a Dominican convent, in whose priory church Lady Zdislava was buried in 1252. Her brother-in-law, Jaroslov Marquard, was soon after inspired to found another Dominican convent in his home town of Turnov.[89] Two of the rare Danish examples of known Dominican convent founders were both nobles. Johannes Ebbesen of the Hvide family, formerly the king's marshal, donated a large sum of money for the construction of a priory in Roskilde before going on a crusade to the Holy Land in the late 1220s,[90] and the Danish seneschal Laurids Jonsen Panter funded the construction of the priory in Vejle around 1325, to be followed by his son Peder Lauridsen thirty years later, who paid for a new priory church in stone instead of the wooden church raised by his father.[91]

One may speculate that the crusader Johannes Ebbesen might have hoped that his pious initiative would help him against the Muslims, just as it has been suggested that Laurids Jonsen founded the convent in Vejle to redeem himself from heavenly anger for his participation in the coup against King Christopher II a few years earlier.[92] A similar motive was apparently the case in Ireland, when the Dominican convent of Sligo was founded in 1252 by the Norman nobleman Maurice Fitzgerald as a penance for this involvement in the death 18 years earlier of Earl Richard Marshal.[93] In the same country, Lady Emmeline de Riddelsford has been

---

88 Koudelka (1956), p. 127.
89 Koudelka (1956), pp. 144-145.
90 Scriptores Rerum Danicarum I, p. 183 (DOPD 1232); Jakobsen (2007), p. 70.
91 Kirkehistoriske Samlinger 2. ser. IV, pp. 587-588 (DOPD 1355 4/10).
92 Gallén (1946), p. 137 with note 4.
93 O'Sullivan (2009), p. 43.

identified as the possible founder of the Dominican convent in Coleraine in 1244, the year after she had become a widow after the quite impious Hugh de Lacy, Earl of Ulster, the salvation of whose soul the foundation may have been intended to help.[94] Certainly, less calculating motives also led noblemen to similar initiatives. In the northern Netherlands, leading local families were initiators of the Dominican convents in Leeuwarden and Winsum; in the case of the former, the foundation took place after young members of the family had simply met Friars Preachers during an educational stay in Paris, and on this basis decided that the friars' devoted service was needed in their home town as well.[95] As pointed out earlier, the two Dutch foundations may also reflect a contemporary need among Church and lay regents for eloquent preachers of the crusade.

The different layers of foundations and not least founders may find their parallel in a study by Tore Nyberg of Benedictine and Cistercian monasteries in eleventh- and twelfth-century Scandinavia, in which he found that while the episcopal foundations achieved a role as spiritual power centres in support of Gregorian ideas, royal and noble foundations mainly functioned as 'house monasteries', whose primary task was to take care of the memorial cult of the founding family.[96] For the Dominicans, this latter function especially seems to be the case for the noble convent foundations, usually from the period 1250-1350. Even in Flanders, the most urbanized region of medieval Northern Europe, scholars have identified a significant role of the nobility in relation to mendicant convent foundations, and among all the mendicant orders especially for the Dominicans. As the nobility moved into the cities, they brought with them the tradition of the twelfth century from the rural districts for the families to establish close relations to one particular monastic convent.[97] With the arrival of the mendicants, this practice became an accessible possibility further down the ranks of the nobility, as it did not require any extensive funding with a great deal of landed estate. Often it was enough to grant the convent a parish church or a chapel already in existence, and a building plot upon which to raise the priory.[98] One should probably, however, be careful not to distinguish too sharply between ecclesiastical and noble convent-founding initiatives, as most high medieval bishops came of prominent noble families, and thus inevitably represented interests and customs from both groups. This can be illustrated by an especially complicated example from the Dominican convent in Šumperk

---

94 O'Sullivan (2009), pp. 40-41.
95 Brada (1982), p. 3.
96 Nyberg (2000).
97 Simons (1987), pp. 74-75.
98 Kłoczowski (1981), p. 77.

(Schönberg), Moravia, founded in 1293 by a certain Johannes, who was an illegitimate son of king Premysl Otakar II of Bohemia, working simultaneously as the king's chancellor and provost of Vyšehrad:[99] in a classification of convent founders, he could thus be categorized as 'royal', 'noble' and 'ecclesiastical'.

Finally, it is worth noticing that a great many foundations of Dominican convents based on royal, princely or noble support occurred on female initiative. A probably highly underestimated reason for the significant success of the Friars Preachers in medieval Europe, at a time when the Church was already well-established with numerous religious branches, appears to be that mendicant fathers in general and Dominicans in particular held a special attraction for many women. The social etiquette of the friars (they usually came from the higher bourgeoisie and lower nobility), combined with their eloquence and deep theological insight, not least with a preference for female saints such as the Holy Virgin, Mary Magdalene, Catherine of Alexandria and Mary's mother Anne, apparently made them extremely popular with many religiously minded women of practically all social classes. When such women had the money, or fathers/husbands/sons with the necessary power and means, several of them initiated the foundation of a convent for the friars in the neighbourhood. A colourful example of this female preference for the Dominicans is found in Ireland, where the baron Jordan de Exeter around 1250 decided to establish a Franciscan house in Strade. His wife, Basilia de Bermingham, who had grown up with close relations to the Dominican convent in Athenry, which her father had founded, wanted the projected house in Strade populated with Dominican friars instead of Franciscans, a wish that her husband at first ignored. At a great banquet, where Jordan's powerful father-in-law was present, Lady Basilia suddenly stood up and proclaimed that she would neither eat nor drink again until she had her way. Since her husband did not want the feast ruined due to her obstinacy, he gave in, and Lady Basilia immediately sent a message off to Rome to have the Franciscan foundation converted to a Dominican one.[100]

Bourgeois and magistrate initiators

Older literature on ecclesiastical history often claims that the success of the new mendicant orders in the thirteenth and fourteenth centuries was closely linked to the contemporary growth of the urban bourgeoisie, and that this was where the friars found their main support. The truth is, however, that studies from all over Northern Europe collectively point to a contrary picture: that urban burgh-

---

99 Koudelka (1956), p. 154.
100 O'Sullivan (2009), p. 44.

ers in most places showed but little interest in the Dominican Order until the fifteenth century, and for the most part had nothing to do with the main series of convent foundations in the preceding centuries. Even in such a highly urbanized and relatively well-documented region as Flanders, out of 27 mendicant convents founded in the period 1225-1350 not a single one of them appears to have had any initial support from the city magistrates or other burghers; land and permission for a foundation were usually offered by the secular Church; funding for the project was given by count and nobility.[101]

The reason for this, perhaps somewhat surprising, absence of bourgeois involvement with high medieval Dominican foundations, could, I think, be two-sided. It was probably not until later in the Middle Ages that the upper bourgeois classes of Northern Europe began to copy the nobility in terms of establishing individual family relations to monastic institutions, with private confessors, perpetual masses, altars and burial places, all well-known bourgeois phenomena from the fifteenth century onwards. Furthermore, city magistrates were generally very reluctant to invite any ecclesiastical institutions within the city walls due to the problem of 'the dead hand', that is the fact that the Church usually did not pay any taxes on its urban land or make any other contributions to the municipal administration, such as the lay citizens were obliged to, which meant that a new major ecclesiastical player on the urban scene was likely to reduce the town income. Especially in the big cities of Flanders and along the north German coast we find such a sceptical attitude among the magistrates. Several Hansa cities, such as Wismar, only admitted the Dominicans after pressure from local princes, and then on an explicit contractual agreement that the friars were never allowed to acquire any houses or sites in the city outside the priory walls.[102]

Whereas private burghers are almost completely lacking in the lists of known Dominican convent founders in high medieval Northern Europe, the anti-fraternal attitude among the urban magistrates was far from universal. For instance in Antwerp and Freiburg the city magistrates joined in with local clergy and lay lordship in inviting the Dominican Order,[103] and in the Irish cities of Dublin and Waterford, it was the citizens themselves who initiated the Dominican foundations. The people of Waterford, for instance, asked for and acquired permission from King Henry III to turn an old royal tower into a priory site for the Friars Preachers.[104] In some western and central European cases, we are even

---

101 Simons (1987), p. 244.
102 Kleiminger (1938), pp. 15-17.
103 Freed (1977), p. 34.
104 O'Sullivan (2009), p. 33.

told why the magistrates took this positive attitude. When the city council of Bern in Switzerland invited the Friars Preachers in 1269, it was for the friars to establish themselves in their city, "... just like you have done in other cities, which now bask in the glory of the friars' sacred house."[105] Likewise, the council of Saint-Julien in western France in 1240 asked the friars to make their way to their town, "As we have experienced from trustworthy testimonials that cities and towns, which you favour with your presence, soon improve in both spiritual and temporal matters."[106] I have not found similar explicit invitations from urban magistrates in Northern Europe, but it is my feeling that especially during the fourth and last of my proposed series of convent foundations, that of the period 1275 to 1350, many of Northern Europe's smaller and newer towns became aware of the value of housing a mendicant convent.[107] In the course of the thirteenth century, the presence of at least one mendicant convent was to be expected in any decent town, and in their on-going internal competition for municipal privileges, it became important to have a convent of mendicants as to claim status as 'a real town'.[108] For instance, several Dominican convent foundations in Bohemia seem to coincide with the time when the towns concerned were granted official urban status and privileges,[109] and in Denmark too, it is probably no coincidence that the three small towns of Halmstad, Holbæk and Vejle all acquired both a Dominican convent and their first town privileges within a few years during this period.[110]

However, there were also more religious, if perhaps no less calculating, motives for a city magistrate to invite the Dominican Order. In Lübeck, one of the largest and most important cities of medieval Northern Europe, the city council decided to found a Dominican convent in 1229, with a priory church dedicated to St. Mary Magdalene, because she had led the Lübeck army to victory against the Danes at the battle of Bornhøved in 1227, by letting her clothes shield the eyes of the Lübeck soldiers from the sun at a critical moment during the battle. In the same way, the Dominican convent of the neighbouring town Meldorf was founded in 1319 on the initiative of the people of Ditmarsken, after Mary Magdalene had led them to victory against the count of Holstein.[111]

---

105 Freed (1977), p. 46.
106 Lawrence (1994), p. 104.
107 Also Vöckler (1991), pp. 7-8.
108 Freed (1977), pp. 46 and 53.
109 E.g. Nymburg *c.* 1257, Kolín *c.* 1260, Brod *c.* 1272, and Pilsen *c.* 1300. Koudelka (1956), pp. 147-149 and 153.
110 Jakobsen (2008), pp. 184-186.
111 Jensen (1874), pp. 120-122.

Concluding remarks

To conclude, when searching for the founders of monastic convents, such as for the Dominican Order in high medieval Northern Europe, one should keep in mind that there was usually more than just one main initiator involved. An example of this phenomenon is given in the unusually well-described founding history of the Dominican priory in Athenry, which began in 1241. The Anglo-Norman magnate, Meiler de Bermingham, bought a site for the priory in the newly conquered region of Connaught for 160 marks, while giving a similar amount of money for the construction of the priory along with some English cloth, wine and horses. All his knights and men-at-arms were endorsed to help the building project in whatever way they could, and it soon developed into a 'joint venture' reaching far beyond the House of Bermingham. Six other magnates, most of them Gaelic and thus potential opponents of Bermingham, each financed the construction of the refectory, the dormitory, the chapter-house, the cloister, the infirmary and the priory guest-house. In addition to this, Archbishop Florence MacFlainn of Tuam personally paid for the construction of 'a house for scholars' at the priory, probably meaning a school of theology, for which the archbishop also established a set of rules.[112] A late medieval inscription in a window in the Dominican priory church of Wismar tells that the convent here was founded back in 1293, when Fr. Dietrich von Hameln and a group of friars were called to Wismar by the city mayor and Duke Heinrich of Mecklenburg. The duke gave the order a suitable site in the city, which was soon improved with the help of local burghers. In all, the inscription claims, both lay and clergy warmly welcomed the friars to Wismar.[113] Although in this particular case, contemporary sources indicate that this was a somewhat rose-coloured description made by the friars in a later time, and that the duke practically had to force the convent foundation upon a most reluctant secular clergy and city magistrate,[114] the mix of initiators presented may indeed have been the typical set-up in many places.

In general, the following set of involved parties was needed to establish a new Dominican convent. The general chapter and provincial chapter of the Dominican Order itself had to permit it, as did the local bishop, and usually these two parties were the initial initiators of a new foundation project. Lay sovereigns, such as kings, dukes, counts or other well-off nobles, were needed to support the project financially, and the town magistrate had to allow the friars inside the urban area of municipal jurisdiction. It probably differed greatly

---

112 O'Sullivan (2009), pp. 33-34.
113 Kleiminger (1938), pp. 10-11.
114 Kleiminger (1938), pp. 13-20.

how much each of the four parties was engaged in a particular convent foundation, but eventually their positive or at least acquiescent involvement was always necessary.

As I have aimed to show, many different interests could be involved in a Dominican convent foundation. Bishops and lay rulers both wanted the friars to strengthen orthodox Latin Christianity among the laity; bishops and canons wanted to benefit from Dominican knowledge on theology and the art of preaching; some kings, princes and city magistrates saw the mendicant orders as valuable alternatives to the secular church ruled by the bishops, and the most learned friars were frequently used as advisers and diplomats in secular affairs; the priory churches constituted potential and prestigious burial places and 'memoria cult'-centres for elite lay families; and the priories added important prestige for towns struggling to receive or maintain urban privileges. Depending on regional variations, the convent foundations could also be aimed at missionary activities and promotion of the crusades; supporting the secular church in its pastoral obligations, e.g. in relation to linguistic minorities; and of course the most famous initial objective of them all: to control and fight heresy. But then again, cynical historians of our time, such as myself, tend to ignore the more devoted and religious reasons for welcoming a convent of Dominican friars, and I will therefore end by quoting the English historian Bede Jarrett, who in 1921 gave this reason for the Order of Preachers' success in his home country, which he believed to be something unique for England: »*Nowhere else had they so quickly so many priories. Perhaps the native love of preaching and of good sermons made them so popular.*«[115]

Literature

Sources
Acta Pontificum Svecica, ed. L.M. Bååth (Stockholm, 1936-57).
DD: *Diplomatarium Danicum,* various editors (København, 1938–).
DN: *Diplomatarium Norvegicum*, various editors (Oslo, 1849-1976).
DS: *Diplomatarium Suecanum*, various editors (Stockholm, 1829–).
DOPD: *Diplomatarium Ordinis Predicatorum Dacie (online)*, ed. J.G.G. Jakobsen, http://www.jggj.dk/CDSD.htm (2007-).
Hákonar saga Hákonarsonar (Håkon Håkonssons Saga), ed. M. Mundt (Oslo, 1977).
'Magnúss saga lagabætiss' (Magnus Lagabøter's Saga), ed. Gustav Storm, in *Islandske Annaler indtil 1578* (Oslo, 1888).
Regesta Norvegica, various editors (Oslo, 1898-).
Scriptores Rerum Suecicarum medii aevi, various editors (Uppsala, 1818-76).

---

115 Jarrett (1921), p. 23.

Scriptores Rerum Danicarum medii aevi, ed. J. Langebek & P.F. Suhm (København, 1772-1878).

All the Scandinavian-Dominican instances referred to in the article with source publication references are also published online on the *Diplomatarium OP Dacie* (DOPD), to be accessed from www.jggj.dk/CDSD.htm.

Studies
d'Avray, David L., *The preaching of the friars - Sermons diffused from Paris before 1300* (Oxford, 1985).
Berger, Thomas, *Die Bettelorden in der Erzdiözese Mainz und in den Diözesen Speyer und Worms im 13. Jahrhundert - Ausbreitung, Förderung und Funktion*. Quellen und Abhandlungen zur mittelrheinischen Kirchengeschichte 69 (Mainz, 1995).
Brada, Menno, *Dominicanen in Winsum* (Leusden, 1982).
Brett, Edward Tracy, *Humbert of Romans - His life and views of thirteenth-century society* (Toronto, 1984).
Carstenn, Edward, *Geschichte der Hansestadt Elbing* (Elbing, 1937).
De Pue, Piet, *Geschiedenis van het oud Dominikanenklooster te Brugge (1233-1796)* (Leuven, 1981).
Foggie, Janet P., *Renaissance religion in urban Scotland - The Dominican order, 1450-1560* (Leiden, 2003).
Freed, John B., *The Friars and German Society in the Thirteenth Century* (Cambridge (USA), 1977).
Friske, Matthias & Blandine Wittkopp, 'Strausberg Dominikaner', in *Brandenburgisches Klosterbuch*, 2, ed. H.-D. Heimann & al. (Berlin-Brandenburg, 2007), pp. 1243-1254.
Gallén, Jarl, *La Province de Dacie de l'ordre des Frères Prêcheurs 1 - Histoire générale jusqu'au Grand Schisme* (Helsinki, 1946).
Grzibkowski, Andrej, 'Early Mendicant Architecture in Central-Eastern Europe. The present state of research', *Arte Medievale – Periodico internazionale di critica dell'arte medievale* 1 (1983), pp. 135-156.
Gyürky, Katalin H., *Das mittelalterliche Dominikanerkloster in Buda*, trans. Zsuzsa Vágó (Budapest, 1981).
Hallerdt, Björn, *Svartbrödraklostret i Stockholm* (Stockholm, 2006).
Hinnebusch, William A., *The early English Friars Preachers* (Rome, 1951).
Historia ordinis predicatorum in Dacia, ed. J.G.G. Jakobsen, http://www.jggj.dk/HOPD.htm (2007).
Jakobsen, Johnny Grandjean Gøgsig, 'Da prædikebrødrene kom til Holbæk - Om de mulige bevæggrunde og samtidspolitiske forhold bag en dominikansk klosterstiftelse på Sjælland i starten af senmiddelalderen', *Kirkehistoriske Samlinger* 2003, pp. 7-35.
Jakobsen, Johnny Grandjean Gøgsig, 'Om de dominikanske prædikebrødre og deres kloster i Roskilde', *Historisk Årbog for Roskilde Amt 2006* (2007), pp. 59-92.
Jakobsen, Johnny Grandjean Gøgsig, *Prædikebrødrenes samfundsrolle i middelalderens Danmark* (Odense, 2008). Ph.D. thesis, accessible for download on http://www.jggj.dk/phd-afhandling.pdf.

Jakobsen, Johnny Grandjean Gøgsig, 'Hvornår oprettedes dominikanerklosteret i Haderslev? - En genopdaget indskrift bekræfter en formodning om prædikebrødrenes ankomst', *Kirkehistoriske Samlinger* 2010, pp. 197-204.
Jakobsen, Johnny Grandjean Gøgsig, 'Venerunt fratres predicatores - Notes on Datings of the first Dominican Convent Foundations in Scandinavia', *Collegium Medievale - Interdisciplinary Journal for Medieval Research* 24 (2011), pp. 5-22.
Jakobsen, Johnny Grandjean Gøgsig, 'Kirker og religiøsitet i middelalderens nordvestsjællandske købstæder', *Fra Nordvestsjælland 2011* (2012), pp. 11-35.
Jarrett, Bede, *The English Dominicans* (London, 1921).
Jensen, H.N.A., *Schleswig-Holsteinische Kirchengeschichte nach hinterlassenen Handschriften*, 2 (Kiel, 1874).
Jongkees, Adrian Gerard, *Staat en Kerk in Holland en Zeeland onder de Bourgondische hertogen 1425-1477*. Bijdragen van het Instituut voor Middeleeuwsche Geschiedenis der Rijks-Universiteit te Utrecht, 21 (Groningen, 1942).
Kirkehistoriske Samlinger, various editors (København, 1849-).
Kłoczowski, Jerzy, 'Dominicans of the Polish Province in the Middle Ages', in *The Christian Community of Medieval Poland*, ed. Jerzy Kłoczowski (Warsaw, 1981), pp. 73-118.
Kłoczowski, Jerzy, *A History of Polish Christianity* (Cambridge, 2000).
Knoll, Franziskus, *Geschichte der Dominikaner in Köln bis 1899*, Dominikanerkloster Heilig Kreuz in Köln, accessed June 1 2012, http://www.dominikanerkloster-koeln.de/24/Kloster/Die-Dominikaner-in-Koeln.htm.
Koudelka, Vladimír J., 'Zur Geschichte der böhmischen Dominikanerprovinz im Mittelalter' (2), *Archivum Fratrum Praedicatorum* 26 (1956), pp. 127-160.
Lawrence, Clifford Hugh, *The Friars - The impact of the early mendicant movement on Western society* (London & New York, 1994).
Machilek, Franz, 'Reformorden und Ordensreformen in den böhmischen Ländern vom 10. bis 18. Jahrhundert', in *Bohemia Sacra - Das Christentum in Böhmen 973-1973*, ed. Ferdinand Seibt (Düsseldorf, 1974), pp. 63-80.
Madej-Anderson, Agnieszka, *Repräsentation in einer Bettelordenskirche – Die spätmittelalterliche Bildtafeln der Dominikaner in Krakau* (Ostfildern, 2007).
Martin, Herve, *Les ordres mendiants en Bretagne (vers 1230- vers 1530) - Pauvreté volontaire et prédication à la fin du moyen-âge* (Rennes, 1975).
McGuire, Brian Patrick, *Da Himmelen kom nærmere - fortællinger om Danmarks kristning 700-1300* (København, 2008).
Moorman, John R.H., *Church Life in England in the Thirteenth Century* (Cambridge, 1945).
Mould, Daphne D.C.P., *The Irish Dominicans - The Friars Preachers in the history of Catholic Ireland* (Dublin, 1957).
Nielsen, Erik Levin, 'Viborg Sortebrødrekirke – En teglstensbygning fra biskop Gunners tid', *Viborg Stifts Årbog* 1974 (Viborg, 1974), pp. 15-49.
Nyberg, Tore, 'Der Deutsche Orden und der Birgittinerorden', in *Der Deutsche Orden in der Zeit der Kalmarer Union 1397-1521*, ed. Z.N. Nowak (Torun, 1999), pp. 169-181.
Nyberg, Tore, *Monasticism in North Western Europe, 800-1200* (Aldershot, 2000).
Nyberg, Tore, 'De benediktinske klostergrundlæggelser i Norden', in *Tidlige klostre i Norden*, ed. Lars Bisgaard & Tore Nyberg (Odense, 2006), 13-30.
O'Sullivan, Benedict, *Medieval Irish Dominican Studies*, ed. Hugh Fenning (Dublin, 2009).

Originally published as articles in the *Irish Rosary* 1948-1953.

Radtke, Christian, 'Untersuchungen zur Lokalisierung und zur Gründungsgeschichte des Schleswiger Dominikanerklosters', *Beiträge zur Schleswiger Stadtgeschichte* 19 (1974), pp. 49-63.

Radzimiński, Andrzej, 'Kirche und Geistlichkeit im Ordensstaat in Preußen um die Wende von 14. zum 15. Jahrhundert', in *Der Deutsche Orden in der Zeit der Kalmarer Union 1397-1521*, ed. Z.N. Nowak (Torun, 1999), pp. 151-167.

Riising, Anne, *Danmarks middelalderlige prædiken* (København, 1969).

Schenkluhn, Wolfgang, *Architektur der Bettelorden - Die Baukunst der Dominikaner und Franziskaner in Europa* (Darmstadt, 2000).

Simons, Walter, *Stad en apostolaat - De vestiging van de bedelorden in het graafschap Vlaanderen (ca. 1225-ca. 1350)* (Brussel, 1987).

Simons, Walter, 'Bedelordenkloosters in het Graafschap Vlaanderen - Chronologie en topografie van de bedelordenverspreiding voor 1350', *Sacris erudiri* 30 (1988), pp. 5-203.

Stüdeli, Bernhard, *Minoritenniederlassung und mittelalterliche Stadt - Beiträge zur Bedeutung von Minoriten- und anderen Mendikantenanlagen im öffentlichen Leben der mittelalterlichen Stadtgemeinde, insbesondere der deutschen Schweiz*. Franziskanishe Forschungen, 21 (Werl, 1969).

Søvsø, Morten, 'Århus sortebrødreklosters senmiddelalderlige kapitelsal', *Anno Domini Middelalderarkæologisk Nyhedsbrev* 10 (2004), pp. 97-106.

Taylor, Larissa, *Soldiers of Christ - Preaching in Late Medieval and Reformation France* (New York, 1992).

Undset, Sigrid, 'Klosterliv, *Årbok 1987* (Foreningen til norske fortidsminnesmerkers bevaring, Oslo), pp. 8-32.

Vöckler, Matthias, 'Einige Anmerkungen zur Entstehung und Bedeutug der Termineien der Bettelmönche im mittelalterlichen Thüringen', *Mitteilungen des Oberhessischen Geschichtsvereins Giessen* 2. ser. 76 (1991), pp. 1-11.

Vorberg, Axel, *Beiträge zur Geschichte des Dominikanerordens in Mecklenburg 1 - Das Johanniskloster zu Rostock*. Quellen und Forschungen zur Geschichte des Dominikanerordens in Deutschland, 5 (Vechta, 1911).

Walther-Wittenheim, G. von, *Die Dominikaner in Livland im Mittelalter* (Rome, 1938).

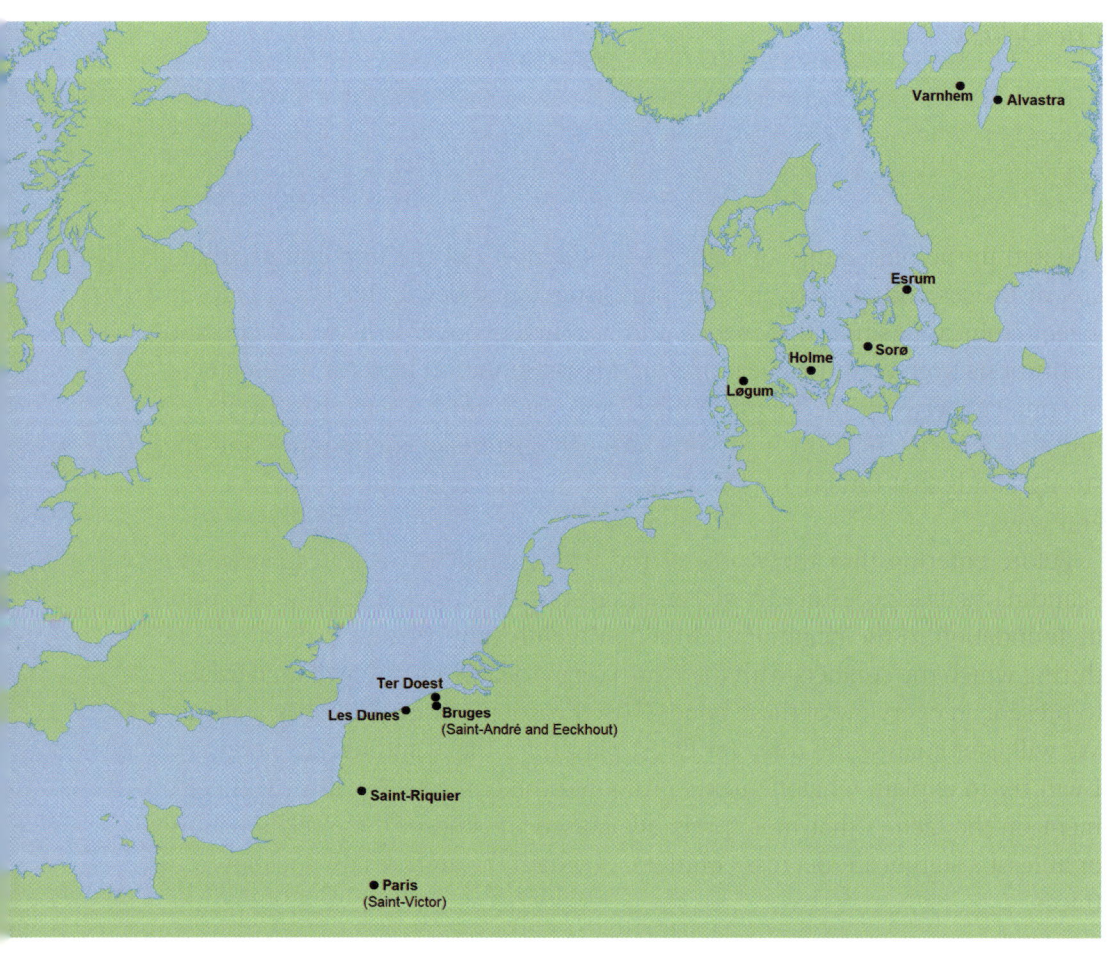

Monastic locations cited in the article.

The Cistercian Network: the Flemish Abbey of Ter Doest and Scandinavia

Eric Delaissé

Situated in the old county of Flanders, to the north of the important harbour city of Bruges and close to the sea, the Cistercian abbey of Ter Doest enjoyed a geographical position that made various contacts possible between men and institutions from countries near and far. My presentation looks at the existence of contacts between the Flemish abbey and the Danish Cistercian dwellings, but also at other relationships with Swedish Cistercian monasteries and the strong bonds that united Ter Doest and the Scandinavian episcopate in a general way.

Before entering into the world of the relationship between Ter Doest and Scandinavia, it is necessary to take an interest in the situation of the abbey from its foundation to the beginning of the fourteenth century, that is to say an era during which the contacts with the North seem to fade out. We will then be able to present an overview of these bonds, based particularly on the abbey archives. We will later analyse the roles Ter Doest played for the Scandinavian clergy and I will try to explain what elements promoted the contacts. Finally, I will comment on the factors that most probably caused the end of these relationships, or at least a significant decrease of them, of which the archives do not show any traces.

Brief historical account and presentation of the abbey

The abbey finds its origins in a little chapel probably built in the early eleventh century. This chapel was called "Capella Thosan" and was dedicated to Saint Bartholomew. It marks the starting point of the Benedictine priory and the Cistercian abbey that were to take its place.

In 1066, Baudri, bishop of Tournai, agreed to the request of the local lord, Lambert de Lissewege, to allow the foundation of a Benedictine priory on the site. He entrusted the chapel to the abbot of Saint-Riquier (France, département de la Somme) to send some founding monks. Yet this request does not seem to have been carried out; the explanation is certainly the decline of Saint-

Riquier. Bishop Evrard from Tournai subsequently decided to grant the site to the Cistercians in order to found a monastery on 29 March 1174. Consequently, in 1175, twelve monks and three lay brothers of the Cistercian abbey of Les Dunes arrived at Ter Doest under the leadership of Abbot Hacket. The abbey of Saint-Riquier did not accept the loss of the site and lodged a complaint with Rome. In 1177 a financial agreement was reached by the parties. The wish of the bishop of Tournai was to be fulfilled: the site would be Cistercian from now on.[1]

Ter Doest reached its peak in the thirteenth century and had business contacts with England, the Empire and the Scandinavian countries.[2] One of the major sources of this abbey's wealth was the enormous flocks of sheep bred by the monks. Additionally Ter Doest possessed several ships, which were precious instruments in its economic activities notably with England. Cistercians were also famous for their technical feats and the monks from Ter Doest did not make an exception to this rule. They indeed made a name for themselves thanks to their remarkable qualities as dyke builders.[3]

At the dawn of the fourteenth century, Ter Doest's wealth belonged to the past: the abbey was heavily in debt and this situation led to the resignation of Abbot Arnoul Neyhensys in July 1300. This change of circumstances cannot be explained solely by the building work carried out by this abbot. When the war broke out between the King of France and the Count of Flanders, Guy de Dampierre, the monastery had to contribute to the supply of goods to the Count's troops and Ter Doest was obliged to take out a loan in order to survive.[4] At the beginning of the fourteenth century, the violent conflicts between the monks and lay brothers also left their mark on the abbey.[5] During these internal rivalries, Abbot Guillaume V of Cordewaeghen was seriously wounded in November 1308 when the lay brother Guillaume de Saeftinge (famous for his acts against the French army during the Battle of Kortrijk in 1302) set upon him with a scythe. The abbot, who had to retire to the infirmary, resigned shortly after these tragic events. After his attack on Guillaume V, the same lay brother killed the cellarer. Thus the difficulties arising in the Cistercian order at that time also struck this abbey that had once been so thriving: the fame of Ter Doest belonged to the past.

---

1   De Ganck and Huyghebaert (1966), p. 325-327.
2   Hoste (1993), p. 11.
3   De Ganck and Huyghebaert (1966), p. 327.
4   Vermander (1957), p. 146; De Ganck and Huyghebaert (1966), p. 337.
5   Donnelly (1949), p. 37.

Overview of the contacts of Ter Doest with Scandinavia

Numerous archival sources of Ter Doest and Les Dunes (Coxyde), its mother abbey, are housed in the Grand Séminaire of Bruges[6] established on the refuge site of Ter Doest, in the buildings of the Cistercian community that was founded in Bruges at the beginning of the seventeenth century after the merger of the abbeys of Ter Doest and Les Dunes.[7] These very rich archives preserve the memory of numerous contacts that existed between the abbey and the Scandinavian world. Besides these, re-transcribed inscriptions from tombs that have disappeared today also prove the existence of such contacts.

Table 1. Contacts between Ter Doest and Scandinavia, 1225- c. 1300

Date	Source	Author	Editions
1225	Funeral inscription		De Visch (1656), p. 320
1227 (Sept.)	AGSB 604	Eustache, Prior of Ter Doest	*Cronica et cart. de Dunis*, p. 531; Weale (1867-1868), pp. 103-104 ; *DD*, I: 6, n° 69.
1227	AGSB 601	Abbots of Esrum & Sorø	*Cronica et cart. de Dunis*, p. 530; Weale (1867-1868), pp. 104-105 ; *DD*, I: 6, n° 70.
1231? (09.08)	AGSB 626bis	Archbishop Uffo of Lund	Weale (1867-1868), pp. 107-109; *Mekl. UB*, X, n° 7162; *APS Cam*, n° 25; *DD*, I: 6, n° 122.
1231 (21.12)	AGSB 50	Nicolas, Abbot of Saint-André etc.	*APS Cam*, n° 26; *Cronica et cart. de Dunis*, pp. 131-132; Weale (1867-1868), pp. 105-109 ; *DD*, I: 6, n° 126.
1266 (30.09)	AGSB 1003	Guy de Bourgogne, cardinal and legate of the Holy See	*Cronica et cart. de Dunis*, pp. 600-605 ; *DD*, II: 2, n° 39.
1273 (28.08)	AGSB 1116	Henry, Bishop of Linköping	*Cronica et cart. de Dunis*, p. 620.

---

6   When we give reference numbers of records housed at the Grand Séminaire Archives' of Bruges, we abbreviate them as »AGSB«. The dates of all the records mentioned in this contribution have been checked on the basis of the originals. They do not always correspond to those given by the editions, which are sometimes erroneous.

7   Schockaert (2003), pp. 427-430.

Date	Source	Author	Editions
1280 (04.09)	AGSB 1185	Aquinus, clerk (of Linköping)	*APS Cam*, n° 62.
1280 (22.11)	AGSB 1186	Bertrand Amalric, chaplain	*APS Cam*, n°63.
1281 (05.06)	AGSB 1194	Henry, Bishop of Linköping	*APS Cam*, n° 64 and (incomplete) in *DD*, II: 3, n° 6.
1282 (May)	Vatican Archives Collect. 213	Pontifical administration	*APS Cam*, n°65 and in *DD*, II: 3, n° 33.
1282? (03.06)	AGSB 1210	John, Archbishop of Trondheim	*DN*, 17, n° 872.
1282 (18.09)	AGSB 1199	Brynolf, Bishop of Skara & Bero, Abbot of Varnhem	*APS Cam*, n° 66; *DN*, 17, n° 873.
1282 (19.09)	AGSB 1201	Henry, Bishop of Linköping	*APS Cam*, n° 68.
1282 (19.09)	AGSB 1200	Ingundus, Provost of Tjust & Brynniolfus, chaplain	*APS Cam*, n° 67.
1282 (14.10)	AGSB 1203	John, Archbishop elect of Uppsala & Jacob, Dean of Bruges	*APS Cam*, n° 70; *DN*, 17, n° 874.
1283 (10.02)	AGSB 1200	Brynniolfus, chaplain	*APS Cam*, n° 71.
1283 (23.02)	AGSB 1212	Chapter of Trondheim	*DN*, 17, n° 875.
1283 (11.04)	Riksarkivet A. 3 O.I. 21	Henry, Bishop of Linköping	*DS*, 1, n° 761.
1284 (18.04)	AGSB 1217	Eric II, King of Norway	*DN*, 17, n° 876.
1284 (22.05)	AGSB 1220	Endridus, canon in Trondheim	*DN*, 17, n° 877.
1284 (22.08)	AGSB 1224	Torphim, Bishop of Hamar	De Visch (1656), pp. 318-319.
1285	Funeral inscription		Van de Putte, Ferdinand & Carton, Charles-Louis (1845), p. 16.
1300 (18.08)	AGSB 383	Jarundus, Archbishop of Trondheim	*Cronica et cart. de Dunis*, p. 226; *DN*, 17, n° 885.
Between 1292 and 1300	Ms Brugge, Stadsbibliotheek, 418, fol. 515r (n° 922).	John, Bishop of Tournai	*Codex Dunensis*, n° CCCLXI.

Contacts with Denmark

Death of Peder Jakobsen, Bishop of Roskilde
The inscription on the tomb of Peder Jakobsen,[8] who was bishop of Roskilde and who died at Ter Doest, is the first trace of contact we can find. It was transcribed by the scholar and historiographer Charles de Visch, who was a Cistercian of Les Dunes. The latter included it in his famous work *Bibliotheca scriptorum sacri ordinis cisterciensis* (1656):

> Hic iacet Petrus Episcopus Roschildensis, cognatus Regis Daciae, qui cruce signatus, in itineratione ad Domini sepulchrum, hoc in loco obiit.

These lines tell us that the bishop was a relative of the King of Denmark and that he died at Ter Doest while he was taking the cross to Christ's tomb. Peder Jakobsen obviously stayed at the monastery during a stop-over in Bruges. Nevertheless, Charles de Visch explains that the bishop of Roskilde's ship suffered a storm which cast him on the Flemish coast. The historiographer also informs us of having noted the date of his death on the gravestone: Jakobsen died on 19 May 1218. Yet this is surely a printing or reading error as the bishop actually died in 1225. Finally, de Visch states that he was buried at Ter Doest in the monks' choir close to the high altar and that his remains were transferred to the new abbey of Les Dunes.[9] This shows that during the seventeenth century, the Cistercians from Bruges felt much respect for him since they wanted to keep his memory alive.

A sum of money to be sent to the King of Denmark on behalf of the Queen of France
Many records concern a sum of money to be sent to the King of Denmark on behalf of the Queen of France.

By means of a record dated from September 1227, the Prior of Ter Doest, Eustache, makes it known that a hospitaller named Gaufroy deposited at the abbey a sum of 549 sterling marks at the request of the Queen of France, to be transferred to the King of Denmark.[10]

Another record from the same year, but this time originating from Danish abbots from Esrum and Sorø, tells us about the course of events. The Danish Cis-

---

8 This concerns Peder Jakobsen and not Peder Suneson, as William Henry James Weale noted in his article; Weale (1867-1868), pp. 102-103. See also Kornerup (1878), pp. 311-318.
9 De Visch (1656), p. 320.
10 AGSB, no. 604. Editions in *Cronica et cart. de Dunis*, p. 531 and in Weale (1867-1868), pp. 103-104; DD 1:6 no. 69.

tercians state that the abbey of Ter Doest which had received in deposit a sum of 540 sterling marks via the hospitaller Gaufroy from the Queen of France, transferred it to the hospitaller Henry for the King of Denmark.[11]

These records show on the one hand that the abbey of Ter Doest played an important role in the financial transactions and that it enjoyed the trust of a political personality such as the Queen of France and on the other hand they reveal the presence of Danish abbots from Esrum and Sorø in the abbey. The circumstances of their stay are unexplained but we may suppose that they were on their way to the General Chapter of their order of Cîteaux.

A sum owed to Rome, entrusted by archbishop Uffo of Lund
Another record from the archives of the Bruges Grand Séminaire demonstrates the role played by Ter Doest in the financial transactions that concern Scandinavia. This record dated, from Ribe on 9 August [1231], was written by Archbishop Uffo of Lund and his suffragan bishops and is addressed to Pope Gregory IX.[12] They express their gratitude to him for making a special concession by asking his writer, Master Simon, to collect a sum of just one thousand marks of silver as compensation for the pontifical tithe due to the difficulties that had hit Denmark – for example the imprisonment of the king, some bishops and many noblemen, and the epidemic that swept through the herds of livestock. In addition, they explain that since money and gold were in the possession of their enemies, they had been forced to melt down their copper coins in order to extract from them the modest quantity of silver they contained. Once the sum had been collected, they transferred it to the harbour of Ribe to send it to Ter Doest and entrust it to Master Simon on his arrival.

On 21 December 1231, Nicolas, abbot of Saint-André, Goswin, abbot of Eeckhout, Guillaume, provost of Saint-Donatien, Robert, Dean of Saint-Donatien and the chapter of Saint-Donatien (Bruges) tell us that – in their presence – the abbot and some monks from Ter Doest, who had received in deposit a certain sum of money from the Danish Cistercian abbots of Holme and Løgum for the account of Master Simon, paid it out to him.[13] The record also explains that since the abbot and the monks did not know him, copies from records were

---

11 AGSB, no. 601; Editions in *Cronica et cart. de Dunis*, p. 530 and in Weale (1867-1868), pp. 104-105; DD 1:6 no. 70. See also: Van Hollebeke (1863), pp. 47-48.
12 AGSB, no. 626bis (this record was unfortunately not found amongst the archives during my visits in spring 2011). Editions in Weale (1867-1868), pp. 107-109 and in Meklenburgisches Urkundenbuch X, no 7162 as well as in *APS Cam*, no. 25; DD 1:6 no. 122. See also Van Hollebeke (1863), p. 54.
13 AGSB, no. 50. Editions in *APS Cam*, no. 26 and in *Cronica et cart. de Dunis*, pp. 131-132 as well as in Weale (1867-1868), pp. 105-109; DD1:6 no. 126.

provided for security reasons: one from the Pope to all prelates of Denmark and the other from these bishops to the Pope.

Here again, the abbey of Ter Doest plays a central role as an intermediary for financial transactions. Once more, Danish Cistercians have been associated with these and this reveals the good health of the Cistercian network.

The interdict lies heavy on Denmark

Over the next thirty-five years the archives of Ter Doest do not mention any contact with Scandinavia and no trace of communication with Denmark can be found. It is a record written on 30 September 1266 in Schleswig that interrupts this silence.[14] The text that was written by Guy de Bourgogne (former abbot of Cîteaux), cardinal-priest of S. Lorenzo in Lucina and legate of the Holy See, deals with the interdict that places a heavy burden on Denmark. The record does not talk about any link with Ter Doest but is a logical sequel of the intervention of Guy in the conflict that opposed Erik V Glipping, King of Denmark, and Jakob Erlandsen, Archbishop of Lund. Nevertheless, the presence of this record in the archives of the abbey shows the interest of Ter Doest in the political and ecclesiastical situation of Denmark.

Contacts with Sweden

A number of records attest to the privileged relationships that existed between Ter Doest and the bishopric of Linköping. In the Bruges Grand Séminaire archives a record is also to be found from the bishop of Skara. Some of the records from the Episcopal world also reveal the existence of links between the Swedish Cistercian establishments and the Flemish abbey.

Cistercian and episcopal contacts

In a record written in Bruges on 28 August 1273 Bishop Henry of Linköping explains that Sylvester, abbot of the Cistercian monastery of Alvastra, with whom he was sailing with a view to attending the general chapter of the order, made for Bruges while he was suffering from a serious illness and that he died in Ter Doest a few days later. The same bishop points out that nothing from Sylvester was left in Ter Doest except his seal that had to be returned.[15]

Another record from Swedish individuals attests to contacts between the Flemish abbey and the Scandinavian Cistercians. Indeed in the Bruges Grand Sémi-

---

14 AGSB, no. 1003. Editions in *Cronica et cart. de Dunis*, pp. 600-605 and DD 2:2 no. 39.
15 AGSB, no. 1116; edition in *Cronica et cart. de Dunis*, p. 620. See also Van Hollebeke (1863), p. 96; De Ganck and Huyghebaert (1966), p. 334.

naire archives, a record is to be found which was written by Bishop Brynolf of Skara and Abbot Bero of the Varnhem Cistercian monastery. The record was written there on 18 September 1282.[16] The bishop and abbot point out that deprived of his privileges, pallium and seal by royal decree, Archbishop John of Trondheim designated John, archdeacon and archbishop elect of Uppsala, as procurator with the power to ask to be given back the deposit entrusted to Ter Doest.

Another series of records in Bruges from the Ter Doest archives concern the contacts of the abbey with Scandinavia – in particular Sweden and Norway – but the Cistercian monks of that area no longer appear in them. These records illustrate the essential part played by Ter Doest as a go-between in relation to several financial matters. They show the trust that it enjoyed as well. In a general way we can say that these elements disclose the reputation of Cistercian abbeys and the influence they could exert in fields far removed from the spiritual. Let's run through these records in quick succession.

Bishop Henry of Linköping and his entourage
On 4 September 1280 Aquinus, clerk to Bishop Henry of Linköping, agreed to the transfer by the abbot of Ter Doest to Bertrand Amalric, a canon in Rheims, chaplain to the Pope and collector of subsidies for the Holy Land in Denmark and Sweden, the sums of money that had been entrusted to the monastery.[17] In a record from Bruges dated 22 November 1280[18] the said Bertrand Amalric pointed out that although Bishop Henry of Linköping had deposited 350 silver marks at Ter Doest he found only 183 marks in the bags even though they had been sealed by Aquinus. Therefore, there is no reason to question the integrity of the abbey. The Pope's chaplain requested that in the event the bishop or someone sent in his name should come and complete the payment by Whitsun, the sum must be delivered to the John de Crusolis de Monte Pessulano Society in Paris, and the latter would hand it over to the Saint-Victor monastery in the same city.

A record dated 5 June 1281 also attests to the relationship between Bishop Henry of Linköping and Ter Doest.[19] In this text the Swedish prelate asks the

---

16 AGSB, no. 1199. Editions in *APS Cam*, no. 66 and in DN 17:873. See also Van Hollebeke (1863), p. 111.
17 AGSB, no. 1185. Edition in *APS Cam*, no. 62. This edition erroneously states the date as 11 September 1280 although the record is in fact dated from the fourth »feria« before the nativity of the Virgin, that is to say the 4 September. See also Van Hollebeke (1863), p. 108.
18 AGSB, no. 1186. Edition in *APS Cam*, no. 63. See also Van Hollebeke (1863), pp. 108-109.
19 AGSB, no. 1194. Editions in *APS Cam*, no. 64 and (incomplete) in DD 2:3 no. 6. See

Cistercian abbot to agree to the deposit of what will be entrusted to him in his name. He ends up by assuring the abbot to fulfill his wishes. The Pope's accounts for May 1282 show that a certain sum of money is also mentioned that the bishop must hand in to Ter Doest.[20] The same bishop is again to be found in the Ter Doest archives in relation to a record dated 19 September 1282 concerning other money deposited with the Flemish Cistercians.[21]

The abbey seems to enjoy a certain degree of trust with regard to money matters and also various objects. Indeed, in a Ter Doest record from 19 September 1282 the provost of Tjust, Ingundus, and the chaplain to the bishop of Linköping, Brynniolfus, preparing for a trip to the Holy Land, entrust the prior with some personal belongings.[22] The latter are carefully enumerated: notably some mattresses and linen. The two men also consider what should happen to their deposit in case they should not return from their trip. The follow-up story to this is also known thanks to another record in the archives. Dated 10 February 1283, it originates from the aforementioned Brynniolfus who declared that he had got back what he had entrusted to the abbey before he left for the Holy Land.[23]

Bishop Henry of Linköping is found one last time in 1283. On 11 April of that same year the Swedish prelate is drawing up his last will and testament in Marseille, and he mentions the abbey of Ter Doest.[24] The condition of the testament does not permit the reader to ascertain more information than that.

Contacts with Norway

Numerous contacts have also existed within the world of the Norwegian bishoprics, most notably with regard to the archbishop of Trondheim, and the bishops of Hamar and Oslo.

Archbishop John of Trondheim

A record written in Bruges on 14 October 1282 by John, archdeacon and archbishop elect of Uppsala, and Jacob, Dean of Bruges, explains that a sum of 25 and a half pounds had been deposited in Ter Doest on behalf of archbishop

---

also Van Hollebeke (1863), p. 109.
20 Editions notably in *APS Cam*, no. 65 and in DD 2:3 no. 33.
21 AGSB, no. 1201. Edition in *APS Cam*, no. 68. See also Van Hollebeke (1863), pp. 110-111.
22 AGSB, no. 1200. Edition in *APS Cam*, no. 67. See also Van Hollebeke (1863), p. 110.
23 AGSB, no. 1200 (this record is kept under the same number as the previous one because they relate to the same matter). Edition in *APS Cam*, no. 71. See also Van Hollebeke (1863), p. 112.
24 This very damaged testament is edited in DS 1:761.

John of Trondheim by his clerk Thorberg, and that the sum had been paid back to Gudbrand, also clerk to the archbishop and a student in Paris.[25] The record is filed together with another concerning the same subject. The latter, the exact date of which is not specified, originates from the Norwegian archbishop and is addressed to Baudouin, vice-prior in Ter Doest.[26]

Concerning the deposits by Archbishop John of Trondheim three other records can be cited. The first is from 23 February 1283, written by the chapter of Trondheim.[27] The second originates from King Eric II of Norway and is dated Bergen 18 April 1284.[28] The third could unfortunately not be found when I visited the archives in spring 2011, yet according to the inventory of the records kept at the Library of Bruges Grand Séminaire, it is dated 22 May 1284, and originates from Archbishop John of Trondheim.[29] The latter piece of information appears to be erroneous since the said archbishop died at the end of 1282. Despite the loss of the original record, we can correct the inventory thanks to the edition in *Diplomatarium Norvegicum*: this originates from a certain Endridus, canon in Trondheim.

Other Norwegian bishops
Another Norwegian episode is the presence and the death in Ter Doest of Torphim, bishop of Hamar, then in exile.[30] The prelate wrote his last will and testament in the abbey on 22 August 1284, and its vidimus notably drawn up by John, archdeacon of Uppsala, which is still kept amongst the monastery's archives.[31] The bishop died on 8 January 1285, and his body was interred in front of the main altar in the abbey church.[32] The original inscription on his tomb is lost but a transcription survives:[33]

Hic jacet dominus Thorphimus, ex regno Norwegiae, civitatis Hamariae episcopus, qui pro jure ecclesiae de terra sua exulatus et in mari naufragatus, hic tandem veniens pauper et attenuates, per triginta septimanas infirmatus, hospitans et amore Christi, misericorditer sustentatus, sancto fine quievit anno Domini MCCLXXXIV, VI Idus Januarii. Anima ejus requiescat in pace.

---

25 AGSB, no. 1203. Editions in *APS Cam*, no. 70 and in DN 17:874. See also Van Hollebeke (1863), pp. 111-112.
26 AGSB, no. 1210. This record was written in Trondheim on the 3rd June without a precise year (probably 1282). Edition in DN 17:872.
27 AGSB, no. 1212. Edition in DN 17:875. See also Van Hollebeke (1863), p. 112.
28 AGSB, no. 1217. Edition in DN 17:876. See also Van Hollebeke (1863), pp. 112-113.
29 AGSB, no. 1220. Edition in DN 17:877. See also *Inventaire* (1857), p. 60.
30 Brouette (1978), pp. 133-136; De Visch (1656), pp. 316-320.
31 AGSB, no. 1224. Edition notably in De Visch (1656), pp. 318-319.
32 De Visch (1656), p. 318; Van Hollebeke (1863), pp. 113-117.
33 Van de Putte & Carton (1845), p. 16.

A record from Bruges dated 18 August 1300 from Archbishop of Trondheim Jarundus is the last item about Scandinavia filed in the Grand Séminaire.[34] It entitles the Ter Doest monks to grant forty days' indulgences on Sundays and Feast days when they preach in or outside the monastery.

A last record attesting to the links between Scandinavia and the Flemish monastery comes from a cartulary kept in the public library of the city of Bruges.[35] The record is incomplete but mentions the Ter Doest community. In this record John, bishop of Tournai, entitles Eyvindus, bishop of Oslo, to bestow holy orders in his diocese. Unfortunately it cannot be dated with any precision but must have been written between 1292 and 1300. This estimation is based on the fact that John was bishop of Tournai from 1292 until 1300, while Eyvindus was bishop of Oslo from 1288 to 1303.

Analysis

The different records and the funeral inscriptions that have been discussed above enable us to establish that the contacts of Ter Doest with Scandinavia seem to be spread over three chronological phases that each correspond to one of the three kingdoms of Scandinavia. The first of these periods is the Danish period that lasted from 1225 to 1266; the second is Swedish and is illustrated by the records written between 1273 and 1283; and finally the third period is Norwegian and lasted from 1282 to 1300.

Although these different phases have unequal durations, it has to be noted that some of them are livelier than others. The Danish period for instance, which can be traced as late as 1266, concentrates its activity in the period up to 1231: as we said earlier, the record from 1266 deals with the interdict that was a burden on Denmark. It does not concern the Flemish abbey. Consequently, the Danish period of communication between Ter Doest and this country actually lasts from 1225 to 1231, i.e. six years. With regard to Sweden, the period is approximately ten years, as the oldest record dates from 1273 and the most recent one from 1283. The Norwegian phase appears to be the longest: 18 years.

Another point that must be made is the fact that the contacts of Ter Doest with the Scandinavian Cistercians especially concern Denmark and to a lesser extent Sweden. In contrast no trace from the Norwegian Cistercians could be found in the archives of the Flemish abbey: it is evident that the records dealing with Norway are all concerned with the episcopal sphere. Furthermore this

---

34 AGSB, no. 383. Editions in *Cronica et cart. de Dunis*, p. 226 and in DN 17:885.
35 MS Brugge, Stadsbibliotheek, 418, fol. 515r (no. 922). Edition in *Codex Dunensis*, no. CCCLXI.

is the case for most records concerning Sweden. If the Danish contacts mainly involve Cistercians, none of them deals with Cistercian matters, but each time abbeys from this religious order appear as intermediaries in financial issues. Each preserved record that shows this situation illustrates a "tandem" system of Danish monasteries facing the abbey of Ter Doest: in one case it is the abbots of Esrum and Sorø who state they received a sum entrusted to the Flemish abbey by the Queen of France to be given to the King of Denmark, and in the other case, it is the abbots of Holme and Løgum who entrusted to Ter Doest a sum owed to the Pope.

End of contacts between Ter Doest and Scandinavia
Several questions can be asked regarding the end of Ter Doest's contacts with each of the Scandinavian countries, and more precisely with the Cistercian institutions in these countries. They cannot be answered easily but the interdict that hung over Denmark – to which a record kept in the Flemish abbey attests – is probably one of the elements which accounts for this change. It is also necessary to wonder about the plight of the Cistercians themselves and to ascertain if the role they played in society still enabled them to enjoy the sort of trust necessary to produce important financial transactions. In order to do so let us consider the situation of Danish monks and the abbey Ter Doest.

Danish Cistercians who had experienced a period of considerable growth in the course of the twelfth century met with a lot more difficulties in the following century. Prof. McGuire has indeed shown to what extent – particularly from the middle of the thirteenth century onwards – the monks' conditions had changed.[36] At that time aristocrats no longer gave their main favour to Cistercians, in fact – what is worse – they regretted their ancestors' donations. The phenomenon is marked from the 1230s, which corresponds to the date of the last surviving record attesting to actual Danish links with Ter Doest. But the plight of Danish Cistercians had also become difficult with regard to other important components of society. This is the case with the monarchy with which troubles started to arise when the Cistercian settlements manifested their support for Archbishop Jacob Erlandsen, and it was also the case with the episcopate with which a number of abbeys went through severe conflicts. It can be seen that the Danish Cistercian monks no longer enjoyed a privileged situation which allowed them to exercise certain tasks, for example financial transactions on behalf of the king or bishops with whom relationships sometimes became hostile. Another element may account for the growing scarcity or even the absence of contacts between Danish Cistercians and Ter Doest from a certain peri-

---

36 McGuire (1982), p. 144.

od onwards, and that is the distance progressively adopted by Danish Cistercian monasteries with regard to the order to which they belonged. Indeed Danish Cistercians expected little of the General Chapter at the end of the thirteenth century and thereafter showed themselves less and less attentive to the overall structure and functioning of the order.[37] In this context Danish abbots may have made less frequent visits to the annual chapter in Cîteaux, and thus had less reason to stop over in Bruges and so to visit the abbey of Ter Doest. It must be noted, however, that this sort of stopover at the abbey does not necessarily entail the writing of a record there by Danish monks and the keeping of it there today. Links may have continued to exist even though these were no longer of the same nature, that is to say economic.

As far as the status of Ter Doest is concerned it must be said that it was brilliant throughout the thirteenth century as the abbey reached its zenith at that time. As we have explained the abbey maintained business relations with numerous countries, and this situation continued throughout the whole of the thirteenth century, i.e. for over fifty years after the last record was written that is filed with relation to Denmark. Indeed we have seen that important contacts of a financial nature existed until 1300, notably with Sweden and Norway. It is at the beginning of the fourteenth century that these contacts seem to disappear. The situation here is certainly to be accounted for by the fact that Ter Doest had to face a large number of difficulties. The abbey had become fragile on account of severe difficulties encountered with lay brothers, but it was above all heavily in debt. Mismanagement but also the heavy conflict between the Count of Flanders and his suzerain the King of France account for the bad financial health of the Flemish monastery. In this context it is easy to understand that Ter Doest was no longer capable of ensuring financial transactions on behalf of foreign sovereigns and bishops. The abbey probably no longer enjoyed the necessary trust either. Hence the type of transactions evoked would notably be carried out by merchants or financial experts, mostly Italian bankers working in Bruges.[38]

Conclusion

The Cistercian abbey of Ter Doest had privileged relations with the Scandinavian countries. Its location, close to the sea and to the important harbour of Bruges, probably played a major role in developing close contacts between the Flemish Cistercians and the Scandinavian clergy. Actually, it seems that the ecclesiastics

---

37 See the numerous examples cited in McGuire (1982), pp. 165-166.
38 See also Despy (1952), pp. 95-109 (principally pp. 97-101); Nyberg (1990), pp. 131-146.

from the Northern countries were used to calling at Bruges and to staying in Ter Doest, when travelling to Rome, the Holy Land, or Burgundy in order to attend the General Chapter of the Cistercian Order. It is likely that these repeated passages to the monastery generated an atmosphere of confidence between the Flemish monks and the Danish, Swedish and Norwegian clerks.

These relations are revealed by numerous archival sources of Ter Doest. In addition to these, two funeral inscriptions attest to the death at Ter Doest of important Scandinavian ecclesiastical personalities who were buried there. All the indications supporting these relations are from the thirteenth century when the abbey was in its golden age. It is worth noting that the relations between the Flemish abbey and the Scandinavian world went through three phases: a Danish period (1225-1266), a Swedish period (1273-1283) and finally a Norwegian one (1282-1300). The deep changes of the society and of the monastic world, for example the severe difficulties of Ter Doest at the beginning of the fourteenth century, brought to a halt the contacts which were previously so numerous.

The sources stress that the monks of Ter Doest had relations with the Scandinavian episcopal milieu in general as well as with Danish and Swedish Cistercian abbeys. Often, indeed, the abbey of Ter Doest played the role of an intermediary for the Scandinavian clergy who entrusted it with considerable sums of money intended for Rome, or personal items while travelling further. It is of interest that pure financial transactions of Denmark were also channelled through the Danish Cistercian monasteries and the abbey of Ter Doest, although these transactions were without any real connection to monastic issues. We can thus observe that if the contacts with Scandinavia were essentially of a financial nature, Ter Doest had no financial interest for itself.

Literature

Manuscript sources
Archives du Grand Séminaire de Bruges: 50, 383, 601, 604, 626bis, 1003, 1116, 1185, 1186, 1194, 1199, 1200, 1201, 1203, 1210, 1212, 1217, 1220, 1224.
MS Brugge, Stadsbibliotheek, 418, fol. 515r (n° 922).

Edited sources
APS Cam: *Acta Pontificum Svecica*, I, *Acta Cameralia*, ed. Ludvig Magnus Bååth (Stockholm, 1936).
Codex Dunensis: *Codex Dunensis sive diplomatum et chartarum medii aevi amplissima collectio*, ed. Joseph Marie Bruno Constantin Kervyn de Lettenhove (Bruxelles, 1875).
Cronica et cart. de Dunis = *Cronica et cartularium monasterii de Dunis*, ed. Ferdinand Van de Putte and Désiré Van de Casteele (Bruges, 1864).

DD: *Diplomatarium Danicum,* various editors (Copenhagen, 1938 –).
DN: *Diplomatarium Norvegicum,* various editors (Oslo, 1847-1992) *(online version: http:// www.dokpro.uio.no/dipl_norv/diplom_field_eng.html).*
DS: *Diplomatarium Suecanum,* various editors (Stockholm, 1829-).
Meklenburgisches Urkundenbuch, ed. Verein für Meklenburgische Geschichte und Alterthumskunde (Schwerin, 1863 –).
Weale, William Henry James, 'Abbaye de Ter Doest – Note sur les relations qu'elle eut avec le Danemark', *La Flandre. Revue des monuments d'histoire et d'antiquités* 1 (1867-1868), pp. 102-111.

Studies
Aubert, Roger, 'Guy de Bourgogne', in *Dictionnaire d'histoire et de géographie ecclésiastiques,* t. 22 (Paris, 1988), cols. 1257-1262.
Brouette, Emile, 'Note sur Torfinn, évêque de Hamar', *Cîteaux. Commentarii Cistercienses* 29 (1978), pp. 133-136.
De Ganck, Roger and Hughebaert, Nicolas, 'Abbaye de Ter Doest, à Lissewege', in *Monasticon belge,* t. 3, *Province de Flandre Occidentale,* vol. 2 (Liège, 1966), pp. 317-351.
Despy, Georges, 'Bruges et les collectories pontificales de Scandinavie et de Pologne au XIVe siècle', *Bulletin de l'Institut Historique Belge de Rome* 27 (1952), pp. 95-109.
De Visch, Charles, *Bibliotheca scriptorum sacri ordinis cisterciensis* (Cologne, 1656).
Donnelly, James S., *The Decline of the Medieval Cistercian Laybrotherhood* (New York, 1949).
Eberhard Mayer, Hans, 'Ein Bischof geht einkaufen: Heinrich von Linköping im Heiligen Land', *Zeitschrift des Deutschen Palästina-Vereins* 124 (2008), pp. 51-60.
Eubel, Conrad, *Hierarchia catholica medii aevi... ab anno 1198,* 8 vols (Münster, 1913- 1978), vol. 1. Also in *Brepolis Medieval Encyclopaedias - Europa Sacra Online* (http://www.brepolis.net).
Hoste, Anselm, *De handschriften van Ter Doest* (Steenbrugge, 1993).
Inventaire des chartes, bulles pontificales, privilèges et documents divers de la Bibliothèque du Séminaire épiscopal de Bruges (Bruges, 1857).
Kornerup, J., 'Om den roskildske biskop Peder Jacobsøns skibbrud og død paa kysten af Flandern i aaret 1225', *Aarbøger for nordisk oldkyndighed og historie* (1878), pp. 311-318.
McGuire, Brian Patrick, *The Cistercians in Denmark* (Kalamazoo, 1982).
Nyberg, Tore, 'Skandinavisches in den spätmittelalterlichen Niederlanden', in *Brügge – Colloquium des Hansischen Geschichtsvereins: 26-29 Mai 1988,* ed. Klaus Friedland (Cologne-Vienne, 1990), pp. 131-146.
Schockaert, Thomas-Eric, *De abten der Cisterciënzerabdij Onze-Lieve-Vrouw-Ten-Duinen te Koksijde 1107-1627* (Koksijde, 2003).
Van de Putte, Ferdinand and Carton, Charles-Louis, *Chronique de l'abbaye de Ter Doest* (Bruges, 1845).
Van Hollebeke, Léopold, *Lisseweghe, son église et son abbaye* (Bruges, 1863).
Vermander, Marcel, 'Handelsbedrijvigheid der abdij Ter Doest', *Cîteaux in de Nederlanden* 8 (1957), pp. 139-146.

Monastic locations cited in the article.

"Ex magno devotionis fervore…"
Danish Cistercians and the Apostolic Penitentiary in the Later Middle Ages

Kirsi Salonen

Is it possible to find medieval documents regarding the Danish Cistercians that Brian McGuire has not exploited in his studies? The answer to this question is, incredibly, positive. The medieval holdings of the archives of the Apostolic Penitentiary in Rome[1] do indeed include some still unknown documentation concerning members of the Cistercian Order in the territory of the medieval church province of Lund. The aim of this essay is to offer some glimpses of these documents.

The Apostolic Penitentiary

The Apostolic Penitentiary was a papal office whose competence included various issues regarding sin and contravening the norms of ecclesiastical legislation. Christians could turn to the Penitentiary when they had issues of conscience or canon law to resolve. The Penitentiary had apostolic authority to grant four different types of grace:
1) Absolutions for those who had broken the regulations of canon law in a particularly serious way and the handling of the matter was entrusted to the pope, as for example with cases of clerical homicide or apostasy.
2) Dispensations that allowed Christians to act against the regulations of the Church: for example, to enter an ecclesiastical career despite an impediment such as illegitimacy, minority, or bodily defect.
3) Licenses that allowed Christians to deviate from observing certain ecclesiastical norms in matters mainly concerning the exercise of one's Christian

---

1 Archivio della Penitenzieria Apostolica (henceforth: APA) is situated in the Palazzo della Cancelliera close to the famous piazza, Campo de'fiori, in the heart of Rome. The use of the material in the archives of the Penitentiary is restricted, because the collections may contain matters of conscience, but since 1984 it has been possible to obtain a permit to use the material.

faith: for example, to confess to a priest other than one's own father confessor or to consume meat or dairy products during fasting periods.
4) Official declarations: for example, that a cleric was not guilty of murder despite an (unjust) accusation or that a monastic profession was void, if the person concerned had been forced to take the monastic vows.[2]

According to these powers, the Penitentiary granted graces in numerous different matters including marriage, illegitimacy, priestly ordination, violence, apostasy, and confessing. Since the competences of the Penitentiary included many matters relevant for monks and nuns, it is no wonder that Cistercians also used the services of this papal office – including Cistercians from the territory of the Danish church province of Lund.[3]

The medieval copy books of the Penitentiary office include thousands and thousands of documents which are abbreviated copies of the original petitions directed to and approved by the officials of the Penitentiary.[4] The petitioners who turned to the Penitentiary came from the whole territory of Latin Christendom. In the second half of the fifteenth century they numbered over 200.000, and included laymen and ecclesiastics, as men and women.[5]

---

[2] For the history, functioning and competence of the Penitentiary in the Middle Ages, see for example Göller (1907, 1911); Schmugge, Hersperger & Wiggenhauser (1996); Salonen (2001); Salonen & Schmugge (2009).

[3] The Danish church province of Lund included, in addition to the archdiocese of Lund, the dioceses of Aarhus, Børglum/Aalborg, Odense, Ribe, Roskilde, Schleswig, and Viborg.

[4] The records of the office from the 1450s until the 1540s consist of c. 100 copy books, which are internally divided into different sections containing petitions related to a specific matter. The most common petition categories in the registers are: *de matrimonialibus* (about marriages), *de diversis formis* (concerning various types of cases), *de declaratoriis* (about declarations), *de defectu natalium* and *de uberiori* (matters related to illegitimacy), *de promotis et promovendis* (about ordinations), and *de confessionalibus* (licence to choose a personal confessor). Registering the different types of instances under specific titles is a technique that can only be found in the Penitentiary registers, not in the other medieval papal register series. The division of the cases into different petition categories was probably made for practical reasons, for easing the tracing of the decisions of the office, if there was need to consult the records later. Concerning the registers of the Penitentiary, see for example Salonen (2001), pp. 425-426; Salonen & Schmugge (2009) pp. 3-7, 17-20.

[5] Salonen & Schmugge (2009), p. 19.

The Petitions of Danish Cistercians: a concise review

The medieval holdings of the Apostolic Penitentiary include c. 780 petitions from the Danish church province.[6] There are a dozen documents in which Danish Cistercians appear as petitioners. Unlike the Swedish Cistercians[7], who turned to the Penitentiary at the same time, the Danish Cistercian supplicants include one nun, namely sister Catherina Pedersdatter from Slangerup on Sjælland. The proportion of nun petitioners reflects the proportion of convents in Denmark meant for male and female, since of the fourteen Cistercian monasteries in Denmark, eleven were intended for monks and three for nuns.

Some Cistercian monasteries are better represented in the Penitentiary documents than others. There are indeed as many as five documents regarding the monastery of Øm (or in Latin: *Care Insule*) in the diocese of Aarhus. The monastery of Esrum in Sjælland (diocese of Roskilde) appears in two petitions, while the monastery of Vitskøl in Jutland (diocese of Viborg) is mentioned in one petition. Other monasteries are not identifiable on the basis of their names, since only the diocese where the monastery is situated is mentioned in the petition, and in some Danish dioceses there was more than one Cistercian monastery. On the basis of the diocese specification only the monastery of Holme, the sole Cistercian monastery on Funen (diocese of Odense), can be identified. Even though not all Cistercian monasteries are present in the Danish documentation, it can be concluded that the Danish Cistercians clearly possessed knowledge about the competency of the Penitentiary and in case of need they used its services, since circa half of the Danish Cistercian monasteries are mentioned in the documentation. Similar proportions also figure among the Penitentiary cases regarding Swedish Cistercians.[8]

The Penitentiary office was founded in the thirteenth century, but the archives of the office date only from a much later period. The systematic registers of incoming and approved petitions are preserved only from the mid-fifteenth century and continue until 1585.[9] Understandably, however, the Penitentiary records contain no Danish documents from the period after the Reformation

---

6   APA, Reg. Matrim. et Div. 1-100; On the Scandinavian Penitentiary material in general, see Ingesman (2009). The number of cases from the Danish territory is relatively high in respect of the cases from the same time period from the Swedish church province of Uppsala (c. 450 documents) and the Norwegian church province of Nidaros/Trondheim (c. 150 documents). The Swedish Penitentiary material is edited in *Auctoritate Papae* and the Norwegian material in *Synder og pavemakt*.
7   Concerning the Swedish Cistercians' petitions to the Penitentiary see *Auctoritate Papae*, pp. 123-126.
8   *Auctoritate Papae*, p. 124.
9   See note 4.

(1536 in Denmark).¹⁰ The earliest Danish Penitentiary case regarding Cistercians can be dated to the 1460s and the latest to the 1520s, which means that Danish Cistercians have turned to the office throughout the whole period of the Later Middle Ages. We can therefore say that the Danish Cistercians fit well to the general "Danish" trend in the Penitentiary material.

What did the Danish Cistercians petition for from the Penitentiary?

Predictably, among the broad spectrum of cases the Penitentiary could deal with surveyed above, some of the petition types are more characteristic of monks and nuns than some others. For example apostasy was an ecclesiastical crime typical for members of monastic orders, while marriage dispensation cases involved only laymen.[11]

Even though the Penitentiary is considered as the "tribunal of conscience", turning to the office did not automatically mean that the petitioner had done something bad that he regretted. In fact, a large proportion of the clients of the Penitentiary were petitioning for devotional reasons for some kind of license or dispensation. I will begin the analysis of the documents related to Danish Cistercians with the examples of Cistercians who petitioned the Penitentiary with regard to such devotional matters.

The Penitentiary had the power to grant Christians so-called confessional letters, which allowed the holder of the letter to choose a confessor and confess to him instead of being obliged to confess to his or her parish priest, which was the usual practice according to canon 21 of the Fourth Lateran Council in 1215. This provision stipulated that each Christian had to confess his or her sins at least once a year to his or her parish priest and not to anyone else.[12] If a person could not confess to his parish priest for some good reason, such as absence from his or her parish due to constant travelling, a confessional letter from the pope made it possible to turn instead to another priest. The Penitentiary granted thousands of such letters during the Later Middle Ages.[13]

One of the recipients of a confessional letter was Nicolaus, the abbot of the Cistercian monastery of Øm in the diocese of Aarhus.[14] It is even possible that Abbot

---

10 The last Danish Penitentiary document dates from 27.6.1534. APA, Reg. Matrim. et Div. 83, fol. 5r-6r. The corresponding original petition, which surprisingly has also survived, is edited in *Acta Pontificum Danica* 7, no. 6475.
11 Salonen (2001), pp. 215-216, 417-418.
12 Canon "Omnis utriusque sexus", in *Conciliorum Oecumenicorum Decreta*, p. 245.
13 On the Penitentiary and confession letters, Salonen & Schmugge (2009), pp. 64-68.
14 APA, Reg. Matrim. et Div. 8, fol. 362v (dated 20.12.1460).

Nicolaus had travelled to Rome to spend Christmas there, since the other papal register series reveals that he had been granted a papal license to carry a portable altar only four days later than his petition to the Penitentiary had been approved. These two license types can be considered as a kind of "souvenir from Rome".[15]

Another abbot of the same monastery, Cristernus Martini, petitioned the Penitentiary for another kind of devotional favour. Like his predecessor Nicolaus, Christernus also wished to use a portable altar and asked for a license to possess and use one. Christernus did not direct his request to the Apostolic Chancery as Nicolaus did, but to the Penitentiary, and his request was successful.[16] Portable altars were meant for persons who wished to celebrate or participate in the celebration of the Holy Mass in non-consecrated places. Their use in Scandinavia became more and more common in the course of the fifteenth century. Earlier they were used mainly by the high nobility or high-ranking ecclesiastics, but later many members of religious orders or even parish priests received the permit to use portable altars.[17]

Two further Danish Cistercians can be included in the group of persons who have turned to the Penitentiary for devotional reasons. Both of them desired to receive a dispensation that would allow them to take priestly orders, which according to the regulations of canon law they could not receive due to some kind of defect that disqualified them from priestly functions.[18]

Brother Nicolaus Johannis alias Thome from the diocese of Aarhus[19] had to petition for dispensation from his birth defect, as the Church did not allow illegitimate children to become priests unless they received a papal dispensation. Since the pope had delegated these powers to the Penitentiary, it became one of the main offices in whole of Christendom for granting such graces.[20] Brother Nicolaus needed a dispensation from illegitimacy since he was the fruit of an adulterous relationship between an unmarried man and a married woman (*de soluto et coniugata genitus*).[21]

---

15 *Acta Pontificum Danica* 3, no. 2200 (dated 16.12.1460). Abbot Nicolaus is the only Danish Cistercian in the Penitentiary material who can also be identified in other medieval sources.
16 APA, Reg. Matrim. et Div. 32, fol. 266v (dated 15.4.1483).
17 Norberg (1982); on the Penitentiary and portable altar, Salonen (2001), pp. 209-210, 369.
18 On the Penitentiary and different kinds of questions regarding problems in obtaining priestly ordinations, see Salonen & Hanska (2013).
19 The name of the monastery of Nicolaus is not given in the Penitentiary document but since the petitioner is said to come from the diocese of Aarhus, we must be dealing with the monastery of Øm.
20 Regarding the Penitentiary and illegitimacy, see Schmugge (1995).
21 APA, Reg. Matrim. et Div. 9, fol. 303r (dated 26.7.1461).

Similarly to illegitimate children, the Church did not allow men with any kind of physical fault to receive priestly ordinations either. This was the reason why Brother Johannes Andree from the archdiocese of Lund[22] turned to the Penitentiary. He was not suitable for an ecclesiastical career because he was not bodily perfect and needed a dispensation that he could receive the orders despite his physical defect. Johannes told to the Penitentiary that he had cut off his testicles thinking that he could thus better serve God (*credens se obsequium prestare Deo sibi virilia amputavit*). His good intentions made him, however, unqualified for priesthood because of his physical defect and he had to ask for dispensation so that he nevertheless could become a priest.[23]

About half of the Danish Penitentiary documents regarding the Cistercians refer to problems in the monastic life, since more than a few brothers and sisters considered leaving their monasteries or had already done so and were consequently guilty of apostasy.[24] The only female petitioner, Sister Catherina Pedersdatter, explained to the Penitentiary that she had left her monastery, Slangerup, without license and lived a secular life for a time (*monasterium ipsum illicentiata exivit*). Life outside the walls of the nunnery had, however, been a disappointment to her, since she turned to the Penitentiary and explained that she had had second thoughts and was willing to return to her monastery (*cupit ad ovile redire*). But before she could do so, she needed absolution from the excommunication she had incurred by committing the crime of apostasy. The Penitentiary granted such a grace to the repentant Sister Catherina.[25]

Another Danish Cistercian had difficulties within his monastery which resulted in much more serious problems. Brother Nicolaus Olaij, priest from the diocese of Aarhus, explained in his petition to the Penitentiary that he had joined a certain monastery of the Cistercian Order (*in quodam monasterio dicti*

---

22 This document does not indicate which monastery was in question. There were two Cistercian monasteries in the territory of the archdiocese of Lund: Herrevad and Ås.

23 APA, Reg. Matrim. et Div. 55, fol. 726v-727r (dated 18.5.1510). Regarding the Penitentiary and bodily defects, see Salonen & Hanska (2013), pp. 8-9, 122-130, especially 127-128 regarding the lack of testicles. This case might seem very particular, but defects in genitals or testicles appear relatively frequently in the Penitentiary sources. Cutting off one's testicles was without doubt not common in the Middle Ages, but similar stories occur nevertheless regularly in the Penitentiary records.

24 Petitions regarding apostasy or the need to change one's monastery or even order are relatively common among the Penitentiary records and all monastic orders are represented among the petitioners. Concerning the Penitentiary and apostasy or transfer, see Salonen (2001), pp. 138-144; Salonen & Schmugge (2009), pp. 32-33, 138-141.

25 APA, Reg. Matrim. et Div. 16, fol. 100v (dated 14.7.1468).

ordinis)²⁶ where after a time he also received priestly ordination. However his life in the monastery turned out to be a nightmare, due to certain quarrels (*pretextu certarum rixarum*), because of which some of his monastic brethren had wounded him, captured him, and put him in jail. As if all this was not enough, the abbot of his monastery had subsequently expelled him from the monastery and from the order. Thereafter Brother Nicolaus had joined the Dominican Order, where he wished to stay. Since the regulations of canon law did not allow such a spontaneous change of monastic order without a special papal license, Nicolaus was afraid of having committed the crime of apostasy and thus having become irregular. He therefore turned to the Penitentiary and asked for absolution and a dispensation that would allow him to stay in the Dominican Order.²⁷

The petition of Nicolaus is a good example of the controversies in monasteries and to what kind of problems this might lead when they escalated. But life was not complicated only for brothers within the Cistercian Order, for the Penitentiary documentation includes testimony of problems within other orders as well. In fact, Brother Mathias, son of Mathias, a subdeacon from the monastery of Øm is an example of a reverse situation. Brother Mathias explained in his Penitentiary supplication that he had earlier joined the Order of Saint Benedict, from which he escaped without a permit (*ab eo sine licentia auffugisset*). He did not want to leave the monastic life, but joined the Cistercian Order and, at the moment of making his petition, he had already lived in the monastery of Øm for three years and intended to stay there (*per triennium moram traxit ac moram trahere intendit*). But leaving his first monastery had caused his excommunication and irregularity, from which he petitioned for absolution and dispensation so that he could receive the priestly orders and serve in the monastery in that role.²⁸

These three persons had in common the fact that they wanted to continue their monastic life despite the problems they had encountered. But not all Penitentiary petitioners who had left the Cistercian Order wanted to return to the monastic life. In order to continue their lives outside their monasteries, such men needed a papal declaration which stated that they were not bound to the monastic rule. Such a declaration guaranteed them all their rights in

---

26 Also in this case the name of the monastery is not given. If Nicolaus has stayed in the same diocese, Aarhus, where the monastery he had joined was situated it must be a question of the monastery of Øm. But since Nicolaus had left his first monastery and moved to another one, he might also have moved from the territory of one diocese to another, which means that it is not possible to detect which Cistercian monastery he had entered.
27 APA, Reg. Matrim. et Div. 56, fol. 379v-380r (dated 19.9.1511).
28 APA, Reg. Matrim. et Div. 16, fol. 83v (dated 2.4.1468).

secular society: they could inherit from their parents, marry legally, and their offspring would be considered legitimate if they decided to continue their lives as laymen; they could act as parish priests if they were already ordained to the priesthood.

Such declarations, which are relatively common among the Penitentiary documents, were requested by two Danish ex-Cistercians, who had both chosen to continue in their ecclesiastical career. Mathias Jacobi had entered the monastery of Esrum as a novice and realized that the monastic life was not for him and wanted to leave the monastery within the novice year (*infra annum probationis exire voluit*). The abbot of Esrum did not want to let him go and had even ordered him to be flagellated (*abbas tamen dicti monasterii eum pluries propter ea flagellari fecit*) in order to force him to stay in the monastery. According to his petition, the use of force had made him stay in the monastery of Esrum for a few years more, after which he escaped from the place and wished to continue his ecclesiastical career as a secular priest.[29] A similar but fortunately less violent story was told by Olaus Petrus from the island of Fegge (*de insula Ffegge*), a priest from the diocese of Odense. Olaus had been introduced as a small boy to the monastery of St Bernard of the Cistercian Order.[30] When he came of age, he retracted his profession and left the monastery (*captata oportunitate domum ipsum exivit*). Since he had meanwhile been ordained to priesthood, he, too, wished to receive a declaration that he was not bound to the Cistercian Order but could continue his life as a secular priest. Unlike many other clients of the Penitentiary, Olaus had even travelled to Rome and pleaded his case personally in the papal curia (*ad Romanam curiam venit*).[31]

Two further Danish Cistercians petitioned the Penitentiary to receive a letter of declaration. Their motivation was not that of leaving the order but they had more serious reasons for their requests – they had been involved in events that led to the death of another person. Being guilty of the death of someone meant for priests that they became irregular and could no longer officiate at the altar or hear confessions. The only way to restitute the right to continue in an ecclesiastical career for a priest accused of the death of someone was to receive a declaration that stated that even though they were involved in sad events, they could not be considered guilty of murder because of certain extenuating

---

29 APA, Reg. Matrim. et Div. 55, fol. 190r (dated 23.4.1510).
30 The petition does not mention the name of the monastery but just its patron Saint. Saint Bernard was at least the patron of the monastery of Tvis in the diocese of Ribe. His case is a good example of how people moved around, since his petition gives Odense as his present home diocese.
31 APA, Reg. Matrim. et Div. 72, fol. 647v (dated 13.6.1524).

circumstances – such as the death's being an accident or the fact that they had acted in self-defence in a situation they could not escape.[32]

Brother Cristernus Mathei from the monastery of Øm in the diocese of Aarhus told the Penitentiary that he had participated in a party and when the evening became too advanced, he wanted to return to his monastery. A friend of his, layman Thomas, wanted to join and accompany him home. The men walked together and Thomas carried weapons since the path was not safe (*balistam quandam unacum gladio pro sua deffensione* [sic] *portabat*). At a certain point, when the road became more dangerous, Thomas asked Cristernus to take one of the weapons, a loaded cross bow, for his defence, which he did and the men walked further. The road they were walking was dark and suddenly Brother Cristernus slid in the mud. As he fell down with the weapon in his hand he pressed the key of the cross-bow with the consequence that the bolt was fired and hit Thomas, wounding him (*lapso pede corruit et amota clave dicte baliste que tensa erat cum iaculo ... dictum laicum amicum suum cum illo iaculo percussit et vulneravit*). The wound was lethal and Thomas died after a few weeks. Since it was Cristernus who had held the weapon in his hands when it fired, he felt guilty and was afraid that he could be blamed for the death of his friend. Since it was a question of pure accident, he asked the Penitentiary for a letter of declaration in his favour that would state that he was not guilty of the death of Thomas.[33]

Similarly sad was the story told by the other Danish Cistercian, Brother Henningus of Esrum from the diocese of Roskilde, requesting a similar grace. He explained that he had been the tutor of a small boy and one day he had punished the boy by beating him with a stick (*eumque quibusdam virgis in illis partibus consuetis verberasset*). The beating had caused the boy some wounds in his buttocks, which Brother Henningus afterwards wanted to medicate. For medicating the skin of the boy, Brother Henningus had to use some lotion, which he needed to soften by holding it above the flame of a candle (*certam unctionem ... cum candela incesu mollificare cupiens*). While doing so a drop of hot wax from the candle fell accidentally onto the skin of the little boy who started moving. Henningus tried to hold him tight by squeezing him upon the chest (*ipsum cum manu supra pectus per vim tenuit*) so that he could continue the medication. Unfortunately, his attempt to try to protect the boy from being hurt was so harsh that the boy died after couple of hours, due to the hard pressing. Since Brother Henningus had not intended to kill the boy and he had even satisfied his parents for their loss (*cum consanguineis dicti defuncti amicabiliter concordavit*), he

---

32 On the Penitentiary and declaratory letters in murder cases, see Salonen & Schmugge (2009), pp. 49-53.
33 APA, Reg. Matrim. et Div. 16, fol. 176r-v (dated 14.11.1468).

considered himself not guilty and wanted to have an official declaration testifying to that effect.[34]

Danish Cistercians in minor roles

All the above examples are from cases in which Danish Cistercians figure in the role of the petitioner. The Danish Penitentiary material also includes documents in which Cistercians are mentioned in some role other than as supplicants.

One of the roles in which a Cistercian appears in a Penitentiary document is that of a local expert to whom the final resolution of a tricky case at home was entrusted. There were numerous cases where the officials of the Penitentiary could not make a definitive decision, due to lack of information or access to local witnesses. In such cases the Penitentiary made a preliminary decision in favour of the petitioner, but entrusted the final decision in the case to local ecclesiastical authorities. They were supposed to examine the details mentioned in the Penitentiary letter and if they found everything to be correct, they could pronounce the previous decision of the Penitentiary officials to be valid. If they found out that the details in the letter were incorrect or that the petitioner had not told the Penitentiary the whole truth, they had the power to declare the preliminary decision of the Penitentiary void.[35]

The Danish material reveals that the Penitentiary used Cistercians as referees in some cases. The abbot of Tvis monastery (*abbas monasterii sancti Bernardi alias Tviscloster*), for example, was used as an expert together with two canons from Viborg. They were asked to examine the case of layman Johannes Friis from the diocese of Børglum, who had asked for a declaration that his previous marriage with Botilda, daughter of Johannes Svensson, should be regarded as void and that, consequently, he could remarry.[36]

More unfortunate is the role of a (nameless) Cistercian abbot in the petition of a certain layman, Johannes Raa from the diocese of Roskilde. After the petitioner Johannes, the poor abbot in some sense played the second main role in the petition. Johannes petitioned the Penitentiary namely for an absolution because he had incurred an automatic excommunication after he had beaten up the aforementioned abbot.[37]

---

34 APA, Reg. Matrim. et Div. 49, fol. 392r-v (dated 5.3.1501).
35 On the role of the commission in the Penitentiary cases, see Salonen, *The Penitentiary*, 79-83.
36 APA, Reg. Matrim. et Div. 47, fol. 465r-v (dated 14.5.1499).
37 APA, Reg. Matrim. et Div. 37, fol. 156v (dated 12.1.1488). There is a slight misinformation in this document. The text of the petition says directly that the victim of the assault

The fact that monks appear in Penitentiary documents in the role of victim of an assault by laymen or co-monks is not unusual, as parallel examples from the Swedish material and of members of other monastic orders have demonstrated.[38]

Conclusion

These earlier unknown documents not only revealed to us the identities of a handful of until now unknown Danish Cistercians but they also give us glimpses of their devotional needs as well as problems they faced in the Later Middle Ages. The petitions of the Danish Cistercians do not contain any great surprises but it can be concluded that their petitions fit very well into the picture we in general have of the petitions of the Swedish Cistercians.

These documents include all the most common petition types typically directed to the Apostolic Penitentiary by Christians from all over Latin Christendom: the need to enter a monastic career despite certain ecclesiastical impediments, daily difficulties in enduring the monastic life, and persons who needed a confirmation of innocence. Some of the petitioning Cistercians had committed severe crimes and sins, testimony to the fact that the Cistercians were not above illicit behaviour.

On the other hand, some of the Danish Cistercians, like Abbots Nicolaus and Cristernus of the Øm monastery, presented their petitions to the Penitentiary for purely devotional reasons. Therefore the Penitentiary documents should not be considered only as testimony of the crimes the Danish Cistercians had committed. Indeed, we have to remember that even those petitioners who turned to the Penitentiary because of a crime did so because they regretted what they had done and wanted to be liberated from the burden of sin. Therefore these documents offer good testimony of how the Danish Cistercians petitioned the Penitentiary out of great devotional fervour (*ex magno devotionis fervore*) as Brother Henningus expressed it is his supplication.

---

had been the abbot of the monastery of Skov of the Cistercian Order (*manus violentas ... in quondam abbatem monasterii Skow ordinis Cisterciensis iniecit*). The monastery of Skov was, however, not a Cistercian but a Benedictine abbey. Therefore it seems obvious either that the layman was not aware of which order the Skovkloster belonged to, or that it was the abbot of another Cistercian abbey in Roskilde diocese. In any case, the document says that the abbot was a Cistercian.

38 Concerning the Swedish material regarding the members of different monastic orders, see *Auctoritate Papae*, pp. 115-137.

Literature

Manuscript sources
APA: Archivio della Penitenzieria Apostolica, Registra matrimonialium et diversorum 1-100.

Printed sources
Acta Pontificum Danica. Pavelige aktstykker vedrørende Danmark 1316–1536, vol. 1-7, ed. L. Moltesen, Alfr. Krarup, and Johs. Lindbæk (København, 1904–1943).

Auctoritate Papae. The Church Province of Uppsala and the Apostolic Penitentiary 1410–1526, ed. Sara Risberg, Introduction by Kirsi Salonen, Diplomatarium Suecanum, Appendix. Acta Pontificum Suecica II, Acta Poenitentiariae (Stockholm, 2008).

Conciliorum Oecumenicorum Decreta, ed. J. Alberigo, P.-P. Joannou, C. Leonardi, and P. Prodi (2nd edn., Freiburg, 1962).

Synder og pavemakt. Botsbrev fra den Norske Kirkeprovins og Suderøyene til Pavestolen 1438-1531, Diplomatarium Poenitentiariae Norvegicum, ed. Torstein Jørgensen and Gastone Saletnich (Stavanger, 2004).

Studies
Göller, Emil, *Die päpstliche Pönitentiarie von ihrem Ursprung bis zu ihrer Umgestaltung unter Pius V.* (Roma, 1907, 1911).

Ingesman, Per, 'The Apostolic Penitentiary and the Nordic Countries: The Importance of a New Source Material', in *Itinéraires du savoir de l'Italie à la Scandinavie (X^e-XVIe siècle): Études offertes à Elisabeth Mornet,* ed. C. Péneau (Paris, 2009), pp. 33-49.

Norberg, Rune, 'Resealtare', in *Kulturhistorisk leksikon for nordisk middelalder* 14 (2nd edn., Viborg, 1982), pp. 77-79.

Salonen, Kirsi, *The Penitentiary as a Well of Grace in the Late Middle Ages: The Example of the Province of Uppsala 1448–1527* (Saarijärvi, 2001).

Salonen, Kirsi, & Ludwig Schmugge, *A Sip from the 'Well of Grace': Medieval Texts from the Apostolic Penitentiary* (Washington D.C., 2009).

Salonen, Kirsi, & Jussi Hanska, *Entering a Clerical Career at the Roman Curia, 1458–1471* (Surrey, 2013).

Schmugge, Ludwig, *Kirche, Kinder, Karrieren. Päpstliche Dispense von der unehelichen Geburt im Spätmittelalter* (Zürich, 1995).

Schmugge, Ludwig, Patrick Hersperger & Béatrice Wiggenhauser, *Die Supplikenregister der päpstlichen Pönitentiarie aus der Zeit Pius' II. (1458–1464)* (Tübingen, 1996).

Concluding Remarks:
Monastic Culture in Northwestern Europe in the long thirteenth Century, c. 1150-1350

Brian Patrick McGuire

The Centre for Medieval Studies has now existed at the University of Southern Denmark in Odense for several decades and has succeeded every autumn in offering an international interdisciplinary symposium on an aspect of medieval life and culture. In 2011 the symposium was dedicated to monastic culture in northwestern Europe, and the thirteen papers published in this volume bear witness to the richness and variety of the sources and the research now taking place. Indeed, in looking back at my own contribution to monastic studies from the 1970s and 1980s, it is apparent how much new and valuable work is taking place. In what follows here I will briefly discuss the contents of the symposium and give the reader my own response to its results.

Professor Gert Melville of Dresden University was able to draw on a lifetime of research into monastic life and mentalities, in getting behind what he characterizes as "all those glossy coffee-table books" on monasticism. He combines in an eminent manner the material achievements of monastic life with its spiritual dimension. His central theme is reflected in the title of his paper, "the innovational power of monastic life in the Middle Ages". Professor Melville shows how monks "were adept at forming flexible and innovative solutions in order to attain their goals" . In so doing they insisted that the individual be subject to the community "for the sake of the perfection of one's spiritual welfare and salvation".

Such broad statements are backed up by an impressive array of footnotes, many of which refer to Melville's own publications or those of his colleagues and students, who over a number of years joined him at a centre for monastic studies at Eichstätt. Melville emphasizes the importance of the individual's examination of conscience in the monastic tradition and refers to the *meditationes piissimae* published in Migne's *Patrologia latina* under the works of Bernard but more indicative of late medieval monastic spirituality. He sees how monasticism combined two paths, that of organized community and that of the individual soul's salvation. Monasteries sought to find ways to deal with the self, and this development can be seen both in legal and in spiritual texts.

Professor Melville sees the Cistercian *Carta caritatis* as the first monastic constitution, formulating principles in a rational programme (p. 9). The organisation's "rationality" was intended to foster the individual's spiritual life, and Melville sees monastic organization as making it possible to have "a deeply internalized and often ecstatically lived spirituality" which could be realized "in a radical and even revolutionary way". He alternates between the individual and community in their contributions to each other: in this interchange he finds "internalized faith with the pragmatic organization of life". By providing this environment, monks in Melville's view served medieval society, in promising to "the extra-monastic world a security repository for investments both in piety and in the secular business of economy and politics". Monks were innovators, and their institutions "could profitably be transferred to the secular world". Religious fervour and strict institutional structures were combined in a "seeming paradox" of religiosity and "practical rationality". Professor Melville offered here a classic keynote paper, outlining many of the themes of the symposium. His work combines the interior life of monks and nuns with their communities' development and impact on society around them. It is a onerous task to do justice both to the material and spiritual dimensions of medieval life and to record their interactions, but Melville does so and goes beyond, showing how monastic institutions and individuals made possible the world in which we live.

The Danish Cistercian contribution

The work that I did on the Cistercians in Denmark in the 1970s, which led to the monograph, *The Cistercians in Denmark* (1982), has now been brought up to date by several fresh contributions. Kurt Villads Jensen, the head of the Centre in Odense and one of the organizers of this symposium, based his paper on manuscripts from Løgum abbey in Southern Jutland which are preserved at the Landesbibliothek in Halle. He has taken up the challenge from Anne Riising, whose doctoral thesis from 1969 remained for decades the only available work on medieval sermons in Denmark. Professor Jensen reviews the contents of the sermon manual copied in the late fourteenth century by the monk Peter at Løgum, and he surmises that it was a Cistercian who wrote the original sermons. The sermon manual reflects "a continuous meditation or a continuous dialogue which took place within the monastery". Thus the contents were intended not for the laity, who would have been nourished in a more pedagogical manner, but the monastic community, which was used to ruminating over Biblical texts and considering their possible implications.

Professor Jensen asks why there is little about penitence and assumes that this near silence is a result of the fact that life in the monastery was penitential in itself and so the practice did not require "to be further elaborated upon". The author makes excellent use of the Swedish professor Alf Härdelin's understanding of monastic theology: monks made use of clusters of words or pictures, meditated on them, and demonstrated their implications. These results led to "some basic themes of action". Kurt Villads Jensen shows how the collection was meant for the monks themselves and not for outside preaching. Thus the sermons allow us to approach "the lived life and mental world of the Cistercians in Løgum". I agree, and this paper in itself makes it clear that we are just beginning to appreciate the place of sermons in monastic and pastoral life in medieval Denmark. In this area the Swedes, with their wonderful Vadstena collection, are far ahead of us.

Eric Delaissé from the Catholic University of Louvain presents another aspect of Danish Cistercian life in his study of contacts between Danish monasteries and the Flemish abbey of Ter Doest. This monastery's geographical placement meant that it was a strategic stopping place for Scandinavian clergy and especially abbots on their way south, as in attending the General Chapter at Cîteaux in Burgundy. Delaissé has looked at the sources found today at the Grand Séminaire at Bruges, beginning in 1225. He detects a Danish period from 1225-1266, a Swedish one from 1273-83 and a Norwegian one from 1282-1300. For the Danish Cistercians he sees contacts with Esrum and Sorø on Zealand as well as with Holme on Funen and Løgum in Southern Jutland. These sources tell of sums of money entrusted for safekeeping to Ter Doest, which does not seem to have functioned as a modern bank in taking or giving interest but simply took on the obligation out of a sense of solidarity within the Cistercian Order.

For Sweden we hear of an abbot of Alvastra on his way to the General Chapter who became ill and died at Ter Doest. Otherwise Ter Doest appears mainly in terms of its willingness to look after sums of money. The references to Swedish churchmen, however, for the most part refer to bishops or their chaplains and not to monks. The same is the case with Ter Doest's contacts with Norway. The archbishop of Trondheim in 1282 deposited a sum through his clerk, and other Norwegian bishops also had contacts with the Cistercian house.

For the three Scandinavian monarchies, it is only for Denmark that the records of Ter Doest provide information about the activities of the Cistercians. Contacts ended after the last decades of the thirteenth century, probably as a result of the problems the Cistercians experienced in Denmark at this time, with families that refused to hand over lands willed to the monasteries by their ancestors and bishops making demands on the monks. Delaissé assumes that the abbots attended the General Chapter less frequently, and he refers to my own conclusion from 1982, that the Danish houses became more isolated. In a larger sense the economic crises of the fourteenth century also seem to have limited contacts not only between Danish Cistercian houses and Ter Doest but also between Swedish and Norwegian ecclesiastics and the Flemish abbey.

The most interesting result of this study is found in its final sentence: even if Ter Doest in its contacts with Scandinavia mainly had financial dealings, it "had no financial interest for itself". The transfer of money was, as it were, "on the house", a far cry from the financial institutions of today which generally take a hefty payment for even the most banal services to their customers. In these sources for Ter Doest we see the functioning of the Cistercian Order, bonds between Scandinavian Cistercians and Southern Europe, and the willingness of an abbey to function as a financial facilitator.

For a much later period, the last medieval decades leading up to the coming of the Reformation in Denmark in the 1520s, Kirsi Salonen from the University of Turku in Finland provides a fascinating journey through the Apostolic Penitentiary's records. This "tribunal of conscience" established by the papacy in the thirteenth century provides information especially in the later Middle Ages that sheds light on Cistercian life. We hear how in the later fifteenth century a Cistercian monk received a dispensation for his illegitimate birth in order to function as a priest. In 1468 there is the case of a Cistercian nun who had left her monastery at Slangerup in Northern Zealand and then regretted her decision. She wanted to return and was given permission to do so. Another such case is that of Nicolaus Olaij, who joined an unnamed Cistercian monastery in Denmark but had difficulties with the brethren and was expelled. He joined the Dominicans and in 1511 asked the Penitentiary to remain there, in spite of his apostasy. We are on the very threshold of the Protestant Reformation, but monastic life in Denmark seems to be proceeding as usual.

The Penitentiary's sources provide insight into a number of individual lives in the Cistercian houses of Denmark and thus shed light on a period where other sources are much less abundant. In my monograph on the Cistercians in Denmark, I stopped soon after 1400, for I found that narrative sources had virtually disappeared, while Professor Salonen here has provided new material about how the Order functioned and individual monks and nuns tried to reconcile their actions and needs with the requirements of monastic life. Kirsi Salonen concludes that the monks and nuns in these sources demonstrate "great devotional fervour", and thus she counters the long-standing myth that the monasteries in the last medieval century were decadent and had lost touch with their original ideals.

One narrative source that I was able to use in my study of Cistercian monasticism in Denmark was the thirteenth-century biography of Bishop Gunner of Viborg, who was the first abbot of Øm Abbey before he was headhunted in 1222 for the episcopal office. Sigga Engsbro of University of Southern Denmark reviews the genre of biography in its medieval context and also looks back on classical models. She takes me to task for an article on Gunner's biography from

1983, when I concluded that there were no viable models for its composition. Instead she points to the writings of Bernard of Clairvaux in terms of the ideals he outlined for the good bishop, and she suggests the likelihood that an immediate literary model may have been Adam of Bremen's *Gesta Hammaburgensis*. This possibility I did consider but rejected. Her paper reviews the question anew, comes to a different result, and thus provides a fresh perspective for appreciating the Gunner biography. It is more beholden to the historical genre of *gesta* than a conventional *vita* in the hagiographical tradition.

I also stand corrected on the theme of *magnanimitas* (a spirit of great generosity) in the Life of Gunner, which Sigga Engsbro sees as being found in other bishops' biographies from the tenth century onwards. She sees the origins of this virtue in Cicero's writings, in contrast to my attempt to show a parallel between scholastic views of the theme derivative of Aristotle's *Ethics*. Here it is encouraging to see a new generation continuing – and correcting – the work I once did. I remember how isolated I felt as a scholar in the Danish milieu. I sent it to the journal *Analecta Cisterciensia*, where it was very quickly published, but there was virtually no interest at the time in Denmark in what I considered to be a remarkable and revealing source showing the contents of one life. Sigga Engsbro's paper shows that at least in Odense there has been a much-needed opening in medieval studies to the individual in his (or her) historical context.

Perhaps the most fruitful contribution Engsbro makes concerns the use of the American medievalist Thomas Noble's phrase "secular sanctity". According to this ideal, lay persons can become saints, and the medieval writer makes an effort to show the qualities that contribute to this state of holiness. Sigga Engsbro might have traced this attempt back to Odo of Cluny's superb tenth century portrait of Count Gerald of Aurillac. As she shows, what is important "is not a saint in the traditional mould…but rather a public figure who through his perfect exercise of office….will attain salvation" (p. 17). This is an apt description of Count Gerald as well as of Bishop Gunner.

Another paper which has a strong Danish Cistercian content is Thomas Riis's "Monasteries as Cultural Centres: The Case of Schleswig-Holstein with Lübeck and Hamburg". He traces the intellectual interests of the Benedictine monastery of Saint John's in Lübeck and the Cistercian house at Ryd in Schleswig. Both monasteries showed an interest in the writing of history: Arnold of Lübeck followed the Danish expansion in the Baltic in the later twelfth and early thirteenth century, while the Ryd Annals provide one of our best narrative sources for the thirteenth century. Thomas Riis shows how the Latin version of the annals and the first Danish version are more anti-German than later Danish ones. Thanks to these annals we get a sense of the author's outlook and indirectly thus can follow the mentalities of Benedictines and Cistercians on the periphery of medieval Denmark and Germany. The Ryd annalist is remarkable for his anti-German prejudice.

While most of the papers in this volume can be classified under the broad category of history of mentalities, Christian Lovén, formerly of the University of Gothenburg and now at Hallands Museum for Cultural History, provides an approach to Swedish and Danish monastic sources in terms of patronage and takes a more legalistic view. His point of departure is the German term *Eigenklöster*, but he considers rights over church property in the context of Susan Wood's study from 2006, *The Proprietary Church in the Medieval West*. He shows how the founders and donors of twelfth century Benedictine and Cistercian abbeys in the two kingdoms often did not hand over the land on which these monasteries were built. The donors seem to have maintained their rights over these properties for some time after the initial foundation. Lovén speaks of monasteries "on unfree ground", a phenomenon he does not find elsewhere in Western Europe. One wonders how or why Danish and Swedish Cistercians and Benedictines accepted this situation, but eventually most abbeys did obtain the full ownership of these primary areas.

With this perspective Lovén offers a revised understanding of how lay patrons presumably continued to exercise a degree of control over the monasteries they helped to found. The author concedes that the very concept of ownership varies tremendously, and it is not clear whether the monks considered their benefactors to be entitled to some degree of control over the lands they had handed over to the monks. As Lovén writes in his conclusion, "The founder gave land but at the same time withheld the monastery site itself". It is only at the end of the period, in the thirteenth century, that the monasteries "reached a basic freedom from lay influence". For those of us who think of the development of monasticism and other ecclesiastical institutions in Scandinavia as parallel with developments elsewhere in Western Europe, Lovén's paper provides a question: was lay patronage so very different and more persistent here than elsewhere?

The Cistercians in Sweden

The Cistercians were, as Catharina Andersson of Umeå University points out, the first monastic order in Sweden. They came from Clairvaux, and by about 1250 there were twelve houses for men and women in the kingdom. Andersson has to deal with the sparse written sources that characterize medieval Sweden, at least until the time of Saint Birgitta, but she has enough material to establish that the Cistercian prohibition of child oblates was probably also followed there. The few cases that may indicate children being accepted into monasteries do not indicate a widespread practice. At the same time she establishes that monks came from the lower aristocracy, as they did elsewhere in Europe. Here Swedish developments are similar to what we find in Champagne and Burgundy, where we benefit especially from the researches of the American medievalist Constance Bouchard. Professor Andersson shows that many monks first were secular priests before they entered the monastery. One can wonder if they sought the quiet and order of monastic existence in order to get away from the demands and possible chaos of parish life! It could be added that the same phenomenon takes place today in the American Trappist-Cistercian monasteries I know: they regularly get vocations from burnt-out parish priests looking for an alternative way of life in prayer, work and community.

One of the most intriguing themes of this article is Catharina Andersson's considerations on "conflicting masculine ideals" in terms of the way manliness was perceived in Swedish medieval society. She draws on a rich literature from 1994 onwards dealing with the expression of masculinity in history, and she contrasts the Cistercian way of life with that of the Order of St. John. I think it is commendable that she allows herself to move into an area that, at least for medieval Sweden, with so few sources must remain speculative. Her approach makes it possible to see the Swedish Cistercians in a European perspective. I would add here that her study of the monks is indebted to James France's 1992 monograph, *The Cistercians in Scandinavia*. This study has been well received by contemporary monastic scholars. Its comparative approach is invaluable for understanding the success of the order in establishing itself in places which the first monks, according to the *Exordium magnum cisterciense*, considered to be totally unsuitable for their way of life.

Another contribution to this volume from Elisabet Regner considers "networks, contacts and change in Alvastra Abbey, c. 1185-1350". She goes back to the renowned Cistercian historian Louis Lekai in his seminal 1977 study that looked upon the interaction of ideals and realities in the history of the order. At the same time she makes use of archaeological finds and thus gives this volume a welcome material content. Her article's very first sentence mentions some of the objects archaeologists have found at Alvastra: "...pilgrim badges from Spain, German stoneware, French ivory carvings, Norwegian coins and seals owned by Swedish nobility". She then traces the history of the excavations at Alvastra since the nineteenth century: here as unfortunately can be the case, a centrally placed archaeologist never wrote the comprehensive report that was awaited from his work. Moving from here to the written sources, Regner traces "a network of friends and benefactors". She considers especially the burials inside and outside the abbey church, since lay persons who invested in the abbey came to insist that after death their remains were to be placed close to the monks. Thus the later Middle Ages saw more burials in the abbey church, a practice that the early Cistercians tried to limit to the founders of monasteries.

The article also touches on the architecture of the abbey buildings in terms of the classic Cistercian plan, and it considers the evidence for trade and international contacts at Alvastra. Elisabet Regner concludes that the monks adapted to new circumstances by accepting lay persons as members of the Cistercian fraternity. I found a similar development in later medieval Danish Cistercian sources, and it would be useful to study the phenomenon on a European basis, in trying to understand how the Cistercians, who in the twelfth century valued being far from the madding crowd, in the last medieval centuries opened their monasteries to lay persons who could benefit them. This article sees such a development in terms of the contrast between the relative stability of the monasteries in the thirteenth century and the changes of the fourteenth, when economic and political crises made their existence much more precarious.

The Dominican surge

The Dominicans in many ways took over from the Cistercians in the thirteenth century as the darlings of the ecclesiastical establishment, and they are represented in this book by two scholars who have frequented University of Southern Denmark at Odense: Johannes Schütz, who was a doctoral student from Göttingen, and Johnny Grandjean Gøgsig Jakobsen, who completed his doctorate at University of Southern Denmark's Medieval Centre and is now a lecturer at Copenhagen University. Schütz demonstrates with great clarity how the Dominicans distinguished themselves as experts in the care of souls, in accord with the aspirations of the Fourth Lateran Council to bring the Gospel to as many baptized Christians as possible. In order to illustrate this commitment, Schütz provides the case of Mathias Ripensis, Matthew of Ribe, in his sermons on wealth and poverty. Thus, as with Kurt Villads Jensen's paper, we have a fresh use of a neglected type of source, the sermon, which is seen as revealing the mentality of a group – for Jensen the Cistercians, for Schütz the Dominicans. He indicates how Mathias makes good use of the stories of Lazarus and the rich man as well as of the emperor Theodosius in order to give historical and theological context to the teachings of the Church. The Dominicans were able through giving sermons, as well as in hearing confessions, to care for the pastoral needs of the laity.

Johnny Jakobsen is concerned not with Dominican preaching but with patronage: "Who ordered the Dominicans?". He asks who sponsored the foundation of the order's houses in Northern Europe from about 1216 and until 1350. He has the advantage of the research he did for his doctoral thesis, but this limited itself mainly to the Danish Dominicans, while he branches out here to the whole of Northern Europe and indicates that he would be able to provide a splendid monograph on this subject, which lacks the study once promised by the legendary Dominican scholar Jarl Gallen.

The Dominicans made themselves useful to lay rulers, and one might think that cathedral clergy would have been jealous of their popularity. Jakobsen, however, shows convincingly that canons were among the most avid patrons of the friars, while urban burghers showed little interest in the Dominicans until the fifteenth century. The old history of conflict between the mendicants and the secular clergy hardly applies in Jakobsen's narrative, which instead of emphasizing the Dominicans as rivals of the cathedral clergy shows how they were often perceived as allies. It is delightful how in this article the author can move from one country to another in illustrating common themes and demonstrate how the Dominicans made themselves useful in the later medieval Church.

Outriders: Norwegian and English monks

The symposium was given further geographical and monastic context thanks to the contributions of Eldbjørg Haug and Mia Münster-Swendsen. The first looks at "Augustinian canons and Benedictine monks in the medieval Stavanger diocese". Eldbjørg Haug, professor at the University of Bergen, has done seminal work on the Augustinian convent of Utstein. She has to deal with a lack of contemporary sources for this house, as well as in dealing with the foundation of Saint Olav in Stavanger, a Benedictine monastery until at least 1171. Her contribution reviews the historiography of monastic life in Norway, and she shows how difficult it is to draw any firm conclusions about the country's monasteries. As for Saint Olav's, she detects influence from the cathedral priory of Winchester, but also here the sources can be challenged and different interpretations emerge. There is no doubt, however, that Norwegian monasticism benefited from English contacts. Two of the three Cistercian houses of the country were founded by the English.

Professor Haug concludes that Saint Olav's may have been founded with priests who looked after a relic of the Winchester saint, Swithun, but she admits that "new evidence may tear down the synthesis that I have presented". As in so much else in Scandinavian medieval history, we poke around in the dark and try to find relationships and explanations when little written source material is available. For Mia Münster-Swendsen, then of Copenhagen University, now at Roskilde, there is not a dearth of sources, but what we do have is eminently confusing. Professor Münster Swendsen draws on earlier work on the "Two Lawrences of Durham" and sees them both in terms of "an intricate web of friends". It is a pleasure to see how she makes use of the concept of friendship and its practice, which I dealt with in my study from 1988, and like a detective she follows her Lawrences through a maze of sources but never abandons friendship as a unifying theme.

The most exciting aspect of the article I find in her comparison of Aelred of Rievaulx's view and experience of friendship with that of the Lawrence who wrote the *Consolatio* on the death of a friend. She sees the latter as "a troubled man", verging on despair, who was "more a courtier than a monk", engaged in "almost perpetual conflict". Certainly Aelred had his conflicts, and the almost complete silence about him in the decades after his death at Rievaulx suggests that his practice of friendship was not appreciated. As I showed in my biography of Aelred from 1994, his immediate legacy was meagre. It is only in the twentieth century that there began to grow up an appreciation of Aelred's contribution to the literature of friendship. Mia Münster-Swendsen sees the difficult side of one of her Lawrences, but Aelred's "warmth and humanity" remain unquestioned.

We can be grateful to Professor Münster-Swendsen for unravelling a complex story and putting it in the context of monastic friendship. Prior Lawrence of Durham emphasized friendship as valuable in itself, while he made use of his friends "in the making of his personal career". The other Lawrence, who became abbot at Westminster, benefited from his network of friendship. England in the middle of the twelfth century witnessed "fierce political and ecclesiastical conflicts". Amid these Professor Münster-Swendsen finds "the functioning of monastic friendship-networks in creating, accelerating and solving disputes".

Conclusion: History is everything

Years ago my Oxford D.Phil. supervisor, Richard W. Southern, said to me with a smile, "History is everything". In reading through these contributions to the Odense 2011 symposium I have thought of these words and seen how they ring true in the context of medieval Scandinavian monastic life and culture. In monasticism we come to a crossroads of medieval society, with monks responding to the needs and yearnings of a much larger population, contributing to networks of friends, jockeying for political protection and patronage, and preserving and protecting a material and spiritual heritage in lands, manuscripts, and buildings. Thanks to the monks and nuns we gain an impression of the thoughts and feelings of our long-dead ancestors and see how their ingenuity and determination were blessed with a spiritual dimension that can still repel or fascinate and attract new generations.

In 1977 when a seminar on Scandinavian life took place at Løgumkloster Højskole (its contributions were never published), some of the participants echoed the old Protestant prejudice against monasticism as not being a genuinely Christian way of life. Celibacy, obedience, and devotion to a daily round of communal prayer were all considered to be a wrongful way of living as followers of Christ, and monks were looked upon as selfish people who shut themselves away from the real world. Today, thankfully, such prejudices about the dark Middle Ages and its ignorant monks are limited to much more ignorant politicians and journalists who revel in the old view. For anyone who has followed recent historical research and writing in Scandinavia and elsewhere, it is clear that monastic life and culture provide a way to study the medieval past and its relevance for us today. Certainly Professor Melville's article shows how this is done, but the other articles in this collection also provide inspiration and stimulus.

It is common for historians when they grow older to formulate the attitude, *Après moi, le déluge*. I remember how Richard Southern frowned upon the changes of the 1970s and felt that the world he had known and loved was collapsing, as one evening on the Walking Street in Copenhagen when we dined at a restaurant and he asked me to change places so that he did not have to look down at the neon lights of a porn shop. Southern, born in 1912, could not accept the "liberating" movements of the 1970s, just as I, born in 1946, cannot accept the "liberating" movements of Facebook and Twitter. I remain aloof, but I refuse to believe that the world I leave behind is a worse place than the one that made me. The fruits of this symposium point to the vivacity and dedication of new generations of historians in meeting and interpreting our medieval friends. It was a privilege for me to be present at the symposium and I hope that the publication of its proceedings will be useful and enlightening for anyone interested in rediscovering our common spiritual and material heritage in medieval monastic life.

Bibliography of Brian Patrick McGuire's published Works

(not including reviews, minor articles for encyclopedias, and newspaper articles)

1973 "Property and politics at Esrum Abbey, 1151-1251", *Mediaeval Scandinavia* (Odense) 6, pp. 122-50.

1974 "Love, Friendship and Sex in the Eleventh Century: The Experience of Anselm", *Studia Theologica* (Oslo, Norway) 28, pp. 111-152.

"Patrons, Privileges, Property: Sorø Abbey's first half-century", *Kirkehistoriske Samlinger* (Copenhagen), pp. 5-39.

1976 "God-Man and the Devil in Medieval Theology and Culture", *Cahiers de l'Institut du moyen-âge grec et latin* (Copenhagen 1976), pp. 18-82 (Trans. into Greek in *Epopteia* 87, 1984, pp. 109-50).

Conflict and Continuity at Øm Abbey. A Cistercian Experience in Medieval Denmark (Museum Tusculanum. Opuscula graecolatina 8, Copenhagen), 152 pp.

1978 "The collapse of a monastic friendship: The case of Jocelin and Samson of Bury", *Journal of Medieval History* 4, pp. 369-97.

"Clairvaux og Nordens cisterciensere i 1100-tallet" (Clairvaux and the Cistercians of the North in the twelfth century) *Løgumkloster Studier* 1, pp. 11-29.

1979 "Structure and consciousness in the *Exordium Magnum Cisterciense*: The Clairvaux Cistercians after Bernard", *Cahiers de l'Institut du moyen-âge grec et latin* 30, pp. 33-90.

English translation, *Universitas Studii Hafniensis: Stiftelsesdokumenter og Statutter 1479* (foundation documents), published by Copenhagen University with Jan Pinborg (Copenhagen), 148 pp.

Editor, *Kulturblomstring og samfundskrise i 1300-tallet* (Center for Europæiske Middelalderstudier, Copenhagen University, reprinted C.A. Reitzel, Copenhagen 1985), 204 pp.

"Dante i Paradis: Det følsomme menneske midt i samfundets krise" in *Kulturblomstring og samfundskrise*, pp. 86-107.

"Efterskrift - Johan Huizinga, Barbara Tuchman og os andre: Hvad skal vi med 1300-tallets krise og blomstring?" in *Kulturblomstring*, pp. 193-204.

"Written Sources and Cistercian Inspiration in Caesarius of Heisterbach", *Analecta Cisterciensia* 35, pp. 227-82.

1980 "Friends and Tales in the Cloister: Oral Sources in Caesarius of Heisterbach's *Dialogus miraculorum*", *Analecta Cisterciensia* 36, pp. 167-247

1981 "The Cistercians and the Transformation of Monastic Friendships", *Analecta Cisterciensia* 37, pp. 1-63.

"Caesar of Heisterbach and the Cistercians as Medieval People", *Noble Piety and Reformed Monasticism*, ed. E. Rozanne Elder. Studies in Medieval Cistercian History 7 (Cistercian Publications: Kalamazoo, Michigan), pp. 81-108.

"Eskild og hans farbrødre" *MIV: Museerne i Viborg Amt* 11, pp. 82-85.

1982 *The Cistercians in Denmark: Attitudes, Roles and Functions in Medieval Society.* Cistercian Studies 35 (Cistercian Publications: Kalamazoo, Michigan), pp. 421.

Triviallitteratur og samfund i latinsk middelalder: Caesarius af Heisterbach (Center for Europæiske Middelalderstudier, Copenhagen), 213 pp.

"Ungdom og omvendelse til munkelivet hos cistercienserne 1153-1223", *Løgumkloster Studier* 3, pp. 7-33, with English summary, pp. 34-5.

1983 "A Lost Clairvaux Exemplum Collection Found: The *Liber visionum et miraculorum* compiled under Prior John of Clairvaux 1171-79", *Analecta Cisterciensia* 39, pp. 26-62.

"The Cistercians and the Rise of the Exemplum in early thirteenth-century France: A Reevaluation of Paris BN MS lat. 15912", *Classica et Mediaevalia* 34 (Copenhagen), pp. 211-67.

"Monastic and Episcopal Biography in the Thirteenth Century: The Danish Cistercian Account of Bishop Gunner of Viborg", *Analecta Cisterciensia* 39, pp. 195-230.

1985 "Manderollen og lærerrollen på universitetet". *Gamle og Nye: Fra forelæser til projektvejleder*, ed. Karen Borgnakke, Per Fibæk Laursen, Chresten Kruchev (Institut for pædagogik, København), pp. 161-70.

Preface to Kirsten Grubb Jensen, *Mennesker og Idealer i Giovanni Boccacios Decameron* (Center for Europæiske Middelalderstudier, Copenhagen University), pp. 7-8.

"Was Bernard a Friend?" *Goad and Nail: Studies in Medieval Cistercian History* X, ed. E. Rozanne Elder (Cistercian Publications, Kalamazoo), pp. 201-27.

"Why Scandinavia? Bernard, Eskil and Cistercian Expansion in the North 1140-80", *Goad and Nail*, pp. 251-81.

"Monastic Friendship and Toleration in Twelfth-century Cistercian Life", *Monks, Hermits and the Ascetic Tradition* (Studies in Church History 22), ed. W. J. Sheils (The Ecclesiastical History Society. Blackwell, Oxford), pp. 147-160.

"A Changed Face of Aelred? A New Attribution of Sermons to the Abbot of Rievaulx", *The Downside Review* (London), pp. 147-50.

"Anders Sunesen og klostervæsenet: kontinuitet eller brud?", *Anders Sunesen: Stormand, teolog, administrator, digter*, ed. Sten Ebbesen (Center for Europæiske Middelalderstudier, København), pp. 27-41.

1986 Editor, *Mennesker i Danmarks og Europas Middelalder*. (Center for Europæiske Middelalderstudier and C.A. Reitzel, Copenhagen), 350 pp.

"Aelred af Rievaulx. Kærlighedens og selverkendelsens ven", *Mennesker i Danmarks og Europas Middelalder*, pp. 21-37.

"Er der mennesker i Middelalderen?", *Mennesker i Danmarks og Europas Middelalder*, pp. 253-67.

"Looking Back on Friendship: Medieval Experience and Modern Context", *Cistercian Studies* 21 (Trappist, Kentucky), pp. 123-42.

"A Letter of Passionate Friendship by Guibert of Gembloux" (with John Benton, California Institute of Technology), *Cahiers de l'Institut du Moyen-âge grec et latin* 53 (Copenhagen), pp. 3-14.

1987 Editor, *War and Peace in the Middle Ages* (Center for Europæiske Middelalderstudier and C.A. Reitzel, Copenhagen).

"Introduction", *War and Peace in the Middle Ages*, 7-12.

"The Church and the Control of Violence in the Early Middle Ages. Friendship and Peace in the Letters of Gerbert, 982-997", *War and Peace in the Middle Ages*, pp. 29-55.

"Introduktion", *Iran, Islam og Vesten i Middelalderen*, red. Kurt Villads Jensen (Center for Europæiske Middelalderstudier. Museum Tusculanums Forlag. Copenhagen), pp. 5-9.

"Forord" and "Morderiske munke i *Rosens Navn* overfor den europæiske middelalders munke", *Om Rosens Navn*, red. Kirsten Grubb Jensen (Center for Europæiske Middelalderstudier. Copenhagen), pp. 7-8, 25-42.

1988 *Friendship and Community: The Monastic Experience 350-1250* (Cistercian Studies 85: Cistercian Publications: Kalamazoo, Michigan), 571 pp. Reprinted 2010, Cornell University Press, with a new introductory chapter covering research since the 1980s.

"Rebirth and Responsibility: Cistercian Stories from the Late Twelfth Century", *Cahiers de l'Institut du Moyen-âge grec et latin* 57 (Copenhagen), pp. 148-58.

"Daily Life in Danish Medieval Monasteries", *Medium Aevum Quotidianum* 15 (Krems, Austria), pp. 14-22.

"Peopling Solitude: Petrarch in Crisis Years 1346-50", *A Literary miscellany. Presented to Eric Jacobsen*, ed. Graham D. Caie and Holger Nørgaard (Publications of the Department of English vol 16. University of Copenhagen), pp. 17-31.

"Taking Responsibility: Medieval Cistercian Abbots and Monks as their Brother's Keepers", *Cîteaux: Commentarii Cistercienses* 39, pp. 249-69.

1989 "The First Cistercian Renewal and a Changing Image of Saint Bernard", *Cistercian Studies* 24 (Gethsemani, Kentucky), pp. 25-49.

"Purgatory, the Communion of Saints, and Medieval Change", *Viator: Medieval and Renaissance Studies* 20 (Center for Medieval and Renaissance Studies, University of California, Los Angeles), pp. 61-84.

"Østens ørkenfædre og Vestens efterligninger", in *Europa og de fremmede i middelalderen*, ed. Kurt Villads Jensen (Center for Europæiske Middelalderstudier, Copenhagen University), pp. 11-26.

"Efterskrift. Festung Europa og de usynliggjorte flygtninge", *Europa og de fremmede*, pp. 225-34.

"Holy Women and Monks in the Thirteenth Century: Friendship or Exploitation?", *Vox Benedictina* 6 (Peregrina: Toronto, Canada), pp. 343-73.

1990 "Spiritual Life and Material Life in the Middle Ages: A Contradiction?", *Mensch und Objekt im Mittelalter und in der Frühen Neuzeit . Leben--Alltag--Kultur. Veröffentlichungen des Instituts für Realienkunde des Mittelalters und der Frühen Neuzeit* 13 (Wien), pp. 285-313.

"Denys of Ryckel's Debt to Bernard of Clairvaux", *Die Ausbreitung kartäusischen Leb-*

ens und Geistes im Mittelalter. Band 1. *Analecta Cartusiana,* ed. James Hogg 63 (Salzburg), pp. 13-34.

"Visioner, venskab og fællesskab hos 1200-tallets hellige kvinder", *Dansk Udsyn* 70 (Askov højskole), pp. 100-18.

1991 *The Difficult Saint: Bernard of Clairvaux and his Tradition* (Cistercian Publications: Kalamazoo, Michigan), 317 pp.

Editor, *Autoritet i middelalderen* (Center for Europæiske Middelalderstudier and C.A. Reitzel, Copenhagen), 200 pp.

"Lyt nu mit barn. Autoritet og oprør i 1100-tallets Vesteuropa", *Autoritet i middelalderen,* pp. 11-34.

"Autoritetsformer i middelalderen og i dag. Opsummering og tilbageblik", *Autoritet i middelalderen,* pp. 183-200.

1992 "An Introduction to the *Exordium Magnum Cisterciense*", *Cistercian Studies Quarterly* 27, pp. 277-98. Trans. into French by Joseph Longton, in Conrad d'Eberbach, *Le grande exorde de Cîteaux ou récit des débuts de l'ordre cistercien,* publié sous la direction de Jacques Berlioz (Brepols/Cîteaux Commentarii cistercienses, 1998), pp. xi-xxxv.

«Lebanese Asylum Applicants in Denmark 1985-1988: Political Refugees or War Emigrants?», *The Lebanese in the World: A Century of Emigration,* ed. Albert Hourani and Nadim Shehadi (Centre for Lebanese Studies and I.B. Tauris, London), pp. 661-84.

1993 "Friendship in Birgitta of Vadstena: Tradition or Renewal?", in *Heliga Birgitta--budskapet och förebilden,* red. Alf Härdelin och Merethe Lindgren. Kung. Vitterhets Historie och Antikvitets Akademien. Konferenser 28 (Stockholm: Almqvist & Wiksell), pp. 153-174.

"Self-Denial and Self-Assertion in Arnulf of Villers", *Cistercian Studies Quarterly* 28, pp. 241-59.

"Loving the Holy Order: Jean Gerson and the Carthusians", *Die Kartäuser und Ihre Welt--Kontakte und Gegenseitige Einflüsse* Band 1, *Analecta Cartusiana,* ed. James Hogg (Salzburg), pp. 100-139.

"La présence de Bernard de Clairvaux dans l'*Exordium Magnum Cisterciense*", *Vies et légendes de Saint Bernard,* ed. Patrick Arabeyre, Jacques Berlioz et Philippe Poirrier. Présence cistercienne. Cîteaux, Commentarii Cistercienses, pp. 63-83.

"Munken, ridderen, bonden: Dannelsesbegreb i middelalderen", *Tidsskriftet Den Frie Lærerskole* 40 (Ollerup), pp. 31-36

1994 *A Guide to Medieval Denmark/Guide til Middelalderens Danmark,* trans. into Danish by Ann Kirstin Pedersen (C.A. Reitzel, Copenhagen), 240 pp.

Brother and Lover: Aelred of Rievaulx (Crossroad Publishers: New York), 186 pp.

Autoritet i middelalderen, (Center for Europæiske Middelalderstudier and C.A. Reitzel, Copenhagen), 200 pp.

"A Saint's Afterlife. Bernard in the Golden Legend and in Other Medieval Collections", *Bernhard von Clairvaux. Rezeption und Wirkung im Mittelalter und in der Neuzeit,* ed. Kaspar Elm (Harrassowitz Verlag: Wiesbaden), pp. 179-211.

"Sexual Awareness and Identity in Aelred of Rievaulx, 1110-67", *The American Benedictine Review* 45, pp. 184-226.

1995 "Venskab og kærlighed i historiens lys", *Kritisk Forum for praktisk teologi* 61 (Copenhagen), pp. 20-31.

"Jean Gerson, the Carthusians, and the Experience of Mysticism", *The Mystical Tradition and the Carthusians* 3, ed. James Hogg, *Analecta Cartusiana* 130 (Salzburg, Austria), pp. 61-86.

"Integration: fra inferno til utopi", *Kultur og politik i dansk og europæisk perspektiv*, ed. Niels I. Meyer, Peter Johannes Schjødt og Pia Krogh Christoffersen (Copenhagen, Fremad), pp. 14-21.

"Who Founded the Order of Cîteaux?", *The Joy of Learning and the Love of God: Studies in Honor of Jean Leclercq*, ed. E. Rozanne Elder (Cistercian Publications: Kalamazoo, Michigan), pp. 389-414.

"The Meaning of Cistercian Spirituality: Thoughts for Cîteaux's Nine-Hundredth Anniversary", *Cistercian Studies Quarterly* 30, pp. 91-110. German translation as "Gibt es eine spezifische Zisterzienser-Spiritualität?", *Cistercienser Chronik* 104 (Bernardus-Verlag, Zisterzienserkonvent Langwaden: 1997), pp. 337-57. Trans. into Spanish, "El Significado de la Espiritualidad Cisterciense: Pensamientos para el IX Centenario de Cîteaux", *Cistercium* 210 (1998), pp. 241-66.

1996 Editor, *The Birth of Identities: Denmark and Europe in the Middle Ages* (C. A. Reitzel and Center for Europæiske Middelalderstudier, Copenhagen), 363 pp.

"Archbishop Eskil and Danish Identity", *The Birth of Identities*, pp. 189-212.

"Afterword: An Embarrassment of Identities", *The Birth of Identities*, pp. 345-60.

"Education, Confession and Pious Fraud: Jean Gerson and a Late Medieval Change", *The American Benedictine Review* 47, pp. 310-338.

1997 "Late Medieval Care and Control of Women: Jean Gerson and his Sisters", *Revue d'histoire ecclésiastique* 92 (Louvain), pp. 5-37.

"Idealer og munkevæsen i europæisk middelalder (Ideals and monasticism in the European Middle Ages)", *Idealer i religion og religionsforskning*, ed. Lene Buck, Oluf Schönbeck (Copenhagen University), pp. 37-47.

"Esrum Kloster: forhistorien og grundlæggelsen", *Bogen om Esrum Kloster*, ed. Søren Frandsen, Jens Anker Jørgensen, Chr. Gorm Tortzen (Frederiksborg Amt), pp. 12-29.

"Sexual Control and Spiritual Growth in the Late Middle Ages: The Case of Jean Gerson", in *Tradition and Ecstasy: The Agony of the Fourteenth Century*, ed. Nancy van Deusen (Institute of Mediaeval Music, Ottawa, Canada), pp. 123-52.

"Flugten fra flygtninge", *Højskolebladet* 16, pp. 252-54.

"Erslev revisited", *Rubicon* 5 (Center for Historie. Odense Universitet, 1997), pp. 4-7.

1998 *Jean Gerson. Early Works*, introduction and translations. Classics of Western Spirituality (Paulist Press, Mahwah, New Jersey, 1998), 482 pp.

«Les mentalités des cisterciens dans les recueils d'exempla du XIIe siècle: Une nouvelle lecture du *Liber visionum et miraculorum* de Clairvaux», in Jacques Berlioz et Marie Anne Polo de Beaulieu, *Les Exempla médiévaux: Nouvelles perspectives* (Honoré Champion Éditeur, Paris), pp. 107-45.

«Danskernes kirke og det nye Danmark», *Dansk Kirkeliv 1998*, 86-88.

"Den ny middelalder: Fra klassekamp til mentalitetshistorie", *Noter. Historielærer-*

foreningen for Gymnasiet og HF 139, pp. 9-14.

"Kristen humanisme: Om behovet for moderne klosterfællesskaber", *Højskolebladet* 2, pp. 3-4.

"*Shining forth like the Dawn*: Jean Gerson's Sermon to the Carthusians", in Carolyn Muessig, ed., *Medieval Monastic Preaching* (London, Boston, Köln: Brill), pp. 37-52.

"Bisperne, flygtninge og kirkens historie", *Arken: Det Teologiske Fakultets Studenterblad* 20, pp. 61-64.

"Making history: Min vej ind i kilderne", in Tove Elisabeth Kruse (red.), *Bud på Historien* (Frederiksberg: Roskilde Universitetsforlag), pp. 19-30.

"Kristen mystik i historisk belysning", *Ikon* 25, pp. 4-6.

1999 "Middelalderens relevans", *Den lyse middelalder. Ti Foredrag om kristen spiritualitet*, red. Hans Jørgen Frederiksen og Kirsten Kjærulff (Forlaget Anis: Frederiksberg), pp. 9-22.

Europa 1000-1300 (with Kim Esmark) (Roskilde Universitetsforlag). 330 pp. Swedish translation: *Tusen År i Europa. Band I 1000-1300.* (Historiska Media, Lund), 363 pp.

"Middelalderstudier og biografier", *Rubicon* 7 (Center for Historie. Odense Universitet, 1999), pp. 5-9.

"Munkenes bøger", *Levende ord og lysende billeder. Den middelalderlige bogkultur i Danmark. Essays,* red. af Erik Petersen (Det kongelige Bibliotek og Moesgård Museum), pp. 105-110.

"Was Alberic the Real Founder of Cîteaux?", *Cistercian Studies Quarterly* 34, pp. 139-56.

"Jean Gerson and Traumas of Masculine Affectivity and Sexuality", *Conflicted Identities and Multiple Masculinities. Men in the Medieval West*, ed. Jacqueline Murray (Garland Medieval Casebooks: New York and London), pp. 45-72.

"Jean Gerson and the End of Spiritual Friendship: Dilemmas of Conscience", *Friendship in Medieval Europe*, ed. Julian Haseldine (Sutton Publishing: Stroud, Gloucestershire, Eng.), pp. 229-50.

2000 "Esrum kloster i 1400-tallet og senmiddelalderens spiritualitet", in Per Ingesman and Bjørn Poulsen (ed.), *Danmark og Europa i senmiddelalderen* (Aarhus Universitetsforlag), pp. 264-81.

"La présence de la Lettre aux frères du Mont-Dieu dans les oeuvres de Jean Gerson", in Nicole Boucher (ed.), *Signy l'Abbaye et Guillaume de Saint-Thierry* (Signy l'Abbaye, France: Association des Amis de l'Abbaye de Signy), pp. 565-74.

"Heloise and the Consolation of Friendship", in Bonnie Wheeler (ed.), *Listening to Heloise. The Voice of a Twelfth-Century Woman* (New York: Saint Martin's Press), pp. 303-21.

"Friendship and Scholarship in Medieval Germany", in Nancy van Deusen, ed., *Medieval Germany: Associations and Delineations* (The Institute of Mediaeval Music: Ottawa, Canada), pp. 29-48.

"Cistercienserne i det 20. århundredes danske historieskrivning", in Inge-Lise Kolstrup (ed.), *Aspekter af dansk klostervæsen i middelalderen* (Aarhus Universitetsforlag), pp. 13-25.

"Absalon's Spirituality: A Man Attached to Holy Men", in Karsten Friis-Jensen and Inge Skovgaard-Petersen, ed., *Archbishop Absalon of Lund and his World* (Roskilde Museums Forlag), pp. 71-87.

"Cistercienserordenens første årtier--splittelse og identitet", in Jens Anker Jørgensen, Henrik Madsen and Brian Patrick McGuire, ed., *Fjernt fra menneskers færden. Sider af Esrum Klosters 850-årige historie* (C.A. Reitzels Forlag: Copenhagen), pp. 151-85.

2001 "Charity and Unanimity: The Invention of the Cistercian Order. A Review Article", *Cîteaux Commentarii Cistercienses* 51, pp. 285-97.

"Religion and Mentality in the High Middle Ages: An Essay on Denmark and Europe", *Medieval Spirituality in Scandinavia and Europe. A Collection of Essays in Honour of Tore Nyberg*, ed. Lars Bisgaard, Carsten Selch Jensen, Kurt Villads Jensen and John Lind (Odense University Press), pp. 87-97.

Mennesker og kultur i Danmarks og Europas middelalder. Introduktion og kildesamling for gymnasiet og HF. Systimes Forlag: Århus), 167 pp.

2002 *Friendship and Faith: Cistercian Men, Women and their Stories, 1100-1250.* Variorum Collected Studies Series. (Ashgate Publishing Aldershot, Hampshire, England:), (reprinted articles on Cistercian topics, with new introduction), 350 pp.

"In Search of Bernard's Legacy: Jean Gerson and a Lifetime of Devotion", *Praise No Less than Charity. Studies in Honor of M. Chrysogonus Waddell*, ed. E. Rozanne Elder (Cistercian Publications: Kalamazoo, Michigan), pp. 285-328.

"Aelred's Attachments: Individual Growth in Community Life," *Das Eigene und das Ganze. Zum Individuellen im mittelalterlichen Religiosentum,* Gert Melville, Markus Schürer (Hg.), (Lit Verlag: Münster, Hamburg, London), pp. 439-65.

"Catechesis as Pastoral Theology: Jean Gerson's *Opus Tripartitum*," *The Living Light* 39 (Washington D.C.), pp. 23-32.

2003 "Patterns of Male Affectivity in the Late Middle Ages: The Case of Jean Gerson", *Varieties of Devotion in the Middle Ages and Renaissance*, ed. Susan C. Karant-Nunn, (Brepols: Turnhout, Belgien), pp. 163-78.

"Bernard of Clairvaux", *A Companion to Philosophy in the Middle Ages*, ed. Jorge J. E. Gracia and Timothy B. Noone (Blackwell, Oxford), 209-14. Paperback, 2013.

"Sandhed og agtelse: Et gensyn med Øm Klosters Krønike", *Bogen om Øm Kloster*, red. Bo Gregersen og Carsten Selch Jensen, (Øm Kloster Museum and Syddansk Universitetsforlag), pp. 47-55.

"Bernard's Concept of a Cistercian Order: Vocabulary and Context," *Cîteaux Commentarii Cistercienses* 54, pp. 225-49.

"Affectivity in Monastic and Scholastic Material Cultures: A Comparison", *Materielle Kultur und Emotionen im Mittelalter*, ed. Gerhard Jaritz, Institut für Realienkunde des Mittelalters und der frühen Neuzeit, Krems an der Donau, (Verlag der Österreichischen Akademie der Wissenschaften: Vienna), pp. 133-49.

2004 "Jean Gerson and Bilingualism in the Late Medieval University," in Peter Andersen (red.), *Pratiques de traduction du Moyen Age.* (Museum Tusculanum, Copenhagen), pp. 121-29.

"Jean Gerson, the Shulammite, and the Maid," in Ann W. Astell and Bonnie Wheeler (eds.), *Joan of Arc and Spirituality*, (Palgrave Macmillan: New York), pp. 183-92.

"When Jesus did the Dishes: The Transformation of Late Medieval Spirituality," in Mark W. Williams (ed.), *The Making of Christian Communities* (Anthem Press, London), pp. 131-52.

"Cistercian Storytelling–A Living Tradition: Surprises in the World of Research," *Cistercian Studies Quarterly* 39, pp. 281-309.

"Aelred of Rievaulx", "Anselm of Canterbury", "Bernard of Clairvaux", "Bernardino of Siena" and "Christina of Markyate", articles in *Holy People of the World: A Cross-Cultural Encyclopedia*, ed. Phyllis G. Jestice (ABC Clio: Santa Barbara, Denver, Oxford).

"Convent Schools (Cathedral Schools)" and "Desiderius Erasmus", articles in *Encyclopedia of Children and Childhood in History and Society*, ed. Paula S. Fass, vol. 1 (Thomson Gale: New York), pp. 249-50 and 266-67.

"A Benedictine-Cistercian Source: The Book Birgitta Kept on her Person", in *Birgittiana* 16 (Napoli), pp. 81-106.

2005 *Jean Gerson and the Last Medieval Reformation* (University Park: The Pennsylvania State University Press), 441 pages.

Den levende middelalder: Fortællinger om dansk og europæisk identitet, (Gyldendal, Copenhagen), 301 pages.

"Visionary Women Who Did What They Wanted And Men Who Helped Them," in Martin Gosman (ed.), *The Prime of Their Lives. Wise Old Women in Pre-industrial Society*. Groningen Studies in Cultural Change, vol. 12. (Peeters: Groningen), pp. 103-22.

"Den intellektuelle som afviger: Jean Gerson og samvittighedens krav", in *De måshe udstødte: Historiens marginale eksistenser*, ed. Lars Andersen, Poul Duedahl and Louise N. Kallestrup. (Aalborg Univeritetsforlag, pp. 93-113.

"Roskilde i europæisk perspektiv", *Historisk Årbog for Roskilde Amt 2005*, pp. 13-36.

"Un legame cistercense: Herbertus di Torres e Cesario di Heisterbach", *Herbertus Archiepiscopus Turritanus. Bollettino de Gruppo di Studi »Herbertus«* 4, pp. 47-64.

"Historiske perioder i gymnasiet: En udfordring og en konstruktion", *Noter. Historielærerforeningen for gymnasiet og HF* 165, pp. 10-14.

2006 Editor, *A Companion to Jean Gerson*, Brill's Companions to the Christian Tradition, vol. 3 (Brill: Leiden & Boston), 431 pp.

"Introduction" and "In Search of Jean Gerson: Chronology of his Life and Works" in *A Companion to Jean Gerson*, pp. xiii-xxvi and 1-40.

"Love of Learning: Remembering Jean Leclercq," *The American Benedictine Review* 57, 41-59.

"Biskop og kloster: Eksemplet Bisp Svend og Øm Kloster," in *Tidlige klostre i Norden før 1200*, red. Lars Bisgaard and Tore Nyberg. (Syddansk Universitetsforlag, Odense), pp. 31-46.

2007 "Venskab i middelalderens kristne tradition", in *Vänner, patroner och klienter i Norden 900-1800. Rapport til 26e Nordiska historikermötet*, red. Lars Hermanson, Thomas Småberg, Jón Vidar Sigurdsson, Jakob Danneskiold-Samsøe (Islands universitetsförlag: Reykjavik), pp. 21-36.

"The Cistercians as a Scandinavian Elite", i *Les élites nordiques et l'Europe occidentael, xiie-xve siècle*, éd. Tuomas M. S. Lehtonen et Élisabeth Mornet (Publications de la Sorbonne : Paris), pp. 113-25.

"A Medievalist Meets Dan Brown's Readers," *Medieval Academy News* no. 155, p. 10.

"Europæisk middelalder" i Ulrik Grubb og Karl-Johann Hemmersam, *Fokus. Kernestof i historie. Fra antikken til reformationen* (Gyldendal: Copenhagen), pp. 95-124.

"Dansk og europæisk identitet i middelalderen", i *Historie & Samfundsfag*, Udgivet af lærere i historie og samfundsfag, pp. 14-17.

"Pilgrimsfærd fra senantikken til højmiddelalderen", i *Pilgrimsspor,* red. Elizabeth Knox-Seith (Højbjerg: Forlaget Univers), pp. 59-64.

2008 *Da Himmelen kom nærmere: Fortællinger om Danmarks kristning 700-1300* (Frederiksberg, Alfa, 2008, reprinted 2009), 262 pp.

"Writing about the Difficult Saint. Bernard of Clairvaux and Biography", *Medeltidens mångfald. Studier i samhällsliv, kultur och kommunikation tillägnade Olle Ferm,* red. Göran Dahlbäck et alii. Sällskapet Runica et Mediaevalia (Stockholm), pp. 267-81.

Contribution as Faculty Opponent for Biörn Tjällen, "Church and nation: a fresh approach", *Svensk Historisk Tidskrift*, pp. 215-20.

Articles in *The New Westminster Dictionary of Church History*, ed. Robert Benedetto (Westminster John Knox Press: Louisville and London): "Avignon Papacy" pp. 64-5; "Pierre d'Ailly", pp. 187-8; "Jean Gerson", p. 269; "Medieval Papacy", p. 488-9.

"De studerende og Matthæusevangeliet", *Bibelselskabet*. Årbog, s. 9.

2009 *Den første europæer. Bernard af Clairvaux* (Alfa, Frederiksberg), 298 pp.

"Monastic and Religious Orders c. 1100-1300", in *The Cambridge History of Christianity. Vol. 4: Christianity in Western Europe c. 1100-c. 1500,* ed. Miri Rubin and Walter Simons (Cambridge University Press), pp. 54-72.

"Cistercian Origins in Denmark and Sweden: The Twelfth Century Founders," in *Itinéraires du savoir de l'Italie à la Scandinavie (Xe-XVI siècle). Etudes offertes à Elisabeth Mornet,* dir. Corinne Péneau (Publications de la Sorbonne: Paris), pp. 85-97.

»Spirituality and Mentality in Medieval Danish Monasteries«, in *Glaube, Macht und Pracht. Geistliche Gemeinschaften des Ostseeraums im Zeitalter der Backsteingotik,* hrsg. Oliver Auge, Felix Biermann und Christofer Herrmann (Rahden/Westfalen: Verlag Marie Leidorf), pp. 273-82.

"The Charism of Friendship in the Monastic Institution: A Meditation on Anselm and Bernard", *Institution und Charisma. Festschrift für Gert Melville zum 65. Geburtstag,* herausgegeben Franz J. Felten, Annette Kehnel und Stefan Weinfurter (Köln: Böhlau Verlag), pp. 425-36.

"Bernard of Clairvaux", in *The History of Western Philosophy of Religion,* ed. Graham Oppy and Nick Trakakis, vol. 2 of *Medieval Philosophy of Religion* (Durham, Eng.), reprinted 2013, pp. 109-119.

"Kærlighed til reglen og til stedet: Øm Klosters Krønike," i *Øm Kloster Museum. Nyhedsbrev* 12, pp. 3-6.

"Writing about the Difficult Saint: Bernard of Clairvaux and Biography," *Cistercian Studies Quarterly* 44, pp. 447-62.

"Den kristne udfordring: Velfærdsstatens ophav", *Helsingør Stift. Jubilæumsbog 50 År,* pp. 79-81.

2011 *Hjælp mig Herre: Bøn gennem 1000 År* (Alfa, Frederiksberg), with Bishop Henrik Christiansen, 285 pp.

Editor, *A Companion to Bernard of Clairvaux*, Brill's Companion to the Christian Tradition, vol. 25, (Leiden & Boston: Brill), 405 pp.

"Introduction", in *A Companion to Bernard of Clairvaux*, pp. 1-17.

"Bernard's Life and Works: A Review", in *A Companion to Bernard of Clairvaux*, pp. 18-61.

"Saint Bernard on the Cistercian Circuit", *Cistercian Studies Quarterly* 46, pp. 67-81.

"St. Joseph in Bernard of Clairvaux and Jean Gerson", in *Joseph of Nazareth Through the Centuries*, ed. Joseph F. Chorpenning, (Saint Joseph's University Press: Philadelphia, Pennsylvania), pp. 49-61.

"Jean Gerson and the Renewal of Scholastic Discourse 1400-1415", in *Knowledge, Discipline and Power in the Middle Ages. Essays in Honour of David Luscombe*, ed. Joseph Canning, Edmund King and Martial Staub, (Brill: Leiden and Boston), pp. 129-44.

"c.1080-1215: Culture and History", in *The Cambridge Companion to Medieval English Mysticism*, ed. Samuel Fanous and Vincent Gillespie, (Cambridge University Press), pp. 29-47.

"In Search of the Good Mother: Twelfth-Century Celibacy and Affectivity," in *Motherhood, Religion, and Society in Medieval Europe, 400-1400. Essays Presented to Henrietta Leyser*, ed. Conrad Leyser and Lesley Smith (Ashgate: Farnham, Surrey), pp. 85-102.

2012 *Spejl og kilde: Den nye spiritualitet*, (Frederiksberg, Alfa), 150 pp.

"Middelalderens relevans. Enhedskirken", i *Middelalderen og i dag: En essaysamling*, red. af Svend Clausen og Christian Troelsgård, (Center for Europæiske Middelalderstudier, Københavns Universitet, 2012) pp. 29-42 (http://middelalderstudier.ku.dk/dokumenter/Middelalderen_og_i_dag.pdf/).

2013 "Bernard of Clairvaux and the Cistercian Mystical Tradition", in *The Wiley-Blackwell Companion to Christian Mysticism*, ed. Julia A. Lamm (Wiley-Blackwell: Malden, MA), pp. 237-50.

"Kærlighed og ægteskab i middelalderens verden", *Bibliana. Bibel og sex*, pp. 46-49.

"Bernard af Clairvaux", in *Oxford Bibliographies in Medieval Studies*, ed. Paul E. Szarmach. (New York, Oxford University Press, 30 September 2013): http://www.oxfordbibliographies.com

"Constitutions and the General Chapter", in *The Cambridge Companion to the Cistercian Order*, ed. Mette Birkedal Bruun (Cambridge University Press), pp. 87-99.

Index

Aachen 182, 191
Abel duke of Slesvig, king of Denmark 112-114, 253
Abraham 111
Abildgaard 114
Absalon Dominican friar 256
Adalbert archbishop of Hamburg-Bremen 62-64, 66, 72
Adam of Bremen 62, 64, 66, 72, 301
Adolf III count of Holstein 108-110, 253
Æbelholt 123, 131, 137-138
Ælfheah bishop of Canterbury 210, 212
Aelred of Rievaulx 40-42, 48-52, 306
Agnes princess of Denmark 254
Åhus 246
Albano 199
Albert archbishop of Livonia 103
Alcinus/Alquinus/Alechinus (Alcuin) 45-46
Alexander III pope 37, 199, 204-205
Alexander II king of Scots 252
Alexander III king of Scots 252
Alvastra 121-122, 149-150, 152-153, 155-156, 160-163, 165, 177-193, 275, 299, 303-304
Ama noble family 185
Åmøy 200
Anastasius IV 36
Anders monk in Varnhem 165, 173
Anders Sunesen archbishop of Lund 244
Anders Torstensson 164
Anglia Dominican province of 250
Anselm of Canterbury 88
Antwerp 261
Aquinus clerk of Linköping 272, 276
Aristotle 57, 64-65, 87-88, 95, 301
Armagh 257
Arnold abbot at Lübeck 108-111, 115, 301

Arnoldus Leodiensis 82
Arnoul Neyhensys abbot of Ter Doest 270
Ås 8
Asmild/Asmiald 72
Asser bishop of Roskilde 137-138
Asmund Lang 160
Athenry 260, 263
Augustine bishop of Hippo see St Augustine
Augustine Dominican prior 256
Avignon 9, 256

Baltic 112, 191, 301
Barbarossa (emperor Frederick I) 109, 112-113
Bartholomäus Thorgelow 107
Basilia de Bermingham 260
Baudouin prior of Ter Doest 278
Baudri bishop of Tournai 269
Beirut 109
Benedict of Nursia see St Benedict
Bergen 198, 200, 207, 248, 278, diocese 205
Berlin 253
Bern 262
Bernard of Clairvaux see St Bernard
Bernhard count of Ratzeburg 109
Bero abbot of Varnhem 272, 276
Bertrand Amalric 272, 276
Birger Brosa jarl 130
Birger Jarl 125-126, 153, 166, 256
Birger abbot of Alvastra 160-161, 172
Birgittine Order 8
Björn Johansson 162
Bo Polen 160
Bodil mother of Peder Bodilsen 125
Boethius 48, 61, 96
Bohemia 244, 253, 257-258, 262

Bologna 242, 245
Bonaventura see St Bonaventura
Bordesholm 106
Børglum 71, 294
Bornhøved 262
Bosjö 138-139, 142
Bosporus 110
Botilla daughter of Johannes Svensson 294
Brandenburg 253
Bremen 103 archbishopric 110 see also Adam
Brian, life of 88
British isles 244
Brittany 246
Bro 127
Browne Willis 37-38
Brunneby 127
Bruges 242, 272-273, 275, 279, 281
Bruno von Schauenburg 223
Brynniofus chaplain 272, 277
Brynolf biskop of Skara 272, 276
Buda 250
Burchard of Ursberg 222-223
Burgundy 136, 166, 282, 299
Buris Henriksen Danish duke 131
Byarum 133
Byzantine empire 109

Cambrai 249
Cana 88, 92
Canterbury 242
Cnut the Great king of England and Denmark 206, 211-212
Carlisle 245
Carmelites 24
Carta caritatis prior 22
Cashel 245
Cathars 220
Catherina Pedersdatter 287, 290
Cecilia Eriksdotter 164
Champagne 303
Chełmno 251
Christ 82
Christine queen of Sweden 127

Christopher I king of Denmark 113, 255-256
Christopher II king of Denmark 254, 258
Christopher III king of the Nordic Union 254
Cicero 61, 64-65, 105-106, 301
Cîteaux 274, 281, 299
Clairvaux 149, 302
Clement IV 249
Clement VI 162
Clement Dominican friar bishop of Dunblane 252
Cluny 13, 166
Coleraine 259
Cologne 242, 249 archbishops 109
Colyton 249
Connaught 263
Conrad archbishop of Cologne 109
Conrad/Konrad bishop of Metz 247
Conradus de Saxonia 82
Constantinople 110
Cracow/Kraków 244-245, 251
Cristiernus Martini abbot of Øm 289, 295
Cristiernus Mathei from Øm 293
Dacia Dominican province 256
Dalby 8
Dan king of the Danes 111
David king of Israel 49
David I king of Scots 41
David McKelly archbishop of Cashel 245
Denmark 10, 81, 109, 111-112, 114, 119-143, 252, 299
Detmar 108
Dietmarsken 114, 262
Dietrich von Hameln Dominican friar 253
Dominicans/Blackfriars 23, 107, 219-235, 241-264, 291, 299, 304-305
Dominicus see St Dominicus
Dominicus cardinal of Santa Croce in Gerusalemme 165
Doter 130
Drogheda 245
Dublin 248, 257, 262
Dunblane 252
Dunkeld 250

Durham 39, 41-42, 305 see also Lawrence(s)

Eckernförde 115
Edward the Confessor king of England 36, 42
Edward II king of England 252
Edward III king of England 252
Egypt 110
Eilaf father of Aelred 40-41
Eirik Ivarsson 203-204, 214
Elblag/Elbing 251
Elof Bengtsson 153
Elof brother of Birger Jarl 153, 166
Elsinore see Helsingør
Ely 210
England 33-34, 82, 190, 242, 249-250, 252, 256, 271, 287
Emmeline de Riddelsford 258
Empire, German se Germany
Endridus canon in Trondheim 272
Erik II the Good/Ejegod king of Denmark 126
Erik III Lam/Agnus king of Denmark 125, 136-137
Erik IV Plovpenning king of Denmark 113, 254
Erik V Glipping king of Denmark 275
Erik the Holy king of Sweden 127
Erik Knutsson king of Sweden 123
Erik count in Sweden 135-136
Erik Valdemarsson duke of Sweden 254
Erik II king of Norway 272, 278
Erling Skakke jarl of Norway 198
Erling Skjalgsson of Sola 204
Ernis of St Victor 47
Esger from Knutstorp 163
Eskil archbishop of Lund 136-137
Eskilsø 129, 131, 137-138, 142
Eskilstuna 170
Esrum 7, 8, 111, 121, 128-129, 136-137, 142, 165, 271, 274, 280, 292-293, 299
Estonia 204
Esztergom 242
Ethelred king of England 212

Eugenius III 35
Europe 10, 13-14, 27, 59, 142, 151, 166-167, 169, 177, 242, 254-255, 270, 303
Eustache prior of Ter Doest 273
Evrard bishop of Tournai 270
Eyvind(us) bishop of Oslo 279
Exeter 249

Fegge/Ffegge island in the diocese of Odense 292
Finland 8, 251
Flanders 262, 259, 261, 269-282
Flastad 133-134, 143
Florence MacFlainn archbishop of Tuam 263
Fogdö St Alban's 132 see also Vårfruberga
Folkungar 185
Fountains 39
France 37-38, 177, 183, 192, 241, 246, 262, 269-270, 273-274, 280-281, 303
Francia Dominican province 248
Franciscans/Greyfriars 23, 103, 122, 160, 203, 241, 250-251, 253-254, 258-260
Frederick I Barbarossa German emperor see Barbarossa
Freiburg 261
Fulda abbot of 109
Fulko 204
Funen/Fyn 126, 287, 299

Gabel see Jablonné
Gallus Marquard von Lemberk 258
Gaudfred 248
Gaufroy hospitaller 273-274
Gautier de Châtillon 106
Gdansk/Danzig 244, 251
Geoffrey of Coldingham 37, 51
Geoffrey Rufus bishop 51
Geoffrey of St Albans 45
Gerald of Aurillac 301
Gere 130
Gerhard of Lübeck 103
Germany 59-60, 76, 82, 108-109, 111-114, 119, 127, 139, 141, 177, 191-192, 246, 253, 261, 270, 302-303

Gerson, Jean 10
Gervase receiver of Hypognosticon of St Mary's York 40, 46
Glasgow 244
Godrich of Finchale 35, 46, 51
Godskalk Falkdal 256
Goswin abbot of Eeckhout 272
Götaland 111, 191
Gottorp 113-114
Great Belt see Storebælt
Gregory the Great see St Gregory
Gregorius IX 274
Gregorius Cardinal Legate 252
Gudbrand clerk 278
Gudhem 8, 122-123, 125, 129-130, 160, 189
Guillaume V de Cordewaeghen abbot of Ter Doest 270
Guillaume provost of Saint-Donatien (Bruges) 274
Guillaume de Saeftinge 270
Guldholm 121, 123-124, 141
Gunner bishop of Viborg 57-78, 251-252, 300-301
Guy de Bourgogne cardinal legate 271, 275
Guy de Dampierre count of Flanders 270
Gyrid Gjurdsdotter 154

Haarlem 253
Hacket abbot of Ter Doest 270
Haderslev 103, 246
Håkon V Magnusson king of Norway 107, 257
Håkan Jonsson Läma 161
Håkan novice 154-155, 169, 173
Håkon IV Håkonsson king of Norway 254-256
Halland 8
Halmstad 262
Halsnøy 198-200, 202, 204, 213-214
Hamar 199, 272, 277-278
Hamburg 103-116, 253, 257, 301
Hamburg-Bremen archbishopric 62
Harald Bluetooth king of Denmark 249
Harald Fairhair king of Norway 197, 200

Hason Dominican friar and prior 257
Heinrich of Mecklenburg count 112, 253, 263
Heinrich of Schwerin count 114-115
Helena queen of Sweden 127-128
Helgeseter 207
Helmold of Bosau 108
Helsingør/Elsinore 254
Henningus at Esrum 293, 295
Henrik bishop of Linköping 271-272, 275-277
Henry VI German emperor 109
Henry II king of England 40
Henry III king of England 255-257, 261
Henry the Lion duke of Saxony 108, 114
Henry Murdac archbishop of York 35
Henry of Blois bishop of Winchester 35
Henry bishop of Lübeck 108
Henry abbot of Esrum 165
Henry hospitaller 274
Hermann Hose 107
Hexham 42
Holbæk 254, 262
Holland 252-253
Holme 274, 280, 287, 299
Holstein 105, 109, 113, 253, 262
Holy Land 251, 258, 277, 282
Honorius III 241
Horsaberg 256
Hovedøya/Hovedøen 207
Hucklum 127
Huge Ripelin de Argentina 82
Hugh de Lacy earl of Ulster 259
Hugh of Paiset archdeacon of York 35
Hugh the Chanter 36
Hugh of St Victor 44-45, 47
Hungary 244, 250
Hugues bishop of Liège 245, 247
Humiliati, order of 220, 222
Hypognosticum 39-41, 44, 49

Iceland 139
Inge king of Sweden 127-128
Ingeborg princess of Denmark, queen of France 256, 273-274, 280

INDEX

Ingeborg daughter of jarl Siward 132
Ingrid Anundsdotter 182
Ingundus provost in Tjust 272, 277
Innocent III 112, 115, 223
Innocent IV 247
Innocent VI 162
Inverness 257
Ireland 250, 252-253, 257-258, 261
Isfrid bishop of Ratzeburg 110
Iwo Odrowaz 245, 251

Jablonné 258, see also Gabel
Jacek Odrowaz 251
Jacob Erlandsen archbishop of Lund 275, 280
Jacob dean of Bruges 222, 277
Jacobus de Benevento 82
Jarler archbishop of Uppsala 244, 251
Jaroslov Marquard 258
Jarundus archbishop of Trondheim 279
Jean Gerson see Gerson
Jerusalem 108-109, 170, 202
Jesus 84, 94-95
Joar coralis 163
Job 87
Johan Sverkersson king of Sweden 129
Johan duke brother of duke Ragvald 127
Johan Erlandsson novice 155, 169, 172
Johanna of Flanders 252
Johannes archbishop of Trondheim 272, 276-278
Johannes archbishop of Uppsala 272, 276-277
Johannes Andree 290
Johannes Dominican friar 256
Johannes Ebbesen (Hvide) 258
Johannes Friis from Børglum 294
Johannes Messenius 133
Johannes Puster 103
Johannes Raa 294
Johannes Svensson 294 see also Botilda
Johannes priest 161
Johannes monk of Alvastra 161-162, 172
John bishop of Børglum 71
John bishop of Tournai 279

John archdeacon of Uppsala 278
John Bale 38
John de Crusolis 276
John of Hexham 37, 52
John Leland 37, 42
John see also Johannes, Jöns
Jonathan friend of king David 49
Jöns abbot of Nydala 154
Jordan de Exeter 260
Josephus 105
Juhel archbishop of Reims 245, 247
Julita 130, 150, 160, 164, 189
Jutland/Jylland 59, 82, 111, 114, 123, 134
Jutta princess of Denmark 254

Kalvø 134-135
Kamien/Kammin 244
Karelia 254-255
Karl Ulfsson 133-134
Karl canon at Hamburg 105
Kilkenny 252
King's Langley 252
Kintyre 256
Klemens Tyrgilsson 170
Knud/Knut the Great king of England and Denmark, see Cnut
Knud/Knut the Holy king of Denmark 126
Knud VI king of Denmark 109
Knut Eriksson king of Sweden 122, 130
Knut Långe king of Sweden 126, 133
Knutstorp 163
Kortrijk (Courtrai) 270
Kristina princess of Norway 256
Kungsälven 8
Kungslena 163

Lambert de Lissewege 269
Lars Boberg 153
Lars Ulfsson (Ama) 192
Laurids Jonsen Panter 258
Lawrence of Durham magister 35-37, 40, 43, 45, 306
Lawrence of Durham prior 34-39, 41-43, 306

Lawrences of Durham 33-55, 305
Lazarus 229, 231, 233, 304
Leeuwarden 251, 259
Les Dunes 270, 273
Lichfield 245
Liège 245, 247
Lille 248
Lincoln 245
Linköping 124, 163, 185, 246, 256, 272, 275
Livonia 109
Løgum 8, 81-99, 105, 108, 121, 274, 280, 298-299
Lommaryd 161
London 242
Louis IX king of France 255
Louth Park 39
Lübeck 103-116, 191, 262, 301
Lucan 105-106
Luke Netterville of Armagh 245
Lund 244-246, 271-272, 285-286, 290, annals 111, prefectus 139
Luther, Martin 14

Magdeburg 245
Magnus Birgersson king of Sweden 153
Magnus Eriksson king of Sweden 254, 256
Magnus Henriksson king of Sweden 127-128
Magnus Erlingsson king of Norway 198-199
Magnus IV Hakonsson the Lawmender king of Norway 201-203, 205, 213, 256
Malente 104
Mällatorp 127
Margareta of Flanders 252
Margareta noblewoman 135-136
Margrete regent of the Nordic Union 254
Mark hundred 155
Marquard/Markwartinger noble family 258 see Gallus, Jaroslov
Marseille 277

Mary, Virgin 95 lamentations 104
Mathias Jacobi 292
Mathias Mathie 291
Mathias monk in Nydala 153, 172
Mathias Ripensis 220, 227-235, 304
Mats Esgersson subprior in Nydala 162, 172
Matthew Paris 45, 206, 255
Maurice Fitzgerald 257-258
Maurice of Rievaulx 44
Mazovia 253
Mechtild married to Duke Abel 112
Meiler de Bermingham 263
Meldorf 262
Metz 247-248
Michael bishop of Włocławek 253
Mieszko II prince of Opole and Mazovia 253
Morlaix 246
Moravia 244
Mosterøy 197, 199

N. former abbot in Roma, Gotland 162
Næstved St Peter's 121, 125
Nanne Kärling novice 156, 173
Nanne 156
Nantes 246
Närke 122, 130
Netherlands 251-253, 259
Neumünster 105-107, 115
Nicholas Breakspear 199, 205, 214
Nicholas Estonian monk 204-205
Nicholas abbot of Øm 68-69, 288-289, 295
Nicholas abbot of Saint-André 271, 274
Nicolaus I prince of Werle 253
Nicolaus Ragvaldi archbishop of Uppsala 164
Nicolaus bishop of Riga 244
Nicolaus Brun 103
Nicolaus Ebbonis 162, 172
Nicolaus Johannis alias Thome 289
Nicolaus Olaij 290-291, 299
Nicolaus Dominican friar 256
Nidarholm 206-207

Nidaros church province 199, diocese 206, church of St Clement 205 see Trondheim
Norway 121, 139, 177, 197-213, 255-257, 272, 276-279, 281-292, 299, 303
Norwich 210
Nydala 122, 124-125, 135, 149-150, 154, 160-163

Odense St Knud 121-122, 126-127, 208, diocese of 287, 292
Odo of Cluny 301
OIav Haraldsson king of Norway 204, 212-213 see also St Olav
Olav Kyrre king of Norway 207
Olav Tryggvasson king of Norway 204, 207, 212
Olaus Petri monk in Alvastra 163, 167, 172
Olaus Petri priest in *Ffegge* 292
Olavus Johannis Franciscan 160
Olmütz 244
Olov Basatömir archbishop of Uppsala 244
Olof Lang 154
Olof [Svensson] novice 152-154, 172
Øm 7, 59, 62, 64, 68-69, 121, 134, 287-288, 291, 293, 295, 300
Opole 253
Øresund (Sound) 111
Origen 88, 107
Orkney islands 201
Osbert of Claire 40
Oslo 254, 277, 279, diocese 198, 206-207
Östergötland 121-122, 152, 177, 185
Östra Aros see Uppsala
Otto IV German emperor 108-110, 115
Otto III margrave of Brandenburg 253
Outremer 111
Ovid 88, 106
Oxford 242
Øystein Erlendsson 199

Paganus 48-49
Palestine 110

Paradise 95
Paris 76-77, 107, 162, 199, 203, 214, 242, 248, 251, 259, 276
Pavia 13
Peder Lauridsen (Panter) 258
Peder Jakobsen bishop of Roskilde 273

Peder Bodilsen 125
Pelhrim bishop of Prague 244
Pembroke 252
Perth 257
Peter of Blois 34
Peter Comestor 88
Peter the Dane 82
Peter the Lombard 87-88, 226
Peter of Moûtier-la-Celle 15
Peter brother of Gyrid 154
Peterborough Chronicle 36
Philip German king 109
Philip IV king of France 256
Philip bishop of Ratzeburg 110
Plato 61, 65
Płock 251
Poland 244, 251, 253
Pomerania 109, 250
Prague 164, 244
Preetz 104-105, 115
Przemysl Ottokar II king of Bohemia 253, 257
Prussia 250-251

Racibórz 253
Radulf of St Albans 45
Ragvald duke in Sweden 127
Ranulf archdeacon 37
Ranulf Flambard of Durham 48
Rasmus Ludvigsson 127-128
Ratzeburg 103, 109-110
Reginald of Durham 35-37, 43, 51-52, 204-205
Reims 245
Reinald bishop of Stavanger 204, 210, 212
Ribe Dominicans 227-235, 246, 274, 304 chronicle of bishops 62

Richard of St Victor 46
Richard Marshal 258
Rievaulx 41-44
Riga 244
Ringsjön 138
Ringsted Our Lady's 121
Riseberga 122, 130-131
Röbel 253
Robert bishop of Esztergom 244
Robert bishop of Moravia 244
Robert Archer Dominican friar 257
Robert of Bridlington 40
Robert of St Albans 46
Roger of Durham 43
Rome 9, 35, 38, 45, 150, 162, 244, 260, 274-276, 282, 285-295
Roskilde 137, 245-246, 254, 258, 273, diocese 287, 293, Our Lady's convent 121
Rostock 253
Rudolf abbot of Julita 160, 173
Rudolf monk at Alvastra 165, 173
Russia 254-255
Ryd 105, 108, 111-115, 141, 301
Ryfylke islands 197

Säby 122, 130, see also Julita
Saint:
St Alban 207
St Albans 36-37, 45, 47, 52
St Anne 260
St Augustine 61, 65, 88, 93, 95, 198, 214
St Barbara bishopric see William
St Bartholomew 269
St Benedict of Nursia 13, 16, 151, 205, 291, rule of 16, 171
St Bernard of Clairvaux 292
St Birgitta 179
St Bonaventure Franciscan Cardinal 82
St Brigit of Kildare 40, 52
St Catherine of Alexandria 260
St Clement in Nidaros 206
St Cuthbert 204-205, 213
St Dominic Guzman 241
St Donatien (Bruges) 274
St Edmund 207
St Gallen abbey plan 23
St Genesius 72
St Gregory the Great 61, 65, 90
St Hallvard 207
Saint-Julien 262
St John, order of 170, 301, 303 see also Teutonic
St John's abbey at Lübeck 105, 108, 303
St John the Baptist 86
St John Chrysostomos 88, 90
St Knud the Holy king of Denmark 208
St Lawrence 197, 206
St Martin 64
St Mary 203, 207, in York 39
St Mary Magdalene 262
St Michael in Schleswig 122-124, 134, 140-141, 143
St Olav 254
St Olav's convent in Stavanger 197-200, 202-205, 208-209, 213-214, 305
St Paul 87
St Riquier 269-270
St Rufus 199, 205
St Swithun 204, 210-214, 305
St Sunniva 207
St Thomas apostle 50
St Thomas Becket 108
St Thomas Aquinas 13, 64
St Victor in Paris 34, 44-45, 47, 52, 137-138, 199, 203
Saddell abbey of Kintyre 256
Sallust 105
Salomon 85, 202
Salomon Dominican friar 24
Sandomierz 244, 251
Sätuna 132
Savonarola 13
Saxo 111
Saxony 113, 256
Scandinavia 8, 10, 119-143, 149, 167, 169, 191, 207, 209-210, 219-235, 254, 269-282, 289, 306
Scania/Skåne 8, 131, 138
Schinkel M. 104

Schleswig/Slesvig 103, 107, 113, 115, 122-123, 140-141, 246, 253, 275, 301
Schleswig-Holstein 103-116, 301
Schönberg 259
Scotland 250, 252, 256-257
Segeberg 105-107, 115
Selja 206-207
Seneca 94
Shetland islands 202
Sigtuna 244, 246-247, 251, 254
Sigurd Dominican friar 255
Sigurd Ullstreng 206-207
Simeon of Durham 36
Simon of St Albans 46
Simon the Preacher Dominican friar 255-256
Simon master 274
Sion, daughter of 85
Siward jarl 131-132
Sjælland 125, 131, 136-137
Skálholt 199
Skänninge 246, 254
Skara 163, 167, 272, 275-276
Sko 122, 126, 133, 142-143
Slangerup 121, 281, 290, 300
Sligo 258
Småland 122, 124, 133, 161, 163
Sminge 134
Söderköping 152, 192
Södermanland 122, 130-131, 164
Sola 204
Sophie queen of Sweden 253
Sorø 121, 128-129, 141, 186, 271, 274, 280, 299
Sound see Øresund
Spain 177, 256, 303
Stavanger 197-214, 305
Stedingers 251 (252)
Stephan king of England 34, 40, 45
Stockholm 122, 192, 254
Storebælt (Great Belt) 111
Strade 260
Strängnäs 164, 167, 246
Strausberg 253
Suetonius 57

Sulpicius Severus 63
Sune [Elofsson] novice 153-154, 157, 166, 172
Sunnhordland 198
Svein Alfivasson king of Denmark 206, 212
Sven bishop of Århus 62-64, 68-71, 76
Sven goldsmith 152
Svend Grate king of Denmark 136
Sverker I the Elder king of Sweden 184-185
Sverre king of Norway 140
Sweden 81, 119-143, 244, 251, 276, 279, 281-282, 299, 303
Switzerland 262
Sylvester abbot of Alvastra 275
Syria 110

Ter Doest 269-282, 299
Terence 106
Teutonic knights 250-256 see also St John
Theodoricus Monachus 206
Theodosius I the Great Roman emperor 230-231, 233
Thidericus Koller 107
Thomas Walsingham 45
Thomas layman at Øm 293
Thord founder of Bosjö 138-139
Thorberg clerk 278
Tjust 277
Tønsberg 257
Torbjörn Kärling 156
Torphim bishop of Hamar 272, 278
Torsten Andreasson 164, 167, 173
Tournai 269-270, 279
Tréguier 246
Trøndelag 139, 206
Trondheim 206, 272, 277, 279, 299
Tuam 263
Turnov 258
Tvis 71, 121, 131, 294, abbot of 294

Uetersen 105, 115
Uffo archbishop of Lund 271, 274
Ulf Gudmarsson 179

Ulf parish priest 162
Ulster 259
Ulvhilde queen of Sweden 184
Uppland 122, 126, 130, 133, 139-140
Uppsala 81, 139-140, 164, 244, 246, 251, 272, 276-278
Utrecht 253
Utstein 197-205, 209, 213-214, 305

Vä 131, 136, 143
Vadeby 127
Vadstena 81, 185
Valdemar I king of Denmark 108, 112, 122, 126, 134-135, 204
Valdemar II king of Denmark 112-114, 127
Valdemar Duke bishop of Schleswig 110, 122-123, 141
Valdemar Birgersson king of Sweden 125-126, 153, 254
Vallentuna 140
Vårfruberga 132, 137, 142-143
Varnhem 8, 121-122, 150, 156, 165, 189, 272
Vartofta 156
Västerås 153
Västergötland 121, 125, 129, 155-156, 160, 163
Vejle 258, 260
Veng 124, 135-136, 141-143
Vergil 105-106
Viborg 245, 251 diocese 287, 300 canons 294
Viby 122-123, 130
Vingåker 164
Visby 246

Vitskøl 66, 69, 71, 287
Vreta 8, 121-122, 127-128, 130-131, 135, 149, 142, 189
Vyborg in Karelia 254

Waldensians 220
Waltham (Essex) 44, 141-142
Waterford 261
Wazo archdeacon 35, 37
Wenzel I king of Bohemia 253
Werle 253
Wessex 208, 214
Westminster 36-38, 40, 42, 45-47, 51-52, 306
Willem II of Holland 253
Willem van Le Plouich bishop of Lille 248
Wilhelm of Lüneburg 110
William Marshal earl of Pembroke 252
William bishop of St Barbara 34-35
William of Æbelholt 123, 137
William of Rievaulx 43-44
William of Saint-Thierry 23-24
William Cumin 34
Wilsnack 191
Winchester 204, 208, 210-214, 245, 305
Winsum 251, 259
Wismar 253, 261, 263
Włocławek 248
Wrocław [Breslau] 244
Würzburg 110

York 52
Yorkshire 188

Zdislava 258 see Marquard